Development Challenges
in a Postcrisis World

ANNUAL WORLD BANK CONFERENCE ON DEVELOPMENT ECONOMICS

Annual World Bank Conference
on Development Economics—Global
2011

Development Challenges
in a Postcrisis World

Edited by
Claudia Sepúlveda, Ann Harrison,
and Justin Yifu Lin

THE WORLD BANK
Washington, D.C.

Edited by Claudia Sepúlveda, Ann Harrison, and Justin Yifu Lin

Professional affiliations identified in this volume, unless otherwise noted, are as of the time of the conference, May 31–June 2, 2010.

ISBN (paper): 978-0-8213-8522-7
ISBN (electronic): 978-0-8213-8730-6
DOI: 10.1596/978-0-8213-8522-7

Library of Congress Cataloging-in-Publication Data has been requested.

Contents

About This Book

Since 1989, the Annual Bank Conference on Development Economics (ABCDE) has provided a forum for the presentation and discussion of new knowledge on development economics. The conference aims at promoting the exchange of ideas among researchers, policy makers, and students interested in development issues and emphasizes the contribution that empirical research in economics can make to understanding development processes and to formulating sound development policies.

Conference papers are reviewed by the editors and are also subject to internal and external peer review. Some papers were revised after the conference to reflect the comments made by discussants and/or participants from the floor. As a result, discussants' comments may refer to elements of the paper that no longer exist in their original form. Most discussant's comments were not revised.

The conference took place in Stockholm, Sweden, from May 31 to June 2, 2010. Fourteen papers were presented at the conference: four keynote addresses and ten plenary session papers, as well as nine commentaries. All of them are gathered in this volume with the exception of three plenary session papers and their respective commentaries that were already committed for publication elsewhere. Unless otherwise noted, participation affiliations identified in this volume are as of the time of the conference.

The conference also featured the launch of the Global Development Debates, a joint effort by the Development Economics Department, Poverty Reduction and Economic Management Network, and the World Bank Institute. The theme of this first debate was "Development Challenges in a Postcrisis World," which was also the theme of the conference. The debate was moderated by Stephanie Flanders from the BBC and had Abhijit Banerjee, Partha Dasgupta, Eric Maskin, James Mirrlees, and Robert Solow as panelists. The discussion was wide ranging and included issues related to globalization, inequality, the role of the state, and the problems of poverty.

The planning and organization of the conference was a joint effort by Sweden's Ministry for Foreign Affairs and Ministry of Finance and by the World Bank.

We gratefully acknowledge timely and valuable contributions by all members of the Steering Committee and other reviewers. We also thank Alan Gelb and Mia Horn for their insightful advice and Julia Hector and Leita Jones, conference organizers, whose excellent organizational skills helped to ensure a successful conference. Finally, we thank the staff of the World Bank's Knowledge and Publishing Division, in particular, Stephen McGroarty and Rick Ludwick, for their efforts and persistence in putting this volume together.

Introduction

CLAUDIA SEPÚLVEDA, ANN HARRISON, AND JUSTIN YIFU LIN*

The twenty-second Annual Bank Conference on Development Economics (ABCDE) took place in Stockholm, Sweden, from May 31 to June 2, 2010. The main theme of the conference was "Development Challenges in a Postcrisis World." The theme reflects the mood and the concerns of the development community as the recent global financial crisis, now widely known as the Great Recession, continued to capture the minds of economists and development practitioners while uncertainties on the strength of the recovery and its long-term implications for development remained.

A crisis presents an immediate challenge that has to be faced but also an opportunity to address long-term problems and to reconsider established conventions. With this in mind, this year's volume includes papers on five areas of inquiry: environment and climate change, development strategies in a post-crisis world, the political economy of fragile states, new ways of measuring welfare, and lessons learned from social programs and transfers.

Working Together in Times of Crisis: Development Aid and the Power of Ideas

The opening addresses by Anders Borg, Minister for Finance of Sweden; Justin Yifu Lin, World Bank Senior Vice President and Chief Economist; and Gunilla Carlsson, Minister for International Development Cooperation of Sweden, all focused on the need for cooperation among countries to overcome development challenges and the importance of research as the foundation for sound policymaking.

In his opening address, Minister Borg reminds the audience that, even during crisis, we need to continue to have ambitious policies when it comes to development. He highlights the important role that the World Bank has played during the crisis

* Claudia Sepúlveda is Lead Economist, Development Economics, World Bank. At the time of the conference, Ann Harrison was Director of Development Policy, Development Economics, World Bank, and Justin Yifu Lin was Senior Vice President and Chief Economist, Development Economics, World Bank.

by increasing lending and draws attention to Sweden's commitment to development reflected in the continual allocation, even in a time of global recession, of 1 percent of its gross national income (GNI) to aid. Minister Berg concludes by pointing out that one of the lessons from the crisis is that all countries and institutions must work together to maintain global economic stability.

Justin Yifu Lin in his address echoes the view by Minister Berg that the world is experiencing the largest development challenge since the Great Depression. In Lin's view, governments have adopted economic measures to stabilize the banking sector and fiscal stimulus packages to avoid the worst-case economic scenarios. The global recovery, however, is still fragile and, therefore, innovative solutions are needed. Lin proposes a global recovery initiative with a focus on infrastructure investments in developing countries. The funds for this initiative should come from high-income and reserve-rich countries. Lin argues that such a program would benefit both high-income and developing countries as infrastructure investments in developing countries would boost exports, manufacturing employment, and growth in high-income countries, while reducing poverty, enhancing growth in the developing world, and facilitating the achievement of the Millenium Development Goals (MDGs). It is a win-win solution.

Lin concludes by quoting John Maynard Keynes's *General Theory of Employment Theory and Money*. In the last sentence of the last chapter, Keynes wrote, "But soon or late, it is ideas, not vested interest, which are dangerous for good or evil." Today, faced with a similar situation in the world economy, Lin acknowledges that the world needs good ideas and the ABCDE can help generate ideas that can make a difference for developing countries and the world.

Gunilla Carlsson, Minister for International Development Cooperation of Sweden, continues in her address the discussion initiated by Borg and Lin, namely the importance of ideas for solving development challenges. Carlsson points out the importance of research as a foundation for sound policy making and calls for increasing a developing country's research capacity and research on development issues, as well as innovative ways to stimulate communication and collaboration among researchers, evaluators, policymakers, and development practitioners to effectively tackle the major global development challenges that we face.

Carlsson concludes by discussing the new initiative by the Swedish government, called Open Aid, to adapt development aid to today's realities and the opportunities that globalization and technological developments have created. This new initiative aims to combat poverty as effectively as possible by opening aid to public control and ideas from sources around the world.

Overcoming the Samaritan's Dilemma in Development Aid

The impact of development aid on growth, poverty alleviation, fostering democracy, and other outcomes has been debated intensively in academic and policy circles, as well as in the press. The late Elinor Ostrom, 2009 Nobel Laureate in Economics, argues that much of aid's disappointing results are related to the incentives generated by development aid institutions. In her view, an understanding of the incentives that confront donors and recipients requires knowledge of the fundamental collective-action problems that these players face. The problems include motivation in the provision of public goods (health, public safety), provision and maintenance of common-pool resources (forest, oceans, etc.), and the Samaritan's Dilemma. Other perverse incentives common in aid include asymmetric power relationships, rent seeking and corruption, and missing information.

Ostrom applies the above framework to analyze and evaluate the incentive structure within the Swedish International Development Cooperation Agency (SIDA) and SIDA-supported projects in India and Zambia. The general findings of these field studies, as well as interviews at SIDA, can be summarized as: a) type of project affects the likelihood of sustainability with infrastructure projects still very attractive to development agencies because they generate immediate benefits and move a large amount of money with low staff time but they may do little else; b) small investments in building human skills can be effective in building productivity and self-reliance if designed well for the local environment; c) feedback from citizens in recipient, as well as donor, countries to their own officials and development assistance staff is lacking; d) motivated staff is not sufficient to overcome the many incentives to spend money rather than time on the project; and e) enhancement of individual learning about sustainability by long-term assignments, continued flow of information about projects, and career advancement based to some extent on past participation on successful projects are needed.

On the basis of these findings, Ostrom concludes by noting that development problems are difficult to tackle and there are no magic bullets to solve collective action problems, but a step forward is to dig into understanding the incentives of each situation, fit what is being done to the local culture and circumstances, and make sure the participants understand the benefits and see them as legitimate.

Learning Growth and Development

As customary in a festschrift, Joseph Stiglitz's paper is inspired by the work of the honoree, Partha Dasgupta. In this case, the topic chosen is innovation because it is central to development and has been a source of concern to Partha and himself since they were graduate students. Stiglitz remembers the heady days in Cambridge when he and his colleagues anticipated "putting a golden nail in the coffin of capitalism." He then proceeds to attempt to do exactly that by arguing that markets by themselves do not yield efficient solutions for promoting innovation in part because knowledge is a public good.

Stiglitz develops a general theory of growth and development based on endogenous learning (with endogenous capital constraints) derived from underlying market imperfections. He argues that such a model with its underlying neoclassical model with well-functioning markets provides a policy framework that is markedly different from that of the Washington consensus. Within this setup, he proceeds to analyze the infant industry argument for protection based on the theory of learning. He concludes that, whether learning is internal or external to the firm, the market equilibrium in general will not be Pareto efficient and, therefore, there is a role for government in correcting the market misallocations.

Given that there are large spillovers and externalities and imperfections in the industrial structure, Stiglitz proposes to create incentives to expand parts of the economy that generate spillovers. Thus, design an industrial policy whose goal is not to pick winners but to identify these externalities and support them. One goal would be to use instruments that give broad-based support, such as the types of subsidies and other forms of support used in East Asia. Since the World Trade Organization (WTO) has restricted the use of such subsidies, he suggests using the exchange rate as a tool of industrial policy.

Weak States, Strong States, and Development

The donor and development communities often mention lack of state capacity as one of the main obstacles for development in weak states. Torsten Persson using the tools of political economy and economic theory presents a unified framework on how to think about fragile or weak states (see Figure). The main question he attempts to answer is why we observe development clusters that tend to combine effective state capacity (fiscal and legal capacity), absence of political violence, and high per capita income.

Persson breaks down this question into three sub-questions: What factors influence effective state capacity? What factors drive political violence? What explains the clustering of state institutions, violence, and income? Persson argues that a state's institutional capacity to levy taxes and support a legal system is constrained by its history of investments in legal and fiscal capacity. Investment in common interest public goods such as fighting external wars, political stability, and inclusive political institutions are conducive to building state capacity. In contrast, civil war and internal conflict are damaging to building state capacity. All of these capacities vary in conjunction with each other because of their common determinants, their inherent complementarities, and the various feedback loops they generate. If a state is good at keeping internal

FIGURE I.1
Determinants of State Capacity and Political Violence

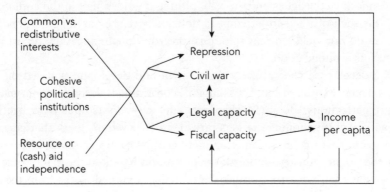

peace, for example, then citizens are more willing to pay taxes, more taxes can pay for a better legal system, and a better legal system helps to keep the peace.

Persson concludes by exploring the implications of this unified framework for the allocation of development assistance. If development assistance is to work, according to the author, the donor's focus should be on whether recipient governments invest in public goods and the fiscal and legal capacity of their governments.

Personal Histories and Poverty Traps

A conventional view of poverty is that individuals' socioeconomic prospects are largely under their own control. Income rewards productive efforts. The observed persistence of poverty across generations, however, has led to an increasing interest in the concept of poverty traps.

Partha Dasgupta tackles this issue by stressing the importance of distinguishing between describing poverty and explaining poverty. Dasgupta's interest is in the latter. In particular, he is interested in understanding the complementarities and circular nature of causal processes, or positive feedback loops, involved in poverty and how they may lead to poverty traps. In a poverty trap, individuals fail to rise or lack access to threshold levels of capital (human, physical, natural, or other) that spur well-being. Dasgupta models the link and positive feedbacks from malnutrition and infectious diseases at an early stage of an individual's life to the lack of acquisition of socioeconomic competencies in early childhood, to its impact on the capacity for physical work and endurance later on life, and to wages and the capacity to obtain the food needed to improve nutritional status given origin in a poverty trap.

Dasgupta concludes by offering five morals from his research on poverty traps: a) the high maintenance costs of good physical and emotional health underlie the existence of poverty traps and b) it is a manifestation of complementarities among the inputs that humans need to survive; c) human capital formation is complementary over time and d) that a personal history has a long reach, affecting not only the person in question but also its descendants; and e) in low-income countries, absolute poverty is a cause and a consequence of unequal distribution of assets.

Environmental Commons and the Green Economy

Both Thomas Sterner and Ramon López characterize the world's current growth pattern as unsustainable and offer potential answers on how to turn this situation around. Sterner starts by recognizing that the hopes for a grand deal were shattered at Copenhagen in December 2009 and that "green growth" has been promoted as an alternative path. He points out that green growth is no magic bullet because growth, green or not, will boost demand for energy and coal is normally the cheapest source. He suggests, however, that, if green growth is taken seriously, it can be viewed as a bridge to facilitate a final (and maybe elusive) global treaty with close to total participation that can deal with the ethical issues of fairness and distribution.

Sterner argues that the costs of climate abatement are sufficiently high to motivate industries and countries to focus on efficiency and, therefore, the need to strive for a unique price of carbon and negotiate a global agreement with close to total participation. This solution will take time. In the meantime, emissions must be reduced, both to reduce pressure on the atmosphere and—perhaps most importantly—to learn. A number of initial steps have been taken, such as experiments with "green" cars, new fuels, energy efficiency in buildings, solar heating, solar and wind power (in the European Union and the United States), and other clean development mechanism projects for new technology in developing countries. China's five-year economic plan, passed in March 2011, championed energy efficiency and pollution reduction as central to its plan for generating economic growth. It is, of course, too early to see the outcome of these initiatives but they clearly demonstrate that economic growth in the coming years will be tied to an emerging low-carbon economy.

Sterner concludes by saying that these actions may be symbolic but are embryonic as well. Green growth is no panacea. It is a new direction, not merely an instrument. He believes that all too soon, the policies applied in many countries will not be tough enough in the absence of a global international treaty that internalizes the global externalities involved. In the end, green growth policies can help bring all countries some steps closer to the necessarily binding global commitment.

Ramon López strengthens Sterner's assessment by presenting mounting evidence that, in the past few decades, the world's pattern of growth and consumption has become unsustainable as the result of the emergence of new industrial giants (NIGs) such as China and India among others, and the increasing scarcity of natural resources in developing countries. These structural changes have entailed a significant tightening of the link between global growth and commodity prices with the world commodity supply becoming more inelastic. López shows that growth in advanced countries has been characterized by a "dematerialization" of its production from manufacturing, forestry, fishing, etc. to services and a "materialization" of consumption. This sharp divergence in the structure of consumption and production in advanced countries has meant an increasing reliance on developing countries as suppliers of primary commodities and manufacturing goods made only possible by the emergence of NIGs. But it also has brought an increasing net demand for food, energy and raw materials. This increased connection between commodity prices and growth after the incorporation of the NIGs has happened at a time when natural resources in developing countries have become less abundant as these countries have become more aware of the environment costs in the ecosystem. Thus, the observed pattern of growth and consumption has advanced countries not by becoming environmentally cleaner but by becoming better at dumping their pollution on the rest of the world.

What will be the impact of the global crisis on the commodity supply curve given the structural change already observed in the pattern of world production and consumption? López argues that the impact will be determined by the macroeconomic policies prior to the crisis, the stringency of environmental regulatory regimes, domestic policies in response to the crisis, and country characteristics associated with factor endowments, population density, and poverty levels. Given that it is too early to have empirical evidence about the impact of the current crisis, he relies on two previous crisis episodes, the 1995 Mexico Peso crisis and the 1997–99 Asia crises, as empirical references. Loópez suggests that the impact of the current crisis is likely to exacerbate environmental scarcities in the developing world and may eventually force further tightening of environmental policies over the long run in response to such degradation. This, in turn, may make the commodity supply curve even steeper in the future, thus reinforcing the sensitivity of commodity prices to world economic growth.

López concludes by pointing out the need to end the support of public policies that discriminate in favor of the "materialization" of consumption. Policies such as a carbon tax, as well as several other consumption taxes that focus on material goods but exclude services, would be steps in the right direction, as well as a dematerialization of public expenditures by increasing the provision of public social goods including education, health, environmental protection, etc.

Post-Crisis Debates on Development Strategy

Openness to trade is a well-accepted component of many successful growth strategies of emerging market economies. Nevertheless, the role that government policies have played in guiding the industrial structural transformation ahead of a country's factor endowment—leapfrogging—have been controversial. Opinions vary but the empirical evidence is scarce in part because it is more difficult to measure the degree of leapfrogging than the extent of trade openness. Shang-Jin Wei and co-authors move forward this debate by providing empirically evidence of whether leapfrogging strategies work.

Wei and co-authors undertake a systematic look at the evidence across countries using gross domestic product (GDP) per capita growth equations for the period 1992–2003 to assess the efficacy of a leapfrogging strategy. To quantify the degree of leapfrogging that an economy may exhibit, they use country's detailed export data instead of production data because the latter is not available for most developing countries in an internationally comparable classification and, when available, has a relatively coarse industrial classification. Leapfrogging is measured using four alternatives indicators: EXPY, the productivity level associated with a country's specialization pattern; a modified EXPY using unit value; EDI, an export dissimilarity index that measures the discrepancy between a country's exports and that of G-3 countries (European Union, Japan, and United States), and ATP, a measure of export sophistication using high-tech exports as the export bundle.

After testing a series of specifications controlling by the initial level of GDP, human capital, institutional variables and using instrumental variable techniques, the authors find a lack of strong and robust support for the notion that a leapfrogging industrial policy strategy can reliably raise economic growth. They conclude by recognizing that there may be individual success stories, but there are also failures and, if leapfrogging is a policy gamble, there is no systematic evidence that suggests that the odds are favorable. Finally, they suggest two areas for further research. The impact of leapfrogging strategies on the "import side" because the use of tariffs and other polices to reduce the import of high tech or high value added products can give domestically produced goods an advantage and versions of leapfrogging strategies, if moderate or subtle, that attempt to exploit latent comparative advantages may be more successful.

The Political Economy of Fragile States

James Fearon revisits the issue posed by Torsten Persson's keynote address, that is, the association of the concept of fragile states with weak institutions and political violence. Even though the concept of fragile states remains murky, aid agencies have produced operational criteria to identify fragile states using, in most cases, governance indicators. Fearon points out that most of the cross-national patterns on the onset of civil war can be explained by putting state capabilities at the center. He explores using three different perceived governance indicators widely used by the developing community—the World Bank Country Policy and Institutional Assessment (CPIA), the Worldwide Governance Indicators (WGI), and the International Country Risk Guide (ICRG)—and whether these governance indicators can be used to predict civil violence in subsequent years.

His empirical strategy consists of logistic estimates of the probability of the onset of civil war or lower-level conflict. The data for civil war and conflicts are obtained from the Uppsala Conflict Data Program (UCDP)/Peace Research Institute Oslo (PRIO) Armed Conflict Dataset. The estimates controlled by population and GDP lagged by one period those affected by oil-producing country, political instability, civil war or conflict in the previous year and governance indictors. The results confirm that a country that was judged in one year to have worse governance than expected given its income level has a significantly higher risk of civil war and conflict during the next five to ten years. This is true for the three sets of governance indicators but is weaker for the CPIA.

In addition, these results have implications for the debate about the causes of civil wars and conflict by supporting the hypothesis that low income per capita is strongly related to conflict risk because it is a proxy for low state capabilities rather than related to a labor market effect by which young people join rebel factions. Fearon concludes suggesting that more research is needed to gauge the impact of governance on other objective indicators of government performance, such as the quality of public goods, education, health, etc.

News Ways of Measuring Welfare

In the mid-1970s, Richard Easterlin, the first modern economist to study happiness, uncovered a seeming paradox: Neither did average happiness levels increase over time as countries grew wealthier nor was there a clear relationship between average per capita GDP and average happiness levels across countries once they achieved a certain minimum level of per capita income.

Daniel Sacks, Betsey Stevenson, and Justin Wolfers revisit the stylized facts on the relationship between subjective well-being and income casting doubt on the Easterlin Paradox. Using the greatest quantity of data available and different datasets covering 140 countries (Gallup World Poll, World Values Survey, and Pew Global Attitudes), they find that within a given country, rich individuals are more satisfied with their lives than poorer individuals and that richer countries have significantly higher levels of average life satisfaction. Studying the time series relationship between satisfaction and income, they also find that economic growth is associated with increases in life satisfaction.

The key innovation of their work is that they focus explicitly on the magnitude of the subjective well-being-income gradient (rather than its statistical significance) and show that the within-country, between-country, and over-time estimates all point to a quantitatively similar relationship between subjective well-being and income. This relationship is robust to different levels of aggregation and different data sets with the gradient for the log of income between 0.3 to 0.4. They also find that income is positively associated with other measures of subjective well-being, including happiness and other upbeat emotions.

They conclude by arguing that the fact that life satisfaction and other measures of subjective well-being rise with income has significant implications for development economists. First and most importantly, these findings cast doubt on the Easterlin Paradox and various theories by suggesting that there is no long-term relationship between well-being and income growth and that economists' traditional interest in economic growth has not been misplaced. Second, the results suggest that differences in subjective well-being over time or across places likely reflect meaningful differences in actual well-being.

Carol Graham, who has studied the topic of happiness extensively and knows its promises as well as its limitations, starts by reviewing all determinants of happiness across and within countries of different development levels. She summarizes the evidence surrounding the debate on the Easterlin Paradox by stating that both sides of the debate may be correct first, because although people in richer countries are happier than those in destitute ones but many things other than income contribute to people's happiness regardless of their level of income, including freedom, stable employment, and good health, which are easier to come by in wealthier countries. Second, the latest studies have used new data from the Gallup World Poll, which includes many more (unweighted) observations from small poor countries in Africa and from transition economies than did Easterlin's original studies (as well as his more recent ones). These countries in particular have relatively low levels of happiness and have had flat or even negative rates of growth over time. Thus, rather than a story of higher levels of income pulling up happiness at the top, it may be one of falling or volatile income trajectories pulling down happiness at the bottom.

Although Graham's research and that of others have established that the standard determinants of happiness demonstrate fairly stable patterns worldwide, it has also shown that people have a remarkable capacity to adapt to both prosperity and adversity. Thus, many people living in conditions of prosperity report to be miserable, while many others living in contexts of remarkable adversity report to be very happy. This adaptation conundrum is one of the main challenges that people advocating happiness as a benchmark for development will have to answer. This capacity to adapt—and the mediating role of norms and expectations—poses all sorts of measurement and comparison challenges, particularly in the study of the relationship between happiness and income. Graham asks if we can really compare the happiness levels of a poor peasant in India, who reports to be very happy due to low expectations and/or due to a naturally cheery character, with those of a successful and very wealthy CEO, who reports to be miserable due to his or her relative rankings compared to that of other CEOs or to a naturally curmudgeonly character?

At one level, it suggests that all happiness is relative. At another, it suggests that some unhappiness may be necessary to achieve economic and other sorts of progress. The examples of migrants who leave their home countries—and families—to provide a better future for their children or of revolutionaries who sacrifice their lives for the broader public good come to mind among others. This also begs more difficult questions. One is whether outside observers, such as development practitioners, should tell the poor peasant in India how miserable he or she is according to objective income measures in order to encourage that peasant to seek a "better" life. A related question is whether we should worry more about addressing the millionaire's misery or increasing the peasant's happiness. Other unanswered questions that must be resolved—or at least further discussed—before happiness can be used a benchmark for progress or as an objective of development policy are the definition of happiness, inter-temporal trade-offs, and cardinality versus ordinality.

Graham concludes that, while all these questions cannot be answered now, the discussion raises issues that are important to development policy and forces us to think deeply about what measures of human well-being are the most accurate benchmarks of economic progress and human development.

Social Programs and Transfers: Are We Learning?

Conditional cash transfers are an increasingly popular strategy for poverty-reduction programs. Countries like South Africa, however, have experimented with cash transfers that are mean tested but unconditional. Ingrid Woolard and Murray Leibrandt review the experience of South Africa on social assistance post-apartheid and the role that unconditional cash transfers have had in reducing poverty and other social outcomes and make recommendations for the future.

The authors start by pointing out that, at the time of the transition to democracy in 1994, the South African social security system (social insurance and social assistance) already was notably well developed for a middle-income country. Since then, the social assistance system has evolved in a way that continued and modified some of the grants (old age pension, disability grant, and foster grant) and replaced the state maintenance grant with the child support grant (CSG). The CSG was introduced in 1998 and was to be paid to the child's primary caregiver based on a means test and immunization requirements. The program, however, had a low take-up rate. Thus, in 2000, the government extended the grant to children seven to fourteen years old.

Since then, the CSG has expanded and older age groups have been gradually been included. From 2010, all income-eligible children born after 1996 will receive CSG until they turn 18 years old. Today, spending on cash transfers is currently at 3.5 percent of GDP, which is more than twice the median spending across developing economies and is the center piece of the poverty-reduction strategy.

The authors show that the reduction in poverty during the post-apartheid period has been associated strongly with the expansion of social grants and that the disbursement of these grants has been strongly redistributive. Also, at the micro level, they show that the money flowing into households through grants has been used in part to improve health and education outcomes for household members other than the direct beneficiary. Such impacts are crucial for longer-run poverty alleviation. At the same time, the evidence on the labor supply effects of grants is more mixed with grants seeming to promote migration in search of employment but also seeming to provide some disincentive for resident, working-age household members to look for work.

The authors conclude by stating that the current system, which focuses on children and the elderly, is something of an artifact of history, rather than a reflection of a coherently designed system. In the absence of a comprehensive social insurance system, prime-age adults can only benefit from social assistance grants if they are disabled or are co-resident with a child or elderly person. They believe that the overriding goal of economic and social policy has to be the assimilation of many more of the unemployed into the labor, but they are cautious about further expansion of social grants to this end. Finally, they also are cautious about the associated imposition of cash conditionalities that are likely to be high in the South African context. They argue that the desire to introduce conditionalities seems to be driven by political economy considerations, that is, the belief that taxpayers may be more likely to support transfers to the poor if they are linked to efforts to overcome poverty in the long term, particularly when the efforts involve actions to improve the welfare of children although they may be expensive to monitor and enforce.

Opening Address

ANDERS BORG

Thank you very much. I would like to welcome you all to Stockholm. This is obviously a very beautiful time, when spring is coming to our country after a long and cold winter.

We have gone through a winter in the global economy over the past few years, and I think we are all hoping that we are seeing the first signs of spring. Politicians will have to deal with this crisis for another few years, and researchers will probably spend a couple of decades trying to understand what really happened and what lessons we can draw from this eruption of dramatic events. Already, we are seeing some potentially serious effects on the fight against world poverty. People always reconsider their spending during an economic crisis, but it is important for us to continue to have ambitious policies when it comes to development.

The World Bank has played a crucial role in responding to this crisis, and the Swedish government will continue its close cooperation with and strong support of the Bank. We are one of the major donors and one of the major contributors when it comes to foreign aid. We believe that individuals and nations have a Samaritan duty to help those who are worse off. And from a practical point of view, development policy is good for the whole world. Every country that achieves self-sustained growth will contribute to world trade, and an open global trade system contributes to the common good.

Sweden contributes 1 percent of its gross national income to foreign aid; we encourage other countries to follow our example. For us, development is about core values. We need free markets to organize societies, price mechanisms, and property rights. We need functioning court systems to help solve conflicts over rights. But we also need social cohesion—a system in which the public sector plays a crucial role. Investments in energy, infrastructure, and education are essential for development, and we assign a high priority to these areas.

One of the main lessons that come out of the crisis is that all these institutions must work together, with a strong emphasis on macroeconomic stability. Unsustainable

Anders Borg is the Minister for Finance of Sweden.

Annual World Bank Conference on Development Economics 2011, Global
© 2013 The International Bank for Reconstruction and Development/The World Bank

macroeconomic imbalances will contribute to more crises in the world economy, so whatever we can do in our own countries to deal with account deficits and government deficits is of utmost importance to promote stability.

Again, welcome to Stockholm. I hope you will spend some inspiring days here and participate in many good discussions on these very important issues of global development.

Opening Address

JUSTIN YIFU LIN

Minister Borg, Minister Carlsson, ladies and gentlemen, it is a pleasure for the World Bank to cohost this year's Annual Bank Conference on Development Economics (ABCDE) together with our Swedish colleagues, and it is my honor to welcome you to the conference. Since its first meeting in 1989, the ABCDE has become the largest gathering of economists from academia, government, international financial institutions, and nongovernmental organizations to exchange new ideas and recent findings on research and to discuss development policies. This 21st ABCDE will have four keynote addresses—on development aid, state capacity, learning growth and development, and poverty traps. We will also have five plenary sessions, ranging from the environment and the green economy to development strategies post-crisis, fragile states, new ways of measuring welfare, and social transfers. In addition, there will be 18 parallel sessions with papers selected from 270 proposals.

This year, we will also launch a global debate, organized by the Development Economics Vice Presidency and the World Bank Development Institute. The debate, titled "Development Challenges in a Post-Crisis World," will feature three Nobel Prize winners—Eric Maskin, James Mirrlees, and Robert Solow—and two distinguished economists—Partha Dasgupta and Abhijit Banerjee. It will be webcast, so many people throughout the world can watch it simultaneously.

We have 600 participants, including 5 Nobel laureates and many potential laureates. As we meet here today, the world is experiencing the biggest development challenges since the Great Depression in 1929. In fact, when the global financial crisis erupted in September 2008, the collapse of equity markets, contraction of global trade, and decline of industrial production in many countries were all more serious than in the Great Depression. However, we had learned our lessons from the past, and governments immediately adopted financial rescue measures to stabilize the banking sector and avoid the worst possible scenarios. At the same time, these

---

At the time of the conference, Justin Yifu Lin was senior vice president and chief economist, Development Economics, World Bank.

Annual World Bank Conference on Development Economics 2011, Global
© 2013 The International Bank for Reconstruction and Development / The World Bank

governments pledged continued support for free trade, despite the rising unemployment in their domestic economies. Many governments adopted fiscal stimulus policies and passed financial restructuring legislation, and now the global economy is recovering.

According to our forecast, the overall growth rate for the global economy in 2010 will be 3.1 percent—a far cry from the 2.1 percent contraction of 2009. Among high-income countries, the 2010 growth rate will be 2.2 percent; among developing countries, it is likely to be 6 percent.

However, the foundation of the recovery is still very fragile. Although the crisis erupted in the financial sector, the challenge has moved to the real sector; specifically, the underutilization of global capacity. In the first quarter of 2010, the U.S. capacity utilization rate was 73 percent and the Euro-zone rate was 72 percent—both about 10 percent below normal. A similar situation exists in a number of middle-income countries (but not in China, India, or Brazil). With excess capacity, we know that the unemployment rate will be high and the incentive for private sector investment will be low. In this situation, the financial sector will still be under stress because of the danger of nonperforming loans, and slow growth will mean that some countries will have sovereign debt pressure.

So the world is facing a dilemma. In high-income countries, with high underutilization of capacity, it is necessary to have a fiscal stimulus; however, this stimulus may cause public debt to rise very rapidly. But if governments adopt an early exit strategy from the stimulus measures, there is a danger of a double-dip recession, which can cause financial trouble or even a sovereign debt crisis. This dilemma will spread to the developing countries, because if the high-income countries continue their fiscal stimulus measures, the increasing public debt will have a crowding-out effect in the financial sectors and interest rates will rise, which will increase the cost of growth in developing countries. If the high-income countries exit from the fiscal stimulus, the danger of double-dip exists. Declines in the growth rates of high-income countries will also negatively affect developing countries through trade, remittance, and capital flow.

This is an important year for the developing countries in terms of meeting the Millennium Development Goals (MDGs). Seven of the eight goals (except for the first one—reducing the world poverty rate by half) have already been derailed. If developing countries cannot maintain their growth rates, the world will be even less likely to achieve the MDGs.

What are some possible ways out of this global dilemma? We know that a Keynesian type of fiscal stimulus is desirable in the face of large underutilization of capacity; the two main challenges are whether the stimulus will be effective in supporting demand and whether the public debt accumulation is sustainable. The effectiveness of fiscal stimulus is related to the so-called Ricardian Equivalence; that is, the government increases spending while the private sector increases saving. As a result, public debt rises but the total demand in the economy may not increase much. The Ricardian Equivalence holds only if government spending does not increase productivity. If productivity increases, it will promote growth. Government revenue will increase and debt can be paid back. In this situation, sustainability, higher taxes, and lower consumption in the future will not be an issue.

But how can we increase productivity through government fiscal stimulus? Two areas have potential. One is related to the green economy, which we will discuss at this conference. The other is related to the infrastructure bottleneck that exists in many countries, especially developing countries. In high-income countries, the scope for investing in infrastructure to release bottlenecks is small, and the green economy alone may not be able to boost demand and absorb the underutilization of capacity. However, in developing countries the opportunity to invest in the green economy and in infrastructure is large, although (except for a few emerging markets, such as China, India, and Brazil) many developing countries are facing constraints in their fiscal situation as well as on their foreign reserves.

Thus, a possibility exists for a win–win situation in which high-income and foreign reserve-rich countries find a way to increase their investments in developing countries. Such investment will boost the demand for capital goods produced in high-income countries and reduce their excess capacity, while promoting growth in developing countries, which will help them avoid the poverty trap and facilitate their achievement of the MDGs. In this spirit, recent capital increases in the World Bank and other regional development banks will support an increase in investment in developing countries; certainly, that is desirable.

This year, we are going to celebrate the 50th anniversary of the International Development Association (IDA). IDA is not just for humanitarian purposes; in the current global situation, it is also an important way to promote growth in low-income countries. Sweden should be complimented for its generous support—the country's 2009 contribution was 1.12 percent of gross national income, which exceeded the 0.7 percent target for high-income countries.

But if we want to emerge from the global crisis, we need more than money. We need ideas so we can select the right projects for the green economy and reduce infrastructure bottlenecks. Education and health are also important—investment in those areas will increase productivity in the future. Not only do we need to select the right areas, we need to have the ability to implement projects. Thus, state capacity and governance issues are also important, and these issues will be discussed at this conference. Overall, I believe this year's conference can make an important contribution to addressing global issues.

In his opening remarks at the 2004 ABCDE, former World Bank President Jim Wolfensohn said, "The field of development economics is a seductive discipline in that it offers those working in it the possibility to make a difference." And 75 years ago, at the height of the Great Depression, John Maynard Keynes published his *General Theory of Employment, Interest and Money*. In the last sentence of the last chapter, he said, "But, soon or late, it is ideas, not vested interests, which are dangerous for good or evil." Today, we face a similar situation in the world economy. The world needs good ideas. ABCDE will help generate ideas that will make a difference for developing countries and for the world.

Opening Address

GUNILLA CARLSSON

Excellencies, ladies and gentlemen. Thank you, Justin.

Let me start by adding my voice to the chorus of welcomes, from Mr. Borg and from the whole of the Swedish government. We are happy to host the ABCDE 2010. For me, it is also a great opportunity to discuss the development challenges of today and tomorrow with some of the greatest minds—that's you.

It is obvious that policy making and action in response to major global challenges should be based on the best available research. And yet, international studies demonstrate that the links between research and policy are not as strong as they need to be. To effectively tackle the current global challenges, there is a great need for systematically researched knowledge—underpinned by context-specific analysis—to guide policy making, political decisions, and implementation. Domestic analytical capacity and country-specific and region-specific expertise through research are key if countries are to take part on an equal footing in international discussions on joint strategies to tackle shared global challenges. The amount and quality of research relevant to developing countries are often insufficient. This is due to the lack of research capacity in the developing countries themselves, but it is also linked to inadequate international production of science-based knowledge concerning poverty-related development issues. Evidence-based policy approaches have a clear potential to strongly affect outcomes in developing countries. Better use of evidence in policy making and practice can help reduce poverty and improve economic performance. Finding innovative ways to make better use of research results in policy making is therefore a necessity.

My hope and expectation is that this ABCDE conference will deepen discussions on how to stimulate communication and collaboration among researchers, evaluators, policy makers, and practitioners in all parts of the world and in different disciplines to effectively tackle the major global challenges we face.

Gunilla Carlsson is the minister for international development cooperation of Sweden.

Annual World Bank Conference on Development Economics 2011, Global
© 2013 The International Bank for Reconstruction and Development/The World Bank

Sweden is proud to cohost this event with the World Bank, one of our main partners in international development cooperation. What distinguishes the World Bank as an institution is its combined role as a knowledge bank and a provider of development finance. One excellent illustration is the Bank's work in low-income countries through its International Development Association (IDA). The International Bank for Reconstruction and Development (IBRD) was established in 1944 to aid the recovery from the destruction of World War II. By the 1950s, it was evident that the poorest countries needed loans on softer terms than IBRD could offer. IDA was established for this purpose in September 1960 with 15 signatory countries, and I am proud to note that Sweden was one of them. Since then, IDA has become the leading source of concessional lending to 79 of the world's poorest countries. IDA credits and grants have totaled over US$200 billion, averaging US$14 billion a year in recent years. IDA is the largest multilateral recipient of Swedish official development assistance. This year, IDA celebrates 50 years of operation, and it has every reason to look back with pride on its achievements.

To give just a few examples, between 2006 and 2009, thanks to IDA, a million additional primary school teachers were trained; more than 7 million people gained access to basic health, nutrition, and population services; almost 8 million women received antenatal care; and 60,500 new piped household water connections were established. In the past five years, IDA has built, repaired, or maintained 60,000 kilometers of rural roads, benefiting 60 million people in low-income countries.

During its 50 years, one-quarter of its borrowing countries have graduated completely from IDA. In 1991, China was IDA's biggest borrower; by 2007, China had not only graduated but had become a donor. Reflecting the increasingly multipolar world economy, I expect to see more new donors following this example, and donors increasing their contributions. The current replenishment round is an opportunity for these emerging donors to play a bigger role. With combined efforts, we can eradicate poverty more quickly. In fact—and with all due respect—I sincerely hope that our successors will not stand here in another 50 years, celebrating 100 years of IDA. After all, the goal of international development cooperation is to render itself obsolete. For this to happen, we need to make the necessary enhancements to IDA's Results Measurement System and make sure it is accompanied by a more robust results framework. We need to work hard together during this replenishment period to achieve the Millennium Development Goals (MDGs). And we must continue to target Africa, the continent that is lagging furthest behind on the MDGs.

Together with other donors, Sweden has encouraged IDA to highlight three particular issues in the coming three years. First, postconflict and fragile states present the greatest development needs and the most challenging circumstances. These are the states in which it is hardest to obtain results, but IDA has to make good use of our money here, too. Second, gender equality must be seriously addressed for IDA's poverty reduction efforts to be as effective as they can possibly be. And third, IDA and the entire World Bank must develop a coherent approach to address climate change. IDA is an excellent expression of multilateral cooperation. It is also the product of the intellectual work of many people, including the participants at this conference. I trust that IDA will continue to evolve—to contribute to a world free of poverty and to translate the latest academic findings into best practices on the ground.

Let me take this opportunity to say a few words about the key priorities for the further improvement of Swedish bilateral aid. As you heard from our minister of finance, we are proud to be the biggest aid donor in the world, but we need other countries to join us to ensure sufficient resources, as well as enough interest and strategies to deal with global poverty.

When I first took office as minister for international development cooperation, I had one overarching priority: to ensure that Swedish aid would be efficient and effective, and would deliver concrete development results for people living in poverty. We have made progress, but I still feel frustrated at times. Why does change come about slowly, or at least slower than we hope and need? Why have we not come further?

One of the first measures I undertook was to limit the number of Swedish partner countries and increase country focus. I have also been very strict in ensuring that Swedish aid is provided in a maximum of three sectors in each partner country. Furthermore, we have launched a strategy for our participation in multilateral development cooperation. A fundamental premise for all these measures was the focus on efficiency, effectiveness, and results. The world is changing rapidly. Looking back only a couple of decades, we take things for granted now that we could only imagine then. The Internet is probably the most obvious example. However—and this is of great concern to me—the way we do development cooperation changes slowly and not at the same pace as the changes in the world. It is only natural that bureaucratic structures are slow to change, but in this area we have no time to lose. Poverty is acute today, and yet here we are, working with development cooperation models developed decades ago. We are trying to improve in many ways. For example, within the EU we are working on division of labor and complementarity, and we are promoting the use of partner country systems to limit transaction costs and increase ownership. This is all very useful and important work. But is it enough?

I think we need to approach development cooperation from a new point of view, and the ABCDE conference can assist in this. A basic issue for me, as minister for international development cooperation, is ensuring that we get the best possible value for our money. I need to know how the resources made available by Swedish taxpayers are spent. I have, therefore, focused on three issues that I believe are key to ensuring effective development cooperation. The first issue is corruption and the absolute need to tackle it. The second is the need for increased measuring and understanding of results from the projects and programs to which we contribute, both as an objective to ensure that we are doing the right thing and as a means to continuously improve our methods and strategies. The third issue is the challenge of development contributions in a changing world, including through innovation in a broad sense of the term.

I have launched an agenda—Open Aid—to address these issues and to further improve Swedish development cooperation. We need increased openness through active transparency that promotes accountability, scrutiny, and improved knowledge about aid. Increased openness to participation promotes innovation and ensures that we receive expertise from different spheres of society. And increased openness promotes cooperation among new and increasing numbers of actors in development. Every aspect of Open Aid is underpinned by transparency, participation, and cooperation.

The Open Aid vision and the reform process in general are ongoing efforts. Your deliberations during these coming days will make an important contribution, and I would like to challenge you to reflect on the matters I've just mentioned. Share your ideas. Agree or disagree. Only then can we be sure that we make full use of the resources around us and that we are equipped in the best way possible to reach our objectives of eradicating poverty and giving every person an opportunity to develop.

Thank you for all the excellent preparations for this conference. Thank you all for coming and, once again, we welcome you to ABCDE Sweden.

Keynote Addresses

Overcoming the Samaritan's Dilemma in Development Aid

ELINOR OSTROM

We all have been in situations where we hear people criticizing aid to developing countries. Some people say, "Don't do it anymore." Others say, "Do it better." There is considerable doubt in the world that development aid is increasing economic growth, alleviating poverty, promoting social development, or fostering democratic regimes. We need to have a positive, sustainable impact, and that is not always happening. So it is important that we dig in and understand why some of our policies are not sustainable and why some people keep saying they need more money, while others say, "Well, we just can't help from the outside. It's got to be from inside." Some focus on how long it takes to make a big impact, while others say the reason for diminished or unsuccessful outcomes is too many perverse incentives. This last reason is most important—many development aid incentives *are* perverse.

In a study of development aid commissioned by the Swedish International Development Cooperation Agency (Sida)—one of the best development assistance agencies in the world—Krister Andersson, Clark Gibson, Sujai Shivakumar, and I did find perverse incentives within the organization. We then checked with our colleagues at the U.S. Agency for International Development (USAID) and the World Bank, and discovered that many of these perverse incentives exist across many development aid agencies. This spurred us to write a book about our findings, which was published by Oxford University Press as *The Samaritan's Dilemma* (Gibson et al. 2005).

First, we need a shared basic definition of "development." What we and many other people mean by development is that people around the world are realizing improved well-being through production and exchange of private goods, as well as cooperation and coordination in providing public goods and common-pool

At the time of the conference, the late Elinor Ostrom was Senior Research Director, Workshop in Political Theory and Policy Analysis, Indiana University.

I want to thank Clark Gibson, Krister Andersson, and Sujai Shivakumar for joining me in the earlier research that provides a foundation for this address. I also want to thank the colleagues who have been working with us on our irrigation and forestry studies around the world, and colleagues at Sida who asked us to do this study, which enabled us to get an inside view of development aid.

Annual World Bank Conference on Development Economics 2011, Global

resources. Most aid personnel agree that governments provide the macroinstitutional environments within which development can be realized. One of the puzzles we are trying to solve is why some of the greatest efforts have not led to enhanced development. At the very heart of trying to achieve development assistance are collective-action problems. In many situations, to move ahead, we need the contributions of many participants in public health, in the management of resources, and in a variety of settings.

What Is a Dilemma?

The Prisoner's Dilemma was devised by Merrill Flood and Melvin Dresher in 1950, and expanded in Mancur Olson's *The Logic of Collective Action* (1965) and Hardin's "The Tragedy of the Commons" (1968). Hardin asked whether benefits can be obtained by a person who is making no contribution while others are contributing. He pointed out the incentive for a person, who can receive free benefits, is not to contribute, which may result in overuse of resources or underprovision of public goods. So there is a potential conflict in most of the real problems of the developing world and in the developed world's ability to solve collective-action problems.

Besides the incentive problems, we have a wide variety of information problems. In many instances, we have missing information. We have situations that are asymmetric—some people hold the information and others who need it do not have access to it. And throughout development aid processes, we have principal-agent problems; for example, when employees who work directly with development activities know more about what they do than their managers but do not share the information. When the real goals of donors and recipient country organizations differ, substantial principal-agent problems can occur.

Part of the problem is motivational—getting honest officials to oversee public goods, sharing knowledge about the process and progress, and knowing that we are providing the public goods. Most provision of public goods involves collective dilemmas, and some people say, "Oh, just turn it over to the government." But that has not always been a successful strategy. Government involvement may be very helpful, but it is rarely sufficient. Also, the provision of common-pool resources also involves the potential for a collective dilemma.

The Samaritan's Dilemma

In 1975, James Buchanan wrote about the Samaritan's Dilemma, pointing out that a person may want to help someone in need but faces the question "Do I or don't I?" The Samaritan tries to think through how the recipient will respond to help. In theory, the recipient has two strategies: put in high effort or put in low effort (figure 1). The equilibrium of a Samaritan's Dilemma game is that the Samaritan gives help and the recipient puts in low effort. The equilibrium in the lower righthand

FIGURE 1.
Samaritan's Dilemma

		recipient	
		high effort	low effort
samaritan	no help	2,2	1,1
	help	4,3	3,4

Source: Adapted from Buchanan 1977, 170.

corner of figure 1 is the highest immediate joint payoff in this situation. Food aid (figure 2) is an example in which people often say, "Gee, this is a terrible dilemma." If the Samaritan provides food relief, the recipient could put in high effort by using it and making an investment in new infrastructure and new ways of harvesting food, because the recipient has the food to support the effort. But the recipient could also just eat the food and not do anything to improve self-support. There are a fair number of documented instances in which people have stopped growing food when relief was made available. This is an example of a bad equilibrium, because the donor is trying to help people develop new agricultural techniques and new ways of producing things rather than just providing them with food.

Most infrastructure construction includes a Samaritan's Dilemma. For instance, the humanitarian provision of health aid can have these kinds of results. So we face the risk that all long-term development might become a Samaritan's Dilemma. We need to be aware of this problem when we think about how we provide aid.

Puzzles Related to Aid

Besides the Samaritan's Dilemma, we may encounter many asymmetric power relationships (Gibson and Hoffman, 2011). Some of our contemporary efforts in developing countries are trying to offset earlier forms of asymmetric power, where we have been concerned about elite capture and how we can overcome it. But sometimes when we try to help, we make it worse.

It is not just that developing countries have problems, and we who have all the knowledge should go in and solve them. We must be aware that these problems are complex, and that we often contribute to them when we try to help. Yes, many of the countries in need of aid lack contemporary, effective institutions, but many have had very effective institutions over a very long time. They have been changed, sometimes by internal mandates and sometimes by our own actions. The development assistance dynamic includes a number of actors in what we call an "octangle," representing the tangle of relationships that can exist (figure 3).

Let us take a look at the octangle in figure 3. A donor government might relate to a recipient government in government-to-government activities. Or there might

FIGURE 2.
An Example of the Samaritan's Dilemma: Food Relief

		recipient			
		high effort		low effort	
samaritan	no food	Save funds, but watch starvation occur despite farmers' hard work.	Try to improve farm productivity but starvation occurs.	Save funds and no results.	Do not try to overcome long-term starvation.
	relief food	Watch farmers improve short-term and long-term nutrition.	Eat relief food and improve farm productivity.	Watch farmers eat but not grow any food.	Eat relief food and do not farm.

Source: Adapted from Gibson et al. 2005.

FIGURE 3.
The International Development Assistance Octangle

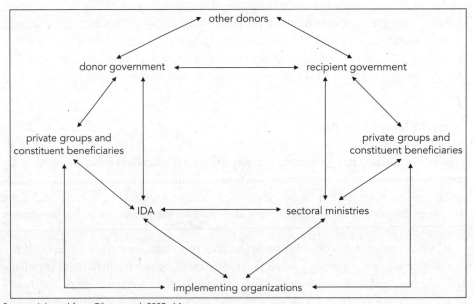

Source: Adapted from Gibson et al. 2005, 64.

Note: IDA = international development agency.

be a triangle that includes other donors. Meanwhile, the development agency within the donor government and the sectoral ministries within the recipient government are relating both hierarchically and across the same level. There are private groups on both sides. And then you have the implementing organizations. We have studied development assistance relationships across many countries and repeatedly found the octangle—the macrostructure always has an element of "tangledness" to it.

Each dyad or triad is subject to motivational, informational, and power problems. Many participants want short-term benefits. If you have a one-year budget, you want results in that year, because you are not going to get more money the next year if you do not spend this year's budget. A failure at any one of the nodes can lead to failure at others, so we can have a system that is working fine until one thing fails and affects others. It is not a self-correcting system. One of the advantages of a market for private goods is that it can self-correct. We need to be thinking about how to add self-correcting mechanisms to the development aid octangle.

We have too many stakeholders and not enough real ownership. The incentives for various participants are problematic, and the beneficiaries are not important stakeholders in the octangle; they are just the recipients. If you are going to try to improve development, recipients/beneficiaries need to be active, or we do not have development.

What Do We Invest in Development Aid?

When we did our empirical work, we chose to do research in two countries we knew very well. Sujai Shivakumar was born and raised in India and had already conducted long-term research there. Clark Gibson had done long-term research in Africa, particularly East Africa. So we chose India and Zambia, Krister Andersson and I have spent considerable time at Sida headquarters in Stockholm, and we have both conducted research in various developing countries. We chose natural resources and the problem of developing agriculture and infrastructure as the basis of our research design. We then asked each country agency—from Sida to the local agencies—to nominate their best projects. We were not able to do a long-term study, so we decided to look at Sida staff rated as their best projects to see whether and how they were handling the Samaritan's Dilemma.

From the field studies and from talking with colleagues across development agencies around the world, we found that infrastructure projects were very attractive to development assistance agencies. This is probably still true, from what I have heard from development assistance colleagues in the past year or two. You can get a budget, you can go out there, you can build a road, and then you can point to that road. You can move large sums of money with a small staff. You may also be able to involve firms from the donor country. USAID, for example, funds a very large number of U.S. firms that do consulting work plus construction and engineering work all over the world.

One comparative example comes from a long study of irrigation in Nepal, more than 200 systems that colleagues and I have studied intensely (Joshi et al. 2000). The agency-based systems that have received huge amounts of financial assistance from various donors are not able to outperform the farmer-managed systems. The farmer-managed systems—built on infrastructure the farmers have constructed out of mud and rocks—produce more food, produce more water for the tail-end farmers, and are economically more efficient than some of the very large donor projects in which the infrastructure has been built for the recipients. The reason: The agency-based projects did not pay attention to property rights and were simply turned over without any effort to understand the incentives needed to keep them going. When we help with infrastructure, we must be very careful to work with the recipients to produce a successful, sustainable project (see Ostrom et al., forthcoming).

We also need to be thinking about how we support human skills to build productivity. How can we design systems so that people who receive funds and produce results get more money in the future, and those who do not produce get less? To achieve this goal, we have to keep records over time, invest in human knowledge, evaluate productivity, and base future projects on results. This investment will be substantial. When officials at USAID, the World Bank, Sida, and other development aid agencies ask me to describe successful development projects, I tell them about an ingenious intervention in Nepal and their reaction is often, "Oh, that would require a very large amount of our human capital, and we don't have that many staff." Most of the successful projects we have studied have involved large amounts of human capital compared with the proportion of engineered capital (Lam and Ostrom 2010). An agency can have a highly motivated staff, young people coming in with new ideas, investments in improvements, and high morale in the home office, but is this enough? I believe that these are necessary but not sufficient conditions for learning how to achieve sustainable development.

Sustainability of a Project

How can the individual in a development agency learn about sustainability, and how can that learning be enhanced? One way is through a long-term assignment. Projects frequently take five to seven years—if a person is there at the beginning or the middle or the end, he or she has a sense of the processes at different stages. We found in most projects we studied that people who were there at the beginning were not there in the middle or at the end, so there was no long-term involvement or learning. But even if a person is not involved in a project over the long term, he or she can pass information along, so the next person knows what happened earlier. Retaining young staff so they work with you for a long time is important, and people have to have a sense that their career advancement is based on performance.

There is often a huge variation in the length of assignments. One person may have a five-month assignment while another has been doing the same job for 18 years. People with longer assignments are often in a headquarters office and never get into the field. Many field assignments last for only one to three years, which means the person is there at the beginning or the middle or the end, with little or no continuity within the project.

A lot of moving around means that staff receive knowledge of what is going on in the recipient country, at headquarters, in infrastructure, and in agriculture, but the rapid shifts back and forth do not allow the person to learn enough about any one area to gain the kind of expertise required for long-term design. When we have asked development aid staff about their assignments, most say the quick turnover rate has an adverse effect. For example, one person told me, "I just started to learn and then they shifted me somewhere else. I was learning the local language, and now I'm in a different place and I don't have the local language." That is a common problem. Also, there is often very little communication or participation in follow-up on a project after a person has moved on to another project.

Another factor in the development assistance world is temporary contracts. And part of that is due to the budget that determines how a project moves forward. For instance, an agency's budget allows a certain amount for a project that must be spent in a year but does not allow the hiring of full-time employees. Many aid personnel are temporary, with contracts ranging from 3 to 12 months. How can an agency maintain continuity on a project and how does one's career move forward when there is a collective-action problem within the organization itself? In this case, no single staff member is responsible for the project's performance. The octangle teaches us that many people and organizations are involved in a project, and the opportunity exists to point fingers and blame others for problems, especially when there is a succession of temporary staff in each organization. I think part of the solution is to establish long-term assignments for staff members. This will also enable more accurate performance evaluation for promotion within the agency.

How can we enhance organizational learning about sustainability? I believe there are five techniques. The first is to evaluate a project at midterm rather than just at the end. If an evaluation occurs at the end of a seven-year project, for instance, there is no chance of improving something that was not working right from the beginning. Problems are not noted until after the project is over. Second, it is very important to involve beneficiaries in evaluations, because they are key actors. If they are not involved, they do not have a voice. They need to receive the reports so they can participate in the discussions and the learning. Third, cumulative knowledge about factors (such as ownership) that lead to sustainability is important. All factors must be included in the evaluations, so the information can build as the project progresses. Fourth, information must be exchanged between the research world and the world of action, and compared among projects within a development aid organization and among similar projects developed by all aid agencies. The fifth technique is to make evaluations useful. Performance criteria should be uniform across evaluations, so knowledge can be accumulated and discussions about improvements can be productive.

How do we learn from the evaluations and how do we make them more useful? Critical reports exist on projects that were evaluated in the late 1990s and early 2000s (Carlsson, Köhlin, and Ekbom 1994; Cracknell 2001). The authors found that evaluations were conducted too late to be useful and did not involve the beneficiaries. My colleagues and I were struck by the lack of ownership. If you are going to have an effective project, the recipients have to have some sense of ownership. I have checked with USAID colleagues and other agency personnel, and they say that evaluation still frequently comes at the very end of a project and rarely involves beneficiaries.

If we decide we are going to work on a certain aspect, we should be sure our evaluation process looks at that aspect. We did a content analysis of 16 evaluation reports to see what they considered factors for success. Of the 16, only one mentioned ownership (Gibson et al. 2005, chapter 11), and most of the reports did not mention sustainability. If we want to build sustainable development projects, we need be doing a thorough analysis of them, sometimes going back 5 or 10 years after project completion to find out what has happened. We have been doing that in some of our research, because we have been studying forestry, irrigation, and other resources in the field where earlier projects were completed. We look at them and record our careful observations; frequently we have found no impact of government management over a 5- to 10-year period but have found that community-managed forests tend to improve forest conditions in the same time period (Chhatre and Agrawal 2008, 2009; Hayes 2006;).

We need to make the evaluations useful and develop some sense of what criteria we should be using. But how do we get back and forth between the university and the world of action? In talking with Sida staff, we found that 85 percent believed evaluations were ineffective, but nothing was happening to change them at that time—lots of informal discussions but no effort to move ahead. And we did not find an internal and self-conscious effort of Sida managers to stimulate learning about factors leading to success or failure of their projects. We also asked about seminars that bring together all the people who are working on infrastructure around the world to talk about why projects work here and not there. We did not find anything like this at Sida, USAID, or other development aid organizations. I do not think we have had a lot of that at the World Bank either. We need to build these sorts of efforts.

Another arena that needs work is the budget process. The main problem is trying to get the money spent each year, because if it is not spent this year, it will not be available next year. This budgetary pressure is a universal problem and one we need to understand. The official policy of most development agencies is to discourage the use-it-or-lose-it approach; however, when project staff have spent all their money by a certain date, they are often feted with champagne or a party. We need to ask ourselves if we are rewarding the wrong behavior and not dealing with the problem.

One way of dealing with the mad dash to use up the money is to continue funding projects. If a project is already out there and we have "leftover funds," let's just keep it going. But that is not always the best strategy. We have found, in general, that the type of project affects the likelihood of sustainability. We studied efforts to transfer electricity over huge transmission lines without charging a fee to households; no income meant that the electricity agency in the country did not have a budget to sustain itself. As a result, it had to go back to the development agency to get more money to continue providing electricity (Gibson et al. 2005, chapter 9). Ed Araral (2009) conducted a fascinating study in the Philippines of more than 2,000 irrigation systems and found the same lack of incentives. If the farmers do not invest in keeping the system going, they can go back to the development agency and ask for help to repair the system that they could have maintained. The development agency usually comes through with new funds. Decentralization has recently become another panacea, but it is not a universal success (Andersson, Gibson, and Lehoucq 2006; Andersson and Ostrom 2008). The Samaritan's Dilemma works itself out in a wide array of settings around the world.

Conclusion

It is important for us to recognize that there are no magic bullets and that these are tough problems. Instead of assuming that we have a panacea and taking action, we have to dig in and understand the incentives of a situation (Ostrom, Janssen, and Anderies 2007). We need to broaden our decision base, and we need multiple strategies, knowing that they will not work in every case (Poteete, Janssen, and Ostrom 2010). It is not easy to overcome these problems. We have to fit what we are doing to local culture and circumstance. And the participants have to understand what we are trying to accomplish and see it as legitimate and something they want to pitch in on (Shivakumar 2005).

So, what can we all do? I think we need to revisit the concepts of ownership and sustainability in terms of how we create projects in which people have real ownership and want to sustain over time, rather than simply handing out money. We need to examine the role of consultants. In our research, we encountered many nongovernmental organizations that were profit makers in disguise, simply trying to find the money. We also need to understand that public goods are different from common-pool resources; that enhancing a market is different from getting health care; and that we accomplish these tasks in different ways. We need to understand the politics. We need to understand the pressure to disperse and spend the money, which is a very big problem. We need to use evaluations more effectively.

Understanding all these factors requires time. We need to help build institutions, but we cannot build institutions primarily from the outside. Yes, we can build the hardware, but in our resource studies around the world, we repeatedly find that hardware is only part of what is needed to achieve development. Without the software of institutions, projects do not do well or last. We need much better work and communication back and forth, and I must say that academia has not functioned as well as it should have. When I go out to study various kinds of problems around the world, some colleagues in my department say, "Why are you studying *that*? You should be studying the government and parliament, not farmers." We need academia to get involved and not just work at official levels of government. We need to be developing the theory and testing it so we are moving ahead. We have a lot of work to do; if we can work together on these issues, I think we will move ahead.

References

Andersson, Krister, Clark Gibson, and Fabrice Lehoucq. 2006. "Municipal Politics and Forest Governance: Comparative Analysis of Decentralization in Bolivia and Guatemala." *World Development* 34 (3): 576–95.

Andersson, Krister, and Elinor Ostrom. 2008. "Analyzing Decentralized Resource Regimes from a Polycentric Perspective." *Policy Sciences* 41: 71–93.

Araral, Eduardo. 2009. "What Explains Collective Action in the Commons? Theory and Evidence from the Philippines." *World Development* 37 (3): 687–97.

Buchanan, James M. 1975. "The Samaritan's Dilemma." In *Altruism, Morality and Economic Theory*, ed. E. S. Phelps. New York: Russell Sage Foundation.

———.1977. *Freedom in Constitutional Contract: Perspectives of a Political Economist*. College Station: Texas A&M University Press.

Carlsson, Jerker, Gunnar Köhlin, and Anders Ekbom. 1994. *The Political Economy of Evaluation: International Aid Agencies and the Effectiveness of Aid*. London: Macmillan.

Chhatre, Ashwini, and Arun Agrawal. 2008. "Forest Commons and Local Enforcement." *Proceedings of the National Academy of Sciences* 105 (36): 13286–91.

Chhatre, Ashwini, and Arun Agrawal. 2009. "Tradeoffs and Synergies between Carbon Storage and Livelihood Benefits from Forest Commons." *Proceedings of the National Academy of Sciences* 106 (42): 17667–70.

Cracknell, B. E. 2001. "Knowing Is All: Or Is It? Some Reflections on Why the Acquisition of Knowledge, Focusing Particularly on Evaluation Activities, Does Not Always Lead to Action." *Public Administration and Development* 21 (5): 371–79.

Gibson, Clark C., Krister Andersson, Elinor Ostrom, and Sujai Shivakumar. 2005. *The Samaritan's Dilemma: The Political Economy of Development Aid*. Oxford, England: Oxford University Press.

Gibson, Clark C., and Barak D. Hoffman. 2011. "Political Accountability and Fiscal Governance in Africa." Working Paper. San Diego: University of California, Department of Political Science.

Hardin, Garrett. 1968. "The Tragedy of the Commons." *Science* 162: 1243–48.

Hayes, Tanya. 2006. "Parks, People, and Forest Protection: An Institutional Assessment of the Effectiveness of Protected Areas." *World Development* 34 (12): 2064–75.

Joshi, Neeraj N., Elinor Ostrom, Ganesh P. Shivakoti, and Wai Fung Lam. 2000. "Institutional Opportunities and Constraints in the Performance of Farmer-Managed Irrigation Systems in Nepal." *Asia-Pacific Journal of Rural Development* 10 (2): 67–92.

Lam, Wai Fung, and Elinor Ostrom. 2010. "Analyzing the Dynamic Complexity of Development Interventions: Lessons from an Irrigation Experiment in Nepal." *Policy Sciences* 43 (1): 1–25.

Olson, Mancur. 1965. *The Logic of Collective Action: Public Goods and the Theory of Groups*. Cambridge, MA: Harvard University Press.

Ostrom, Elinor, Marco Janssen, and John Anderies. 2007. "Going beyond Panaceas." *Proceedings of the National Academy of Sciences* 104 (39): 15176–78.

Ostrom, Elinor, Wai Fung Lam, Prachanda Pradhan, and Ganesh Shivakoti. Forthcoming.

Improving Irrigation in Asia: Sustainable Performance of an Innovative Intervention in Nepal. Cheltenham, UK: Edward Elgar Publishing Ltd.

Poteete, Amy, Marco Janssen, and Elinor Ostrom. 2010. *Working Together: Collective Action, the Commons, and Multiple Methods in Practice*. Princeton, NJ: Princeton University Press.

Shivakumar, Sujai. 2005. *The Constitution of Development: Crafting Capabilities for Self-Governance*. New York: Palgrave Macmillan.

Learning, Growth, and Development: A Lecture in Honor of Sir Partha Dasgupta

JOSEPH E. STIGLITZ[*]

It is a great pleasure to deliver this address to honor my long-time friend and coauthor Partha Dasgupta. Our friendship and collaboration go back some 45 years to the mid-1960s, when we were both students and research fellows at Cambridge. At the time, it was perhaps the most exciting place in economics in the world. To its own luminaries (Robinson, Kaldor, Meade, Champernowne, Farrell, Kahn, and Sraffa, to name but a few) were added a roster of visiting greats: Solow, Arrow, Radner, Minsky, and Diamond. And a younger generation of economists was just emerging, including future stars like James Mirrlees, Geoff Heal, Tony Atkinson, and Partha Dasgupta

We were all enthralled by growth theory, attempting to understand what makes economies grow and why some economies grow better than others. But there was, at the same time, an ongoing debate about capitalism. There was not then the presumption that prevailed for the three decades beginning with Margaret Thatcher and Ronald Reagan—that markets were efficient and stable. On the contrary, one of the memorable moments was when Frank Hahn first derived his results on the dynamic instability of markets;[1] as he put it, he had put the golden nail in the coffin of capitalism. We were concerned too about the inequality and poverty that seemed to accompany capitalism, and about the problems of development. There was still a hope that planning could replace a flawed market.

[*] Joseph Stiglitz is University Professor at Columbia University; chair of the Brooks World Poverty Institute, University of Manchester; and co-president of the Initiative for Policy Dialogue. This keynote address was delivered at the Annual Bank Conference on Development Economics, Stockholm, June 2, 2010. The author owes a long-term debt to Partha Dasgupta for the ideas discussed here and in the many areas on which we have worked together over more than 40 years. I am also greatly indebted to Bruce Greenwald. Much of the research discussed here represents joint work with Greenwald, some of which is reported in our forthcoming book *Creating a Learning Society: A New Paradigm for Development and Social Progress: An Essay in Honor of Kenneth Arrow* (Columbia University Press). The basic ideas were briefly presented in Greenwald and Stiglitz (2006). I am also indebted to Jonathan Dingel, Sebastian Rondeau, and Laurence Wilse-Samson for research assistance. Financial assistance from the Hewlett Foundation is gratefully acknowledged.

Annual World Bank Conference on Development Economics 2011, Global
© 2013 The International Bank for Reconstruction and Development / The World Bank

Even in those heady days, Partha stood out. He tackled new problems and raised new questions, some of which he would pursue in later years. Not since Edgeworth (1925) had an economic theorist tried to think deeply about population policy (Dasgupta 1969). The environment was not the concern that it is today—this was before the oil price shocks of the 1970s turned everyone's attention to the issues. Partha's pioneering work with Geoff Heal defined the field of the economics of natural resources for a generation (Dasgupta and Heal 1979).

The high hopes all of us shared for Partha's future contributions to economics have been more than realized. Year after year, his papers have presented insights into an increasing range of topics, and he has been joined by an increasingly large constellation of collaborators. But most monumental was his work *An Inquiry into Well-Being and Destitution,* (Dasgupta 1993), which identified the nexus between development, growth, inequality, and the environment. No one who read that work or his subsequent related work (e.g., Dasgupta 2001) could ever approach the problems of development as they had before.

Our interests overlapped in many ways; even when we were not writing together, his thinking influenced me. We worked together on issues of taxation,[2] cost-benefit analysis (Dasgupta and Stiglitz 1974; Dasgupta, Blitzer, and Stiglitz 1981), research and development (R&D) and innovation (the subject of this essay) (Dasgupta and Stiglitz 1980a, 1980b, 1981a, 1982, 1988a, 1988b; Dasgupta, Gilbert, and Stiglitz 1983), risk,[3] and natural resources,[4] and on research projects that involved intertwining issues of natural resources, innovation, market structures, and uncertainty.[5] At other times, we worked in parallel; for example, on theories of efficiency wages, on markets with imperfect information, and on theories of social capital.[6] My most recent project, as chair of the International Commission on the Measurement of Economic Performance and Social Progress (Fitoussi, Sen, and Stiglitz 2010), was in many ways inspired by *An Inquiry into Well-Being and Destitution.*

Endogenous Learning and Development: Schumpeterian Economics

It is customary in a *festschrift* to write a paper inspired by the work of the honoree. In this case, there are so many topics I could have chosen. But I shall choose one that I believe is central to development, that has been a source of concern to Partha and me since our days as graduate students, and on which we collaborated extensively in the following years: innovation.[7]

While much of the most widely read work in growth theory of the 1960s assumed exogenous technical progress, that was an assumption of convenience. We spent much time talking about and attempting to model the determinants of the pace of innovation (later called endogenous growth theory).[8]

Solow's seminal work (1957), in which he showed how one could decompose the sources of economic growth, had demonstrated why this task was so important: The vast majority of increases in per capita income were attributable to technological change (the unexplained Solow residual) rather than capital accumulation. To leave unexplained the determinants of technological change was, in short, to leave unexplained most of growth.

In the context of development, the matter was even more compelling. As I have repeatedly noted, what separates developed from less developed countries is not just a gap in resources but a gap in knowledge. The pace at which developing countries grow is largely determined by the pace at which they close that gap. Conventional economics and development theory and practice have given short shrift to these issues. They have focused on how to increase static efficiency; that is, given the state of knowledge within the country, how to move the country closer to its production (or utilities) possibilities curve. This was the focus of the Washington Consensus policies, including trade liberalization. But that meant policy was focusing on something that was, in a sense, of second order importance: gains in moving to the production possibilities curve (say, as a result of trade liberalization) were one-off. Increases in income attributable to higher investment were dwarfed by those attributable to closing the knowledge gap. If one could only understand how to close that gap more rapidly and how to move the knowledge frontier out at a faster pace, one might be able to design policies that would have far larger impacts on standards of living. Ignoring the most important source of increases in income was bad enough; making matters even worse was that policy conclusions focusing only on static considerations and ignoring dynamics were likely to be wrong and misguided. For instance, if technological change is exogenous (and there are no problems of information asymmetries, no environmental externalities, etc.), the presumption is that markets are efficient and the role for government is very limited. But that may not be the case when technological change is endogenous.[9] One of the major objectives of this paper is to explore the design of optimal government interventions.

Trade-offs can exist between static efficiency and dynamics. From the perspective of long-term well-being, it may be optimal to maintain static inefficiencies—possibly forever—because of dynamic benefits that might be generated by such seemingly distortionary behavior.

The idea of static versus dynamic trade-offs is familiar: The patent system introduces an inefficiency in the use of knowledge by restricting its free flow (because knowledge is a public good, with nonrivalrous consumption, when provided to an additional individual it does not subtract from that available to others). Moreover, patents reduce competition and in some cases even give rise to (perhaps temporary) monopolies, which in turn give rise to static inefficiencies. We countenance these inefficiencies in the belief that the restrictions incentivize research and that the dynamic gains outweigh the static costs.[10]

These concerns are even more central to development economics, where the focus of attention should be on how to bring about the transformation of the economy and society (Stiglitz 1998). Learning new ways of producing, of doing business, and of organizing economic, political, and social activities is at the heart of development. Dynamics cannot be ignored. Here we focus more narrowly on "economic learning": improving workers' productivity. In this context, the central issue is *how can developing countries maximize these knowledge-related improvements in productivity or, more accurately, balance out the short-run costs and the long-run gains?* Exploring this issue is the central objective of this paper.

Arrow's (1962a, 1962b) pioneering work provided a framework for analyzing endogenous technological progress: Some progress was the result of deliberate allocation of resources to R&D, while much was learning that occurred as one produced or invested (learning by doing.)[11] Here, we explore the improvements in productivity that result from learning by doing.[12]

Arrow noted that market structure (i.e., whether there was a monopoly or competition) affected incentives to innovate. But market structures themselves are endogenous. Knowledge can be viewed as a fixed cost; sectors in which R&D or learning are particularly important can be viewed as natural monopolies.

In short, if technological progress is endogenous, there is a raft of market failures: Markets are not likely to be perfectly competitive; benefits of research or learning are likely to spill over to others; firms engaged in research will appropriate only a portion of the societal benefits arising from their research; and attempts to strengthen appropriation will introduce further distortions in the economy. Many of these market failures (e.g., those arising from imperfections of competition and the inability to appropriate all the benefits of R&D) may result in underinvestment in research.[13] Yet attempts to correct this problem—for example, through strong patent protection—may result in overinvestment: The private return from obtaining a patent typically exceeds the social return, which is simply the availability of the knowledge shortly before it otherwise would have been available.

Markets may not only invest too much or too little in research, they may invest too much in some kinds of research (me-too patents in the drug industry) and too little in others (especially in basic research).

Analyzing the efficiency of the market is a complex task, and at the time Partha and I embarked on our work, a third of a century ago, few attempts had been made to do so. Remarkably, in spite of the constant praise of the market system's "innovativeness," we found no general theorems on the efficiency of markets with respect to the pace and direction of innovation. In a series of papers, we modeled the interactions between industrial structure and the pace of innovation, viewing them as both endogenous and simultaneously determined (Dasgupta and Stiglitz 1980a, 1980b). Only in such a context could one begin to analyze the efficiency of markets.

We were, I think, greatly influenced by the ideas of Schumpeter (1912, 1943), who had been long neglected by the mainstream. Schumpeter had argued—and we agreed—that if there was virtue in a market economy, it lay more with its dynamism, its ability to innovate, than with the kind of allocative efficiency stressed by the standard Arrow-Debreu model. Schumpeter grasped the dynamic/static trade-off and thus took a more benign view of monopolies. Monopolies could generate the profits necessary to fund research—especially important in an era when financial markets were less developed, and venture capital firms did not exist. Borrowing to finance speculative research was limited because, if the research project failed, there was nothing for the lender to seize. In real estate, at least there is some collateral.

As a result of my research on the economics of information, I had less sanguine views of markets and monopoly. Markets in which information was endogenous were generally not efficient (see Greenwald and Stiglitz 1986). Beginning in the late 1960s, I had explored the nature of these inefficiencies. In Stiglitz (1975a), I showed that there could exist Pareto inferior equilibria, and in Newbery and Stiglitz (1982), we showed that trade restrictions could make everyone in all countries better off. But then, in Stiglitz (1975), I showed that the economics of information and the economics of knowledge were very similar.[14] Both information and knowledge had public goods properties and large associated externalities. Given that we had established the inefficiency of market economies in which information was endogenous, it was also clear that economies in which knowledge was endogenous would also be inefficient. There was a presumption against unfettered markets.

As a point of departure, we wanted to test the robustness of some of Schumpeter's ideas, which for the most part had not been formally modeled but nonetheless had come to be accepted as part of the conventional wisdom. At the same time, we wanted to shed light on some key policy debates.

Economists had long been preoccupied with the dangers of monopolies. Schumpeter dismissed these worries—in his view, in these dynamic settings conventional competition would be replaced by Schumpeterian competition. Competition *for* the market would replace competition *in* the market, and there would be a succession of monopolies. Schumpeter seemed to countenance monopoly: He saw it as a small price in static inefficiency to pay for a greater pace of innovation associated with monopoly.

Our analysis called into the question the way Shumpeter had posed the questions. We argued that if market structure itself were endogenous and affected by, say, the technology of technological progress, the right question was not the effect of monopoly power on innovation but under what circumstances the market structure that emerged endogenously would lead to efficient allocation of resources to innovation. Or, more broadly, what government interventions would enhance societal well-being? Such interventions could take a myriad of forms: antitrust policies, patent laws, government-funded research, or government incentives for research; for example, through the tax system. Until the development of the modern theory of the economics of information, the presumption in conventional economics was that markets, by themselves, result in efficiency (with well-known exceptions, such as those associated with pollution). Schumpeterian competition seemed to create a similar presumption for dynamic economies, in which the center of attention is on innovation.

Our results also called into question much of the conventional wisdom and some of what Schumpeter claimed.[15] For instance, Schumpeter too easily dismissed the distortions that arose from monopoly and underestimated the ability of monopolies to maintain their position. Firms had an incentive and the means to deter entry of rivals and maintain their monopoly (Dasgupta and Stiglitz 1980b, 1988b; Gilbert and Newbery 1982). Some of these actions, though privately profitable, were highly socially costly (Stiglitz 1981, 1987b). Monopolization could result in both short-run inefficiencies and a slower pace of innovation.[16] We wrote about this before Microsoft's abuses became well known. In a sense, our work laid out a framework to evaluate claims about the benefits associated with attempts to limit competition, explaining both the private incentives and the high social costs of these anticompetitive practices.

The Infant Industry Argument for Protection

In a later work, we linked this broad conceptual work to our interest in development and, in particular, to the question of industrial policy and whether innovation and learning[17] provided a justification, for instance, for industrial tariffs (Dasgupta and Stiglitz 1988a). While earlier literature had developed the infant industry argument for protection, conventional wisdom in the previous quarter-century had moved against it.[18]

This reaction was partly for reasons of political economy: The infants never grew up, and the argument often seemed more abused than used (America's ethanol subsidies are a case in point). Not content with these political arguments—especially since the most successful countries, those in East Asia, had arguably employed industrial policies with considerable success—many economists attacked the economics itself.

Critics of infant industry protection argued that learning by itself does not imply a market failure. Firms take learning benefits into account in their behavior. They are willing to produce at a loss, knowing that they will be more competitive in the future.

Dasgupta and I provided what was perhaps the obvious answer to this argument: Firms faced capital constraints. They couldn't borrow to make up for their shortfall. The retort was that even if capital market imperfections existed, it made more sense to correct those imperfections than to create new ones. If the government couldn't correct the market failure, it should subsidize the firms directly rather than through distortionary tariffs.

But Dasgupta and I provided a novel retort to this retort, based on insights from the emerging field of information economics—one to which the critics of industrial policy have never offered an effective reply. We argued that capital market imperfections result from information imperfections, and these information imperfections help explain why subsidies may not work. The government may not know which firms to subsidize, just as the market may not know which firms to lend to; it may not know which firms will be most successful in learning or in R&D. But with a tariff or other trade interventions (such as the exchange rate interventions described below), the firms that believe they will be profitable—with their learning—self-select into the market.[19]

Partha and I thus provided a fully articulated rationale for infant industry protection based on information asymmetries and a theory of learning by doing. But while the model provided a convincing refutation of the critique of the infant industry argument, it did not fully answer the question of when and how the government should intervene (putting aside political economy considerations).

One of the reasons countries engage in infant industry protection is that they want to enter the fast-moving high-growth sectors—sectors with significant learning. The industrial sector is subject to faster learning than agriculture, so countries wanted to move into that sector. But industry was not their current comparative advantage; without some government intervention, they could not enter the industrial sector and therefore could not learn. Unfettered markets can keep a country from entering more dynamic sectors, especially if the learning is external to the firm.

But this argument for infant industry protection is not fully convincing,[20] as all countries will benefit from the learning as a result of lower prices, so long as markets remain competitive. Moving into a more dynamic sector does not guarantee a country greater (innovation) rents.

Consider a two-country, two-good model, in which we assume all persons have the same utility function $\ln U = .5 \ln C_1 + .5 \ln C_2$.[21] Each good is produced by labor alone; the two countries are the same size; and country 1 specializes in good 1, while country 2 specializes in good 2. It is trivial to show that half of global income goes to country 1, half to country 2. If country 1 has rapid technical progress (endogenous or exogenous) but goods are produced competitively, prices will fall in proportion to productivity, so that while revenue per unit produced falls in proportion to productivity, revenue per hour remains the same. Country 2 benefits fully from country 1's learning (Skeath 1993, 1995). It should not envy the other country that has specialized in the seemingly more dynamic sector.

A rationale may still exist for encouraging the more dynamic sector, but it lies elsewhere—with the externalities the tradable high-learning sector generates, for instance, to the nontradable sector. Here we provide the real answer to the critics of industrial policy. Industrial policy is not focused on picking winners, and it is not predicated on the belief that government can do a better job than the private sector of picking winners. It is based on the notion that learning involves spillovers (externalities) that will be imperfectly internalized in a market economy, and that in circumstances in which learning might largely be internalized—where there is a monopoly—the distortions created by the monopoly itself require government intervention.

I present here a general theory of growth and development based on endogenous learning with endogenous capital constraints derived from underlying market imperfections. It is based on joint work with Bruce Greenwald on what we call the "infant economy argument for protection." The theory offers a policy framework that is markedly different from that of the Washington Consensus, which rests on neoclassical models with well-functioning markets in which technology is either fixed or, if it is changing, the changes are simply assumed to be exogenous, unaffected by anything the government might do. The latter theory focuses on the importance of allocative efficiency given a level of technology. Theories of endogenous learning, by contrast, focus on the determinants of learning.[22] Unlike the standard infant industry theory, the theory presented here examines how a society, not just a particular sector, learns.

The theory shows that in some circumstances Schumpeter's criticism of competition may contain a grain of truth; in general, with full competition, the pace of innovation is suboptimal. There may even be a grain of truth in his perspectives on monopoly: Monopolies are more likely to internalize the benefits of learning (R&D), and this factor by itself would suggest a faster pace of innovation. But monopolies constrain production, and that means that they have less incentive to innovate, as Arrow long ago argued. And even with monopoly, there are likely to be important spillovers to other sectors, the benefits of which the monopolist will not take into account. In short, neither unfettered competitive markets nor unbridled monopolies are likely to lead to socially efficient levels of innovation. Government policies—sometimes called industrial policies—are required. In the context of a highly simplified model, we characterize those policies, identifying both broad-based and sectoral policies that would lead to welfare improvements and a higher level of innovation.

Outline of the Paper

I proceed methodically in the analysis of the infant economy argument for protection based on the theory of learning. I first consider a closed economy, explaining why government intervention is desirable. In the context of a closed economy, I first consider a two-period model, and then investigate long-run growth models. Next, I examine the special case of government intervention in the context of monopolistic competition. The remainder of the paper considers an open economy, asking when countries that are stuck in the less dynamic sectors suffer as a result. To answer that question, I construct a model of dynamic trade equilibrium. First I consider a model that contains only tradable commodities, then I introduce nontradables. The remarkable result is that, in the presence of certain policy restrictions, not only might it be desirable for countries to promote exports and not only might exchange rate policy be an effective mechanism for doing so, but it may even pay countries to permanently maintain an exchange rate that is so undervalued that it creates permanent reserve accumulations.

Like much of the modern economics of the public sector, the nature of the optimal interventions depends on the instruments and powers of government. Whether the government can abolish monopolies or undo their distortionary behavior has implications for the desirable levels of research and learning. It makes a difference, too, if the government can raise revenues to subsidize or support research or learning only through distortionary taxation rather than through lump sum taxes. The economics of the second best is of particular relevance here: R&D and learning give rise to market imperfections, and all policies have to take into account the presence of these imperfections (sometimes referred to as distortions) if they cannot undo them. Well-designed distortions in one market can partially offset distortions in others.

I use the word "distortions" with care: Common usage suggests that governments should simply do away with them. But as the term has come to be used, it simply refers to deviations from the way a classical model with, say, perfect information might function. Information is inherently imperfect, and these imperfections cannot be legislated away. Nor can the market power that arises from the returns to scale inherent in research be legislated away. That is why simultaneously endogenizing market structure and innovation is so important. Similarly, the costs associated with R&D (or the "losses" associated with expanding production to "invest" in learning) cannot be ignored; they have to be paid for. Monopoly rents are one way of doing so, but—as I argue here—a far from ideal way. There are ways to impose even distortionary taxes (i.e., taxes that give rise to a loss of consumer surplus) that increase societal well-being and the speed of innovation.

Government Intervention in Closed Economies with Learning by Doing

When there is learning by doing, today's production has benefits for the future. We must ask, will firms take that into account, and what are the consequences of not doing so?

The answers to these questions revolve around whether the learning is internal to the industry or internal to the firm. If learning is internal only to the firm, then the larger the firm, the lower its cost. Each firm is, in a sense, a natural monopoly. There cannot be competition. And, in general, when competition is restricted, market allocations are not efficient. But now there are two inefficiencies: In addition to the static inefficiencies associated with the exercise of monopoly power, there may be dynamic inefficiencies. These may be complex: Products in which firms have more monopoly power will have less production, and the lower production will lead to less learning. Productivity growth in these sectors may, accordingly, be slower.[23] In addition to the static consequence of the loss of consumer surplus from underproduction, there is a dynamic cost: The lower learning and higher costs in subsequent periods associated with monopoly today result in lower output in future periods. Of course, labor not used in the monopolized sector gets displaced to other sectors, but if those sectors are sectors with less learning, the overall rate of growth of the economy is reduced. Moreover, monopoly power will result in lower real wages; lower real wages will normally result in lower equilibrium labor supply; and, if learning depends on production (i.e., increases with labor supply), there will be less learning (slower increases in productivity) even if the monopolized sectors did not have an advantage in learning.

In short, we will typically see lower societal innovation with monopoly *even in the absence of learning spillovers*—that is, even where the monopolist fully internalizes the benefits of learning—for two reasons: (1) because of underproduction in future periods as a result of monopoly power, the benefits that accrue to the monopolist from innovation are lower than they would be with efficient production; and (2) the lower real wages lead to lower production on average and hence less learning. In addition, the pattern of production will be distorted from what is optimal; that is, the pattern that would emerge from a careful balancing of static costs and dynamic gains. If monopoly power is greater in the more dynamic sectors—because those are sectors where the natural monopoly nature of learning is strongest—resources are displaced from learning sectors to others and, again, there is a presumption that the pace of innovation is lower.

On the other hand, if learning is external to the firm—so much so that others in the industry benefit from its learning as much as it does—the industry can be competitive, but because of the externality, there will be underproduction of goods generating (positive) externalities such as learning.

In short, whether learning is internal or external to the firm, the market equilibrium will not, in general, be Pareto efficient. Government has a role to play in correcting the market misallocations.

While the result on the inefficiency of market equilibrium is robust, the result that a competitive equilibrium can exist if there are full spillovers of knowledge is not.

If there are not *full* spillovers, then the firm engaging in learning has a competitive advantage, and the earlier argument about the existence of a natural monopoly is restored. On the other hand, the result that there is always a natural monopoly is also not robust. We can obtain an equilibrium with many firms if the diseconomies of scale are large enough to outweigh the economies of scale in learning.

In the following analysis, we make two important distinctions. The first distinction concerns the structure of the product market. As we have noted, endogenous learning makes some market structures infeasible: In the absence of full within-industry spillovers, a natural monopoly exists. With full spillovers, there can be many firms in the industry; there will be competition, but no firm will take into account the learning benefit its production confers on others. It is possible that the market might best be described as monopolistically competitive, with only one firm in the industry but spillovers to other industries. In this case, we will see two distortions: underproduction as a result of the exercise of monopoly power and underproduction as a result of failing to take into account the learning benefits that accrue to others.

The second concerns the nature of spillovers. Traditional analyses assumed full spillovers within the sector within the country and no spillovers to other sectors or other countries. This is extreme. In fact, the production of any good involves many stages, and some of the stages may involve processes that are similar to those used in another seemingly distinct sector. The result is that innovations in one sector may benefit other sectors that look markedly different. Inventory control and cash management techniques affect virtually every firm in an economy. Just-in-time production or assembly lines are examples of production processes that affect many industries. Sectors that are similar may, of course, benefit more. (Indeed, the same argument holds within a sector. An innovation in one technology in a given sector may have limited spillovers for other technologies—the spillovers may be greater to other products using analogous technologies.)[24] There are equally important economy-wide "technologies." A financial system developed to serve the manufacturing sector may equally serve the rural sector. In the discussion in this and the next section, we use a general formulation that has as limiting cases no and perfect spillovers.

Table 1 outlines the three cases. Most of our attention will focus on the cases with perfect competition and full spillovers, or monopolistic competition and no spillovers.[25]

One of the important methodological implications of the analysis is that not only must one simultaneously consider market structure and innovation (both are endogenous), but the analysis must be conducted within a general equilibrium framework. In a partial equilibrium context, one might conclude—as Schumpeter did—that monopoly was better than competition because it internalized the benefits

TABLE 1. Spillovers and Market Structures

	No cross-firm spillovers	Full cross-firm spillovers
Perfect competition	X (not feasible)	Underinvestment in learning
Monopolistic competition	Restricted output	Both market distortions

of learning, without noting adverse general equilibrium effects (in the simple model presented here, arising from the impacts on real wages and labor supply).

Optimal Resource Allocations with Learning: Basic Intuition

It is easy to describe the efficient resource allocations without learning: In each period, the marginal benefit of producing one more unit of a good must equal its marginal cost. In the case of a good produced by labor alone, the marginal rate of substitution between the good and leisure (which should be the same for all persons) should equal the marginal rate of transformation; that is, the marginal product of labor. With learning, producing or investing more today has future benefits—lower future production costs—and this needs to be taken into account. This can easily be done:

(1) The value of the marginal product + *total* future cost savings = marginal cost today.
This contrasts with the competitive equilibrium without learning, where

(2) The value of the marginal product = marginal cost today;
and with the monopolistically competitive equilibrium with learning, where

(3) Marginal revenue product + future cost savings *to the firm* = marginal cost today.

The competitive scenario neglects all the learning benefits; the monopolistically competitive firms underestimate the static benefit of production, ignore learning benefits to other firms, and, because production may be lower, assign a lower value even to firm cost savings.

Understanding the structure of learning and knowledge dissemination is essential to understanding efficient production. We are concerned with societal learning, not just sectoral or firm learning. For example, some sectors may have stronger learning curves; that is, the elasticity of learning may be larger for a firm. But what matters is not just the ability of a firm or sector to learn but also the benefits that sector (firm) transmits to other sectors (firms) and the extent to which it does not appropriate for itself the benefits of the learning.

If learning in one sector generates more externalities to other sectors than do others, production in that sector should be increased (relative to what it would be in the market equilibrium that ignored these learning externalities) at the expense of others. The dynamic (future) benefits need to be offset against the static (short-run) costs.

Section 1. A Two-Period Model

This section is divided into five parts. First, we consider a "direct control" problem in which government can determine the amount of labor allocated to each sector. Second, we provide a price interpretation of this optimum. Third, we examine some special features of the symmetric sectors case. Fourth, we analyze optimal interventions using standard optimal tax theory (i.e., we investigate indirect control mechanisms through taxes and subsidies), assuming that government can levy lump sum taxes. Finally, we analyze government intervention in more realistic contexts, in which government cannot impose such taxes.

Optimum Learning A simple two-period model in which labor is the only input to production suffices to bring out the major issues.[26] Assume (for simplicity) that utility is separable between goods in the two periods and between goods and labor:

$$W = U(\mathbf{x}^t) - v(L^t) + \delta[U(\mathbf{x}^{t+1}) - v(L^{t+1})], \tag{1}$$

where $\mathbf{x}^t$ is the vector of consumption $\{x_k^t\}$ at time t and L^t is aggregate labor supply at time t. The disutility of work is the same in all sectors, and L^t is aggregate labor input in period t:

$$L^t = \sum L_k^t \quad \text{and} \quad L^{t+1} = \Sigma L_k^{t+1},$$

where L_k^i is the input of labor in sector k in period i.

Production is described by (in the appropriate choice of units)

$$x_k^t = L_k^t. \tag{2}$$

In this simple model, the more output of good j in period t, the lower the production costs in period t + 1. We assume

$$x_k^{t+1} = L_k^{t+1} H^k[L^t], \tag{3}$$

where L^t is the vector of labor inputs at time t $\{L_k^t\}$.

The learning functions H^k and their properties are at the center of this analysis. In the following analysis, two properties of these learning functions will play a central role:

(a) Learning elasticity—how much sectoral productivity is increased as a result of an increase in labor input.

We define

$$h_k = d \ln H^k / d \ln L_k^t. \tag{4}$$

h_k is the *elasticity of the learning curve in sector k*.

(b) Learning spillovers—the extent to which learning in sector i spills over to sector j.

$$\partial H^k / \partial L_j^t > 0, \quad j \neq k, \text{ if there are learning externalities,}$$

while

$$\partial H^k / \partial L_j^t = 0, \ j \neq k, \text{ if there are no learning externalities.}$$

At various points in the discussion, we will find it convenient to focus on two special cases, one with no learning spillovers and one with full learning spillovers. In the special case with no learning externalities, we write, for simplicity

$$x_k^{t+1} = L_k^{t+1} \psi_k (L_k^t). \tag{5}$$

In the other case, with full learning spillovers,

$$H^k = H^j, \text{ all } j, k.$$

Optimization of (1) with respect to L_k^j, $j = t$, $t + 1$ yields (in the obvious notation)

$$U_k^t = v^{,t} - B_k \qquad (6)$$

$$U_k^{t+1} H^k = v^{,t+1}, \qquad (7)$$

where B_k is the learning benefit from increased output (input) into sector k:

$$B_k = \delta \sum U_{jk}^{t+1}(x^{t+1}) L_i^{t+1} H_k^i \qquad (8)$$

The first equation simply says that in allocating labor in the first period, we take into account the learning benefits. $B_k \geq 0$ implies that, so long as there are any learning benefits, production the first period goes beyond the level that would have occurred with static efficiency (which entails $U_k^t = v^{,t}$). Obviously, sectors with more learning benefits expand production more.

To see what that entails more precisely, we focus on three polar cases:

(a) *No spillovers.*

$$H_j^k = 0 \ j \neq k.$$

Then

$$B_k = \delta \xi_k h_k U_k^t(x^t), \qquad (9)$$

where

$$\xi_k = (U_k^{t+1} x_k^{t+1} / U_k^t x_k^t).$$

The magnitude of the learning benefit depends on the discount rate (the larger δ, the more we value future benefits) and the learning elasticity h_k. Indeed, without spillovers, the learning benefit is simply proportional to the learning elasticity.[27]

One might have thought that because of the fixed-cost nature of learning, production in larger sectors would have increased more. But the magnitude of expansion of production entails a careful balancing of the marginal benefit of learning (the dynamic gain) and the marginal costs of the first period distortion (the static cost). The formulas derived in this paper analyze what that entails. In effect, they show that what matters is the learning elasticity and not the scale but changes in the scale between the two periods, captured by the variable ξ_k.

Normally, we would expect that, as a result of productivity increases, consumption of each good will increase. In the case of separability with respect to consumption,

$$U = \Sigma_k u_k(x_k),$$

and the effect on $U_k x_k = u'_k x_k$ of an increase in x_k depends on the elasticity of marginal utility for commodity k, η_k, where $\eta_k = - d\ln u'_k / d\ln x_k$:

$$d\ln U_k \ x_k / d\ln x_k = 1 - \eta_k$$

Because normally $x_k^{t+1} > x_k^t$,[28] ξ_k is greater than or less than unity, depending on whether η_k is greater or less than unity. If marginal utility diminishes slowly, the value of learning is greater.

In the case of the logarithmic utility function, $\xi_k = 1$, so

$$B_k = \delta h_k \, U_k^t(x^t) \tag{10}$$

(b) Full spillovers.

The case of full spillovers can most simply be analyzed by rewriting our maximand (1) as

$$\text{Max } W = U(x^t) - v(L^t) + \delta[U(H(x^t) \, L^{t+1}) - v(L^{t+1})]. \tag{11}$$

For simplicity, we assume homothetic preferences, which allows us to rewrite our utility function $U = U(\phi(x))$ where ϕ has constant returns to scale. This generates the first order condition

$$U^{t} \phi_k - v' = -\delta \, U^{t+1} H_k \sum_j \phi_j (x^{t+1}) L_j^{t+1}$$
$$= U^{t+1} \phi_k [-\delta h_k \xi^* / \gamma_k],$$

where

$$\xi^* = U^{t+1} \phi^{t+1} / U^{t} \phi^t,$$

where

$$\gamma_k = d\ln \phi / d\ln x_k.$$

and where we have made use of the result that with constant returns

$$\sum_j \phi_j (x^{t+1}) L_j^{t+1} H = \sum_j \phi_j (x^{t+1}) x_j^{t+1} = \phi.$$

Obviously, as before, if $U = \ln \phi$, then $\xi^* = 1$ and

$$B_k = U^{' t+1} \phi_k [\delta h_k / \gamma_k].$$

B_k is proportional to the discount factor δ and the learning elasticity h_k, and inversely proportional to the share in total consumption in period t represented by good k (γ_k).

(c) Full spillovers in some sectors and no spillovers in others.

For simplicity, we focus on two sectors, labeled s for spillovers and 0 for no spillovers. Then our maximand becomes

$$\text{Max} \quad W = U(x_s^t, x_0^t) - v(L^t) + \delta[U(H^s (x_s^t) L_s^{t+1}, H^s (x_s^t) H^0(L_0^t) L_0^{t+1}) - v(L^{t+1})],$$

yielding the first order conditions

$$U_s^t - v'(L^t) = \delta H^{s'}(x_s^t) [U_s^{t+1} L_s^{t+1} + U_0^{t+1} H^0(L_0^t) L_0^{t+1}]$$
$$= \delta h^s(x_s^t) [U_s^{t+1} (x_s^{t+1} / x_s^t) + U_0^{t+1} x_0^{t+1} / x_s^t]$$

and

$$U_0^t - v'(L^t) = \delta H^s (x_s^t) U_0^{t+1} H^{0'}(L_0^t) \, L_0^{t+1}$$
$$= \delta h^0 (x_0^t) U_0^{t+1} x_0^{t+1} / x_0^t.$$

Provided that the learning elasticities are similar, learning induces a far larger expansion in the sector with spillovers than the sector without. For instance, with logarithmic utility functions, $U = a_s \log x_s + a_0 \log x_0$, $a_s + a_0 = 1$

$$U_s^t - v'(L^t) = \delta h^s (X_s^t)/X_s^t = \delta h^s U_s^t \left(1 + \frac{\alpha_0}{\alpha_s} \right),$$

while

$$U_0^t - v'(L^t) = \delta a_0 h^0 (X_0^t)/X_0^t = \delta h^0 U_0^t.$$

Price Interpretation The equations describing the optimal allocation of resources have an obvious price interpretation. Let

$U_k^t/v'^t = p_k^t$ = marginal rate of substitution between good k and leisure in period t. Let q_k^t = marginal rate of transformation between labor and good k in period t.

$$q_k^t = 1 \text{ for all k,}$$

and

$$q_k^{t+1} = 1/H^k, \text{ for all k.}$$

Then (7) implies that

$$p_k^{t+1} = q_k^{t+1} \text{ for all k.} \tag{12}$$

In the first-best allocation, in the second period, the consumer price (equals the marginal rate of substitution) equals the producer price (equals the marginal rate of transformation).

The first period allocation is somewhat more complicated. Equation (6) implies that

$$p_k^t = q_k^t - \Omega_k p_k^t = 1 - \Omega p_k^t = 1/(1 + \Omega_k), \tag{13}$$

where Ω_k is the marginal (normalized by the marginal utility) learning benefit from producing more of good k in the first period (this includes the learning benefits to *all* sectors):

$$\Omega_K \equiv B_k/U_k^t = \delta[\sum_j U_j(X^{t+1})L_j^{t+1}H_k^j]/U_k^t$$
$$= \delta \sum \xi_{jk} d \ln H^j/d\ln x_k^t > 0. \tag{14}$$

where

$$\xi_{jk} = \frac{U_j^{t+1} x_j^{t+1}}{U_k^t x_k^t}$$

Optimal production entails producing in the first period beyond the point of the static efficiency condition, where marginal rate of substitution equals the marginal rate of transformation. The extent to which we expand production depends on the direct learning effects *and* on the indirect benefits to other sectors. It is not just the direct learning benefits that count. If a sector has more spillovers to others, we might want to expand its production even if its own learning elasticity is lower.

Consider our two polar cases. First, assume there are no learning spillovers, so $H_j^k = 0$ for $j \neq k$. Then

$$\Omega_k = \delta \, \xi_{kk} \, h_k.$$

In the case of a logarithmic utility function, $\xi_{kk} = 1$. The extent to which the marginal rate of substitution is less than the marginal rate of transformation (i.e., the extent to which production is expanded beyond the level of static efficiency) depends on the elasticity of learning. If marginal utility diminishes rapidly, sectors for which there is a lot of learning will have correspondingly smaller values of ξ_{kk}, diminishing the extent to which output is expanded. The higher d is (the less future utility is discounted), the more important the learning benefits are and thus the higher the level of production the first period.

Second, consider the case with full spillovers. Then where

$$\xi_{kk} = U_j^{t+1} x_{jt+1} / U_k^t x_k^t$$
$$\Omega_k = \delta h_k \xi^* / \gamma_k.$$

If we implement the optimal allocation through a market mechanism, we encounter a problem: Production in the first period has to be subsidized, and the subsidies have to somehow be paid for. If we can impose a lump sum tax on individuals to pay the "learning subsidies," we can achieve the first-best optimum. In later sections, we turn to optimal policies for when we cannot impose lump sum taxes.

The price interpretation is useful because it provides an easy and direct contrast between optimal resource allocations and the competitive equilibrium. (We will discuss the monopolistically competitive equilibrium later.) In the competitive equilibrium,

$$U_k^t / v^{*t} = q_k^t = 1 \text{ for all } k$$
$$U_k^{t+1} / v^{*t+1} = q_k^{t+1} = 1/H^k, \text{ for all } k;$$

that is, production in the first period ignores *all* learning benefits but, conditional on the learning that has occurred, second period production is efficient. Clearly, there will be underproduction in the first period, especially in those sectors in which learning is important.

Symmetric Case The above analysis derived general formulas for analyzing optimal production/learning if government could directly control inputs/outputs in every sector. We also provided a price interpretation of the optimum. Much of our discussion focused on the desirability of increasing activities that generate learning externalities compared with those that did not.

But there is a broader macroeconomic issue: Even if all sectors were identical (symmetric), so that 1/nth of the labor supply ought to (and, in market equilibrium, will) be devoted to each commodity, there may be too little output (labor supply) in the first period. If labor supply is inelastic and the number of goods is fixed at n, in the symmetric equilibrium, 1/nth of the labor force is allocated to each good. It is obvious that the market equilibrium has the efficient amount of learning in each sector; there is no learning distortion, even though there are learning externalities.

This is important, for it illustrates the large discrepancy between partial and general equilibrium analysis. (Partial equilibrium analysis would have led us to the conclusion that there was an underinvestment in learning.)

The symmetric equilibrium also provides an easy context in which to compare the market equilibrium with the optimum. For simplicity, we will assume no spillovers across sectors.

The social welfare maximization problem can be easily written as

$$\text{Max} \quad U^t(L^t/n, L^t/n, L^t/n, \ldots) - v^t(L^t) + \{L^t, L^{t+1}\}$$
$$\delta[U^{t+1}(\psi(L^t)L^{t+1}/n, \ \psi(L^t)L^{t+1}/n, \ \psi(L^t)L^{t+1}/n, \ldots) - v^{t+1}(L^{t+1})],$$

where n is the number of commodities, and where we have assumed separability between labor and goods but not necessarily between goods; where $\psi_k(L_k^t)$ is the learning function giving output per unit input[29]); and where, because of the assumption of symmetry, we can, without loss of generality, drop the subscript on the learning function.

The first order condition can be written

$$\sum U_i^t/n - v^{t'} = U_i^t - v^{t'} = -\delta \sum U_i^{t+1} \psi^*(L_i^t) L^{t+1}/n - -\delta U_i^{t+1} \psi^*(L_i^t) L^{t+1}.$$

In competitive equilibrium

$$U_i^t - v^{t'} = 0,$$

so it is clear that (in general) there is too little production the first period. The only exception is the case where L^t is fixed (i.e., cannot be increased). Then, trivially, the market equilibrium is efficient.

The first order condition for L^{t+1} is

$$U_i^{t+1} \psi(L^t) - v^{t+1'} = 0.$$

In competitive equilibrium, the price is $1/\psi(L_i^t)$, so that, conditional on the state of knowledge in the second period, output is efficient.

If the government were to subsidize first period production by t , so that the first order condition is

$$U_i^t - v^{t'}(1 - \tau) = 0$$

and sets

$$\tau^* = \delta U_i^{t+1} \psi^*(L_i^t) L^{t+1}/v^{t'},$$

raising the revenue through a lump sum tax, then the government can replicate the first best optimum.[30]

It is useful to rewrite the above expression as[31]

$$\tau^* = \delta[v^{t+1'}L^{t+1}/v^{t'}L^t]h$$
$$\approx \delta h[1 + (1+v)H_0\varepsilon_{LW}]/\{1 - [1 + (1+v)H_0\varepsilon_{LW}](1+v)(h\varepsilon_{LW} - 1)\varepsilon_{Lw}^c\},$$

where $\varepsilon_{Lw} = d\ln L/d\ln w$, $\varepsilon^c{}_{Lw}$ is the compensated elasticity of labor supply, $H_0 = H(L^t(\tau))$ when $\tau = 0$, $v = d\ln v'/d\ln L$, the elasticity of the marginal disutility of work, and, as before, $h = \psi'(L^t)L^t/\psi'(L^t)$ is the elasticity of the learning curve.

In the limiting case of the logarithmic utility function, $\varepsilon_{Lw} = 1$, $\varepsilon^c_{Lw} = 1/(1 + v)$ and the above expression simplifies to

$$\delta h / 2,$$

the optimal subsidy is simply related to the discount factor and the elasticity of the learning curve.

Even though we can impose lump sum taxes, subsidies distort static allocations. Optimal interventions balance these static losses with the dynamic gains. The above formulas show the outcomes of this balancing.[32]

Optimal Learning with Optimal Taxation: Lump Sum Taxation So far, we have derived the optimal allocation (assuming that government directly controls production and consumption) and analyzed price interpretations of the resulting equilibrium. It may be useful to redo the analysis using more standard techniques in public finance. We begin by assuming that the government can only impose excise taxes and subsidies and lump sum taxes. The government faces an indirect control problem. With lump sum taxation, assuming that first period subsidies must be paid by a lump sum tax in the first period (i.e., there are no intertemporal budget constraints, so the government cannot borrow from the future to finance this period's deficits), we can write social welfare using the indirect utility function, giving the level of utility as a function of prices and "income":

$$V^t(\mathbf{p}^t, -\textstyle\sum \tau_i x_i) + \delta V^{t+1}(\mathbf{p}^{t+1}_i, 0) \tag{15}$$

$$p^t_i = (1 - \tau_i) \tag{16}$$

$$p^{t+1}_i = 1/H^i, \tag{17}$$

where τ_i is the first period subsidy to commodity j. Under our normalization, in a competitive market without subsidies, the (consumer) price of all goods would be unity; a subsidy on good j of t_j brings down the competitive price to $1 - \tau_j$. In a competitive market, in the second period, the price is just the cost of production.

There are two spillovers from a subsidy on sector j:

1. An increase in the subsidy on commodity j affects demand (and supply) for commodity i. That in turn has two effects: an impact on learning in those sectors (the benefits of which can spill over to other sectors) and an impact on the government's budget constraint; for example, if demand shifts toward highly subsidized products, the government would face a budgetary shortfall, which would necessitate a decrease in the subsidy on some other commodities.
2. The expansion of sector j affects learning in sector i.

It is easy to establish that, provided the sectors are not too different, it pays to subsidize consumption of every good in the first period. But if sectors are very different, it may pay to impose a tax on a sector, even if there is some learning in that sector. If the learning elasticity of a sector is much larger than that of others, and that sector has large spillovers to others, and there is some sector that is a substitute for the high-learning sector, then it may pay to tax that sector, in order to encourage learning in the high-learning sector.[33]

We can easily derive the optimal tax/subsidy rate[34]:

$$-V_{pj}^t - V_I^t[x_j^t - \Sigma\tau_j(dx_j^t/d\tau_i)] - \delta\Sigma_k V_{pk}^{t+1}\Sigma_i((1/H^k)^2)H_i^k dx_i/d\tau_j = 0. \qquad (18)$$

The third term above $[\Sigma\tau_j(dx_j^t/d\tau_i)]$ reflects the spillovers to the budget constraint: the increase in output of sector i affects the aggregate subsidies and, therefore, the aggregate lump sum tax. We define

$$\delta V_I^{t+1}/V_I^t = \rho, \qquad (19)$$

the intertemporal marginal rate of substitution, reflecting the pure rate of time discount plus the diminution of the marginal utility of income as a result of growth. (Normally, d is less than unity, and with growth and diminishing marginal utility of income, V_I^{t+1}/V_I^t is less than unity, so r is less than one.) Then, using the standard "tricks" of optimal tax theory (combining the Slutsky equation with the symmetry of the compensated price elasticities), we can rewrite (18) as

$$-\Sigma_j (\tau_j/p_j) (\partial\ln x_i/\partial\ln p_j)_U = \rho\Phi_i + \chi, \qquad (20)$$

where $\Phi_i = -x_j^t \Sigma_k (L_k^{t+1}/L_k^t) \Sigma_i h_i^k (\tau_i/p_i) (\partial\ln x_j^t/\partial\ln p_i)_U$ is the total net marginal learning benefit from encouraging the consumption (equals the production in a closed economy) of sector j, taking into account potential effects on other sectors, both through induced learning in other sectors (as a result of cross elasticities of demand) and as a result of learning spillovers,[35] and where

$$\chi = \rho\Sigma_{jk}(\Sigma_k x_k^{t+1}((1/H^k)^2)H_j^k) - \tau_j)(dx_j/dI),$$

the net value of learning benefits as a result of an increase in income less the net increase in subsidies as a result of an increase in income (an increase in income will normally lead to an increase in spending).[36]

This can be interpreted similarly to the analogous expression in optimal tax theory: In the absence of learning (where $\Phi_i = 0$ for all i), the percentage deviation of consumption of good i (along the compensated demand curves) should be the same for all goods. Now we will make an adjustment: The percentage deviation should be larger for those sectors with larger marginal learning benefits, but those marginal learning benefits include not just the direct learning benefits but the spillovers to other sectors.

Qualitatively, we can see what is implied by considering the case of separable demand functions with no spillovers:[37]

$$\tau_i/p_i = \chi/\acute\eta_{ii} (1 - \rho h_i \zeta_i), \qquad (21)$$

which, for small h_i, can be approximated by

$$\tau_i \approx \chi (1 + \rho h_i \zeta_i)/\acute\eta_{ii},$$

where $h_i = (\partial\ln H^i/\partial\ln L_i)$, the elasticity of the learning curve; $\acute\eta_{jj} = (\partial\ln x_j/\partial\ln p_i)_U$, the (own) elasticity of (compensated) demand;[38] and $\zeta_i = (L_i^{t+1}/L_i^t)$, the ratio in sector i of labor input the second period to that in the first period.[39] ζ_i is itself a function of τ_i. We can use techniques similar to that employed earlier to show that the optimal subsidy increases with the learning elasticity and the (compensated) elasticity of labor supply, and obviously decreases with the intertemporal price.

(a) A two-sector case

Now let us assume, as before, two sectors: one (denoted by o) that has no learning spillover to the other sector and another (denoted by s) that has a full learning spillover.

Continuing with the assumption of separability of demand functions,

$$\tau_o/p_o = \chi / \acute{\eta}_{oo} (1 - ph_o \zeta_o) \tag{22a}$$

and

$$\tau_s/p_s = \chi [1 + (ph \zeta_o/(1 - ph_o \zeta_o))]/\acute{\eta}_{ss} (1 - ph_s \zeta_s). \tag{22b}$$

If the two sectors have the same learning elasticity and demand elasticity, we will subsidize (expand) sector s (with the spillover), more than sector 0 (without).[40] Similarly, even if sector j has a lower learning elasticity, we may wish to subsidize it more. The extent of spillovers is of first order importance.

(b) Symmetric equilibrium

We can simplify further in the special case of symmetry, discussed above. From symmetry, we know that all will face the same price, so we can write our optimization problem as (using the obvious notation)

$$\text{Max } V^t ((1 - \tau_i), \ldots \ldots, -n\tau_i x_i) + \delta V^{t+1}(c_i(\tau_i, \tau_j \neq i), 0), \tag{23}$$

where c is the cost of production, i.e. $c_i = 1/H_i$, implying

$$-V_I^t(\tau dx_i^t/d\tau) - \delta V_I^{t+1}\Sigma_i((n-1)x_j^{t+1}\partial c_i(\tau_i, \tau_j \neq i)/\partial \tau_{j\neq i} + x_i^{t+1}\partial c_i(\tau_i,\tau_{j\neq i})/\partial \tau_i = 0 \tag{24}$$

or

$$\{- V_I^t(\tau/p) + \delta V_I^{t+1}(L_j^{t+1}/L_j^t) [(n-1)h_{ij} + h_{jj}]\}\{d\ln x_i^t/d\ln\tau\} = 0,$$

where

$$d \ln c_i(\tau_i, \tau_{j\neq i})/d \ln \tau = -[(n - 1) (\partial \ln c_i/\partial \ln x_j)_{j\neq i} + \partial \ln c_i/\partial \ln x_i] d \ln x/d \ln \tau.$$

There are direct benefits of learning (h_{jj}, the own elasticity of the learning curve) and indirect benefits (h_{ij}, the learning spillovers).

There are two solutions. If $d \ln L^t/d \ln \tau = 0$, then (as we argued earlier) there is no reason to interfere with the market. But in the more general case,

$$\tau/1 - \tau = \rho \zeta [(n - 1)h_{ij} + h_{jj}] \tag{25}$$

As before, the higher the learning and the more learning spillovers, the higher the subsidy. If labor supply is very elastic and there is substantial learning, then L^{t+1}/L^t >>> 1, so, again, the higher the subsidy. If there are significant spillovers and many sectors, it is the magnitude of the spillovers that really matters.

No Lump Sum Taxes When government cannot impose lump sum taxes, there may still be room for industrial policies. One sector may have more learning benefits, so that a tax on the other sector to finance a subsidy on the learning sector might be desirable.

Consider the following polar model (which will be expanded on in later sections).[41] There is no learning in sector A (the agricultural sector), but sector M (manufacturing) has a learning function $c(L_M)$, and there are full spillovers to sector A. (Greenwald and Stiglitz [2004] argue that it is plausible that not only does manufacturing have a higher learning elasticity ($h^A < < h^M$) but that there are larger cross-sector learning spillovers from manufacturing to agricultural than vice versa.) Thus, continuing within the optimal tax framework of the previous section, we seek to

$$\text{Max } V^t((1 - \tau_M), (1 + t_A), 0) + \delta V^{t+1}(c(L_M), c(L_M), 0) \qquad (26)$$

$$\{\tau_M, t_A\}$$

where $\tau_M x_M = t_A x_A$, $dt_A/dt_M = (x_M/x_A) + \tau_M(d(x_M/x_A)/d\tau_M$
where, as before, τ_M is the subsidy on manufacturing and t_A is the tax that must be levied on agriculture to pay for the subsidy. This implies that

$$V_I^t\{x_M^t - x_A^t(dt_A/d\tau_M)\} = -\delta V_I^{t+1}c'(L_M)(x_M^{t+1} + x_A^{t+1})dx_M^t/d\tau_M. \qquad (27)$$

The LHS of (27) is the cost of the subsidy/tax—the distortion in consumption patterns—while the RHS is the learning benefit. Optimality requires that the (static) marginal cost of a subsidy equal the (dynamic) marginal benefit.

As expected, if $c' = 0$, the solution to (27) entails $\tau_A = t_m = 0$: There is no scope for distortionary taxation. But if the RHS of (27) is positive, it is optimal to tax A (agriculture) to expand M (manufacturing), provided $(\beta_M + \beta_A) > 0$:

$$\tau_M = -h\rho(L^{t+1}/L_A^t)\beta_M/(\beta_M + \beta_A) \geq 0 \qquad (28)$$

where, as before, $\rho = \delta V_I^{t+1}/V_I^t$, the discount rate for future income, reflecting both the pure discount factor δ and the normally lower marginal utility of income at $t + 1$ relative to t as a result of growth, and where[42]

$$\beta_M = d\ln x_M/d\ln \tau_M \geq 0, \text{ and}$$

$$\beta_A = -d\ln x_A/d\ln \tau_M \geq 0 .$$

These are total derivatives, taking into account the indirect effect of the increased price of agricultural goods. Thus, normally we expect the subsidy to increase consumption of manufacturing and reduce the consumption of agricultural goods. It follows that

$$(d\ln(x_M/x_A)/d\ln \tau_M = \beta_M + \beta_A.$$

This is the total change in relative consumption of the two goods as a result of the imposition of the subsidy on M paid for by a tax on A, the magnitude of which depends on the elasticity of substitution. If the elasticity of substitution is zero, then $\beta_M + \beta_A = 0$.[43]

When the elasticity of substitution is zero, ther are neither benefits nor costs associated with the imposition of the subsidy/tax scheme. With a small elasticity of substitution, because the distortion is low and a tax subsidy is required to elicit significant shifts toward manufacturing, it appears that a high subsidy is desirable.

Again, we obtain the result that the larger the learning elasticity (h) the larger the subsidy, and the larger the sensitivity of consumption of manufacturing to a subsidy, the larger the subsidy.

Alternatively, the government may be able to borrow, even if private individuals cannot. It can impose taxes the second period to repay the cost of first period subsidies. Take the symmetric case. The government seeks to maximize

$$\text{Max } V^t \left((1 - \tau i), \ldots \ldots, 0 \right) + \delta\, V^{t+1}\left((1 + ti)\ \mathbf{ci(\tau i,\ \tau j \neq i)},\ 0 \right)$$

$$\text{s.t. } \Sigma \tau_i x^t_i\, (1 + r) = \Sigma t_i\, x_i^{t+1},$$

where r is the interest rate the government has to pay. In the symmetric case, we can, without loss of generality, simplify by assuming only one commodity; dropping the subscripts, we have $\tau x^t\, (1 + r) = t\, x^{t+1}$.

The first order condition is

$$\tau[V^t_I\, x^t - \delta(1 + r)\, V^{t+1}_I\, x^t\, [1 + \beta^t + \beta^{t+1}]] + \delta\, V^{t+1}_I\, x^{t+1}\, c'x^t\, \beta^t = 0,$$

where, in the obvious notation,[44]

$$\beta^t = d\ln x^t/dn\ \tau > 0$$

and

$$\beta^{t+1} = -d\ln x^{t+1}/dn\ \tau,$$

or simplifying

$$\tau\, [1 - \rho(1 + r)\, [1 + \beta^t + \beta^{t+1}]] + \rho(\, L^{t+1}/L^t)\, h\, \beta^t = 0.$$

$[1 - \rho(1+ r)\, [1 + \beta^t + \beta^{t+1}]]$ is the benefit of borrowing money this period to be paid back next period. It is negative if r is high or ρ is small. We focus on the case where, in the absence of learning benefits, it would not be beneficial to borrow, that is,

$$\rho(1 + r)\, [1 + \beta^t + \beta^{t+1}] > 1.$$

In that case, if there is learning, there is an optimal subsidy (financed by borrowing), given by

$$\tau^* = \rho(L^{t+1}/L^t)\, h\, \beta^t/\, \rho(1 + r)\, [1 + \beta^t + \beta^{t+1}] - 1 > 0.$$

The subsidy is higher the higher the learning elasticity h; the lower the interest rate; and the more sensitive first period consumption (production) is to the subsidy (i.e., the higher β^t is).

Section 2. Long-Term Growth

Finite period models have gone out of fashion in economics in favor of infinite period models. To make such models tractable, however, requires much more special parameterizations, so that in practice neither model is really more general than the other. If there is to be a steady state with learning, since the output per unit of labor is increasing steadily, for the labor supply to any sector to be constant, either (a) the labor supply must be inelastic and relative prices must be constant or (b) utility of consumption must be logarithmic. Logarithmic utility functions have the unattractive property that the share of expenditure on each commodity is fixed. Normally, relative prices will be constant only with full spillovers (one of the cases we focus on, but clearly not general). Alternatively, we can focus on asymptotic behavior; for instance, where the fraction of a person's (society's) time spent working in any particular sector approaches some bound. But again, these asymptotes are often of limited interest in the short run (and we are always in the short run), especially since in the general case of these models, asymptotic allocations of labor to certain sectors go to zero.

The problems posed by learning models are even more complicated in the case of, say, an exponentially growing population. Of course, with a finite earth, such models face a problem of asymptotically infinite density, which is, to say the least, uncomfortable. But more formally, if learning depends on labor input and labor input is always growing, then growth is always increasing, unless there is magically just the right amount of offsetting diminishing returns. One can find parameterizations in which this occurs, but we should not be fooled—they are very special.

Indeed, there is no theoretical reason to expect the episodic large innovations that have transformed our economy—electricity, computers, the automobile—to occur with regular periodicity and appropriate magnitude to sustain anything approximating a steady state.

In our own lifetime, we have seen dramatic transitions in the rate of population growth, to the point where it is even declining in many advanced industrial countries. There is a general consensus that the global population will level off (will *have* to level off) at around 9 billion.

In short, we shouldn't take steady-state models excessively seriously. They are meant to help us think through trade-offs. In some cases—for instance, when we are focusing on issues of the demographic transition—more insight might be obtained from looking at N period models, where population is expanding in earlier periods and stationary in later periods. On the other hand, with a high enough discount, the distant future is of little moment, and a model focusing on the short run may provide a good approximation.

In the paragraphs below, we briefly explore special cases in which a steady state exists. We structure the cases so that whatever is optimal at time t is optimal at time t + 1; in that case, policy is directed at choosing the optimum steady state. In all the cases, the central result is that it is optimal to permanently impose distorting taxes to encourage production in the learning sector.

In the previous sections, we have explored models in which the government directly controls outputs (inputs), in which it has indirect control through taxes but can impose lump sum taxes, and in which it cannot impose lump sum taxes. We have also explored models in which learning is symmetric or asymmetric. In this section, we investigate only two cases; the results can easily be generalized to the other contexts.

Logarithmic Utility Functions We first assume a logarithmic utility function

$$u^t = \Sigma \alpha_i \ln x_i^t, \ \Sigma \alpha_i = 1$$

and

$$W^t = u^t - v(L^t),$$

which at each moment of time implies (in static maximization)

$$\alpha_i/x_i^t = p_i v'(L^t),$$

which in turn implies that

$$x_i^t p_i = \alpha_i/v'(L^t).$$

Expenditure shares are proportional to α_i and don't depend at all on costs. We focus on the direct control problem where the government sets $\{\upsilon, L\}$, where υ_i is the share of total labor allocated to the production of good i. In the short run, as before, we assume the cost of each good is unity. Then

$$W^t = \Sigma_i \alpha_i \ln \upsilon_i^t + \ln L - v(L) \equiv W_o,$$

from which it follows that static optimization entails $\upsilon_i^t = \alpha_i$, and $1 = v'(L^*)L^*$. Note that the short-run optimum L does not depend on productivity.

We assume that, as before, productivity at time t + 1 is related to productivity at time t by a learning function, which we now write as

$$P_i^{t+1} = P_i^t \ H_i^t(\upsilon L),$$

where P_i^t is output per unit labor at time t and υL is the vector of labor inputs. If L and υ are the same at t and t + 1, then

$$u^{t+1} = u^t + \Sigma \alpha_i \ln H_i^t(\upsilon L) = u^t + g(\upsilon L).$$

g (υL) is the overall rate of productivity increase (measured here in terms of utility). It should be clear that, given the structure of the model, if υL is optimal for time t, it is optimal for time t + 1. We can write discounted utility[45]

$$W = \Sigma \ W^t \ \delta^t = [W_o + \delta \ g/1 - \delta]/(1 - \delta),$$

from which it follows that W is maximized when

$$\partial W_o/\partial \upsilon_i + (\delta/1 - \delta) \ \partial g/\partial \upsilon_i = 0$$

$$\partial W_o/\partial L + (\delta/1 - \delta) \ \partial g/\partial L = 0,$$

from which it follows that we expand production beyond short-run utility maximization the most in sectors that increase g the most; in this model, industrial policy is a permanent feature of the economy. Moreover, we increase work (labor supply) beyond the level of short-run utility maximization.

It is easy to derive the implications for some special cases. Assume that there are two sectors, A and M, and there is learning only in the M sector. Then

$$g = \alpha_M \ln H(\upsilon_M L)$$

and the optimum value of

$$\upsilon_M = \alpha_M[1 + h\delta/1 - \delta]/[1 + \alpha_M h\delta/1 - \delta],$$

where $h = d \ln H/d\ln \upsilon_M L$.

The greater h, the larger the larger the fraction of labor allocated to manufacturing. When $h = 0$, as expected, $\upsilon_M = \alpha_M$. By the same token, work at each date is expanded beyond the static level, to the point where

$$1/L - v' = -h\delta\ \alpha_M/(1 - \delta)L < 0,$$

(the static marginal disutility of work exceeds the value of the marginal output), or L^{**} now satisfies

$$Lv' = 1 + h\delta\ \alpha_M/(1 - \delta) = (1 - \alpha_M)/(1 - V_M^t)$$

Fixed Labor Supply, No Lump Sum Taxation In the second case, the labor supply is fixed and lump sum taxes are not allowed. There are two sectors, denoted A and M. Here, we have an additional problem in steady-state analysis: If there is differential growth in labor productivity in the two sectors, one sector gets a smaller, diminishing share of overall expenditures, except in the special case of unitary elasticity of substitution (the logarithmic utility case just analyzed.) Accordingly, we focus on the case with full spillover, so that relative prices remain unchanged, and with homotheticity, so do relative shares. We assume a homothetic utility function of the form

$$U = U(x_M, x_A) = x_A^{-\eta+1}\ u(x_M/x_A), 0 < \eta < 1,$$

where, as before, η is the elasticity of marginal utility. As before, we impose a subsidy at the rate t on manufacturing paid for by a tax at rate t on agriculture. We can write the indirect utility function then as $V(1 - \tau, 1 + t, I)$. Static utility maximization entails maximizing V with respect to τ:

$$dV/dt = - x_A\ \tau\ (d(x_M/x_A)/d\ \tau)\ V_I$$

$$= - x_M\ (d\ln\ (x_M/x_A)/d \ln \tau)\ V_I$$

$$= - x_M\ [\beta_M + \beta_A]\ V_I$$

Static efficiency entails, as before, $\tau = 0$.[46] But now assume that there is learning only in the manufacturing sector but perfect spillover to the agricultural sector. Productivity growth is thus $H(x_M)$. Again, we have structured the model so that the optimal subsidy at time t is the optimal subsidy at t + 1, and the present discounted value of utility is given by

$$U_0/1 - \delta - H^{-\eta+1},$$

which is maximized at

$$\partial \ln \frac{U_0}{\partial} \tau + \left[\frac{(1-\eta)H^{-\eta+1}}{1-\partial-H^{-\eta+1}} \right] (\partial(\ln H/\partial \ln x_M))(\mathrm{d}\ln x_M/\mathrm{d}\tau) = 0.$$

The above expression can be used, as before, to derive the optimal subsidy rate.

Cumulative Experience We take a somewhat different approach in which changes in productivity are based not directly on current production but on the change in cumulative experience. (Effectively, Arrow's original model was of this form.) That is, we write, in the absence of spillovers,

$$Q^k(t) = H^k (t) L^k (t),$$

where now, say, productivity depends on discounted cumulative experience E according to the function

$$H^k(t) = [E]^{b^k}$$

where b^k is the elasticity of productivity with respect to experience in sector, and where experience E is defined by[47]

$$E = [\textstyle\int_o^t L_k(x)e^{-z(t-x)}dx],$$

capturing the notion that experiences a long time ago have limited relevance for productivity today. In steady state, it is obvious that

$$g^k = \mathrm{d}\ln Q^k/\mathrm{d}t = (b^k + 1) \, n,$$

where n is the rate of growth of population. Even though learning is endogenous, we obtain the standard Solow result that the long-term sectoral growth rate is determined by the rate of growth of population. The fact that learning is affected by experience is still important, because the aggregate growth rate is affected by the allocation of resources. Assume, for instance, individual logarithmic utility function

$$W^t = \Sigma \alpha_i \ln x_i^t - v(L^t), \ \Sigma \alpha_i = 1,$$

exponential labor force growth at the rate n, and a social welfare function of the form

$$W = \int \exp \{- r + n\}W^t,$$

where r is the discount rate, r > n + g, where g is the rate of growth of utility (output, if U has constant returns to scale). In steady state,

$$W = W^*/n + g - r.$$

With learning, in steady state, W is increasing at the rate

$$g = \Sigma \alpha^k (b^k + 1) \, n.$$

Clearly, allocating more labor to sectors with higher learning elasticities will lead to higher rates of growth of utility. As before, let υ_i and g be the fraction of the labor supply allocated to sector i. For simplicity, we can express W^* (in steady state) as a function of $\{L, \upsilon\}$. Then, if we want to choose the allocation that

$$\text{maximizes } W^*\{L, \upsilon\}/n + g\,(L, \upsilon) - r$$

$$\{L, \upsilon\},$$

implying that we distort the allocation of $\{L, \upsilon\}$, relative to static utility maximization, to increase long-run growth.[48] The optimum balances the two effects. Because increasing L increases cumulative experience, it increases productivity, and long-term social welfare maximization takes this into account. Like an increase in the savings rate in the standard Solow growth model, an increase in L does not, however, have any effect on long-term growth rates. The allocation of labor does.

Asymmetric Equilibria and the Advantages of Specialization Learning, as we have noted, introduces nonconvexities, which may make it desirable for countries to specialize. The learning curves introduced in the previous section suffer from diminishing returns and therefore don't capture this effect. If, for instance, there were two commodities, with $\alpha = \frac{1}{2}$, then, $\upsilon^* = \frac{1}{2}$.

Assume that

$$H^k(t) = [\textstyle\int_0^t L^k(x)e^{-z(t-x)}dx]^b \text{ if } E \geq E^*$$
$$= \hat{H} \text{ if } E < E^*$$

and (E) is a convex function, such that $\hat{H}(0) = 1$, $\hat{H}(E^*) = E^{*b}$.[49]

Assume further that

$$u^k = \log x^k \text{ if } x^k \geq 1$$

$$= 0 \quad \text{otherwise}$$

where now x^k represents individual consumption. (We introduce this assumption because otherwise, as x^k goes to zero, the marginal utility of consumption goes to infinity, and we always produce both goods.)

It follows that if L is small enough, then optimality may require, say, $\upsilon_1 = 1$, $\upsilon_2 = 0$. The economy specializes in one of the two commodities. As we specialize in commodity 2, H^2/H^1 becomes small (there is no cumulative experience in producing good 2), so it becomes optimal both statically and dynamically not to produce good 1.

Cumulative Learning from Output A slight variant of the previous model focuses on output rather than input. The difference arises from that fact that with learning, output grows more rapidly than input.[50] Assume now that the relevant measure of "experience" is

$$E = [\int_0^t Q^k(x)e^{-z(t-x)}dx]$$
$$H^k(t) = [\int_0^t Q^k(x)e^{-z(t-x)}dx]^b,$$

so in steady state (where the same fraction of labor is allocated to any sector every year)

$$g^k = bg^k + n = n/1 - b,$$

where it will be remembered that $b < 1$. If $b > 1$, faster growth begets faster growth of experience, which begets even faster growth of output. The economy is unstable, with potentially super-exponential growth. While the steady states of this model look very much like those of the earlier models, in which experience is based on labor input, more general versions of this model can give rise to multiple short-run equilibria. Assume that $H^k(E)$ does not have constant elasticity.[51] Then, assuming that at each date, L is fixed,

$$g^k = h(E) \, d\ln E/dt + n + d\ln \upsilon^k/dt.$$

Since E and $d\ln E/dt$ depend on g^k, there can be short/medium rate high-growth scenarios: A high level of expansion of a sector can lead to a higher elasticity of learning (e.g., if there is learning by learning), which supports the higher expansion of the sector. The implications for optimal policy are similar to those discussed earlier: Even if two sectors initially appear symmetric, it may be optimal to focus on one of the two sectors to increase learning; but now it is possible that the increased growth induced by the faster learning is further reinforced by a higher learning elasticity.

Monopolistic Competition

A similar analysis applies to a model with monopolistic competition. In the previous models, there was competition and learning was external to the firm, so that each firm put no value on the learning generated by its production activities. In this model, there is only one firm in each sector, but there are a sufficiently large number of products that each firm can take the wages and prices of other firms as given. As before, industrial policy depends on the set of instruments available to the government; for example, whether it can undo the effects of monopoly and whether it can impose lump sum taxes. Here, we assume that the government can do nothing about the monopoly power of each firm but that in setting, say, a subsidy for any product, it takes into account that markets are distorted as a result of monopolistic competition.

The major difference between this case and those analyzed in the previous section is that if there are no cross-sector learning externalities, the monopolistically competitive firm internalizes the learning externality. However, the firm still does not internalize cross-sector demand effects. We begin the analysis, however, by focusing on the case in which these can be ignored. The firm sets

$$(p_i^t + x_i^t \, dp_i^t/dx_i^t) = 1 - \delta x_i^{t+1} H_i^i/(H^i)^2 \tag{29}$$

or

$$p_i^t(1 - 1/\acute{\eta}_i) = 1 - \delta \zeta_i h_i$$

or

$$p_i^t = [1 - \delta \zeta_i \, h_i]/(1 - 1/\acute{\eta}_i), \tag{30}$$

where (as before) $\zeta_i = L^{t+1}{}_i/L^t{}_i$, the ratio of the input into sector j at time t to that at t + 1, $h_i = d\ln H^i/d\ln L_i^t$, the (own) elasticity of productivity with respect to labor input (the learning coefficient) and $1/\acute{\eta}_i = - \, d\ln p_i/d\ln x_i$, the elasticity of demand.

The monopolist obviously doesn't take into account the consequences of his production/pricing decisions on the learning of other firms—either through spillover effects or through market effects. The latter can be important in the case of a nonseparable demand function. But he does take into account his own learning, and so sets a price lower than he would if there were no learning. Firms with more elastic demand functions charge a lower price (and produce more the first period); but firms with a more inelastic demand show a greater sensitivity to learning (i.e., all firms lower their price as h increases, but those with a higher markup—lower price elasticity—lower their price more. They have to, in order to expand output.)

The nature of the overall market distortion is, however, complex. For instance, in the second period, because of the exercise of monopoly power, the benefits of learning will be smaller. But, given the lower level of output in the second period, ignoring spillovers, the firm appropriately values the benefits of learning, which it sees, at the margin, as saving labor.[52]

There can be distortions in both total labor supply in the first period and in its allocation. Consider, for instance, a symmetric equilibrium in which all firms have the same demand and learning elasticities. The effect of monopolistic competition is to change real wages in the first period. If first period labor supply elasticity is zero, this has no effect on learning. An awareness of the learning benefits drives up the real wage, but that is all that happens. First and second period output is unchanged. But if there is a positive elasticity of labor supply, the analysis becomes more interesting. In the case of myopic monopolistic competition (where no weight is given to the value of future learning), first period real wages are lowered as a result of monopoly power, labor supply is lowered, output is lowered, and learning is thereby lowered. *With myopic monopolies, monopoly is unambiguously worse than competition; even though neither takes into account the benefits of learning, growth is higher with competition than with monopoly.*

With nonmyopic monopoly, whether learning (growth) is higher with monopoly depends on whether

$$[1 - \delta\, \zeta_i\, h_i]/(1 - 1/\acute{\eta}_i) < \text{or} > 1, \tag{31}$$

that is, on whether

$$d\, \zeta_i\, h_i > \text{or} < 1/\acute{\eta}_i. \tag{32}$$

If the elasticity of demand is low, the elasticity of learning is small, or the rate of discount is high, then monopoly is worse than competition, even though the benefits of learning have been internalized.

The general principles of government intervention should be clear. Government has to correct two market failures and must be careful that in correcting one, it does not exacerbate the other. Focusing only on learning, optimal policy entails encouraging production in the first period by a production subsidy financed (if possible) by a lump sum tax. If a lump sum tax is not possible but the country can borrow, it pays to finance the first period subsidy with a second period tax.

Precise prescriptions for the design of optimal intervention depend on what the government can do. For instance, if the government can impose a nondistortionary profits tax and use it to subsidize production in the first and second periods, it can presumably fully undo the effects of monopoly. If it can undo the effects of second period monopoly, the formulas derived earlier can be used.

If it can only, say, impose a lump sum tax to finance a commodity subsidy in the first period, then it seeks to

$$\underset{\{\tau\}}{\text{maximize}}\ V^t(\mathbf{p}^t, -\Sigma\tau_i x_i) + \delta V^{t+1}(\mathbf{p}_i^{t+1}, 0) \tag{33}$$

where

$$p_i^t = \kappa_i(1 - \tau_i) \tag{34}$$

$$p_i^{t+1} = \kappa_i/H^i \tag{35}$$

where

$$\kappa_i = 1/(1 - 1/\acute{\eta}_i), \tag{36}$$

the monopoly markup over marginal cost. When we introduce a subsidy, we undo the first period monopoly distortion and correct the underinvestment in production/learning distortion.[53] If we could impose similar corrective taxation in the second period, we could achieve precisely the equilibrium described earlier for the competition case. If not, we have to take into account the fact that the benefits of learning are lower, because future production is lower. Hence, in general, optimal subsidies will be lower.

The more interesting case is that in which there are two sectors, one (manufacturing) with a full learning spillover and the other (agriculture) with no learning. In this case, it can be shown that not only is a subsidy on manufacturing desirable, there is even some presumption that it should be larger with monopoly than with competition.

We now have

$$\text{Max } V^t(\kappa_M (1 - \tau_M), \kappa_A (1 + t_A), 0) + \delta V^{t+1}(\kappa_M c(L_M), \kappa_A c(L_M), 0) \qquad (37)$$

$$\{\tau_M\},$$

where, as before, the subsidy to manufacturing is financed by a tax on agriculture.

$$V_I^t\{(\kappa_M - \kappa_A)\, x_M - \kappa_A x_A \tau_M d(x_M/x_A)/d\tau_M)\} \qquad (38)$$
$$= -\delta V_I^{t+1} c'(L_M)(\kappa_M x_M^{t+1} + \kappa_A x_A^{t+1}) dx_M^t/d\tau_M,$$

where, it will be recalled,

$$dt_A/d\tau_M = (x_M/x_A) + \tau_M d(x_M/x_A)/d\tau_M.$$

The following differences from the earlier equation (27) are apparent:

(a) The change in relative prices may correct or exacerbate a distortion in relative consumption caused by differences in demand elasticities. In the case where demand elasticities are the same, the LHS of (38) simplifies to

$$- \tau_M(d(x_M/x_A)/dt\tau_M)\, \kappa_A x_A \,,$$

which is negative.

(b) Lowering costs has a multiplicative effect on prices in the next period, so the benefits of learning are enhanced. In the case where demand elasticities are the same, the benefits are multiplied by a factor $\kappa_M = \kappa_A$. Moreover, an increase in the subsidy leads to a decrease in the price by a multiple (and an increase in the price of the agricultural good by a corresponding multiple), so that with monopoly, $dx_M^t/d\tau_M$ is much larger than with competition. Moreover, under normal assumptions, c' with monopoly is higher but $x_M^{t+1} + x_A^{t+1}$ is smaller, because real wages are smaller and productivity is lower.

Open Economy

The most interesting context for analyzing government intervention is that of a small, open, developing economy. The question is, should it use trade policy (tariffs or foreign exchange intervention)? Such policies change the structure of the economy. Can it do so in ways that will enhance learning and promote welfare? And even if it can, are these the best instruments available?

Two-Sector Economy

First, consider a two-sector economy, comprising agriculture and manufacturing, in a Ricardian world in which labor is the only input to production. In the simplest version of this model, the country can produce both goods and exchange some of the tradable goods for imports.

The developing country is small relative to the global economy and is assumed initially to have a comparative advantage in the agricultural good. The agricultural good has no direct learning potential but industrial production has considerable learning potential, and the benefits of learning spill over perfectly to the agricultural sector. This is important, because it means that the relative price of agriculture and industrial goods remains fixed.

In the absence of protection (or some other industrial policy), the small developing country specializes in agriculture and hence has no growth. It stagnates, while the large developed country continues to grow. The gap between the two increases over time.[54]

With protection—say, in the form of quotas—the country produces some of the industrial good, generating some learning, which spills over to the rest of the economy. There is a static inefficiency, but so long as the learning is sufficiently great, the static inefficiency is more than offset by the dynamic benefits.

Assume, for instance, that the labor supply is (in the absence of intervention) fixed at unity (this is just a normalization);[55] that a fraction of the labor force π is assigned to the industrial sector; that the short-term productivity in the industrial sector relative to that in the advanced industrial country is $\gamma < 1$ (where we have normalized productivity abroad at unity); and that a proportion of the production of the agricultural sector λ is traded for industrial goods from the developed country (at a price of unity). Then, at any moment in time,

$$U = \alpha_M \ln M + (1 - \alpha_M) \ln A \tag{39}$$

$$= \alpha_M \ln (\pi \gamma + (1 - \pi)\lambda) + (1 - \alpha_M) \ln ((1 - \lambda)(1 - \pi)) = U^*.$$

It is easy to show that U is maximized at $\pi = 0$; that is, the country specializes in the production of agricultural goods. This is the conventional static result.[56]

But now we assume that the country's rate of productivity increase is $g(\pi)$, $g' > 0$; that is, the rate of productivity growth increases with the size of the industrial sector. There is full spillover from the industrial sector to the agricultural sector. Because of this assumption (and a similar assumption in the global market), the country's comparative advantage remains with agriculture. The problem facing the country in the next period is essentially the same problem facing the country this year. If consumption of both goods at t + 1 is (1 + g) times consumption at t, $U^{t+1} = U^t + \ln (1 + g)$. Hence, if δ is the discount rate, the present discount value of utility is[57]

$$W \equiv [U^* + \delta(\ln (1 + g)/1 - \delta)]/(1 - \delta). \tag{40}$$

And it is no longer the case that maximizing social welfare (W) entails $\pi = 0$. It immediately follows that

$$\partial U^*/\partial \ln \pi + G \, g \, \delta/(1 - \delta) = 0, \tag{41}$$

where $G = d\ln g/d\ln \pi$, which implies that, so long as $G > 0$ (there is a marginal benefit to learning) optimality requires that $\pi > 0$: The dynamic benefits of learning exceed the static costs. Industrial policies pay off. The greater the learning elasticity and the higher δ (the lower the discount factor), the higher π; that is, the higher the optimal static distortion.

This framework requires industrial policies that allow for a limited industrial sector, even though the country has a comparative disadvantage in that sector in the short run and, in this model, even in the long run. That is, in our Ricardian model, with full spillovers, technological change does not change the country's comparative advantage. The fact that the country's industrial sector never becomes competitive (the infant never grows up) is not necessarily an argument against industrial policies, when the learning spillovers are great enough.

In this model with a linear technology, the easiest way to implement the desired level of domestic production is through a quota, which ensures that at the equilibrium price, the desired amount of manufactured goods are produced at home. With increasing costs, there exists an optimal tariff, which would result in the desired level of domestic production.

Nontraded Sector

Finally, we consider a variant of the canonical Ricardian model in which there are three goods: exports, imports, and a nontradable. Government intervention can affect either the price of tradables relative to nontradables or the price of imports relative to exports.

A slight variant of the previous model yields precisely the same results. Let us assume a more general homothetic utility function, with the obvious notation

$$U^* = U(M, A, NT)$$

$$= U\left((\pi\,\gamma + (1 - \pi - \theta)\lambda),\ (1 - \pi - \theta)(1 - \lambda),\ \theta\right),$$

where now θ is the fraction of the labor force allocated to the nontraded sector.

We again get the result that U^* is optimized at $\pi = 0$. But again, if the rate of learning is a function of the size of the industrial sector π, the economy should produce industrial goods even though those are not its comparative advantage.

We now consider what happens when international trade agreements restrict the use of industrial policies. The only instrument left is the exchange rate. Lowering the exchange rate simultaneously decreases the price of exports in foreign currency, leading to an increase in the demand for exports, and increases the price of imports (in domestic currency, relative to the price of nontraded goods). It thus encourages substitution away from imported consumption goods. Increased exports and reduced imports lead to a trade surplus.

In a two-period model, this means that the country consumes less than it could in the initial period, offset by increased consumption in the later period.[58] As in the earlier models without trade, the static distortion (consuming less than what would normally maximize utility, based on the equality of the marginal rate of substitution and the interest rate) is justified by the dynamic benefits—producing more of the export good, say, leads to more learning, which generates a higher level of consumption in the second period than would otherwise be possible. This is true even though the range of instruments has now been restricted so the social cost of intervention is higher.

But if the learning effects are strong enough, even in an infinite period model, the benefits of expanding exports are sufficiently great that it may be possible that optimal policy requires the country to build up reserves forever, never to use them (essentially like throwing money away). We construct a model in which each period the world looks as it did the previous period, so that if it is desirable to have a surplus at time t, it is desirable to have a trade surplus at time t + 1. (Of course, in a more general dynamic model, it may be desirable to have trade surpluses initially, to be spent at later dates.)

Denote the exchange rate by e. Taking labor as our numeraire, and noting that by our choice of units the price of the nontraded goods is also unity (in the absence of taxes and subsidies, which, by assumption, are precluded), the price (and therefore the level of consumption) of the industrial and agriculture good are simply a function of e.

Hence, we obtain

$$U^* = U[M(e), A(e), NT(e)], \tag{42}$$

where consumption of agricultural goods is equal to production minus exports:

$$A(e) = (1 - \pi - \theta)(1 - \lambda), \tag{43}$$

where, it will be recalled, λ is the share of production exported, and where consumption of the industrial goods is production plus imports, m,

$$M(e) = \pi\gamma + m. \tag{44}$$

Static utility maximization requires

$$(1 - \pi - \theta)\lambda - m = S \geq 0, \tag{45}$$

where S is the balance of payments surplus.

((45) is the balance of payments constraint.)

In a static model, U^* is maximized, subject to (45) (the balance of payments constraint), $1 \geq \lambda \geq 0$, $1 \geq \pi \geq 0$, and $1 \geq \theta \geq 0$. It is easy to show in the static model (i.e., with no learning) that free trade is optimal and the balance of payments constraint is binding:

$$\pi = 0, S = 0, \lambda > 0. \tag{46}$$

The equilibrium exchange rate can easily be calculated. In equilibrium, full income is

$$y = \theta + e(1 - \theta) = y(e, \theta).$$

$$NT(e, y(e, \theta)) = \theta \tag{47a}$$

$$X = 1 - \theta - A(e, y(e, \theta)) \tag{47b}$$

$$m = I\,(e,\, y(e,\, \theta)) \tag{47c}$$

$$X = m \tag{47d}$$

where X = exports, and where NT(e, y(e, θ)), A(e, y(e, θ)) and I (e, y(e, θ)) are, respectively the demand for nontraded goods, agricultural goods, and industrial goods, and where, because of the lack of comparative advantage in manufacturing, in the absence of government intervention, the country imports all manufactured goods. (47b) – (47d) can be re-expressed as a function relating e and θ:

$$1 - \theta - A(e,\, y(e,\, \theta)) = I\,(e,\, y(e,\, \theta))$$

or

$$1 - \theta = A(e,\, y(e,\, \theta)) + I\,(e,\, y(e,\, \theta)). \tag{48}$$

(48) and (47a) can be solved simultaneously for e and θ. Equations (47a) through (47d) can then be solved simultaneously for the full equilibrium. We assume the government controls e, and that the rate of growth depends on Q_M, the output of manufacturing goods, which in turn depends on e.

In the dynamic model, we can write again

$$W \equiv [U^* + \delta(g)/1 - \delta)]/(1 - \delta). \tag{49}$$

We now maximize W with respect to e (recognizing the effect of e on Q_M) to obtain an equation parallel to (41):

$$\partial \ln U^*/\partial \ln e + G\, g\, \delta\, (d\ln Q_M/d\ln e)/(1 - \delta) = 0. \tag{50}$$

If δ g G (dln Q_M (e)/dln e) > 0, it means that at the optimum e, $\partial U^*/\partial \ln e$ < 0.

Once learning is taken into account, it may pay to have a lower exchange rate than the equilibrium exchange rate described earlier. A lower exchange rate will mean that exports will increase and imports decrease, and (with the usual restrictions on demand functions) there is a trade surplus. It pays to perpetually accumulate reserves—to run a surplus—because of the learning benefits. (To repeat: This requires that no other instruments are available to promote learning; for example, through exports.)

In our Ricardian model, with constant returns to scale, small changes in the exchange rate have no effect on production of the industrial good, given the developing country's comparative and absolute disadvantage in its production. But lowering the (real and nominal) exchange rate enough makes the industrial good competitive. Define e** as the exchange rate at which firms are just indifferent between producing industrial goods and importing them. Assume that at e** the government can choose a level of industrial output, Q_M^{**} > 0. Then we can solve for the equilibrium allocation of labor to the nontraded sector:

$$NT(e^{**},\, y(e^{**},\, \theta^{**})) = \theta^{**}.$$

The equilibrium level of exports is[59]

$$X = 1 - \theta^{**} - A(e^{**}, y(e^{**}, \theta^{**})) - Q_M^{**}/\Upsilon),$$

while the level of imports is

$$m = I(e^{**}, y(e^{**}, \theta^{**})) - Q_M^{**}.$$

At every value of Q_M^{**}, we can calculate S:

$$S = X - m.$$

Then the optimal level of Q_M^{**}[60] solves

$$W^{**} = \max_{\{M^{**}\}} \{U[I(e^{**}), A(e^{**}), NT(e^{**})] + \delta(\ln(1+g)/1-\delta)\}/1-\delta \qquad (51)$$

subject to

$$S \geq 0.$$

In general, the constraint will not be binding.

If $W^{**} > W(e^{*})$, it pays to lower the exchange rate to e^{**}. If the optimum Q_M^{**} is such that

$$1 - \theta^{**} - A(e^{**}, y(e^{**}, \theta^{**})) - (Q_M^{**}/\Upsilon) > I(e^{**}, y(e^{**}, \theta^{**})) - Q_M^{**},$$

it pays the country to accumulate a perpetual surplus.

We should emphasize the sensitivity of this analysis to the assumptions that we have imposed to allow for a steady-state analysis. A fuller analysis would take into account the fact that as the country closes the knowledge gap between itself and the advanced industrial countries, learning benefits may decrease, perhaps to the point at which the cost of running a surplus—the lost utility from the foregone consumption—exceeds the learning benefit. The country might then want (as in our two-period model) to consume its accumulated surplus. Other factors would also affect the country's desired level of surplus. A country with an aging population might want to put aside savings and then, as the aging population enters into retirement, reduce that surplus. Such demographic transitions are not analyzed well in steady-state models.[61]

Some countries have been criticized for contributing to global imbalances by accumulating excessive reserves. In static models, it has seemed irrational for developing countries—suffering from capital shortages and with constrained consumption—to do so; just as it has seemed peculiar that the United States, with an aging population, is running long-term deficits. This paper shows, however, that once dynamic learning benefits are taken into account, with sufficient constraints on industrial policies (such as those imposed by the World Trade Organization), the accumulation of reserves by a developing country (beyond a level required for precautionary reasons to manage global volatility) may be reasonable if the learning benefits are large enough. Interestingly, while this policy leads to a lower level of imports initially because of the induced growth, over the longer run, the country's level of imports is actually increased.[62]

Concluding Comments

I have argued here that what matters for development is *learning* and, more broadly, technical progress and a developmental transformation. I have focused on a simple model of learning, but even within that simple model, we have seen how much of recent conventional wisdom about development strategies is overturned. The standard paradigm has focused on eliminating market distortions—ensuring that the economy is on its static production (or, more generally, utility[63]) possibilities curve, based on a given level of knowledge. More important in the long run, however, is moving the possibilities curve outward—for advanced industrial economies by advances in technology; for developing countries by closing the knowledge gap between advanced industrial countries and developing countries; and for all countries by ensuring that all firms are employing best practices[64] as rapidly as possible. Moving toward the frontier (for instance, by eliminating all tariffs and quotas) might entail slowing down the pace of outward movement of the frontier—and slower long-run growth. In the former case, there is but a one-time gain.

A full analysis of what makes for a learning economy would take us beyond this short paper. We can *learn to learn* (Stiglitz 1987c)—we can enhance our learning capacities. Just as what we produce may affect how much we learn, it may affect how we learn to learn. Just as "roundabout means of production" (to use Böhm-Bawerk's terminology) may be more efficient, roundabout means of learning may be more efficient: We can learn more efficiently if we first learn how to learn.[65]

Once one recognizes the importance of learning and developmental transformation (Stiglitz 1998), analysis must go beyond economics. Education can either reinforce norms of *statis* or persuade young people that change is possible and give them tools with which to bring about and cope with change. A variety of institutions and institutional arrangements can either promote or prevent the development of a culture of change.[66]

In this paper, we have focused on the economics of learning. From the earliest literature on endogenous technological change—when the public-good nature of knowledge, the problems of appropriability, and the pervasiveness of spillovers were recognized—it was apparent that markets on their own were not likely to be efficient and that the overall efficiency of the market would depend on market structure in rather complex ways—with monopolies restricting output but internalizing the benefits of learning. Schumpeter recognized that this was a problem in the second best.[67] He tried to defend monopoly on the grounds (in modern language) that it partially solved the appropriability problem and the problems posed by imperfect capital markets. While the question is in some sense not appropriately posed (market structure should be viewed as endogenous, and in the absence of full spillovers, competitive markets may be hard to sustain), this paper shows that even though monopolists internalize their own learning benefits, the distortion associated with underproduction (monopoly pricing) may lead to less learning than in a competitive market with optimal intervention.

Until this paper, most of the growth literature has focused on aggregate models in which the scope for allocative decisions was very limited (e.g., sectoral allocations played little role in aggregate growth rates). Insufficient attention has been paid to the design of policy interventions and the parameters on which they should depend to correct systemic market failures, especially in the presence of cross-sectoral spillovers. This paper has provided a simple context in which market distortions—on both the aggregate supply of labor and its allocation—can be analyzed and the kinds of interventions (typically second or third best interventions, predicated on the existence of certain restrictions on the set of admissible policies) that might address them.

The paper thus provides both a case for industrial policies and the beginning of an analysis of the optimal design of such policies. Many of the results are not surprising, though the simplicity of the forms of intervention (at least in some limiting cases) is striking. Simple formulas akin to those arising in the theory of optimal taxation are derived. The size of the static distortions (reflected in subsidies) increases, as expected, with learning elasticities and knowledge spillovers—with the latter taking on a particularly prominent role. Patterns of subsidies are affected, too, in easily understandable ways by patterns of demand interdependence. Intertemporal trade-offs are captured by the pure rate of discount as well as the rate at which marginal utility of income diminishes as a result of increasing productivity (which, in turn, depends on the elasticity of marginal utility and the rate of progress), with the intuitive result that the smaller the value at the margin of future consumption, the less distortion (the smaller the subsidy) to induce learning. But now the intertemporal trade-off is partly endogenous and other factors come to play a role, especially the elasticity of labor supply. Indeed, in the limiting case of symmetric learning and demand functions, we have shown that regardless of the learning elasticity, if the elasticity of labor supply is zero, the market equilibrium may be Pareto efficient. More generally, the magnitude of interventions also depends on labor supply elasticities. A particular complicating factor which we have noted is that, given the nonconvexities naturally associated with learning, optimal intervention may lead to asymmetric equilibria, even when all demand and learning functions are symmetric.

We noted that one of the standard objections to industrial policies in the past has been political: the potential for misuse. This poses an important trade-off. Broad-based measures such as exchange rate interventions require only that the government ascertain that the sectors that would be encouraged by such interventions have more societal learning benefits than the sectors that would be discouraged—and there is ample evidence that that is the case (evidenced by the success of export-led growth strategies). Firms and sectors within the economy self-select, and the expansion of firms and sectors with greater learning enhances the dynamism of the economy. On the other hand, more targeted interventions can lead to even more learning and faster rates of growth. No intervention completely "solves" the political economy problem: Sectors that benefit from exchange rate intervention may lobby for the maintenance of that intervention even in the absence of learning benefits. And some countries have shown that they can manage the political economy problems of more targeted interventions. The East Asian countries did so by using rule-based systems in which interventions were linked to past export success.

In any case, no government can completely absolve itself of the necessity of addressing the issues with which we have been concerned. For while we have focused on the use of taxes and subsidies to alter the structure of production and encourage more learning, different government investments in infrastructure, technology, and education affect different industries differently. In making such decisions, we argue that the government should take into account impacts on societal learning that will shape the country's dynamic comparative advantage.

We have focused on a model with a single factor of production: labor. The early learning literature[68] focused on learning through investment. Obviously, if countries learn through investment, there is an argument for encouraging investment, especially in sectors that have a greater learning elasticity and greater spillovers. Standard international trade arguments demonstrate that taxes on imports, if imports are labor-intensive, will drive up wages and lower interest rates, thus encouraging more investment (Korinek and Servén 2010).

We have emphasized the importance of developing policies that maximize effective learning. In our simple model, we have assumed that different sectors have different learning curves, with different spillovers to other sectors. Identifying these learning functions is necessary to design appropriate government policies. Elsewhere, Greenwald and Stiglitz (forthcoming) have discussed some of the factors that contribute to greater learning and greater spillovers. We argue that the manufacturing sector may have both greater learning potential and greater spillovers. Different countries may have different learning elasticities. Countries that are too distant in technology may have more difficulty closing the gap than countries that are somewhat closer, while for some countries there is little gap to close. Hence, learning elasticities (at least in some sectors) may be low for both the least developed countries and those that are near best practices.

Our simplified model also circumvents a central question: learning toward what end? Much of technological change in advanced developed countries has been directed toward saving labor, which is viewed as the "scarce factor." In developing countries, however, labor is in abundance—levels of unemployment are often high. A reduced demand for labor exacerbates the problem of unemployment. To put it another way, in these situations, the shadow wage and the market wage may differ. Innovation responds to market wages; innovation in the advanced industrial countries responds to the high market wages there.

It has long been recognized that technologies that are appropriate for developed countries may be less appropriate for developing countries. This means that developing countries may have less to learn from developed countries than is sometimes supposed;[69] their learning and research should be directed not so much at saving labor (the shadow price of which may be very low) as at saving capital and natural resources, and protecting the environment.[70]

Four decades ago, when we were thinking about these issues at Cambridge, Tony Atkinson and I introduced the concept of "localized technological change. (Atkinson and Stiglitz 1969). Technological change affected only certain production processes. An innovation could improve, for instance, some very advanced technologies but leave traditional technologies largely unaffected. Indeed, as noted earlier in this paper, the spillovers might be greater to advanced technologies in other sectors than to simple (say, nonautomatic) processes in the same sector.[71] This has an important implication: If developing countries resort to learning and adapting technologies created for circumstances prevalent in developed countries, the advances may be of limited value to their own economies. Emerging markets and developing countries need to develop their own research and learning capacities so they can improve the technologies that are appropriate to their economic circumstances. Thus, the point of industrial policies is not just to catch up to the advanced industrial countries, but to promote advances in technology that are appropriate to their circumstances and enhance their ability to make additional advances in these technologies.

Figure 1 illustrates an isoquant with two technologies, one (A) appropriate to a high-wage economy, the other (B) appropriate to a low-wage economy. Advances in technology in the advanced industrial economy move A downward (lower labor requirements per unit of output) but leave B unchanged. If the developing country simply borrows (say, with a lag) technology from the advanced industrial country, it initially gets no benefit (if it produces the good at all, it continues to use the unchanged technology B) until the cost savings from lower labor costs are so overwhelming that the country switches to A.

The fact that the country's technology remains unchanged implies that if it did not initially have a comparative advantage in the good (say, the industrial product), its comparative disadvantage may increase over time. But even if the country does not have a comparative advantage in the good and never will, the nontraded sector (or the agriculture sector) might benefit from spillovers.

If, however, the country is able to develop its own learning capacities (e.g., through industrial policies, which might seem inefficient in the short run), it can

FIGURE 1.

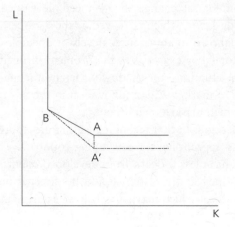

start improving technology B. Moreover, with capital scarce, the improvements will be directed at saving capital, not labor. Indeed, the improvements in its technology, if rapid enough, could change its comparative advantage. But even if that did not happen, the spillovers to the other sectors—reducing, say, capital but leaving labor inputs unchanged—would have far greater benefits than those generated from borrowing technology from the advanced industrial country.

The distortions in the bias of innovation are even greater when it comes to saving on environmental resources because of the massive mispricing of these resources. With no costs associated with carbon emissions, why would there be any incentive to reduce them? Social costs associated with the macroeconomic variability linked to dependence on imported resources whose prices are highly variable may be far greater than the private costs. This provides another rationale for government policies designed to encourage less dependence on such inputs—and another rationale for industrial policies.[72]

These environmental impacts are important for all countries but especially for developing countries, as Dasgupta's work repeatedly emphasizes.

This brings me back to one of the themes I raised earlier, a theme central to Dasgupta's work. What matters is not gross domestic product but quality of life, well-being, and sustainability.[73] What that entails—and how it can be increased—should and can be the subject of rational inquiry. Dasgupta has led the way in showing us how that can be done. For that, and for all his other contributions, we are grateful.

Notes

1. Later published; see Hahn (1966). Karl Shell and I extended this result in Shell and Stiglitz (1967).

2. In particular, on the questions of when production efficiency was desirable, the optimal supply of public goods in the presence of distortionary taxation, and "third best" approaches to optimal taxation when there were constraints on the set of feasible taxes. See especially Dasgupta and Stiglitz (1971, 1972).

3. See, for instance, Dasgupta and Stiglitz (1977), where we showed that the presumption in favor of tariffs over quotas did not hold in the face of uncertainty and incomplete insurance markets.

4. This included a large study done for the Department of Energy (Dasgupta et al. 1977).

5. See Dasgupta, Heal, and Stiglitz (1980); Dasgupta and Stiglitz (1981b, 1981c, 1982); Dasgupta, Gilbert and Stiglitz (1982, 1983). In many of these studies, we found that the study of natural resources provided a concrete context within which we could investigate issues of broader concern.

6. See, in particular, a paper published in a volume edited by Partha in an area in which he has devoted much of his time during the past decade: Stiglitz (2000).

7. Moreover, the techniques (and second best reasoning) employed below are those we employed in our joint papers on public finance (see note 3).

8. Perhaps most notable was the work of Kaldor (1957) and Kaldor and Mirrlees (1962); and that of Karl Shell and William Nordhaus (Shell 1966, 1967; Nordhaus 1969a,

1969b). Also influential were Uzawa (1965), Arrow (1962a, 1962b), and Nelson and Phelps (1965). My own paper with Tony Atkinson (Atkinson and Stiglitz 1969) was influenced by Kaldor. I discuss these developments at greater length in my 1990 paper. For a more recent contribution to the theory of endogenous growth, with some perspectives on the intervening literature, see Stiglitz (2006a).

9. Indeed, Arrow (1951) and Debreu (1959), in their proofs of the Pareto efficiency of the market economy (the first fundamental theorem of welfare economics), assumed that technology was fixed, or at least that changes in technology were exogenous. As I explain below, there are good reasons to believe that when technical change is endogenous, the market equilibrium will not be Pareto efficient.

10. Whether and under what conditions that is so is, of course, another matter. Elsewhere, I have argued that intellectual property rights may actually impede innovation, especially if they are not well designed. See Henry and Stiglitz (2010) and Stiglitz (2006b, 2008). The adverse effects may be particularly marked in developing countries. See Stiglitz (2004, 2012).

11. There is a large empirical literature on the evidence for learning by doing, cited in Arrow (1962a) and Solow (1997). See, in particular, Hirsch (1952), Alchian (1963), and Argote and Epple (1990). For additional theoretical work, see, for instance, Fudenberg and Tirole (1982), Spence, (1981), Cabral and Riordan (1994), and Besanko et al. (2010).

12. Arrow assumed that learning was a by-product of investment. We simplify by assuming that it is a by-product of production (the input of labor). We comment briefly on how assuming it was a by-product of investment would alter our conclusions. See also Korinek and Servén (2010). Solow (1997) provided an insightful discussion of the Arrow model and its limits, as well as a bibliography of some of the research on learning by doing that occurred in the intervening 35 years, including the work of Levhari (1966, 1967), Sheshinski (1967), and Young (1991, 1997).

13. More accurately, they result in less R&D or less learning than would occur in the first best situation; given the lower output associated with monopoly, conditional on the monopoly power persisting, the optimal degree of investment in R&D is lower.

14. This was one of the central points made in my 1974 lecture before the Association of University Teachers of Economics in Manchester (Stiglitz 1975a). In November 1978, I elaborated on the problems arising from the public-good nature of knowledge in a lecture to an InterAmericn Development Bank-CEPAL meeting in Buenos Aires (published later as Stiglitz 1987a). Knowledge is a special kind of public good—a global public good, the benefits of which could accrue to anyone in the world. After developing the concept of international public goods in an address to a UN meeting in Vienna (Stiglitz 1995a), I applied that concept to knowledge (Stiglitz1999).

15. For a broad overview, see my introduction to the 2010 edition of Schumpeter's classic *Socialism, Capitalism, and Democracy*.

16. A point I discussed more extensively in chapter 5 of *Making Globalization Work* (Stiglitz 2006b).

17. Our thinking in this area was greatly influenced by Kenneth Arrow, who first developed the theory of learning by doing in his classic paper (Arrow 1962a). I studied general equilibrium theory under Arrow at MIT, and he visited Cambridge in 1969–1970, when Dasgupta and I were both working there.

18. Dasgupta, in his carefully reasoned exposition of the appropriate role of government in *An Inquiry into Well-Being and Destitution* (1993), seems to express some misgivings as to whether the government should undertake industrial policies.

19. This is not to suggest that self-selection processes would necessarily be efficient. Indeed, in the absence of coordination, there can easily be too few or too many competitors for the patent prize. While the price system may provide an effective way of coordinating production and consumption in a static model, it does not and cannot do the same with respect to innovation. The virtue of such self-selection processes was, however, that the costs of any mistakes fell (for the most part) on those undertaking the research project. Still, markets demand compensation for risk-bearing, so innovation is retarded. For a broader discussion of these issues in the context of R&D, see Stiglitz (2008).

20. We put aside for the moment the earlier objection—that if firms would eventually have a comparative advantage in the industrial sector, they should have an incentive to invest in learning today. We return to this issue later in the paper.

21. What is essential in this example is the unitary elasticity of substitution. There are problems in modeling long-term economic growth with nonunitary elasticity of substitution and differential rates of growth of productivity. With an elasticity of substitution less than unity, the high-productivity growth sector's share of global gross domestic product shrinks to zero; while with an elasticity of substitution greater than unity, it expands to unity. Both limits are uninteresting. At the same time, it is unsatisfactory simply to assume a unitary elasticity of substitution. A finite period model of the kind presented below avoids this modeling dilemma.

22. Important inquiries investigating the relationship between learning spillovers, growth, trade, and government policy include Young (1991), Hoff (1997), Hausmann and Rodrik (2003), and Hausmann, Hwang, and Rodrik (2007).

23. Though given the lower level of production, the level of investment in learning/R&D may be optimal.

24. Atkinson and I (1969) thus described learning as "localized." Because countries differ, too, some learning that may be relevant in one country may be of limited benefit in other countries. Most changes in technology, however, could confer benefits across borders. And, as we have noted, improvements in skills (techniques) in one sector have spillover benefits to other sectors in which analogous skills are employed. Hidalgo and colleagues (2007) recently characterized the product space, attempting to identify the "capabilities" that different sectors have in common. Presumably, if two products entail similar capabilities, learning that enhances a particular capability in one sector will have spillover benefits to related sectors for which that same capability is relevant.

25. If there are spillovers across sectors (products), but spillovers external to the firm are not full, there is a natural multiproduct monopoly (under our assumptions of linear technology) as a result of these natural economies of scope. These economies of scope and scale and offsetting diseconomies of scope and scale (e.g., arising from limits of the span of control and the benefits of managerial specialization) help define the boundaries of firms.

26. Later, we discuss how the results are changed if learning is related to investment, as in Arrow's original paper.

27. While this is precisely true in the case of logarithmic utility functions discussed below, in the more general case, the analysis is somewhat more complicated because of the endogeneity of ξ_k.

28. Under normal circumstances, growth (an increase in H, productivity) will lead to an increase in consumption; but matters are slightly more complicated, as first period consumption is subsidized because of the benefit of learning. If H_0, the increase in productivity with no subsidies, is large relative to $\delta\, h_k$ (the value of the learning benefits), then $x_k^{t+1} > x_k^t$

29. Recall that in terms of our previous notation, ψ is the special case of H where there are no spillovers.

30. $U_i^t - v^{t'} = -\tau^* v' = -\delta U_i^{t+1} \psi'(L_i^t) L^{t+1}$

31. The symmetric equilibrium can be treated as if there were a single commodity. Without loss of generality, we then write $U^{'t} = U_i^t$. From the first order condition for L^t, recalling that, in equilibrium, $x^t = L^t$

    $U'^t(L^t) - v^{t'}(L^t)(1 - \tau) = 0,$

    we can derive

    $\text{dln } L^t/\text{dln } \tau = (\tau/1 - \tau) / v + \eta = = (\tau/1 - \tau)\varepsilon_{Lw}^c$, where ε_{Lw}^c is the compensated elasticity of supply of labor, where $v = \text{dln } v'/\text{dln } L$ and $\eta = -\text{dln } U'/\text{dln } x$. This is consistent with our earlier notation where η_k is the elasticity of marginal utility with respect to commodity k, and, in the homothetic case, where η is the elasticity of marginal utility with respect to ϕ. From the first order condition for L^{t+1}, recalling that $x^{t+1} = H(L^t)L^{t+1}$,

    $HU'^{t+1}(HL^{t+1}) - v^{t'}(L^{t+1}) = 0,$

    we can derive

    $\text{dln } L^{t+1}/\text{d ln } H = (1 - \eta)/v + \eta = \varepsilon_{Lw},$

    from which it follows that

    $\text{dln } L^{t+1}/\text{d ln } L^t = h(1 - \eta)/v + \eta = h\,\varepsilon_{Lw}.$

    Hence, at $\tau = 0$,

    $v^{t+1'}L^{t+1}/v^{t'}L^t \approx 1 + (1 + v)H_o\varepsilon_{Lw}.$

    $\text{dln } [v^{t+1'}L^{t+1}/v^{t'}L^t]/\text{d ln } \tau = (1 + v)\{h\,\varepsilon_{Lw} - 1\}(\tau/1 - \tau)\,\varepsilon_{Lw}^c,$

    Hence

    $v^{t+1'}L^{t+1}/v^{t'}L^t \approx [1 + (1 + v)H_o\,\varepsilon_{Lw}]\{1 + (1 + v)\{h\,\varepsilon_{Lw} - 1\}(\tau/1 - \tau)\,\varepsilon_{Lw}^c\}.$

32. These formulae provide a characterization of the equilibrium, but it is important to note that, in general, the elasticities can themselves depend on taxes/subsidies.

33. Since, in the first period (omitting the superscript t), $\Sigma p_i x_i = L + \Sigma \tau_i x_i$, at $\tau = 0$,

    $\Sigma\, dx_i/d\,\tau_j = dL/d\tau_j > 0$. Both the income and substitution effects lead to an increased labor supply.

34. We make use of the fact that $V_{pi} = -V_I x_i$.

35. $\Sigma V_{pk}^{t+1} \Sigma((1/H^k)^2)H_i^k dx^t/d\,\tau_j = -V_I^{t+1} \Sigma x_k^{t+1} \Sigma((1/H^k)^2) H_i^k dx_i^t/d\,\tau_j =$

    $= -V_I^{t+1} \Sigma x_k^{t+1} \Sigma((1/H^k)^2) H_i^k [(\partial x_i^t/\partial\tau_j)U - x_j(dx_i^t/d\,I)]$

    $= -V_I^{t+1} \Sigma x_k^{t+1} \Sigma((1/H^k)^2) H_i^k (\partial x_i^t/\partial\tau_j)U + x_j \Xi$

    where $\Xi \overset{\text{def}}{=} V_I^{t+1} \Sigma_k x_k^{t+1} ((1/H^k)^2)\Sigma_i H_i^k (dx_i^t/d\,I).$

    $\Phi_j \overset{\text{def}}{=} \Sigma x_k^{t+1} \Sigma((1/H^k)^2) x_j^t H_i^k(\partial \ln x_j^t/\partial \ln \tau_i)U$

    $= -\Sigma_k x_k^{t+1} \Sigma_i((1/H^k)^2) x_j^t H_i^k(\tau_i/p_i)(\partial \ln x_i^t/\partial \ln p_i)U$

    $= -x_j^t \Sigma_k (L_k^{t+1}/L_k^t) \Sigma_i h_i^k (\tau_i/p_i)(\partial \ln x_i^t/\partial \ln p_i)U,$

    where, as before, $h_i^k = \text{dln } H^k/\text{dln } L_i^t.$

    With separable demand functions and no spillovers, this simplifies to

    $\zeta_j h_j \acute{\eta}_{jj} (\tau_j/p_j),$

    where ζ_j, h_j, and $\acute{\eta}_{jj}$ are defined below.

36. To derive (10), we make use of the Slutsky equation: $dx_i/dp_j = (\partial x_i/\partial p_j)_U - x_j(dx_i/d\,I).$

37. One must take care in interpreting this and other optimal tax/subsidy formulas in this paper, because the variables on the right-hand side are typically not constants but functions

of the subsidy rate itself. Still, they provide insights into the determinants of the appropriate subsidies for optimally designed subsidies.

38. The notation is deliberate: η is the elasticity of marginal utility. The first order condition for consumption, with constant elasticity, can be written $-\eta \ln x = \ln v' + \ln p$. If v' is constant, then $-\eta \ln x = \ln p$, so $d\ln x/d\ln p = 1/\eta$. Thus, if income effects are small, there is a simple relationship between the elasticity of marginal utility of consumption of good i and the elasticity of (compensated) demand.

39. With a positive wage elasticity, ζ_j is normally greater than unity. If there is zero labor elasticity and a logarithmic utility function, then $\zeta_j = 1$ all j. If a sector has elasticity of demand less than unity, ζ for that sector is less than unity. In the symmetric case,

    $d\ln L^{t+1}/d\ln H = (1 - \eta)/v + \eta,$

    $d\ln L^{t+1}/d\ln L^t = h(1 - \eta)/v + \eta$

    Hence at $\tau = 0$,

    $L^{t+1}/L^t \approx 1 + H_o(1 - \eta)/v + \eta,$

    $d\ln L^t/d\tau = (1 - \tau)\, d\ln L^t/d\ln w$

    Hence

    $L^{t+1}/L^t \approx \{1 + H_o(1 - \eta)/v + \eta\}\,[1 + tt)\,d\ln L^t/d\ln w].$

40. The term ζ_i complicates the analysis slightly. With the larger subsidy, L_s^t is increased, which by itself decrease ζ_s, dampening τ_s. Sector "0" benefits from its own learning, and this term by itself increases ζ_0 if the elasticity of demand is greater than unity and decreases it if the elasticity of demand is less than unity. With a positive wage elasticity, ζ_i would, in the symmetric case, be greater than unity, which in turn increases subsidies; the larger the labor supply elasticity, the larger the subsidy.

41. This model is, in fact, the limiting case of the two-sector model discussed earlier (with a sector 0 with no spillovers and a sector s with full spillovers), under the special case that $h_o = 0$: there is no learning in the nonspillover sector. It is straightforward to generalize the results to the case in which there is some learning in the nonspillover sector. In this special case, we relabel the sectors, so s = M (for manufacturing) and 0 = A (for agriculture).

42. Alternatively, we can write $\beta_M = (d\ln x_M/d\ln (p_M/p_A))(\delta \ln (p_M/p_A)/d\ln \tau_M)$, where $d\ln (p_M/p_A)/d\ln \tau_M$ can be calculated in a straightforward way. Similarly for β_A.

43. Relative consumptions x_M/x_A is just a function of relative prices $(1-\tau_M)/(1 + t_A)$:

    $x_M/x_A = Q((1 - \tau_M)/(1 + t_A))$. The elasticity of substitution is defined as $d\ln (x_M/x_A)/d\ln (1 - \tau_M)/(1 + t_A))$, where $dt_A/d\tau_M = (x_M/x_A) + \tau_M(d(x_M/x_A)/d\tau_M$.

44. Both of these are total derivatives, taking into account the direct effect of the change in τ and the indirect effect on the tax in the next period (t).

45. $u^{t+n} = U_o + n\,g$. $\Sigma\, n\, g\, \delta^n = \Sigma\, \delta\, g\, \delta^n/1 - \delta = \delta\, g/(1 - \delta)^2$

46. Recall the definitions of β_M and β_A above.

47. For convenience, we switch to continuous time. Analogous results hold in the discrete time version.

48. The full intertemporal maximization problem is somewhat more complicated and can be analyzed using standard techniques.

49. The simplest form is $\hat{H} = 1$ for $E < E^*$; that is, there is no learning. There is then a discontinuity at E^*.

50. As we noted earlier, Arrow's original model focused on learning through investment. But with the capital output ratio fixed, cumulative investment grows with output.

51. Long-run steady states require asymptotically constant elasticities.

52. In particular, the value of ζ_i is sensitive to the elasticity of demand, the amount of learning in this sector, the elasticity of labor supply, what happens in other sectors, and so on. As we have noted, $p^t_i = (1 - \delta \zeta_i h_i)/(1 - 1/\acute{\eta}_i)$. On the other hand, $p_i^{t+1} = 1/H^i(1 - 1/\acute{\eta}_i)$. If $H^i = 1/(1 - \delta \zeta_i h_i)$, the price would be the same both periods. The smaller the elasticity of demand, the higher the mark-up, so the larger the sensitivity of price to any differences between H^i and $1/(1 - d \zeta_i h_i)$.

53. For instance, in the absence of learning, by setting $\kappa_i (1 - \tau_i) = 1$, or $(1 - \tau_i) = 1/\kappa_i$ or

    $\tau = 1 - 1/\kappa_i = 1/\acute{\eta}_i$, we can correct the monopoly distortion.

54. It is easy to modify our model to allow a steady-state degree of disparity: all we have to assume is that knowledge diffuses freely from the developed to the less developed country with a lag of N years.

55. As we noted earlier, the assumption of a fixed labor supply is, however, not innocuous.

56. $d \alpha_M \ln (\pi \gamma + (1 - \pi)\lambda) + (1 - \alpha_M) \ln ((1 - \lambda)(1 - \pi))/d \pi =$

    $\alpha_M (\gamma - \lambda)/(\pi \gamma + (1 - \pi)\lambda) - (1 - \alpha_M)/(1 - \pi) \leq 0$ for $\pi \geq 0$ (provided $\gamma < 1$); at $\lambda = \lambda^*$, where λ^* is the solution to

    $d \alpha_M \ln (\pi \gamma + (1 - \pi)\lambda) + (1 - \alpha_M) \ln ((1 - \lambda)(1 - \pi))/d \lambda$

    $= \alpha_M (1 - \pi)/(\pi \gamma + (1 - \pi)\lambda) - (1 - \alpha_M)/(1-\lambda) = 0$

57. $U^{t+1} = U^t + \ln (1+g)$, and, using the same techniques employed earlier,

    $W = \Sigma U^*[(1 + t(\ln (1+g)))]\delta^t$, from which (40) follows directly.

    If U is not logarithmic but exhibits constant elasticity with respect to the scale of consumption (as before), with the elasticity of marginal utility of η, there is a parallel analysis.

58. In our simple model, we assume individuals cannot borrow or lend, and simply solve a period-by-period static utility maximization problem, determining the allocation of current income among the three commodities. But it would be easy in principle (complicated in practice) to generalize the results to cases that include individual borrowing and lending, with precise effects depending on the structure of preferences (e.g., on separability of utility functions.)

59. Because of the inefficiency in the production, it takes, in effect, $1/\gamma$ units of domestic labor to produce 1 unit of industrial good. Hence, exports are the output of agricultural goods minus the consumption of agricultural goods, where the output of agricultural goods is total labor supply, less the input into nontraded goods and into the industrial sector.

60. In effect, the supply curve is effectively horizontal at e^{**}.

61. One other interesting aspect characterizes the optimum pattern of reserve accumulation. If, in the earlier stages of development, learning benefits are sufficiently large that the country accumulates a surplus, using the indirect utility function, at the margin, an increase in the price of tradables (a further reduction in the price of nontradables) has a positive effect—it receives more for what it sells; while in later periods, when the country has a trade deficit (using up its surplus), a decrease in the exchange rate (the price the country has to pay for the goods it buys) has a negative effect. This provides further impetus for lowering exchange rates (further below equilibrium levels that would prevail in the absence of intertemporal effects) in earlier stages and increasing them later—exacerbating patterns of "global imbalances."

62. An analysis of the full global general equilibrium effects of such policies, if pursued by enough developing countries to have systemic effects, is beyond the scope of this paper.

63. The utility possibilities curve gives the maximum level of utility for an individual given the level of utility of others.

64. As Greenwald and Stiglitz (forthcoming) point out, even in advanced industrial countries, most firms operate well below best practices.

65. Operationally, we can think of dividing the learning period into two subperiods. In the first, we devote ourselves to improving our learning skills; in the second, we use those learning skills to learn about the subject at hand. (Here, we ignore the problem posed by the possibility of infinite regress: we can learn how to learn how to learn. . . .)

66. Sah and Stiglitz (1989a,1989b), Stiglitz (1995b), and Hoff and Stiglitz (2001) show that there can, in fact, be multiple societal equilibria. Hoff and Stiglitz (2010) use recent results in psychology to underpin an analysis of the interactions between prior beliefs and societal change, explaining how some societies can become trapped in a seemingly dysfunctional equilibrium for an extended period, while other societies seem to evolve more smoothly. Politics and economics also interact: Repressive and authoritarian societies are, in a fundamental sense, incompatible with the kind of questioning of authority that is associated with a dynamic learning society. See Stiglitz (2010b).

67. Before the term "second best" had come into fashion through the work of Meade (1955) and Lipsey and Lancaster (1956–1957).

68. See, in particular, Arrow (1962a). See also Solow (1997).

69. There is an old (and largely forgotten) literature on the determinants of the factor bias of technological change. For a more recent attempt to develop a general theory of the endogenous determination of the factor bias and the equilibrium level of unemployment, using a variant of the efficiency wage model, see Stiglitz (2006a).

70. Some might argue that with globalization, the price of capital has become the same everywhere in the world. But this view ignores the importance of information and other market imperfections, the effect of which is to make the effective price of capital higher in some countries than in others. See, for example, Greenwald and Stiglitz (2003).

71. Indeed, that is one of the reasons we have emphasized cross-sector learning spillovers in this paper.

72. This is a lesson Europe learned at some cost: It might have been privately profitable to become dependent on Russian oil, but it was socially costly.

73. This was, of course, the thrust of the *Report of the International Commission on the Measurement of Economic Performance and Social Progress*. See Fitoussi et al. (2010).

References

Alchian, Armen. 1963. "Reliability of Progress Curves in Airframe Production." *Econometrica* 31: 679–693.

Argote, Linda, and Dennis Epple. 1990. "Learning Curves in Manufacturing." *Science* 247: 920–913.

Arrow, Kenneth J. 1951. "An Extension of the Basic Theorems of Classical Welfare Economics." In *Proceedings of the Second Berkeley Symposium on Mathematical Statistics and Probability*, ed. J. Neyman, 507–532. Berkeley: University of California Press.

———. 1962a. "The Economic Implications of Learning by Doing." *Review of Economic Studies* 29: 155–173.

———. 1962b. "Economic Welfare and the Allocation of Resources for Invention." In *The Rate and Direction of Inventive Activity: Economic and Social Factors*, ed. R. Nelson, National Bureau of Economic Research (NBER). Princeton, NJ: Princeton University Press.

Atkinson, Anthony B., and Joseph E. Stiglitz. 1969. "A New View of Technological Change." *Economic Journal* 79(315): 573–578.

Besanko, David, Ulrich Doraszelski, Yaroslav Kryukov, and Mark Satterthwaite. 2010. "Learning-by-Doing, Organizational Forgetting, and Industry Dynamics." *Econometrica* 78: 453–508.

Cabral, Luis, and Michael Riordan. 1994. "The Learning Curve, Market Dominance, and Predatory Pricing." *Econometrica* 62: 1115–1140.

Dasgupta, Partha S. 1969. "On the Concept of Optimum Population." *Review of Economic Studies* 36(107): 295–318.

———. 1993. *An Inquiry into Well-Being and Destitution.* New York: Oxford University Press.

———. 2001. *Human Well-Being and the Natural Environment.* New York: Oxford University Press.

———. 2005. "Economics of Social Capital." *Economic Record.* 81(s1): S2-S21.

Dasgupta, Partha S., Charles R. Blitzer, and Joseph E. Stiglitz. 1981. "Project Appraisal and Foreign Exchange Constraints." *Economic Journal* 91(361, March): 58–74.

Dasgupta, Partha S., Richard Gilbert, and Joseph E. Stiglitz. 1981. "Energy Resources and Research and Development." In *Erschopfbare Ressourcen,* edited by Horst Siebert, Vol. 108, 85–108. Berlin: Duncker and Humbolt.

———. 1982. "Invention and Innovation Under Alternative Market Structures: The Case of Natural Resources." *Review of Economic Studies* 49(4): 567–582.

———. 1983. "Strategic Considerations in Invention and Innovation: The Case of Natural Resources." *Econometrica* 51(5, September): 1430–1448.

Dasgupta, Partha S., and Geoffrey Heal. 1979. *Economic Theory and Exhaustible Resources.* Cambridge: Cambridge University Press.

Dasgupta, Partha S., Geoff Heal, and Joseph E. Stiglitz. 1980. "The Taxation of Exhaustible Resources" In *Public Policy and the Tax System,* ed. G. A. Hughes and G. M. Heal, 150–172. London: George Allen and Unwin.

Dasgupta, Partha S., Geoff Heal, Joseph E. Stiglitz, Richard Gilbert, and David Newbery. 1977. *An Economic Analysis of the Conservation of Depletable Natural Resources.* Prepared for the Federal Energy Administration, May.

Dasgupta, Partha S., and Joseph E. Stiglitz. 1971. "Differential Taxation, Public Goods, and Economic Efficiency." *Review of Economic Studies* 38(2, April): 151–174.

———. 1972. "On Optimal Taxation and Public Production." *Review of Economic Studies.* 39(1, January): 87–103.

———. 1974. "Benefit-Cost Analysis and Trade Policies." *Journal of Political Economy* 82 (1, January–February): 1–33.

———. 1977. "Tariffs Versus Quotas As Revenue Raising Devices Under Uncertainty." *American Economic Review* 67(5, December): 975–981.

———. 1980a. "Industrial Structure and the Nature of Innovative Activity." *Economic Journal* 90(358, June): 266–293.

———. 1980b. "Uncertainty, Market Structure and the Speed of R&D." *Bell Journal of Economics* 11(1, Spring): 1–28.

———. 1981a. "Entry, Innovation, Exit: Toward a Dynamic Theory of Oligopolistic Industrial Structure." *European Economic Review* 15(2, February): 137–158.

———. 1981b. "Market Structure and Resource Extraction Under Uncertainty." *Scandinavian Economic Journal* 83: 318–333.

———. 1981c. "Resource Depletion Under Technological Uncertainty." *Econometrica* 49 (1, January): 85–104.

————. 1982. "Market Structure and Resource Depletion: A Contribution to the Theory of Intertemporal Monopolistic Competition." *Journal of Economic Theory* 28(1, October): 128–164.

————. 1988a. "Learning by Doing, Market Structure, and Industrial and Trade Policies." *Oxford Economic Papers* 40(2): 246–268.

————. 1988b. "Potential Competition, Actual Competition and Economic Welfare." *European Economic Review* 32(May): 569–577.

Debreu, G. 1959. *The Theory of Value.* New Haven, CT: Yale University Press.

Edgeworth, Francis Y. 1925. *Papers Relating to Political Economy*, Vol. III. London: Macmillan and Co. Ltd.

Fitoussi, Jean-Paul, Amartya Sen, and Joseph E. Stiglitz. 2010. *Mismeasuring Our Lives: Why GDP Doesn't Add Up.* New York: The New Press. Available at http://www.stiglitz-sen-fitoussi.fr/en/index.htm (accessed November 17, 2010).

Fudenberg, Drew and Jean Tirole. 1982. "Learning-by-Doing and Market Performance." CERAS D.P.8, Ecole Nationale des Ponts et Chaussees, 1982.

Gilbert, R. J., and D. M. Newbery. 1982. "Preemptive Patenting and the Persistence of Monopoly." *American Economic Review* 72(3): 514–526.

Greenwald, Bruce, and Joseph E. Stiglitz. 1986. "Externalities in Economies with Imperfect Information and Incomplete Markets." *Quarterly Journal of Economics* 1(2, May): 229–264.

————. 2003. *Towards a New Paradigm in Monetary Economics.* Cambridge, UK: Cambridge University Press.

————. 2006. "Helping Infant Economies Grow: Foundations of Trade Policies for Developing Countries." *American Economic Review: AEA Papers and Proceedings* 96(2): 141–146.

————, eds. Forthcoming. *Creating a Learning Society: A New Paradigm for Development and Social Progress (An Essay in Honor of Kenneth Arrow).* New York: Columbia University Press.

Hahn, Frank. 1966. "Equilibrium Dynamics with Heterogeneous Capital Goods." *Quarterly Journal of Economics* 80: 633–646.

Hausmann, Ricardo, and Dani Rodrik. 2003. "Economic Development As Self-Discovery." *Journal of Development Economics* 72(2): 603–633.

Hausmann, Ricardo, Jason Hwang, and Dani Rodrik. 2007. "What You Export Matters." *Journal of Economic Growth* 12(1): 1–25.

Henry, Claude, and Joseph E. Stiglitz. 2010. "Intellecutal Property, Dissemination of Innovation, and Sustainable Development." *Global Policy* 1(1, October): 237–251.

Hidalgo, C. A., B. Klinger, A.-L. Barabási, and R. Hausmann. 2007. "The Product Space Conditions the Development of Nations." *Science* 317(5837, July): 482–487.

Hirsch, Werner. 1952. "Manufacturing Progress Functions." *Review of Economics and Statistics* 34: 143–155.

Hoff, Karla. 1997. "Bayesian Learning in an Infant Industry Model." *Journal of International Economics* 43(3–4): 409–436.

Hoff, Karla, and Joseph E. Stiglitz. 2001. "Modern Economic Theory and Development." In *Frontiers of Development Economics: The Future in Perspective*, ed. G. Meier and J. Stiglitz, 389–459. Oxford: Oxford University Press.

————. 2010. "Equilibrium Fictions: A Cognitive Approach to Societal Rigidity." *American Economic Review* 100(2, May): 141–146. Extended version available as Policy Research

Working Paper 5219, World Bank Development Research Group, February 2010, available at http://www-wds.worldbank.org/external/default/WDSContentServer/IW3P/IB/2010/02/26/000158349_20100226083837/Rendered/PDF/WPS5219.pdf. Accessed February 16, 2011.

Kaldor, Nicholas. 1957. "A Model of Economic Growth." *Economic Journal* 67: 591–624.

Kaldor, Nicholas, and James A. Mirrlees. 1962. "A New Model of Economic Growth." *Review of Economic Studies* 29: 174–192.

Korinek, Anton, and Luis Servén. 2010. "Undervaluation Through Foreign Reserve Accumulation: Static Losses, Dynamic Gains." Policy Research Working Paper 5250, World Bank, Washington, DC.

Levhari, David. 1966. "Extensions of Arrow's Learning by Doing." *Review of Economic Studies* 33(2): 31–38.

———. 1967. "Further Implications of Learning by Doing." *Review of Economic Studies* 33: 31–38.

Lipsey, R. G., and Kelvin Lancaster. 1956–1957."The General Theory of Second Best." *Review of Economic Studies* 24(1): 11–32.

Meade, James E. 1955. *Trade and Welfare.* London: Oxford University Press.

Nelson, Richard R., and Edmond S. Phelps. 1965. "Investment in Humans, Technological Diffusion and Economic Growth." Discussion Paper 189, Cowles Foundation, Yale University, New Haven, CT.

David and Joseph E. Stiglitz. 1982. "The Choice of Techniques and the Optimality of Market Equilibrium with Rational Expectations," *Journal of Political Economy*, 90(2): 223–246.

Nordhaus, William D. 1969a. "An Economic Theory of Technological Change." *American Economic Association Papers and Proceedings* 59(May): 18–28.

———. 1969b. *Invention, Growth and Welfare: A Theoretical Treatment of Technological Change.* Cambridge, MA: MIT Press.

Sah, R., and J. E. Stiglitz. 1989a. "Technological Learning, Social Learning and Technological Change." In *The Balance Between Industry and Agriculture in Economic Development,* ed. S. Chakravarty, 285–298. London: Macmillan.

———. 1989b. "Sources of Technological Divergence Between Developed and Less Developed Countries." In *Debt, Stabilizations and Development: Essays in Memory of Carlos Diaz-Alejandro,* ed. G. Calvo, 423–446. Oxford: Basil Blackwell, Ltd.

Schumpeter, Joseph A. 1912. *Theorie der Wirtschaflichen Entwicklung.* Leipzig: Duncker and Humbolt. Translated in 1934 as *The Theory of Economic Development: An Inquiry into Profits, Capital, Credit, Interest and the Business Cycle.*

———. 1943. *Capitalism, Socialism and Democracy,* New York: Harper.

Shell, Karl, 1966, "Toward a Theory of Inventive Activity and Capital Accumulation." *American Economic Association Papers and Proceedings* 56: 62–68.

———. ed. 1967. *Essays on the Theory of Optimal Economic Growth.* Cambridge, MA: MIT Press.

Shell, Karl, and Joseph E. Stiglitz. 1967. "Allocation of Investment in a Dynamic Economy." *Quarterly Journal of Economics* 81(November): 592–609.

Sheshinski, E. 1967. "Tests of the Learning-by-Doing Hypothesis." *Review of Economics and Statistics* 49: 568–578.

Skeath, Susan. 1993. "Strategic Product Choice and Equilibrium Traps for Less Developed Countries." *Journal of International Trade and Economic Development* 2(1): 1–26.

————. 1995. "A Role for Trade Policy? Markets with Informational Barriers to Entry." *International Trade Journal* 9(2): 247–271.

Solow, Robert M. 1957. "Technical Change and the Aggregate Production Function." *Review of Economics and Statistics* 39(3, August): 312–320.

————. 1997. *Learning from "Learning by Doing": Lessons for Economic Growth.* Palo Alto, CA: Stanford University Press.

Spence, A. Michael. 1981. "The Learning Curve and Competition." *The Bell Journal of Economics* 12(1): 49–70.

Stiglitz, Joseph. 1975a. "The Theory of Screening, Education and the Distribution of Income." *American Economic Review* 65(3, June): 283–300.

————. 1975. "Information and Economic Analysis." In *Current Economic Problems: Proceedings of the Association of University Teachers of Economics, Manchester, 1974,* ed. J. M. Parkin and A. R. Nobay, 27–52. Cambridge, UK: Cambridge University Press.

————. 1981. "Potential Competition May Reduce Welfare." *American Economic Review* 71(2, May): 184–189.

————. 1986. "Theory of Competition, Incentives and Risk" In *New Developments in the Analysis of Market Structure,* ed. J. E. Stiglitz and F. Mathewson, 399–449. Cambridge, MA: MIT Press.

————. 1987a. "On the Microeconomics of Technical Progress." In *Technology Generation in Latin American Manufacturing Industries,* ed. Jorge M. Katz, 56–77. London : Macmillan Press Ltd.

————. 1987b. "Technological Change, Sunk Costs, and Competition." *Brookings Papers on Economic Activity* 3: 883–947.

————. 1987c. "Learning to Learn, Localized Learning and Technological Progress." In *Economic Policy and Technological Performance,* ed. P. Dasgupta and P. Stoneman, 125–153. Cambridge, UK: Cambridge University Press.

————. 1990. "Comments: Some Retrospective Views on Growth Theory." In *Growth, Productivity, Unemployment: Essays to Celebrate Bob Solow's Birthday,* ed. Peter Diamond. Cambridge, MA: MIT Press.

————. 1995a. "The Theory of International Public Goods and the Architecture of International Organizations." Background Paper No. 7, Third Meeting, High Level Group on Development Strategy and Management of the Market Economy, United Nations University – World Institute for Development Economics Researcg, Helsinki, Finland, July 8–10.

————. 1995b. "Social Absorption Capability and Innovation." In *Social Capability and Long-Term Economic Growth,* ed. Bon Ho Koo and D. H. Perkins, 48–81. New York: St. Martin's Press.

————. 1998. "Towards a New Paradigm for Development: Strategies, Policies and Processes." Ninth Raul Prebisch Lecture delivered at the Palais des Nations, Geneva, October 19, 1998, UNCTAD. Chapter 2 in *The Rebel Within,* ed. Ha-Joon Chang, 57–93. London: Wimbledon Publishing Company, 2001.

————. 1999. "Knowledge As a Global Public Good." In *Global Public Goods: International Cooperation in the 21st Century,* ed. Inge Kaul, Isabelle Grunberg, and Marc A. Stern, United Nations Development Programme, 308–325. New York: Oxford University Press.

————. 2000. "Formal and Informal Institutions." In *Social Capital: A Multifaceted Perspective,* ed. P. Dasgupta and I. Serageldin, 59–68. Washington, DC: World Bank.

————. 2004. "Towards a Pro-Development and Balanced Intellectual Property Regime." Keynote address presented at the Ministerial Conference on Intellectual Property for Least

Developed Countries, World Intellectual Property Organization (WIPO), Seoul, October 25, 2004. Revised and updated version forthcoming in *Institutional Design for China's Innovation System: Implications for Intellectual Property Rights,* ed. D. Kennedy and J. E. Stiglitz. New York : Oxford University Press.

———. 2006a. "Samuelson and the Factor Bias of Technological Change." In *Samuelsonian Economics and the Twenty-First Century,* ed. M. Szenberg, L. Ramrattan, and A. Gottesman, 235–251. New York: Oxford University Press.

———. 2006b. *Making Globalization Work.* New York: WW Norton.

———. 2008. "The Economic Foundations of Intellectual Property." *Duke Law Journal* 57 (6, April): 1693–1724. Sixth annual Frey Lecture in Intellectual Property, Duke University, February 16, 2007.

———. 2010a. "Introduction." In *Capitalism, Socialism and Democracy* by Joseph A. Schumpeter, ix–xiv. London: Rutledge.

———. 2010b. "A Social Democratic Agenda for a More Dynamic Indian Economy: Creating an Innovative and Learning Society." The 2010 Jawaharlal Nehru Memorial Lecture, New Delhi, November 18, 2011. (Published version forthcoming.)

———. 2012. "Institutional Design For China's Innovation System: Implications For Intellectual Property Rights." In *Law and Economic Development with Chinese Characteristics: Institutions for the 21st Century* ed. D. Kennedy and J. E. Stiglitz. New York: Oxford University Press.

Uzawa, Hirofumi. 1965. "Optimum Technical Change in an Aggregate Model of Economic Growth." *International Economic Review* 6(1): 18–31.

Young, Alwyn. 1991. "Learning by Doing and the Dynamic Effects of International Trade." *Quarterly Journal of Economics* 106: 369–406.

———. 1993. "Invention and Bounded Learning by Doing." *Journal of Political Economy* 101: 443–472.

Weak States, Strong States, and Development

TORSTEN PERSSON

My topic, at least partly, is weak or fragile states, which is one of the themes of this conference. It is also a central concept in the development policy community. International organizations such as the World Bank, the European Union, and many national aid organizations—such as the United Kingdom's Department for International Development and the Swedish International Development Cooperation Authority—have special initiatives for weak states.

What do we mean by weak states? We mean states that cannot do much. They cannot support the most basic economic functions; they find it hard to raise any substantial revenue; they have a hard time delivering health and education to the population; and they have problems maintaining law and order. Unfortunately, this is not a rare phenomenon: about 10 percent of countries in the world (20–30 states) are seriously weak or have failed, and others are quite close (figure 1).

The map is from a 2008 Brookings Institution study. It shows, in black, three states considered to have failed: Congo, Somalia, and Afghanistan; and in dark grey, seriously weak states, from Haiti on the left to North Korea. Lighter shades of grey are other weak countries and those at risk of becoming weak.

The inability of a state to deliver in various dimensions is strongly linked to income per capita and to violence of various sorts. Weak states typically have massive poverty and are plagued by conflict and violence. On the other end of the spectrum, the developed countries have it all: Incomes are high, institutions work, policies are in good order, and conflicts tend to be resolved peacefully.

There is a very strong clustering of state capacity in various dimensions: We see few strong economies among the weak states and few weak economies among the strong states. We have a multidimensional problem—perhaps *the* development problem—in this clustering of low income, violence, and dysfunctional institutions.

Torsten Persson is the Ragnar Söderberg Chair in Economic Sciences at the Institute for International Economic Studies, Stockholm University

Annual World Bank Conference on Development Economics 2011, Global

FIGURE 1.
Map of the Weakest States

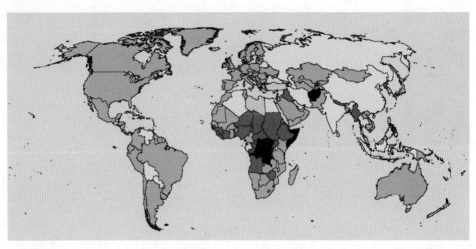

Source: Brookings Index of State Weakness, 2008.

The state does many things, but we can broadly classify its activities into two types: extractive and productive. The extractive capacity of the state is related to its ability to raise taxes from broad bases, such as income or value-added taxes. For this to work, the state requires an infrastructure that includes various compliance institutions, monitoring, and knowledgeable administrators. What about productive capacity? This includes the infrastructure to enforce contracts or protect property rights and to make the private economy work better, as well as the physical infrastructure that supports the private sector; for example, roads and the electrical grid.

Let me illustrate with two specific measures. One is *fiscal capacity*, which I will measure with total taxes as a share of gross domestic product (GDP). This will be an average from the late 1970s onward, using data from the International Monetary Fund. The other is *legal capacity*, which I will measure with an index for the protection of property rights—an average over the 1980s and 1990s, using data from the International Country Risk Guide (ICRG). This index is quite often used in the macro-development literature. These measures are special in some ways, but I could have used a host of other proxies for the extractive and productive capacities, and the graph would be similar to figure 2.

In this figure, we see fiscal capacity (the total tax take) on the vertical axis and legal capacity (the property rights protection index) on the horizontal axis. It is clear that these are strongly positively related to each other, ranging from Haiti at the lower southwest corner up to Sweden in the upper northeast corner. So much for the idea that there is a trade-off between large government and supporting the private economy in other ways. To see the clustering with income, consider the color of these dots: The light grey dots demark countries with high income per capita in 1980; the dark grey ones represent those with low income; and the hollow ones,

FIGURE 2.
State Capacity and Income

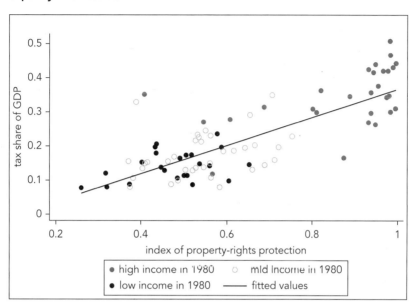

those with middle income. The colors line up pretty well, and we can easily see the correlation between income and the two forms of state capacity.

Figure 3 shows the prevalence of violence in its most extreme form: civil war. The light grey dots represent countries that have not had any civil war since 1950, while the dark grey dots represent countries that had at least one instance of civil war during this period. Again the clustering is pretty evident.

How do we understand these strong patterns in the data? We have to pose and answer three general questions. First, what drives the building of different state capacities and why do these capacities move together? Second, what forces drive political violence? And third, what drives the correlation among institutions, income, and violence?

I will be presumptuous enough to use this opportunity to describe some research I am doing with Tim Besley from the London School of Economics on the economics and politics of state building and political violence. We are trying to understand the observed clustering of income, institutions, and violence, with the goal of building a new theory and uncovering some new evidence. Ultimately, we hope to bring the notion of state capacity into the mainstream of economics. In this talk, I will only be able to scratch the surface, but I will try to give you an idea of our theoretical approach and the predictions we have come up with, and show you some correlations in the data. If you want the gory details, you can go to our Web pages and look at various research papers, either published or very much in progress. We hope to publish a book in 2011 based on the Yrjö Jahnsson lectures we will give in Helsinki two weeks from now.[1]

FIGURE 3.
State Capacity and Civil War

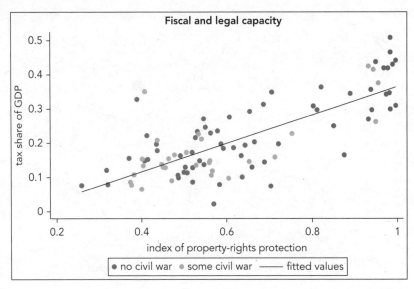

Now, let me next talk about the origins of state capacity and the origins of violence, and how they fit together.

State Capacity

In terms of existing research, I think we can say that state capacity is ignored or, at best, assumed in mainstream economics. The literature on the macroeconomics of development views income per capita—and not state institutions—as the central outcome to be explained and discussed. When it comes to fiscal capacity, the capacity to raise revenue from certain tax bases is basically assumed in various branches of economics. Yes, there are some constraints on taxation, but they tend to come from incomplete information or from incentives in the political system. Similarly, the administrative capacity to enforce contracts and protect investors generally tends to be assumed in finance and microeconomics.

On the other hand, there is considerable focus on state capacity in political and economic history. In particular, the fiscal powers of the state are deemed important in and of themselves—important for military success and important for state development generally. Perhaps the most famous expositor of these ideas is Charles Tilly, the political sociologist, who wrote a lot about how war can be a major motive to build the fiscal capacity of the state and coined some wonderful sayings, such as "War made the state and the state made war", Tilly (1990). But this branch of research largely ignores the building of legal capacity.

Besley and I decided to set up a simple model framework to help us think about state capacity formation. A basic idea in this framework is to distinguish between underlying institutions and the policymaking they enable. So, an incumbent government's choice of taxation and regulation would be limited by its fiscal and legal capacity, and constrained by the political institutions in place. Incumbents in this setting can invest in fiscal and legal capacity—we think about state building as a purposeful and forward-looking activity, as investments made by the incumbent government, but these investments are made under uncertainty about the future. You don't really know how revenue will be used in the future. Will it be spent on public goods or will it be spent on redistribution? You don't really know the levels of non-tax revenue in the future: How much revenue will be available from resource rents and aid? And you don't really know about future incumbency: Will you continue to hold power, or might power be held by an opposition group?

This approach identifies three kinds of situations or states. One is common-interest states. Here government revenue is basically used for public goods; for example, defense against the threat of an external conflict. In this situation, any incumbent group is going to invest in fiscal capacity.

The second is a redistributive state, in which government revenue, at least on the margin, is used to redistribute in the broad sense: giving favors to some groups in society (such as the incumbent's own group) at the expense of other groups. Here, the incumbent government is more or less constrained by the prevailing political institutions. In the redistributive state, the incumbent group invests in fiscal capacity because there is enough political stability.

Finally, there are weak states, in which government revenue is again used for redistribution. In such states, political institutions tend to be noncohesive, and there are high levels of political instability. In this situation, no incumbent group will want to invest in the fiscal capacity of the state.

Another general finding that comes out of this analysis is a complementarity result: investment in one type of state capacity tends to reinforce the other. The idea is that, if future fiscal capacity is higher, there are additional fiscal benefits of building legal capacity, which of course will expand market income and hence the tax base. Similarly, if future legal capacity is higher, market incomes and tax bases will be higher. This, in turn, will increase the motivation to invest in fiscal capacity. Thus, if you do more of one type of state building, you tend to do more of the other.

The implications of such complementarity are immediate. First, it's a natural way to think about the forces behind the observed clustering of various capabilities of the state. Second, it tells you that if you find determinants for one form of state capacity, they should also determine the other capacity of the state. I will briefly discuss the major determinants that our approach suggests; the primary relationships are illustrated in figure 4.

A first determinant is the *structure of interests* in society: common versus redistributive interests. If common interests are strong—say, because a society wants to defend itself against an external enemy—most incumbents will invest in the fiscal capacity of the state to raise revenue for these urgent needs. By complementarity, you will also get more investments in legal capacity. This is essentially the Tilly idea expanded by complementarity with the productive side of the state.

FIGURE 4.
Determinants of State Capacity

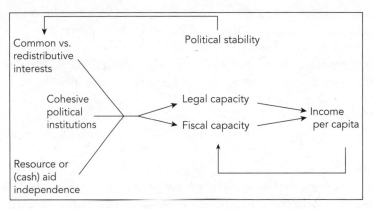

Do the data reflect this simple prediction? Let me show some partial correlations between common-interest spending and state capacity without any pretense that we are isolating a causal effect. I am going to gauge the past demand for public goods by the prevalence of war, the idea being that if in the past a country fought a lot of wars, it probably faced a large risk of war. These are conditions under which you expect a lot of state capacity to be built in the past, meaning that you would expect to see a lot of it today. If we use the Correlates of War data set, we can go back as far as 1816 or to independence of the state, whichever is later. For each state, we measure how many of those years it was involved in external war. Then we correlate that share, partially, with the tax share (fiscal capacity) and the property rights index (legal capacity) shown in figures 2 and 3. To get the partial correlation, we hold constant some other determinants of state capacity, such as cohesive political institutions, plus legal origin and continental location.

Figure 5 shows the two partial correlation plots. On the horizontal axis in each graph, you have the share of years in external war (actually, the residual of that share) once you have held the other variables constant. On the vertical axis on the left-hand graph, you have the residual of the tax share of GDP. The partial correlation is indeed positive. The slope is about 1, meaning that a country that spent 10 percent more of its history at war is currently raising 10 percent higher tax revenue as a share of GDP. Similarly, for the measure of legal capacity, in the right-hand graph, there is a relatively strong positive correlation: Variation in legal capacity is associated with variation in external conflict.

The second determinant is the *cohesiveness of political institutions*. The idea here is that, if incumbent groups are strongly constrained by checks and balances in the political system, or if opposition groups are well represented, the outcome tends to be more cohesive with less emphasis on redistribution and more emphasis on public goods. Because of this, there is also more investment in both types of state capacity.

If we take a look at the data, again, we can see the partial correlation between a measure of the cohesiveness of political institutions and state capacity. As a measure of the former, I will use constraints on the executive from the Polity IV data set,

FIGURE 5.
External War and State Capacity

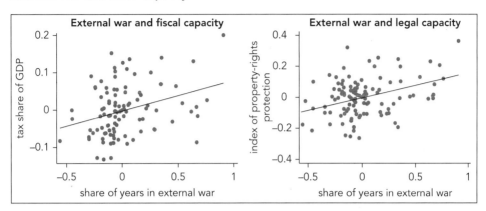

which goes all the way back to 1800. We look at the period from 1800 (or independence) until the present and ask how large a share of those years a country had the highest score in the Polity IV data set on constraints on the executive variable. (If we use the prevalence of parliamentary democracy instead, the results are similar.)

Figure 6 relies on the same approach as figure 5; that is, we control for other variables and look at the partial correlations between cohesive political institutions and both types of state capacity. To the left, we have the relationship between years with high executive constraints and fiscal capacity; to the right, the same relationship with legal capacity. Again, the positive correlations are evident. The slope in the fiscal capacity graph is about 0.1, meaning that if the state had cohesive political institutions for half of its history, it is currently raising about 5 percentage points more revenue as a share of GDP. The legal capacity index also shows quite a substantial variation associated with these political institutions.

As a third determinant, consider *political stability*. The idea is that, if you don't have a lot of common interests and you don't have very cohesive political institutions, redistribution is the main spending activity of governments. If the political situation is very unstable, investments in legal and fiscal capacity might come to a halt. An incumbent group contemplating expanding the state realizes that a stronger state might be used against its own group, and the probability of such a strike-back is higher if opponent groups are likely to hold power in the future. So we see a negative association between political instability and capacity building in this particular situation. In many developing countries, of course, this is intimately associated with the prevalence of political conflicts. I will return to this point.

What about *economic structure*? If you hold the level of income constant, the structure of the economy—in particular, its resource dependence or independence, or its dependence on cash aid—starts to play a role. If you have a large share of resource income or aid, there is less motivation to invest in fiscal capacity or legal capacity, because the prospective tax bases are also going to be smaller.

Let's instead hold economic structure constant and think about the level of income. Clearly, higher income levels mean higher market incomes and higher

FIGURE 6.
Political Institutions and State Capacity

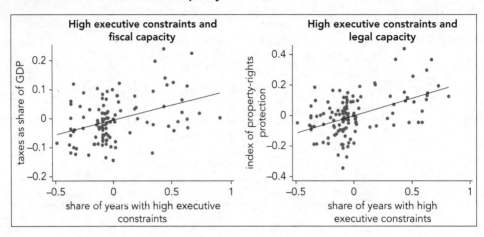

prospective tax bases. Incumbent groups then have greater motivation to invest in legal and fiscal capacity. However, that argument takes income as given, and there will be an association in the other direction as well, where legal and fiscal capacities themselves affect income.

Let us return to the clustering of income and state capacity shown in figure 2. We have the possibility that low income can cause weak states because low prospective market incomes and tax bases reduce the motivation to invest in the state. But weak states can also cause low income. Low legal capacity renders incumbents unable to support markets, and that tends to keep income down. Low fiscal capacity can lead to costly forms of redistribution. If the incumbent government is interested in redistributing toward its own group and doesn't have the ability to use a broad tax-transfer scheme, it will use other means that may be very inefficient, such as tariffs or cumbersome regulations, and that will tend to keep income down. Because of this two-way feedback between income and state capacity, we can get into virtuous or vicious circles that can easily produce clusters of strong states in strong economies or weak states in weak economies.

Figure 4 illustrates the argument I have made so far. Imagine a change over time, a period of foreign threat, and a political reform introducing more cohesive political institutions. This can lead to greater investments in the state, which feed back to income, which feeds back to additional motivation for building the state. I think you can see the possibility of a virtuous circle in operation.

Political Violence

So far we have not considered the origins of political violence. One motivation starts from a juxtaposition with external violence. In the argument I just made, a risk of external violence can promote state building because it boosts the common interest at the expense of redistributive or group interests. Of course, internal political violence is very different. Rather than a manifestation of common interest, it is a manifestation of an extreme redistributive struggle. We intuitively feel that conditions leading to such struggle may entail very different incentives to invest in the state. Another motivation, given the state capacity framework I have outlined, is that we want to partly endogenize political instability. Finally, a better understanding of political violence is valuable in and of itself.

First, we consider some basic facts about civil war and repression, which are, sadly, quite common. Civil war is usually defined as two-sided violence between the government and some insurgency group(s). If you look at the data set compiled by the Peace Research Institutes in Uppsala and Oslo, you find that, in a panel of country-years since 1950, about 10 percent of those observations are classified as associated with civil war. Repression, on the other hand, is one-sided violence—typically, various infringements on political rights that governments engage in to raise their probability of staying in power. A very drastic measure of repression would be purges: the elimination by killing or imprisoning of political opponents. In the data set compiled by Arthur Banks, about 8 percent of the country-years since about 1950 are associated with such repression. However, if you include milder forms of repression, as documented by Amnesty International or the U.S. State Department, the incidence is much higher.

Figure 7 illustrates two main patterns in the data. On the left, it shows the prevalence of these two forms of internal violence over time, measured on the horizontal axes. On the vertical axes, we find the share of countries that are involved in civil war or in repression in each year from 1950. Clearly, there is a lot of time variation, and to some degree these two pictures look like mirror images. When civil war is on the rise, repression is on the fall. It is only after 1990 that the world unambiguously becomes a better place, in the sense that both forms of violence are down. The right part of the figure shows the prevalence of violence by country. For each country, we compute the share of years in which it is involved in civil war or repression, then plot these shares against (the log of) GDP per capita on the horizontal axis. Clearly, civil war is predominantly a phenomenon among the poorest countries, while repression tends to set in mostly at middle income levels. Across both time and countries, there is a sense of substitutability between these two forms of violence.

Political science has dealt with the determinants of violence for many years; only recently have economists become involved. Some theory in the literature applies to civil conflict, but I would say that in general it has little role for institutions, including state capacities. There are also large empirical literatures on civil war and repression, but they have relatively weak connections to theory, so it's a bit difficult to interpret the results. (Of course there are exceptions to this quick and self-serving literature review; one is the work by Jim Fearon that you will hear about in the next session.) However, this empirical work tends to take income as given, even though it is very likely that both violence and income have similar determinants. Think about the literatures on the resource curse: one about income, the other about civil war. Also, the literatures on civil war and repression are largely separate, even though both forms of violence seemingly reflect the fact

FIGURE 7.
Prevalence of Civil War and Repression over Time and Countries

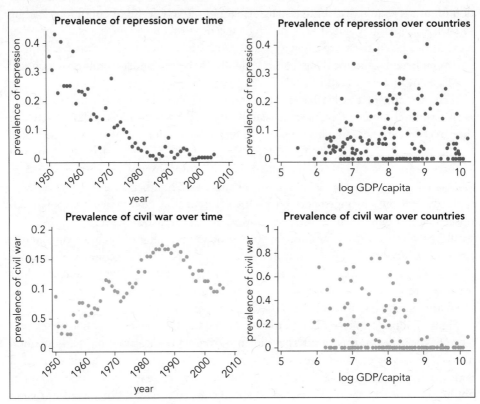

that institutions are not capable of resolving conflicts of interest in society in a peaceful way.

Tim Besley and I have tried to think about a theoretical framework to address these issues. Our approach has been to build a framework to analyze political violence and then to embed it in the earlier framework for state capacities. Our theoretical approach to political violence is pretty simple. There can be investments in violence by both incumbent and opposition groups. Both groups face a trade-off when they invest in violence. On the one hand, you incur some costs by hiring soldiers at going wages; on the other hand, you raise the probability of controlling policy and redistributing in your own group's favor.

What are the main drivers of conflict in this simple framework? When do we observe violence, and of what type? Our theory identifies three possible regimes: peace, repression, and civil war. Under *peace*, no group invests in violence. This regime will be seen when real wages are high, aid or resource rents are low, public goods are valuable, or political institutions are cohesive. It is too expensive to arm, there is not enough redistribution to fight over, or the winner's share isn't much larger because it is constrained by political institutions. The next outcome is *repression*—the incumbent, but not the opposition, takes to violence. Here real

FIGURE 8.
Determinants of Political Violence

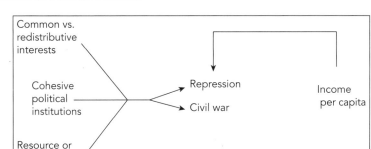

wages are lower, aid or resource rents are higher, public goods are less valuable, or there is less protection of minority interests. And finally there is *civil war*, when there is more at stake or fighting is cheap, so both the incumbent and the opposition groups resort to violence.

Thus, we find that the roots of repression and civil war are largely common, a prediction supported by our empirical work. How are the drivers of conflict related to the drivers of legal and fiscal capacity? Figure 8 illustrates our approach and an interesting result. Essentially, the factors we identified as crucial for the motivation to invest in the state are the same ones that drive the likelihood of repression and civil war. But there is an important difference: All the factors that increase the motivation to invest in the state diminish the incidence of repression and civil war. Conversely, when conditions are not conducive to investments in the state, they are conducive to investments in violence.

Putting the Pieces Together

What happens if we put the two frameworks together and simultaneously consider investments in state capacity and political violence? We predicted that we would see a negative correlation between state capacities and political violence for two reasons. On the one hand, as we have seen, low state capacities and political violence have similar basic determinants. On the other hand, if there is a high degree of political violence, this tends to raise political instability and further diminish the motivation to build strong state institutions, at least in redistributive or weak states.

Figure 9 shows the situation reflected in the data. The top two graphs reproduce figure 5, with its positive correlations between the incidence of external war and fiscal and legal capacity. The bottom two graphs show the partial correlations between the incidence of civil war and fiscal and legal capacity, which are computed in an analogous way. These correlations are negative rather than positive. Of course, there is no claim of causality here: The whole point of the earlier analysis is that these outcomes are jointly determined.

FIGURE 9.
Different Types of War and Fiscal Capacity

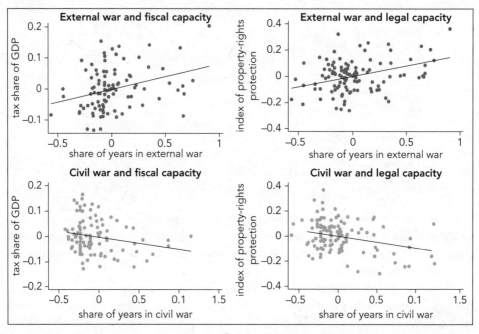

What do we learn from putting the pieces together? Earlier I posed three questions. (1) What drives the building of different state capacities, and why do these capacities move together? I have suggested some determinants of investments in the state—such as common interests and cohesive political institutions—and I have suggested that different state capacities tend to be complements. (2) What forces drives political violence? I have suggested that the determinants coincide with those driving state capacity investments, although with an opposite sign. (3) What drives the clustering among institutions, income, and violence? According to our simple analysis, one driver is the joint determinants of state capacity and violence. In addition, we have two-way feedbacks between income and state capacity and between income and political violence.

The full analysis is illustrated in figure 10, which shows the common drivers of the two forms of state capacity and the two forms of violence, as well as the feedbacks via income. The chart suggests why we might observe snowballing processes with virtuous or vicious circles—producing clusters of strong states in strong economies and nonviolent societies, and clusters of weak states in weak economies and violent societies.

Are there are any lessons here for foreign intervention and development assistance? I have described very early and ongoing work, so there are no rough and ready policy conclusions, but we are approaching a comprehensive way of thinking about various forms of development assistance in different types of states. Let me give six examples. The main lesson we will learn is a very conditional one: The effect of the

FIGURE 10.
Putting the Pieces Together

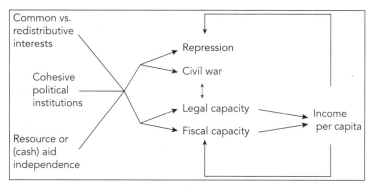

intervention depends crucially on both the type of intervention and the kind of state where it is made.

First, consider conventional development support in the form of cash aid to the government. If this is done in a common-interest state that is cash-constrained, it is very likely to help raise state building and improve policy and welfare. On the other hand, if the state is redistributive or weak, we will see little effect on state building and improvement in policy, and we may see a higher risk of repression or civil war because of the higher stakes of larger budgets.

The second kind of support is infrastructure or project assistance. This looks a bit more promising through the lens of our framework. In a best-case scenario, where such interventions raise local incomes, they can work like investments in productive state capacity, strengthening the motivation to build the state and lessening the risk of violence.

The third type of intervention, which is quite common, is military assistance to the government. According to our simple framework, this is like giving an additional advantage to the government, which can use the government budget to finance the army, while the rebels have to raise their own funds. With a higher return on the incumbent group's investment in violence, we would likely observe a larger range of outcomes with government repression, unless we happen to be in a common-interest state that does not have the propensity to violence in the first place.

A fourth intervention type is a post-conflict settlement. In our framework, this works a bit like cohesive political institutions; that is, it protects the minority and cuts the gains to the winner of a conflict. This would be the case if (a) we are in a conflict-prone, redistributive, or weak state; and (b) such a post-conflict settlement is credibly expected. If those conditions hold (which is a big "if"), the expectation of a post-conflict settlement might reduce the risk of conflict and investments in violence, and thereby strengthen the motivation for state building.

A fifth kind of intervention is direct assistance in capacity building, as many aid agencies are doing with various initiatives. According to our analysis, this intervention type might be quite helpful in common-interest states that already make investments in the state, but it is probably not sustainable in the weak states where it is most needed.

Finally, we can think about various forms of conditionality; for example, conditioning assistance on free multiparty elections. In our framework, this approach might increase political instability, at least from the viewpoint of the incumbent group. Therefore, it could raise the risk of repression and weaken state building, unless electoral reform is combined with other political reforms toward stronger constraints on executives.

I have described some very humble first steps. Many things remain to be done. For example, we should integrate other types of state capacity, such as the ability to provide basic health care and education. This would permit further insights into the clustering of state institutions. As another example, so far we have taken political institutions as given, but in the long run nothing is given and everything is endogenous. It is thus essential to study motives for political reforms. When do we see movement toward more accountability or better representation? When are such reforms introduced? Are they a quid pro quo for significant expansion of taxation, as some important political science literature suggests? If so, this would suggest additional complementarities between state capacity and political institutions.

It is our hope that giving economists some new analytical tools will help them wrap their minds around the crucial concepts of state capacity and political violence, and their role in development. We hope that our framework will also help members of the development community think about assistance to weak or fragile states.

Note

1. Torsten Persson's website is www.iies.su.se/~perssont, and Tim Besley's website is www.econ.lse.ac.uk/staff/tbesley/index_own.html

Reference

Tilly, Charles. 1990. *Coercion, Capital, and European States, AD 990–1990*. Cambridge, MA: B. Blackwell.

Personal Histories and Poverty Traps

PARTHA DASGUPTA

The persistence of poverty in a world that has otherwise and elsewhere enjoyed enormous income growth since World War II remains a puzzle. It wasn't absurd to imagine, as many development economists did in the 1980s, that growth in income in poor economies would trickle down to lift even the poorest out of the mire, but it hasn't happened. Today, the World Bank estimates that more than 1.3 billion people live on less than $1.25 a day, the Bank's rough-and-ready measure of absolute poverty.

Motivation

In speaking of an "economy," I cast a wide net. The economy could be a village, a district, a province, a nation, or even the whole world. A household could be poor in a village that is otherwise prosperous, just as a village could be poor even if the country is not, or a country could be languishing with a per capita income of 800 international dollars in a world where more than a billion people enjoy an average income of over 35,000 international dollars. It is frequently argued that in such a situation outside help is needed if the poor are to lift themselves out of poverty. Others question this argument. But all would seem to agree that the form any such help should take can be determined only when the unit to be assisted is identified (a household or an village or entire country) and the pathways by which lives get shaped are well understood.

When development economists talk of poverty, they have absolute poverty in mind (the 1.3 billion mentioned above). But social scientists in Europe and the United States also worry about poverty in their lands. Because context matters, social activists are quick to point out that poverty means different things to different

Partha Dasgupta is Frank Ramsey Emeritus Professor of Economics at the University of Cambridge and Professional Research fellow at the University of Manchester.

In preparing this keynote lecture, I benefited greatly from conversations and correspondence with Patrick Bateson, Peter Gluckman, and Trevor Robbins.

Annual World Bank Conference on Development Economics 2011, Global

people—that poverty is multidimensional. But if there is something common in a wide-ranging notion, it is not senseless to use one name for it.

The question is whether there *is* something of significance in common. One feature that could be thought to be common is *persistence*. That absolute poverty persists along family lines in rural communities in poor countries is not a controversial claim, even though few longitudinal studies among urban populations prove the claim. Some studies suggest that even in high-income countries poverty is inherited, in that people don't move in and out of poverty periodically (Creedy and Kalb 2006). But I have been unable to find reliable work covering a wide range of places that has determined whether there are lock-in effects, in the sense that the poor on average remain poor and do not enjoy periodic spells of prosperity and the well-off on average remain well-off and do not periodically become poor.

It is the job of theorists to predict what the data would reveal if someone were to look for them. Over the years, I have tried to understand the twin presence of poverty and wealth in poor countries by studying a variety of metabolic and socioecological pathways that would lead to persistent poverty (Dasgupta 1993, 1997, 2000, 2003, 2009). The processes giving rise to those pathways operate at different speeds and at various, often overlapping, spatial scales. And they are highly nonlinear, involving positive feedback. In some cases, the positive feedback is a reflection of fixed costs. For example, the maintenance energy in human metabolic processes is substantial (see below), as are the overhead labor hours in running a household in a world where water cannot be obtained by turning on a tap, where energy is not available at the flick of a switch, and where cooking is a vertically integrated activity. The common feature in all these processes is that the innumerable class of inputs required daily by humans are *complements* of one another. My theme here is the role those complementarities play in dividing populations. The theory I sketch shows why we should expect deep poverty to have a strong tendency to persist across generations.

I am concerned with the absolute poverty experienced by what is commonly referred to as the "bottom billion." Along the way, I shall connect with recent findings by James Heckman and his colleagues on the complementarities that divide populations even in wealthy societies (e.g., Cunha and Heckman 2007; Cunha, Heckman, and Schennach 2010).

Framing Poverty

In studying absolute poverty, it is necessary to go beyond income to the access people have to basic amenities. When you do that, you discover that in low-income countries only 68 percent of people have access to clean water and 39 percent to sanitation facilities; the corresponding figures for high-income countries are 99 percent for both (table 1). Such amenities are the universal determinants of human well-being. If instead you were to study figures for the constituents of well-being, you would discover that in low-income countries 28 percent of children under five years old are wasted and 44 percent are stunted. The corresponding figures in even upper-middle-income countries are 4 percent and 14 percent, respectively (table 2).

TABLE 1. Access to Clean Water and Sanitation, 2006

	Access	
	Clean water (%)	Sanitation (%)
Low-income countries	67	39
South Asia	87	33
(India)	89	28
Sub-Saharan Africa	58	31
China	88	65
High-income countries	99	99
World	86	60

Source: World Bank 2010, table 2.18.

TABLE 2. Prevalence of Child Undernutrition, 2000–08

	Percentage of children under 5		
	Wasted	Stunted	Low birth weight ($\leq$ 2.5 kg)
Low-income countries	28	44	15
South Asia	41	47	27
(India)	44	48	28
Sub-Saharan Africa	25	43	14
China	7	22	2
United States	1.3	4	8
World	23	35	15

Source: World Bank 2010, table 2.20.

These numbers tally with general impressions. The geographic distribution of absolute poverty makes for curious viewing of the world's map, as does the character of that poverty. Globally, the proportion of those who are underweight at birth is 14 percent, which is about the same as the figure for low-income countries. The corresponding figure in the United States, 8 percent, looks disquietingly high (table 2). In numbers, the bulk of the world's poor, when identified in terms of income, are still found in China and South Asia: 47 percent of children in South Asia are stunted and 27 percent are underweight at birth, whereas the corresponding figures in Sub-Saharan Africa are 43 percent and 14 percent, respectively (table 2). And yet, the proportion of people without access to clean water in South Asia is 33 percent, whereas the corresponding figure in Sub-Saharan Africa is 31 percent (table 1). I do not have a satisfactory understanding of some of the puzzling differences in the statistics, but elsewhere I have sought a partial explanation in terms of differences in the socioecological environments in South Asia and Sub-Saharan Africa (Dasgupta 1993, 2000, 2003).

In the world of the poor, fertility is high. The total fertility rate (TFR) in low-income countries is 4.2, compared with a world average of 2.5 (table 3).[1] Being in

TABLE 3. Maternal Burden 2008

	Total fertility rate	Maternal mortality (per 100,000)
Low-income countries	4.0	790
Sub-Saharan Africa	5.1	900
South Asia	2.9	500
China	8	45
High-income countries	1.8	10

Source: World Bank 2010, table 2.19.

excess of 2.1, the global TFR is still above the long-term replacement level. In South Asia, the TFR has fallen to 2.9, but in Sub-Saharan Africa it is a high 5.1, with a number of countries experiencing TFRs around 7. To see how great the cost of high TFRs is for women, consider that in Africa a successful birth involves at least two years of pregnancy and breastfeeding. In a country where the TFR is, say 7, about half of a woman's reproductive years would be spent either carrying a child in her womb or breastfeeding it. And we have not allowed for unsuccessful pregnancies. In those circumstances, employment outside the home is not an option.

An absence of reproductive health facilities in poor countries has meant that maternal mortality rates are high. In several poor countries, maternal mortality is the largest single cause of death among women in their reproductive years, and nutritional anemia plays a central role. In Sub-Saharan Africa, one woman dies for every 110 births. In contrast, the maternal mortality rate in Europe is one death per 20,000 births (table 3).

Contemporary data from more than 180 countries indicate that gross domestic product (GDP) per capita is negatively correlated with TFR (Schultz 2006). Much has been made of that in the demographic literature and by the media. The problem is that the relationship is a correlation, nothing more. It is no good using the correlation to recommend that countries should raise incomes if they wish to reduce fertility; the underlying reasons why household incomes are very low could also be the factors that encourage high fertility rates. Income and fertility are both endogenous variables.

Description

Although absolute poverty is usually defined as a state of affairs in which a person has very little income, a large contemporary literature has arrived at the following conclusion: "In the world of the poor, people don't enjoy food security, are stunted and wasted, don't live long, can't read or write, don't have access to easy credit, are unable to save much, aren't empowered, can't insure themselves well against crop failure or household calamity, don't trade with the rest of the world, live in unhealthy surroundings, are poorly governed, and experience high birth rates."[2]

We should add that the poor often reside in fragile ecosystems (Millennium Ecosystem Assessment 2003). Even absolute poverty is multidimensional.

We will call the passage above *description*. Although we can all agree on it, it offers little guidance for action. It doesn't say what is a cause and what is an effect; it doesn't distinguish between proximate and deep causes; it doesn't say what is a variable and what is a parameter in the environment in which the poor reside; and it doesn't say whether variables can be interpreted in samples to move together over time (time series data) or across parameter values at a point in time (cross-sectional data). Above all, the passage doesn't help us identify the pathways that lead to a state of affairs where *description* holds.

Analysis

Description suggests that poverty and riches have multiple causes; however, the temptation to seek monocausal explanations for the twin presence of poverty and wealth in our world is so powerful that even development experts haven't always been able to overcome it. But mutual causation has implications for interpreting data. Of course, people's lives are subject to many processes. One category—creating metabolic pathways—works at the level of the individual person. The pathways are based on physiological links connecting (1) undernourishment and a person's vulnerability to infectious diseases, (2) nutritional status and physical and mental development among children, and (3) nutritional status and work capacity among adults.

Another class of processes, operating at a spatially localized level, is site-specific. It involves a combination of ecological and socioeconomic pathways, giving rise to reproductive and environmental externalities. These processes are influenced by the local ecology. The theory based on them acknowledges that the economic options open to a poor community in, say, the African savannahs are different from those available to people in the Gangetic plains of India. Although policies and institutions shape the forces people face, the local ecology also shapes them.

Among ecological and socioeconomic processes, some involve positive feedback among poverty, population growth, and degradation of the local natural resource base. But poverty, population growth, and environmental degradation are not the prior causes of each other; over time, each influences and is influenced by the others. The two broad categories of positive feedback are able to coexist in a society because, except under conditions of extreme nutritional stress, nutritional status doesn't much affect fecundity.[3]

Those who are caught in poverty traps don't necessarily spiral down further. For most of them, there is little room below to fall into—many are already undernourished and susceptible to diseases. Modern nutrition science has shown that relatively low mortality rates can coexist with a high incidence of undernutrition and morbidity. To be sure, many people die from causes traceable directly to their poverty. But large numbers continue to live under nutritional and environmental stress. Moreover, people tend not to accept adverse circumstances lying down. So it is reasonable to assume that they try their best to improve their lot. In some situations, human responses to stress lead to successful outcomes. However, because I am talking about poverty traps, I will identify conditions under which the coping mechanisms people adopt are not enough to lift them out of the mire. Turner and Ali (1996), for example, have illustrated the possibility by showing that in the face of population pressure in Bangladesh, small landholders have periodically adopted new ways of doing things to intensify agricultural production. The authors have shown, however, that this has resulted in an imperceptible improvement in the standard of living and a worsening of the ownership of land, the latter probably owing to the prevalence of distress sales. These are the kinds of findings that the perspective I explore here anticipated and was designed to meet.

Externalities associated with people's coping strategies can amount to significant differences between private and social returns to various economic activities. Where reproductive behavior is pro-natalist, the private returns of having large numbers of children are high in contrast to the social returns. Similarly, where communities degrade their natural resource base, collective endeavors to maintain the base are unable to withstand the pressure of private malfeasance. And so on.

Complementarities

In a wide range of cases, the complementarities among the drivers of metabolic and socioecological pathways manifest themselves as fixed costs. When an individual maintains nutritional balance, somewhere in the region of 60 percent to 75 percent of his or her energy intake is spent on maintenance, which is a fixed cost of being alive. The remainder is used for work and discretionary activities.[4] Nutritionists refer to those metabolic fixed costs as "maintenance costs" and sometimes as "resting metabolic rates." About a third of maintenance costs can be traced to the energy expenditure associated with the innumerable brain activities that are synchronized in ways complex adaptive systems generally organize themselves. Those activities are complementary to one another—destroy key steps of a neural pathway, and the brain's overall performance worsens discretely.

Complementarities have been much studied in education. It is common today to say that it's not much use providing classrooms for children if there are no teachers to teach them; or that it's no good providing classrooms and teachers if children come to school hungry and are unable to concentrate; or that it's not much use providing classrooms and teachers and free school meals if the children have been damaged by iodine deficiency during infancy. The return on investment in each of those factors would be low if any of the other factors were in short supply. It's easy to recognize complementarities in the case of classrooms and teachers, because both must be available at the same time. It's less easy to recognize complementarities when they operate sequentially, stretching back to the distant past of a person's life. Complementarities across time give rise to irreversibilities in human development.

Another implication of complementarities is that in the world of the poor, each item in *description* reinforces the others, implying that productivity in labor effort, ideas, capital, land, and natural resources is low and remains low. The lives of the poor are filled with problems every day. On the flip side, the same factors give rise to virtuous feedback, meaning that the rich suffer from no such deprivation. People in the rich world face what today are called "challenges." An implication of the complementarities and the positive feedback they give rise to is that in the world of the rich, productivity in labor effort, ideas, capital, land, and natural resources is high and continually increasing. Success in meeting each challenge reinforces the prospects of success in meeting additional challenges.

So, the processes that shape our lives harbor multiple stability regimes. Some display progress even as others do not. The presence of multiple stability regimes means that in certain regions of the space of personal characteristics, the processes violate the *principle of horizontal equity*, so that very similar persons diverge cumulatively to face very different life chances. Horizontal inequity is a manifestation of a divided society, and poverty traps are an extreme form of horizontal inequity. (See the appendix for a stylized example.)

Of the many complementary factors that shape our lives, I want to focus on one broad class that illustrates the stranglehold a person's early life can have on his or her ability to function satisfactorily in later years. Those processes range from malnutrition and infectious disease at the very earliest stages of life to the nonacquisition of socioeconomic competencies in early childhood. I work backward from adulthood through childhood to the prenatal stage of life, and from there to the mother's status. I need to retrace people's lives because if, say, you place a malnourished person next to a healthy person, they won't look similar at all. You would then ask, where is the horizontal inequity that supposedly characterizes poverty traps? The point in tracing a person back to the distant past, one that includes the person's mother's status before conception and perhaps even before that, is to show how small shocks could have had marked cumulative effects in the person's subsequent development. That is the sense in which two very similar individuals can face very different life experiences. Complementarities are the cause of societal breaks.

Adult Health and Productivity

By undernourishment, I mean a combination of inadequate nutritional intake and exposure to a disease environment. Stunting is a reflection of long-term undernourishment, while wasting is a manifestation of short-term undernourishment. Each significantly limits the capacity for physical work, where strength and endurance are needed.

When nutritionists talk of physical work capacity (Collins and Roberts 1988; Ferro-Luzzi 1985; Pollitt and Amante 1984), they mean the maximum power (i.e., maximum work per unit of time) someone is capable of offering. Laboratory methods for estimating maximum power include having a person run on a treadmill and pedal a bicycle ergometer. The most compelling index of a person's physical work capacity is maximal oxygen uptake, usually denoted by the ungainly expression O_2 max. It is the highest rate of oxygen uptake a person is capable of attaining while engaged in physical work at sea level. Maximal oxygen uptake depends on the body's capacity for a linked series of oxygen transfers (diffusion through tissues, circulation of hemoglobin, pulmonary ventilation). It measures cardiorespiratory fitness—the higher the value, the greater the body's capacity to convert energy in the tissues into work (Åstrand and Rodahl 1986). That capacity depends on the metabolically active tissue mass, which is nearly the same as muscle cell mass (sometimes called the cell residue). Clinical tests suggest that O_2 max per unit of muscle cell mass is approximately constant across well-nourished and marginally undernourished people (Viteri 1971). Even among undernourished persons, the difference is not thought to be great. In one set of studies, more than 80 percent of the difference in O_2 max between mildly and severely malnourished people was traced to differences in their muscle cell mass (Barac-Nieto et al. 1980). It is therefore useful to have a measure of O_2 max per unit of muscle cell mass. A rough approximation of this is provided by the maximal aerobic power, which is O_2 max per unit of body weight. As muscle cell mass and lean body mass are related, we do not lose much by not being particular as to which of the two we identify as the chief determinant of O_2 max.[5]

We are, however, trying to identify the determinants of physical work capacity. A person must enjoy good current nutritional status in order to perform well at strenuous physical work, but that isn't sufficient, because one can be healthy but stunted. Of a pair of people with the same body mass index (BMI), the taller person typically possesses greater muscle cell mass; so the O_2 max is higher. Broadly speaking, taller and heavier (but nonobese) people have greater physical work capacity. O_2 max also depends on the level of habitual physical activity (training, in sports parlance), but I ignore this factor here.[6] Maximal oxygen uptake depends as well on the concentration of hemoglobin in the blood. I also ignore that in what follows.[7] O_2 max is usually expressed in liters per minute (l/min). To obtain a sense of orders of magnitude, note that 6 l/min is about as high as this measure can be, while 2 l/min and below are the numbers observed among chronically malnourished people.

O_2 max measures the maximum volume of oxygen the body is capable of transferring per minute. Except for very short bursts, this maximum cannot be reached. The highest level of oxygen transfer a person can sustain over an extended period of eight hours or so is of the order of 35 percent to 40 percent of the O_2 max. There is a relationship between the rate at which a person works (expressed as a fraction of his O_2 max) and his endurance in maintaining that rate of work. The negative-exponential function has been found to be a good approximation, even among undernourished subjects (Åstrand and Rodahl 1986); so, writing the duration of work by T, we have

$$\text{percentage of } O_2 \text{ max} = \exp(-bT). \tag{1}$$

In equation (1), b (> 0) is a constant. Barac-Nieto and colleagues (1980) have found b not to be significantly different among people suffering from degrees of malnourishment ranging from mild to severe. The endurance time for 80 percent of O_2 max in their sample was, on average, 97 minutes, with a coefficient of variation of 12 percent. This means that $b = 0.0023$/min. The suggestion is not that this is a human constant; nor is it claimed that the energy cost of a task does not vary with the rate at which it is performed. All the formula means is that, as a very rough approximation, we can distinguish people's capacity for physical activities in terms of their physical work capacity, which I define below.

Let P denote physical work capacity, and V the maximal oxygen uptake (O_2 max). From equation (1) we conclude that

$$P = KV\exp(-bT), \tag{2}$$

where K is a positive constant. The total quantity of work a rested individual is capable of performing is then $PT = KVT\exp(-bT)$, which attains its maximum value at $T = 1/b$. I conclude that if we are interested in aggregate work, the duration of work should be $1/b$. If $b = 0.0023$/min, $1/b = 7.2$ hours. I do not know whether, among healthy people in western industrialized countries, a seven-hour day has been arrived at from such a consideration as this.

For strenuous work, those with a low O_2 max need to be close to their physical work capacity. That means their hearts must beat at a fast rate. They are then overtaxed and incapable of maintaining the pace of work for long. This is reflected in equation (2). Consider as an example the well-known series of studies by G. B. Spurr and his colleagues on chronically malnourished adult males and nutritionally normal control subjects among sugarcane cutters, loaders, and agricultural workers in Colombia (Spurr 1990). Nutritional status was assessed on the basis of, among other things, weight-for-height, skinfold thicknesses, total body hemoglobin, and daily creatinine excretion. Roughly speaking, the first three indexes reflect current nutritional status, while the fourth picks up nutritional history to an extent (e.g., taller people have greater muscle cell mass). A stepwise multiple regression analysis with the data revealed that O_2 max is positively related to weight-for-height, total hemoglobin count, and daily creatinine excretion; it is negatively related to skinfold thicknesses. The chronically undernourished subjects ranged from mild to intermediate to severe. Approximate values of their O_2 max were, respectively, 2.1 l/min, 1.7 l/min, and 1.0 l/min. The average O_2 max of the nutritionally normal sugarcane cutters was 2.6 l/min. This is about as clear as any evidence we can hope to find for the thesis that undernourished people suffer from depressed levels of O_2 max.

Consider an activity whose oxygen cost is 0.84 l/min. The nutritionally normal group could sustain it at 0.32 of O_2 max, whereas the remaining three groups would have to sustain it at 40 percent, 50 percent, and 80 percent, respectively, of their O_2 max. At those rates, the nutritionally normal group could work for 8 hours, and the three malnourished groups for 6.5 hours, 5 hours, and 1.5 hours, respectively.

All this bears on physical work capacity and endurance, not physical productivity, although one would expect that they are closely related for unskilled manual work. And they are. For tasks such as sugarcane cutting, loading and unloading, and picking coffee, it is possible to measure physical productivity directly in terms of the amount done. Indeed, payment for such work is often at a piece rate. A wide body of evidence links nutritional status to productivity in these occupations. In their work on Colombian sugarcane cutters and loaders, Spurr and his colleagues (Spurr 1990) found height, weight, and lean body mass (roughly, O_2 max) to be significant determinants of productivity measured by daily tonnage of sugarcane delivered. Measuring productivity (W) in units of tons per day, O_2 max (as before, V) in liters per minute, and height (H) in cms., and denoting the percentage of body weight in fat by F, their most-preferred specification was:

$$W = 0.81\ V - 0.14\ F + 0.03\ H - 1.962. \tag{3}$$

In related work, Immink and colleagues (1984) found stature (and thus lean body mass and O_2 max) to be positively correlated with the quantity of coffee beans picked per day, the amount of sugarcane cut and loaded, and the time it took to weed a given area.

I turn now to economic investigations. In their study of a sample of both men and women workers in urban Brazil, Thomas and Strauss (1997) reported that height has a strong positive effect on market wages. That is consistent with the findings of Immink and colleagues (1984) and Spurr (1990), because wages would be expected to bear a positive association with productivity. The relationship between height and productivity is significant because height is not a variable for an adult, so there is less ambiguity about the direction of causality. However, investigators have usually studied the links between current nutritional status and productivity. In a sample of factory workers producing detonator fuses in India, Satyanarayana and colleagues (1977) found weight-for-height to be the significant determinant of productivity. Deolalikar (1988) found strong effects of weight-for-height on both productivity and wages among agricultural workers in South India. The elasticity of farm output with respect to weight-for-height was estimated to be approximately 2, and the elasticity of wages in the region was 0.3–0.7, where the lower value reflects the effect in peak seasons and the higher value in slack seasons, when the tasks are different. In a study of farm workers in Sierra Leone, Strauss (1986) found that energy intake has a positive effect on productivity up to about 5,200 kcal per day. He also found that a worker who consumed 5,200 kcal per day was twice as productive as one who consumed 1,500 kcal per day. Strauss did not report on differences in nutritional status among workers. But if we assume that the workers were in energy balance, we could interpret differences in daily intake as mirroring a combination of differences in nutritional status and the energy expended in the tasks that were accomplished. Thomas and Strauss (1998) found that BMI is positively correlated with wages among Brazilian laborers.

I noted earlier that the energy required for maintaining human life is substantial and that only 25 percent to 40 percent of a person's daily energy intake is spent on discretionary activities—work and leisure. Maintenance costs (resting metabolic rates) are higher for taller people of equal BMI. That is the cost side of healthy persons. On the other hand, they are more productive. It can be shown that because maintenance costs are substantial, markets aren't able to easily eliminate undernutrition, because the undernourished are at a severe disadvantage in their ability to obtain their daily requirements. Since their capacity to work is impaired, they are unable to offer the quality of work necessary to obtain the food they need to improve their nutritional status. Maintenance costs imply that it isn't possible for everyone in an economy that in the aggregate is poor to attain reasonable nutritional status. Thus, over time, undernourishment can be both a cause and a consequence of falling into a poverty trap (Dasgupta and Ray 1986). Moreover, because undernourishment displays hysteresis (there is a further positive feedback between nutrition and infection), Dasgupta and Ray's analysis implies that we should expect poverty to be dynastic. The theory is that once a household falls into a poverty trap, it is hard for descendants to emerge from it.

Childhood Experiences

One way a person can economize on energy expenditure is by reducing physical activities. Mild to moderately wasted preschool children under free-living conditions have been observed to spend more time in sedentary and light activities than their healthy counterparts. They have been found to rest longer and to play more often in a horizontal position. A Jamaican study found stunted children in the age group 12–24 months to be significantly less active than their nonstunted counterparts. The energy saved was comparable to the energy cost of growth at that age. At an extreme, when we observe little children in poor countries lying expressionless on roadsides and not even brushing the flies off their faces, we can infer that they are conserving energy. Among preschool children, the first line of defense against low energy intake would appear to be reduced physical activity. Such behavioral adaptation is not learned; humans are wired that way. Little children by the wayside no more consciously husband their precarious hold on energy than bicyclists solve differential equations to maintain balance.

Chavez and Martinez (1979, 1984) reported that among infants from poor households in rural Mexico, differences in activity levels were marked from about six months of age between those who received nutritional supplements and the control group. Supplemented children made more contact with the ground, slept less during the day, spent more time outdoors, and began playing almost six months earlier. The thesis here is that low nutrition intake depresses activity and isolates the infant or child from contact with the environment and from sources of stimuli of vital importance to both cognitive and motor development. It is significant that the control group in the Chavez-Martinez study was only moderately undernourished.

Motor development is the process by which a child acquires basic movement patterns and skills, such as walking, running, jumping, hopping, throwing, kicking, and holding something. In normal circumstances, children develop these fundamental motor patterns by the age of six or seven years. It is through such movement patterns and skills that many childhood experiences, especially learning and interpersonal relationships, are mediated (Grantham-McGregor 1990). During infancy and early childhood, interactions between the mother and child are of critical importance in this development. This is where the cost of anemia and low energy intake on the part of mothers makes itself felt. Since housework and production activities are mandatory, reducing discretionary and child-rearing activities offers the mother a way of maintaining her energy balance. To be sure, societies differ in the way people other than the mother are involved in a child's upbringing, but in all societies the mother is an important figure in a child's cognitive and motor development.

Long-term malnutrition among infants is especially associated with cognitive development. Dietary deficiencies of iron and iodine in the first two years of life are known to create problems that cannot be reversed by adequate diet in later years (Benton 2010). Under conditions of severe undernourishment (marasmus or marasmic kwashiorkor), both motor development and cognitive development are hampered in infants. Severe malnutrition affects development of the brain, which experiences rapid growth starting at around 10 weeks of pregnancy and continuing in spurts to about three or four years of age (Benton 2010). Fetal iodine deficiency is well known to damage the central nervous system. Equilibrium reactions ("righting reflexes") are functions of the cerebellum and play an important role in the development of motor control. Some of the damage is extremely difficult to reverse and may indeed be irreversible (Kar, Rao, and Chandramouli 2008; Walker 2005). For example, even after six months of nutritional rehabilitation of infants hospitalized for severe malnutrition, Colombo and Lopez (1980) observed no recovery in their motor development (see also Celedon and de Andraca 1979). It is possible that anatomical changes that have been observed are retardation rather than permanent injury, but this is not known with any certainty.[8]

Among schoolchildren, matters are somewhat different. Peer pressure tends to counter the instinct for reducing physical activities, especially among boys. But even for school-aged children, reduced activity is a line of defense. Studies indicate that in school-aged children the low energy expenditure associated with nutritional deficiency can be traced to low body weight; their basal metabolic rates are low. In addition, the development of lean body mass among undernourished children is retarded, which has a detrimental effect on their capacity to work as adults. Marginally malnourished boys don't appear to experience lesser muscle function. Their low capacity for work is due to the fact that their lean body mass is low.

On a wider front, malnutrition and infection have been found to have a pronounced detrimental effect among schoolchildren on such cognitive processes as attention and concentration. Much evidence exists showing that children who suffer from nutritional deficiencies and infections perform poorly in aptitude tests. In extreme cases, nutritional deficiencies affect the central nervous system (Levitsky and Strupp 1995). In less extreme cases, the matter isn't one of brain function; frequent absence and attrition affect learning as well (Bhargava 1994; Pollitt, 1990).

Intertemporal complementarities also exist along nonmetabolic pathways. In a wide-ranging study, Cunha and Heckman (2007) developed a theoretical framework to accommodate the fact that ability gaps between individuals and across socioeconomic groups appear at an early age for both cognitive and noncognitive skills. Studies have shown that enhancements of family environments improve the early development of cognitive as well as socioemotional competencies among children (e.g., perseverance, confidence, motivation, self-control). These competencies are retarded in adolescence if they are not acquired in early childhood (see Cunha, Heckman, and Schennach 2010, and the references there).

Prenatal Experiences

The nature versus nurture or genes versus environment controversy has been recognized as meaningless (Bateson and Martin 1999; Ehrlich 2000). Many important changes to gene expression occur during the first weeks of pregnancy. The DNA experiences epigenetic changes in the first week in particular. These changes determine the pattern of gene expression that not only controls the next stage of the fetus's development but also many of the person's attributes throughout life. The mother's long-term nutritional status determines how she mobilizes nutrients to support fetal development. So the experiences that shape an adult start before birth and perhaps even before the mother's birth. In pioneering work, David Barker and colleagues (Barker et al. 1989a, 1989b, 2002) found that rates of ischemic heart disease in England and Wales were more closely related to mortality conditions that prevailed when heart patients were born than to recent conditions. The hypothesis is that maternal conditions in the prenatal period have an important impact on the emergence of later cardiovascular disease.

What are the signatures of prenatal experiences? Although it would be astonishing if a single scalar index at birth could summarize prenatal experiences, a substantial body of work has shown that birth weight is a reasonable indicator of prenatal conditions.[9] In addition, studies that were based not only on birth weight confirm that food deprivation in the womb affects adult metabolism and cardiovascular health; in fact, it has been found to have adverse effects even on age-associated declines in cognitive functions.[10]

What mechanisms would determine the association between prenatal conditions and the cardiovascular-metabolic cluster of chronic diseases? Barker and colleagues (2002) suggested that insufficient energy during fetal development triggers biased apportioning of the available energy to brain development. Maternal stress may be communicated to the fetus via alterations of placental blood flow and changes in energy available for fetal growth, compromising the development of other organs, including kidneys, pancreas, and adipose tissue. For example, small babies have fewer nephrons in their kidneys, fewer beta cells in their pancreases, and lower fat cell numbers than their peers who are larger at birth. However, many of the deleterious adult outcomes of small birth size appear to be related to altered insulin sensitivity and activity of the hypothalmic-pituitary-adrenal (HPA) axis. Both these systems are important modulators of energy metabolism. A good deal of attention has been paid in recent years to pathways that involve the extent to which insulin sensitivity and the reactivity of the HPA axis are established in utero; the potential for maternal nutritional status to affect those aspects of metabolic physiology; and the cellular mechanisms by which the effects are mediated (Ellison 2010). Between 24 and 42 weeks of gestation, the developing brain is particularly vulnerable to nutritional deficiency, owing to the rapid development of vital neurological processes, including synapse formation. And yet, at that time, the developing brain also demonstrates its greatest degree of plasticity (Georgieff 2007).

What accounts for that aspect of fetal development? One possibility is that beginning as early as the first weeks after conception and continuing into early infancy, the fetus reads key features of its environment and prepares to adapt to an external world that can vary dramatically in its level of safety, self-sufficiency, and danger. When early experiences prepare a developing child for conditions involving high levels of stress or instability, the body's systems retain that initial programming and put the stress response system on a quick response and high alert status. Under those circumstances, the price of short-term survival could be longer-term health. This is called the "fetal programming hypothesis," and it has generated much interest in phenotypic plasticity and the mechanisms that govern it.[11]

Gluckman, Hanson, and Spenser (2005) have proposed that the apparent paradox of adaptive developmental processes yielding pathological results can be resolved if (1) the adaptive processes are aimed at adjusting the organism's physiology to a predicted postnatal environment, and (2) there is a mismatch between the predicted and actual postnatal environment. The hypothesis is that the fetus can sense the environment into which it can expect to be born from maternal signals. The availability of food is one such signal; maternal stress reflected in hormonal changes is another; and fluid deprivation and oxygen availability are others. The authors' point is that there are selection advantages in trying to match the physiology we develop in our plastic phase of development to the environment we may inhabit. This can lead to paradoxical responses, as when a fetus that is "expecting" a strongly constrained environment enters a world where food is abundant. Obesity and the onset of type-2 diabetes are familiar phenomena today. In a wide-ranging work, Gluckman and Hanson (2006) call the maladaptive response *mismatch,* a kind of programming that explains why diets rich in protein and calories have been known to have adverse effects among children of low birth weight. The authors suggest that conditions in utero may reflect not merely maternal conditions at the time but also the mother's sensitivity to those conditions. For example, the energy available to the fetus is affected by maternal undernutrition and the sensitivity of the mother's own physiology to variation in the energy available to her. Maternal sensitivity to energy availability, in turn, may be partly a consequence of the conditions *she* faced in utero, which in turn would depend on *her* mother's sensitivity to energy availability, and so on.[12]

Much medical research on prenatal development has been conducted on subjects in high-income countries. There, the issue isn't usually a question of maternal energy deficiency. Stress, anxiety, or depression during pregnancy have been linked to lower birth weight and subsequently even to psychopathology (Fumagalli et al. 2007). Maternal stress has been found to be associated with increased basal HPA-axis activity in the offspring at different ages, including six months, five years, and ten years. Increased activation of the HPA axis causes the adrenal gland to produce glucocorticoids. These are important for normal brain maturation, but elevated levels impair brain development and functioning. Some of these conditions are reversible, and the effects of prenatal stress are often moderated by the quality of postnatal care; others are not (Cottrell and Seckl 2009). Chronic exposure to stress hormones—whether it occurs during the prenatal period or in infancy, childhood, adolescence, adulthood, or old age—has an impact on brain structures involved in cognition and mental health (Evans and Schamberg 2009; Lupien et al. 2009;

Rice et al. 2010). The fact that there are many pathways to low birth weight perhaps explains why the incidence of low birth weight remains high in rich countries (table 2).

Morals

What morals do we take away from this account? The following seem to be worth commending:

1. The high maintenance costs of good physical and emotional health underlie the existence of poverty traps.
2. From (1) it follows that in low-income countries, absolute poverty is both a cause and a consequence of unequal distributions of assets.
3. High maintenance costs are manifestations of complementarities among the inputs that humans need for survival. Maintenance costs are higher among people who are fortunate enough to flourish.
4. The acquisition of human capital is continuous and cumulative. Formally speaking, investments in human capital are complementary over time. Complementarities across time give rise to irreversibilities in human development. Nutritional insults at the earliest stages of life have a marked effect on a person's subsequent ability to acquire human capital. If governments and international organizations believe human capital formation is important, they should treat all periods of a person's life with respect.
5. From (4) we can conclude that personal history has a long reach, affecting not only the person in question but also any descendants.

These observations bring us back to the point with which I began: that a person's current productivity is a function of the person's nutritional and morbidity history. A reasonable index of a person's productivity over time would be the present-discounted sum of the person's output of work. The reckoning should start from the earliest stages of the person's life. The computation is no doubt very, very hard, but there is no escaping it.

Much international attention has been given to saving lives in times of collective crisis in poor countries. This is as it should be. International agencies have also paid attention to keeping children alive in normal times through public health measures, such as family planning counseling, immunization, and oral rehydration. This too is as it should be. The fact that many poor countries fail to do either does not mean that the problems are especially hard to solve. In fact, they are among the easier social problems—they can be addressed without any major modifications to the prevailing resource allocation mechanism. The much harder problem for intellectual design, political commitment, and administration is to ensure that those who are conceived have a chance for a healthy life. This is a problem whose solution brings no easily visible benefit. But the stunting of both cognitive and motor capacity is a prime hidden cost of energy deficiency and anemia among children and, one step removed, among mothers. It affects learning and skill formation, and thus future productivity. The price is paid in later years, but it is paid.

Appendix: Poverty Traps and Horizontal Inequity

Poverty traps are a sharper notion than horizontal inequity. To illustrate the differences at the nutrition-productivity interface, we consider a stylized example.

Denote time by t (≥ 0). The present is $t = 0$. Consider someone whose nutritional status at t is a scalar, $H(t)$. Let $J(H,q)$ be a person's income, where q is a (scalar) parameter reflecting the person's socioecological environment. We suppose that $dJ(H,q)/dH > 0$ and that J shifts vertically upward with increases in q. Let $R(H)$ denote the person's nutrition requirement (expressed in units of income). We assume $dR(H)/dH > 0$, to reflect the fact that a person's resting metabolic rate increases with body size. A person's health, when viewed as a stock, is assumed to obey the deterministic differential equation,

$$dH(t)/dt = J(H(t),q) - R(H(t)), \qquad H_3 > H(t) > H_1,$$

and if, for any t^*, $H(t^*) = H_1$ (resp. H_3), then $H(t) = H_1$ (resp. H_3) for all $t \geq t^*$. H_1 and H_3 are absorbing states.

Because the resting metabolic rate is positive, $R(H_1) > 0$ and $J(H,q) = 0$ in the neighborhood of H_1. In figure 1, $J(H,q)$ and $R(H)$ have been so drawn that they intersect once, at H_2. The system defined by (A1) has three equilibria: H_1, H_2, and H_3. Among them, H_2 is unstable, whereas H_1 and H_3 are stable. Someone whose

FIGURE 1. Nutrition-Based Poverty Trap

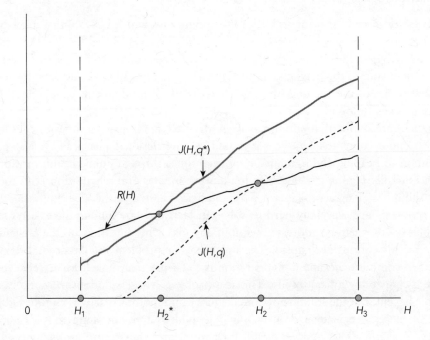

initial health status $H(0)$ is even slightly in excess of H_2 would enjoy improvement in health status, while someone for whom $H(0)$ is even slightly less than H_2 would be trapped in a deteriorating situation. It follows that there could be people in the neighborhood of $H(0)$ who are similar but who face widely differing fortunes. The example exposes the limitations of studies that view the quality of life at a single point in time. Similar people wouldn't remain similar if they were to experience widely different life histories. The principle of horizontal equity could not be applied to them at later times. This is one reason why the principle, as traditionally formulated, has little ethical bite. When assessing an economy, the lives of its citizens should be viewed as a whole, not studied at a frozen moment in time.

What might q reflect? It could reflect factors that are exogenous to the economy, such as rainfall, as well as factors that are exogenous to the person but endogenous in the economy, such as the effectiveness of property rights, the extent to which government and communities have in place effective support systems, the degree to which markets are open to the person, and the person's nonlabor assets, including education. And we can add the extent to which the person has reasons to trust others and to which others trust the person.

If public policies improve q, J would move up vertically. If the schedule were to rise sufficiently high ($q = q^*$), it would not intersect $R(H)$, and H_3 would become the sole (stable) equilibrium point of the system defined in (A1). Welfare support (be it communitarian or state-based) and income guarantees would be another set of mechanisms by which $J(H,q)$ could be lifted. These are among the various pathways by which nutrition-based poverty traps have been eliminated in a number of countries.

Notes

1. TFR is the number of live births a woman would expect to give if she were to live through her childbearing years and to bear children at each age in accordance with the prevailing age-specific fertility rate. If TFR were 2.1 or thereabouts, population would stabilize in the long run.

2. See, for example, Sen (1999); Narayan et al. (2000); Banerjee, Benabou, and Mookherjee (2006); Banerjee and Duflo (2007); and—since its inception in 1990—every annual edition of the United Nations *Human Development Report*.

3. For a more detailed account, see Dasgupta (2000).

4. See WHO (1985) for estimates of mean protein-energy requirements among the genders, occupations, and age groups.

5. The mass of muscle tissue and muscle constitutes about 40 percent of body weight and 50 percent of lean body mass.

6. Unskilled laborers in poor countries are often slight and weak, but they are never out of shape; sedentary workers are often out of shape.

7. A classic article on iron-deficiency anemia and its effect on physical work capacity is Basta et al. (1979).

8. The study of the effect of malnutrition on mental development is fraught with difficulties of interpretation. On this, see the chapter by S. M. Grantham-McGregor in Waterlow

(1992). For wide-ranging reviews of the consequences of chronic energy deficiency, see Schurch and Scrimshaw (1987).

9. For more on the fact that birth weight does not capture many salient aspects of the fetal experience and can in certain ways even mislead, see the summary in Schulz (2010). Ellison (2010) provides an excellent overview of the literature.

10. Bateson and Martin (1999) offer an excellent general account. For studies of the consequences for fetal development of the Dutch Hunger Winter (1944-1945), see Roseboom, de Rooij, and Painter (2006) and Rooij et al. (2010).

11. See the excellent review by Shonkoff, Boyce, and McEwen (2009). They note that the origins of many adult diseases can be found adversities in the early years of life, which establish "biological memories" that weaken physiological systems and produce latent vulnerabilities to problems that emerge well into later adult years.

12. The question whether fetal programming is adaptive remains controversial. Some see these effects as disruptions of optimal development with permanent consequences-developmental pathologies that may be more frequent in novel evolutionary environments (Barker 1994; Barker et al. 2002).

References

Åstrand, P. O., and K. Rodahl. 1986. *Textbook of Work Physiology*. New York: McGraw Hill.

Banerjee, A. V., R. Benabou, and D. Mookherjee, eds. 2006. *Understanding Poverty*. New York: Oxford University Press.

Banerjee, A., and E. Duflo. 2007. "The Economic Lives of the Poor." *Journal of Economic Perspectives* 21(1): 141–168.

Barac-Nieto, M., G. B. Spurr, H. W. Dahners, and M. G. Maksud. 1980. "Aerobic Work Capacity and Endurance During Nutrition Repletion of Severely Undernourished Men." *American Journal of Clinical Nutrition* 33(11): 2268–2275.

Barker, D. J. P. 1994. *Mothers, Babies, and Disease in Later Life*. London: BMJ Publishing.

Barker, D. J. P., C. Osmond, J. Golding, D. Kuh, and M. E. Wadsworth. 1989a. "Growth *in utero*, Blood Pressure in Childhood and Adult Life, and Mortality from Cardiovascular Disease." *British Medical Journal* 298: 564–567.

Barker, D. J., J. G. Eriksson, T. Forsen, and C. Osmond. 2002. "Fetal Origins of Adult Disease: Strength of Effects and Biological Basis." *International Journal of Epidemiology* 31: 1235–1239.

Barker, D. J. P., B. D. Winter, C. Osmond, B. Margetts, and S. J. Simmonds. 1989b. "Weight in Infancy and Death from Ischaemic Heart Diseases." *Lancet* 2 (86663): 381–383.

Basta, S., S. Soekirman, D. Karyadi, and N. S. Scrimshaw. 1979. "Iron Deficiency Anemia and the Productivity of Adult Males in Indonesia." *American Journal of Clinical Nutrition* 32(4): 916–925.

Bateson, P., and P. Martin. 1999. *Design for a Life: How Behaviour Develops*. London: Jonathan Cape.

Benton, D. 2010. "The Influence of Dietary Status on the Cognitive Performance of Children." *Molecular Nutrition and Food Research* 54(4): 457–470.

Bhargava, A. 1994. "Modelling the Health of Fillipino Children." *Journal of the Royal Statistical Society A* 157: 417–432.

Celedon, J. M., and I. de Andraca. 1979. "Psychomotor Development during Treatment of Severely Marasmic Infants." *Early Human Development* 3: 267–75.

Chavez, A., and C. Martinez. 1979. "Consequences of Insufficient Nutrition in Child Character and Behaviour." In *Malnutrition, Environment and Behaviour*, ed. D. A. Levitsky. Ithaca, NY: Cornell University Press.

———. 1984. "Behavioural Measurements of Activity in Children and Their Relation to Food Intake in a Poor Community." In *Energy Intake and Activity*, ed. E. Pollitt and P. Amante. New York: Alan R. Liss.

Collins, K. J., and D. F. Roberts, eds. 1988. *Capacity for Work in the Tropics*. Cambridge, England: Cambridge University Press.

Colombo, M., and I. Lopez. 1980. "Evolution of Psychomotor Development in Severely Undernourished Infants Submitted to an Integral Rehabilitation." *Pediatrics Research* 14 (1): abstracts.

Cottrell, E. C., and J. R. Seckl. 2009. "Prenatal Stress, Glucocorticoids and the Programming of Adult Disease." *Frontiers in Behavioral Neuroscience* 3. Open access.

Creedy, J., and G. Kalb, eds. 2006. *Research on Economic Inequality, Vol. 13: Dynamics of Inequality and Poverty*. London: Emerald Publishing.

Cunha, F., and J. Heckman. 2007. "The Technology of Skill Formation." *American Economic Review* (Papers & Proceedings) 97: 31–47.

Cunha, F., J. Heckman, and S. Schennach. 2010. "Estimating the Technology of Cognitive and Noncognitive Skill Formation." *Econometrica* 78 (3): 883–931.

Dasgupta, P. 1993. *An Inquiry into Well-Being and Destitution*. Oxford: Clarendon Press.

———. 1997. "Nutritional Status, the Capacity for Work and Poverty Traps." *Journal of Econometrics* 77 (1): 5–38.

———. 2000. "Reproductive Externalities and Fertility Behaviour." *European Economic Review* (Papers & Proceedings) 44 (4–6): 619–44.

———. 2003. "Population, Poverty, and the Natural Environment." In *Handbook of Environmental Economics, Vol. I*, ed. K.-G. Mäler and J. Vincent, 191–247. Amsterdam: North Holland.

———. 2009. "Poverty Traps: Exploring the Complexity of Causation." In *The Poorest and the Hungry: Assessments, Analyses, and Actions*, ed. J. von Braun, R. Vargas Hill, and R. Pandya-Lorch, 129–46. Washington, DC: International Food Policy Research Institute.

Dasgupta, P., and D. Ray. 1986. "Inequality as a Determinant of Malnutrition and Unemployment, 1: Theory." *Economic Journal* 96 (4): 1011–34.

Deolalikar, A. B. 1988. "Nutrition and Labour Productivity in Agriculture: Estimates for Rural South India." *Review of Economics and Statistics* 70: 406–13.

Ehrlich, P. R. 2000. *Human Natures: Genes, Cultures, and the Human Prospect*. Washington, DC: Island Press.

Ellison, P. 2010. "Fetal Programming and Fetal Psychology." *Infant and Child Development* 19 (1): 6–20.

Evans, G. W., and M. A. Schamberg. 2009. "Childhood Poverty, Chronic Stress, and Adult Working Memory." *Proceedings of the National Academy of Sciences* 10 (16): 6545–549.

Ferro-Luzzi, A. 1985. "Work Capacity and Productivity in Long-Term Adaptation to Low Energy Intakes." In *Nutritional Adaptation in Man*, ed. K. Blaxter and W. C. Waterlow. London: John Libbey.

Fumagalli, F., R. Molteni, G. Racagni, and M. A. Riva. 2007. "Stress During Development: Impact on Neuroplasticity and Relevance to Psychopathology." *Progress in Neurobiology* 81: 197–217.

Georgieff, M. K. 2007. "Nutrition and the Developing Brain: Nutrient Priorities and Measurement." *American Journal of Clinical Nutrition* 85 (Supplement): 614S–620S.

Gluckman, P., and M. Hanson. 2006. *Mismatch: Why Our World No Longer Fits Our Bodies*. New York: Oxford University Press.

Gluckman, P. D., M. A. Hanson, and H. G. Spenser. 2005. "Predictive Adaptive Responses and Human Evolution." *Trends in Ecology and Evolution* 20: 527–533.

Grantham-McGregor, S.M. 1990. "The Relationship between Undernutrition, Activity Levels and Development in Young Children." *In Activity, Energy Expenditure and Energy Requirements in Young Children*, ed. B. Schurch and N.S. Scrimshaw. Lausanne: Nestle Foundation.

Immink, M. D. C. et al. 1984. "Microeconomic Consequences in Energy Deficiency in Rural Populations in Developing Countries." In *Energy Intake and Activity*, ed. E. Pollit and P. Amante. New York: Alan R. Liss.

.Kar, B. R., S. L. Rao, and B. A. Chandramouli. 2008. "Cognitive Development in Children with Chronic Protein Energy Malnutrition." *Behavioral and Brain Functions* 4, article 31. Open access.

Levitsky, D. A., and B. J. Strupp. 1995. "Malnutrition and the Brain: Changing Concepts, Changing Concerns." *Journal of Nutrition* 125(8): S2212–S2220.

Lupien, S. J., B. S. McEwen, M. R. Gunnar, and C. Heim. 2009. "Effects of Stress Throughout the Lifespan on the Brain, Behaviour and Cognition." *Nature Reviews/Neuroscience* 10(6): 434–445.

Millennium Ecosystem Assessment. 2003. *Ecosystems and Human Well-Being*. Washington, DC: Island Press.

Narayan, D., with R. Patel, K. Schafft, A. Rademacher, and S. Koch-Schulte. 2000. *Voices of the Poor: Can Anyone Hear Us?* Oxford: Oxford University Press.

Pollitt, E. 1990. *Malnutrition and Infection in the Classroom*. Paris: UNESCO.

Pollitt, E., and P. Amante. 1984. *Energy Intake and Activity*. New York: Alan R. Liss.

Rice, F., G. T. Harold, J. Boivin, M. van den Bree, D. F. Hay, and A. Thapar. 2010. "The Links Between Prenatal Stress and Offspring Development and Psychopathology: Disentangling Environmental and Inherited Influences." *Psychological Medicine* 40(2): 335–345.

Rooij, S. R. de, H. Wouters, J. E. Yonker, R. C. Painter, and T. J. Roseboom. 2010. "Prenatal Undernutrition and Cognitive Function in Late Adulthood." *Proceedings of the National Academy of Sciences* 107(39): 16881–16886.

Roseboom, T., S. R. de Rooij, and R. Painter. 2006. "The Dutch Famine and Its Long-Term Consequences for Adult Health." *Early Human Development* 82: 485–491.

Satyanarayana, K., A. N. Naidu, B. Chatterjee, and N. Rao. 1977. "Body Size and Work Output." *American Journal of Clinical Nutrition* 30(3): 322–325.

Schultz, T. P. 2006. "Fertility and Income." In *Understanding Poverty,* ed. A. V. Banerjee, R. Benabou, and D. Mookherjee. New York: Oxford University Press.

Schulz, L.C. 2010. "The Dutch Hunger Winter and the Developmental Origins of Health and Disease." *Proceedings of the National Academy of Sciences* 107(39): 16757–16758.

Schurch, B., and N. S. Scrimshaw, eds. 1987. *Chronic Energy Deficiency: Consequences and Related Issues*. Lausanne: Nestlé Foundation.

Sen, A. 1999. *Development as Freedom*. Oxford: Oxford University Press.

Shonkoff, J. P., W. T. Boyce, and B. S. McEwen. 2009. "Neuroscience, Molecular Biology, and Childhood Roots of Health Disparities: Building a New Framework for Health Promotion and Disease Prevention. *Journal of the American Medical Association* 301(21): 2252–2259.

Spurr, G. B. 1990. "The Impact of Chronic Undernutrition on Physical Work Capacity and Daily Energy Expenditure." In *Diet and Disease in Traditional and Developing Countries*, ed. G. A. Harrison and J. C. Waterlow. Cambridge, England: Cambridge University Press.

Strauss, J. 1986. "Does Better Nutrition Raise Farm Productivity?" *Journal of Political Economy* 94: 297–320.

Strauss, J., and D. Thomas. 1998. "Health, Nutrition and Economic Development." *Journal of Economic Literature* 36(2): 766–817.

Thomas, D., and J. Strauss. 1997. "Health and Wages: Evidence on Men and Women in Urban Brazil." *Journal of Econometrics* 77(1): 159–185.

Turner, B. L., and A. M. S. Ali. 1996. "Induced Intensification: Agricultural Change in Bangladesh with Implications for Malthus and Boserup." *Proceedings of the National Academy of Sciences* 93: 14984–14991.

Viteri, F. E. 1971. "Considerations on the Effects of Nutrition on the Body Composition and Physical Work Capacity of Young Guatemalan Adults." In *Amino Acid Fortification of Protein Foods*, ed. N. S. Scrimshaw and A. M. Altshull. Cambridge, MA: MIT Press.

Walker, C.-D. 2005. "Nutritional Aspects Modulating Brain Development and the Responses to Stress in Early Neonatal Life." *Progress in Neuro-Psychopharmacology and Biological Psychiatry* 29: 1249–1263.

Waterlow, J. C., with contributions by A. M. Tomkins and S. M. Grantham-McGregor. 1992. *Protein Energy Malnutrition.* Sevenoaks, England: Edward Arnold.

World Bank. 2010. *World Development Indicators.* Washington DC: World Bank.

World Health Organization (WHO). 1985. *Energy and Protein Requirements.* WHO Technical Report Series 724, Geneva, Switzerland.

Environmental Commons and
the Green Economy

Voluntary Pledges and Green Growth in the Post-Copenhagen Climate

THOMAS STERNER

A number of features set climate change apart from most environmental problems: It spans several generations, forcing us to think in new ways about intergenerational fairness. More important, it involves a delicate problem of coordination among countries on a global scale. As long as it is very profitable to use fossil fuels, policy coordination must include all major economies. The costs are high enough to make it important to choose policy instruments that encourage efficiency in abatement. Ultimately, this means striving toward a single market for carbon. The importance of getting near-universal adherence to a treaty makes fairness and procedure important, but we know how difficult it is to build a truly global agreement. "Green growth" is promoted as an alternative path. This is clearly the goal, but it is no magic bullet, and it will require clear and stern policy instruments, because economic growth will boost the demand for energy, and coal is typically the cheapest source. In this paper I discuss some necessary ingredients for a long-run global climate strategy; in conclusion, I address the short-run issue of which policies to pursue in the meantime. As we wait for the final (and maybe elusive) worldwide treaty, we must have a policy that makes sense and is not only compatible with but, we hope, will facilitate the development of this worldwide agreement.

Ecosystem Threats to Growth?

Ample evidence exists that climate change presents a dire threat, particularly to many tropical countries, through sea-level rise, increased storm frequency, increased temperature, and decreased rainfall in areas where conditions for agriculture and even survival are already stretched to the maximum. Glacial melting is another grave

Thomas Sterner is professor of environmental economics at the University of Gothenburg in Sweden. Past President of the European Association of Environmental and Resource Economists and a University Fellow at Resources for the Future, Washington DC. Thanks to Christian Azar, Maria Damon, Daniel Slunge, Yonas Alem, Karin Jonson, Jorge Bonilla, Selma Oliveira, Simon Wagura and an anonymous referee for very useful comments on earlier drafts.

Annual World Bank Conference on Development Economics 2011, Global

threat. As glaciers melt, they may change patterns of river flow, which can affect very densely populated areas, with tens and even hundreds of millions of inhabitants. For thorough documentation, see the Intergovernmental Panel on Climate Change (IPCC) 4th Assessment Report (IPCC 2007) or the World Bank *World Development Report 2010* (World Bank 2010) and the studies cited therein.

Most developing countries are deeply concerned about climate change, but they also firmly believe that mitigation should start with the rich countries that bear the largest part of the historical responsibility for emissions. This position has led some to believe, erroneously, that developing countries are uninterested in the issues of global change. Their views on the distribution of burden should not be mistaken for views on climate. For instance, the suggestion that all countries should reduce their emissions by similar percentages clearly favors countries that have large emissions today. If developing countries reject this principle, it does not necessarily have anything to do with a lack of interest in climate damages. In 2009, Prime Minister Meles Zenawi of Ethiopia spoke on behalf of many African nations when he demanded that the industrialized countries that were responsible for most of the historical emissions—countries such as the United States and the United Kingdom—should compensate developing nations for the damage they caused in recent decades to the earth's climate.[1]

The Millennium Ecosystem Assessment (2005) (MA) analyzes a series of additional and often interrelated threats. Finding #1 in the MA synthesis says "Over the past 50 years, humans have changed ecosystems more rapidly and extensively than in any comparable period in human history, largely to meet rapidly growing demands for food, fresh water, timber, fiber, and fuel." According to the MA, more land was converted to cropland in the 30 years after 1950 than in the 150 years between 1700 and 1850. In the past two decades, human activities have dominated the geobiochemical processes of Earth; we dominate many of the processes of photosynthesis; and we have destroyed 20 percent of the world's coral reefs and 35 percent of its mangrove area. The MA goes on to say that although these changes have contributed to net gains in welfare, they have also implied degradation of many ecosystem services, increasing risks of nonlinear changes and the exacerbation of poverty for some groups of people.

The past two decades have witnessed an enormous transformation of the world economy, implying that hundreds of millions of people, particularly in Asia, have left the ranks of the most destitute. This inspires considerable optimism in other countries where poverty is still rampant. It would be a historic tragedy if environmental and resource restrictions stifled this process. However, some environmental problems—notably climate change—definitely could be costly enough to halt economic progress unless they are managed wisely.

In some cases, solutions to several problems may coincide. For example, the same processes might contribute to declining fish or forest stocks and declining biodiversity, so policy measures could be designed to address both problems. However, this is not always the case. Sometimes a technique that would appear to help solve one problem may exacerbate others; thus, the multitude of restrictions suggested by the MA may combine to be a bigger problem than they appear separately. Several alternative energy supply technologies are relevant for the climate area.[2] It may be ineffective to grow biomass on a large scale and with inappropriate conversion technologies. In addition to massive releases of climate gases in the forest-clearing phase, this practice may threaten biodiversity and use land that may be needed for food.

Global Coordination Required

One crucial feature of climate change is that policy must be global because the pollutant is global. Policies that are followed only in some countries will tend to create various forms of "carbon leakage." Policy makers and industries worry about pollution havens and the detrimental effects of environmental regulations on competitiveness; however, not much empirical evidence exists that stricter environmental legislation has induced industry to migrate. In fact, the environmental regulations governing conventional pollutants have, so far, caused only moderate costs to industry compared with drastic cuts in fossil fuel use. But the shadow prices needed to reduce carbon emissions by 50 to 80 percent—and eventually to eliminate them—will be high. If a company could avoid these costs by relocating, it would enjoy a significant competitive advantage.

General equilibrium effects are also a concern, as tougher climate policies in some countries will tend to depress the price of fossil fuels and encourage fossil use in other countries. But the main effect is one of pure arithmetic: If a coalition of countries were to combat climate change (even if this coalition were large and taxed fossil fuel heavily[3]), there would be a risk of significant rebound by developments in the rest of the world economy. If, say, countries representing 80 percent of world emissions were to succeed in reducing their emissions by 50 percent, the effect could still be undone by the actions of the remaining 20 percent of world emitters.

Let us suppose that the smaller "fringe" group experienced economic growth of a few percentage points at the same time world coal and oil prices were falling because of increasing taxation in the climate coalition countries. It would be reasonable to surmise that their use of these commodities (and thus their emissions) would grow at a rate of, say, 6 percent per year. This is less than half the corresponding growth rate of Chinese emissions after 2001. Their emissions would grow so much by 2050 that, in spite of the 50 percent reduction by the main emitters, global emissions would still more than double, and the share of the main emitters would dwindle from 80 to 16 percent (see hypothetical values in table 1).

A smaller fringe group or shorter period would have much less drastic effects, but even if we started with a coalition representing 80 percent of emissions (a broad and ambitious coalition that would be difficult to assemble), developments in the fringe group would be apparent within a decade or two.[4]

TABLE 1. Hypothetical Emissions

	Today	2050
Main emitters	80	40
Fringe group	20	205
Total	100	245

Long-Run Consequences

Let us also briefly deal with the temporal dimension. Anthropogenic emissions are now of such a scale that they have a very big effect on natural processes that have periodicity of tens of thousands of years. Scandinavia was covered by a few kilometers of ice during the last ice age, and land is still rising faster than the sea level in this part of the world, owing to the "rebound effect." (The weight of the ice masses had compressed the land, and it is bouncing back.) By human standards, this movement is so slow that the word "bouncing" seems strange, but it gives some feeling for the time dimension involved. Another example involves the residence time of gases in the atmosphere, which varies in complex ways depending on the gases, their concentration, and other factors. In the case of carbon dioxide, a significant percentage (roughly a quarter) remains for many centuries. The warming also takes many years (decades and centuries) to reach equilibrium, largely owing to the thermal inertia of the oceans. In the historic record for the past half-million years, the carbon content of the atmosphere has oscillated very slowly between 200 and 280 parts per million (ppm). Such a cycle—between two ice periods—would take roughly 100,000 years. Now we are emitting carbon at such a rate that it adds 2 ppm per year (and accelerating), meaning that the corresponding change in carbon concentration takes only a few decades.

Changes in the composition of the atmosphere are causing an increase in the average temperature on Earth, although the processes are delayed and gradual.[5] This increase will have ecosystem effects as local weather, climate zones, wind and rainfall patterns—and thus agro-economic zones—transition.

We are holding the World Bank ABCDE conference in Stockholm. A generation ago, people skied here in the winter. Now, electricity for the snow cannons is the biggest cost for ski resorts, and they even make artificial snow in Piteå on the Arctic Circle. Snow cover is receding toward the poles and mountains, and the Arctic will soon be ice-free in summer.[6] The change is more visible in the far north because temperature variations are magnified there and because, with even a temperature rise of 2 degrees Celsius, ice and snow are replaced by bare ground. However, very dramatic effects are expected in many places on Earth. Some areas that are already hot and arid (for instance, in Africa) may suffer only moderate increases in temperature or decreases in rainfall, but they are already so close to the threshold for what is bearable for humans or feasible for agriculture that the effects may be catastrophic.

In the major flood plains, such as those in Asia, enormous civilizations exist on giant rivers, such as the Ganges and the Brahmaputra. These population centers rely on predictable water flow, but water flow in these rivers is partly regulated by glaciers that are now fast receding. Irregular water flow implies longer periods of drought and increased severity of floods, both of which can be lethal threats in densely farmed areas. Likewise, sea level rise and increased storm damage can hit large, heavily populated areas such as Bangladesh and Bengal in India.

We expect the most dramatic human welfare costs to occur in developing countries, because the people in these countries have less access to skills, resources, and technology for self-protection. To give just one example, climate and other changes have combined to cause dramatic northward migration of ticks that carry Lyme disease and other infections. This situation would be serious but manageable in a country with public health care and good vaccinations. The effect would be much worse in a low-income country.

It should be clear that we must measure the scale of these effects not in years or decades but in centuries and millennia. Even a human generation is short by comparison. This is significant when we turn, as we must, to the issue of intertemporal welfare comparisons. The bottom line for a proactive climate policy is the idea that our generation should make some sacrifices for the benefit of future generations. In this perspective, we need to ask ourselves not only what we wish to do for our children but, more poignantly, for our great-great-grandchildren. The distance in time reduces personal contact and emotional engagement. The issues are also blurred by the limits to our understanding and imagination concerning future technologies and needs, and what will ultimately be perceived as costs and benefits in the future.

In the *Stern Review* (Stern 2006), the biggest source of uncertainty about the "cost" of climate change was the discount rate. We do not know future growth rates or the future distribution of income. We have difficulty valuing the welfare effects today of changes in income that will occur in the distant future. Stern uses a discount rate of 1.4 percent per year, which has been criticized as too low. If we are valuing a cost 200 years away, the difference between using 1.4 percent and 3 percent per year is the difference between 1 billion and 23 billion. Three percent (and even much higher) is definitely a more common discount rate, as in the construction of power plants or roads, but these are not calculations for which we regularly consider many centuries. Some have argued that certain considerations favor low discount factors. One such consideration is that the composition of the economy must change. Growth is the force that underlies discounting. If we have growth for hundreds of years, we will become so much richer that it is hard to conceive and, indeed, misleading, because the growth would have to be accompanied by huge structural changes. Three percent growth for 200 years implies that we would become 370 times richer, but it cannot be that we would use 370 times more steel or meat, and we certainly cannot permit 370 times the emissions of climate gases. Thus, relative prices must change to modify the sectoral composition of the economy. This is akin to using a lower discount rate in the slow-growth sector (Hoel and Sterner 2007, Sterner and Persson 2008).

Cost Efficiency in Climate Policy: The Need for a Unique Price of Carbon

An effective climate policy will be expensive. This does not mean it will be prohibitively expensive or that we should not undertake this cost. On the contrary, the argument is that damages from climate change are likely to be much more costly than abatement and that it therefore makes sense to invest in avoiding them.[7] Those who oppose mitigation sometimes paint a bleak picture, in which people in developed countries are deprived of modern comforts and developing countries are deprived of their prospects for economic growth if we tax fossil fuels. This is wildly exaggerated. The integrated assessment models used to illustrate the costs and benefits typically assume not only continued welfare but continued growth in welfare, even under stringent climate abatement policies. A typical integrated assessment model might conclude that the world economy would grow by 2.9 percent with abatement compared with 3 percent in a hypothetical "business as usual" scenario that neglects climate damages. Although this comparison is grossly inappropriate, precisely because the damages are unaccounted, it is worth noting that even then, world income is assumed to increase. However, instead of taking, say, 100 years for income to increase tenfold, it would take 102 years (Azar and Schneider 2002). Still, we agree that the costs involved are sizable and thus efficiency in climate policy design itself is an important goal.

One of the basic rules of instrument design is that efficiency requires the use of market-based instruments (MBIs) that will ultimately give a simple, single price signal for all countries and sectors (Tirole 2009). This is particularly true if the costs of abatement are heterogeneous. In this case, the cost of abatement, for instance, in avoided deforestation in one country may be very different from the cost of abatement in the forestry or transport or industrial sectors of another country. If there is such a difference, the use of MBIs can save a large share of the total costs by allowing for flexibility in deciding where abatement will be undertaken. The more pronounced the heterogeneity of the costs, the bigger the savings in using MBIs and thus the more important is the predominance of a single carbon price throughout the world (Sterner 2003). The most significant emission reductions may come from technologies yet to be developed. Another very important property of a clear price signal is that it will help incentivize research and development into new technologies, which is fundamental for dynamic efficiency.

It is important to ascertain how heterogeneous abatement costs are. In the meantime, it is reasonable to assume they are quite heterogeneous, because emissions emanate from a wide variety of processes, economic sectors, techniques, and countries. Notice that the broader the definition of the instruments used, the better. If all gases, sectors, and countries are included and if both avoided emissions and captured and stored gases are allowed, a larger number of potential abatement solutions compete. The bottom line is, as usual, that the cheapest solutions are implemented first and costs are saved by avoiding unnecessarily expensive abatement options. Unfortunately, counterarguments can be made against integrating all sectors in one policy instrument. Different rice cultivation methods, for instance, cause widely varying methane emissions. Modifying rice cultivation is probably a cheap way to reduce radiative forcing. However, the uncertainties involved and the degree of complication in monitoring and verification probably make it impractical to include this at present in a carbon trading scheme.

This leads to the next major concern, which is fairness. Suppose it were more "efficient" in the sense just described (lower costs per ton of carbon avoided) to close down the production of bricks somewhere in a small town in Africa or India than to persuade a rich person to drive his SUV less. This example may sound exotic, but it captures the very essence of the issue. We need to ask ourselves whether such an exchange can ever be fair or ethically justified. A simple first answer is that it could be fair and ethically acceptable if it happens through a voluntary exchange in which the users or producers of the bricks are more than sufficiently compensated by the SUV driver. The beauty of MBIs is that, in principle, they can achieve such exchanges efficiently and fairly, with limited transaction costs. However, this would require one policy instrument or scheme broad enough to encompass both the brickmaker and the SUV driver. Designing this type of instrument raises tricky issues about the allocation of rights and about fairness, to which we turn in the next section.[8]

A Fair Share

There is general recognition that a climate treaty must have broad coverage. This does not necessarily imply that each country must be represented in a UN-style negotiation, given the extreme variation in country size. It does imply that we must pull in larger countries, even in the developing world, which requires deep consideration of fairness and equity issues (Aldy and Stavins 2010). Those who take a particular interest in the welfare of the poor should see the opportunity in these facts. Low-income countries that aspire to catch up economically with the rest of the world are understandably apprehensive about emission ceilings. They see them as potential impediments on the road to progress.

Given the historical weight of colonialism, as well as the more recent history of broken commitments by the wealthy countries (for instance, to reach certain percentages in development cooperation assistance), it is natural for developing countries to be wary. Specifically in the climate area, it is also clear that an overwhelmingly large share of historically accumulated emissions come from the countries that are now rich. It is these accumulated emissions that have put us in the predicament we are in. They will cause enormous costs to a number of developing countries. In fact, this effect may already have started: Climate change is a likely factor in regional droughts and desertification, although we cannot yet prove that with certainty, particularly for any given incidence of drought. Still, one can make a strong argument that the rich countries should be prepared to pay some form of indemnity or help pay for adaptation. And responsibility does not end there. Except in a very small number of nations, emissions are still rising. In spite of all the discussions since 1992, the rich world not only continues to emit greenhouse gases, but emits more of them.

Developing countries are wise to be wary. They are confronted with a new and complicated set of issues in which the rich countries appear to be in a considerable hurry to coerce them into binding agreements that might limit their future prosperity. Naturally, they hesitate. A good rule for difficult negotiations is to show that you have all the time in the world and are not interested in a quick deal. Pure arithmetic also implies that risks are greater for fast-growing low-income countries than for slow-growing rich ones.

Even if it were possible to predict whether a country's economy would grow and by how much, it would still be risky to commit to a given emission reduction or emission level, because the commitment implies a cost of unknown size and, therefore, an unknown risk. However, if you do not know whether your economy will grow zero percent or 1 percent, 3 percent, or 10–12 percent, the uncertainty is much greater. The difference over a 50-year period between 2.5 percent and 1 percent growth is a factor of 2. Between 5 percent and 10 percent, the difference is *10-fold* in gross domestic product—and with constant energy intensities, that means 10 times the energy demand. On top of all this, low-income countries are probably less able to adapt, because they lack the technology and infrastructure flexibility to allow for the kind of rapid adaptation to new relative prices.

A worldwide agreement for emission reductions would essentially be the same thing as an agreement on emissions. Considering that emission reductions will be expensive, these emissions will be very valuable, and we will need to develop an allocation mechanism. A number of such principles are possible and have been proposed, but I will limit the discussion here to two: *grandfathering* and *equal per capita allocation*. These mechanisms appear to best exemplify the conflict of interest between rich and poor countries.

Grandfathering

Grandfathering, as applied to greenhouse gas emissions, means that future emission allowances for any agent should be a proportion of past emissions. This approach heavily favors countries with historically high emissions and penalizes low-emitting countries. The United States emits five to six tons of greenhouse gases per capita. Western European countries typically emit a couple of tons per capita (measured as tons of the element carbon per year), while poor countries, such as India and most countries in Africa, emit only a few hundred kilos. When we speak of grandfathered *rights,* we also use the term *prior appropriation*. Perhaps the best-known historical application of prior appropriation is in the water use laws in the western United States, where usage rights and priorities are granted on the basis of when a person first put the water to beneficial use. Under this system, "once a priority user, always a priority user," often to the detriment of those downstream. The most common form of prior appropriation in the climate debate is equal percentage reductions (EPRs). In fact, this is the foundation for much of the Kyoto Protocol and even for more recent climate negotiations. On the surface, EPR might seem to be a fair and "natural" principle in the same sense as a flat tax rate. If we examine it, however, we find significant inequities in this approach.

Under EPR, those who emit more do, in fact, have to abate more (in tons), but they also get to use more of the resource. If a rich country today uses 10 times as much carbon as a poor country and both are forced to reduce by x percent, the inequity will be exactly conserved. The rich country will always get 10 times more of the resource than the poor country will get. The Kyoto Protocol was essentially the result of negotiations that took grandfathering—and EPRs in particular—as their starting point. In reality, the reductions were not equal, but the inequalities did nothing to even out carbon intensities—on the contrary. Australia, with high emission intensity, was allowed an increase of 8 percent, while Canada and Japan were required to reduce by 6 percent, and the United States would have reduced by 7 percent and Europe by 8 percent.[9] The European Union got the biggest reductions, not because it had high emission intensity but simply because the EU was keen on pushing through the deal. Developing and intermediate countries were exempted from numerical emission targets as a result of their appeal to a concept of fairness based on equity. Although I sympathize with the position of the developing countries, I prefer to argue for a (very) high allocation than for these countries, having no ceiling at all. It is unacceptable, as a matter of principle in the long run, for them to have no ceiling at all since they then have no incentives to conserve.

Equal Per Capita Allocation

Countries that see grandfathering as an unfair principle often appeal to one of several other principles. These may include such factors as *endowment* and *need*. Countries that happen to have large hydropower resources or gas resources will find it easier to emit less CO_2 than those whose only endowment is coal. Those with a very cold climate may argue that they need energy for heating. We will not delve too much into this line of reasoning, partly because it quickly becomes overly complex. For now, it is enough to say that if we accept the argument that cold weather warrants high energy use and carbon emissions, similar arguments can be made for countries that are so hot they need air conditioning or countries that happen to have bauxite mines and aluminum industries.

A more tractable and common principle is that of equal per capita allocation. In its simplest form, this means that each person in a jurisdiction receives one equal unit of benefit. "One person, one vote" is an excellent illustration of this concept; it is an idea that underlies many democratic principles. The one child per couple policy in China is another example of equal per capita allocation. Perhaps the best illustration for our purposes is the way oil revenues are allocated in Alaska. Twenty-five percent of Alaskan state oil revenues are paid into a fund, and the dividends are distributed on an equal per capita basis to all state residents. The remaining 75 percent of the funds are used to finance the state budget. Obviously, these funds also benefit the citizens of Alaska, although in ways that are less direct and apparent. I use the Alaska example because Alaskan oil was found fairly recently, and this approach might serve as a model for how to distribute an unexpected windfall profit. Specifically because of its democratic nature, however, this approach appeals much more to poor countries than to rich ones.

Comparing Allocation Mechanisms

Both grandfathering and per capita allocation have logical and intellectual appeal. Both are ubiquitous and can—and will—be defended passionately in a very wide variety of countries and socioeconomic or political contexts. Proponents of grandfathering may say it has the appeal of having already been tested in important permit trading schemes (such as sulfur trading in the United States), and, of course, it was a key component of the Kyoto Protocol. It seemed to be taken for granted as countries compared their percentage reduction offers in the run-up to Copenhagen. On the other hand, equal per capita allocation also has a considerable pedigree.

In our context, grandfathering benefits countries with large emissions or fossil fuel use and equal per capita allocation benefits low-income countries that use little fossil fuel. Table 2 shows the percentage share of global carbon emissions from fossil fuel and population for a number of countries. I have not grouped the countries by any conventional categories but rather for the purpose of this discussion.

The United States has 20 percent of world emissions but less than 5 percent of world population. Fossil-based carbon emissions per capita are 5.2 tons of carbon (tC/cap), four times higher than in China (1.3 tC/cap) and roughly twice as high as in Germany, the United Kingdom, or Japan (2.6, 2.7, and 2.8, respectively). If emission allowances were allocated by grandfathering, the United States would receive 20 percent of the global total; on a per capita basis, it would receive only 5 percent. We can also consider the domestic consequences in the United States if the whole world were to reduce emissions by 50 percent. With grandfathering, the U.S. allocation would be reduced by 50 percent, whereas with equal per capita allocation, its share would be reduced by almost 90 percent.

Any efficient and rational scheme would allow trading, so actual emissions do not necessarily need to be reduced so much—we are speaking here of allocations. The point is that the allocations would generate very substantial flows of revenue. The consequences for India would be generally the opposite of those for the United States. With a per capita allocation, India would get a share equal to its population share (17 percent); with grandfathering, it would receive only 5 percent. If the whole world reduced emissions by half, the Indian allocation would still increase

TABLE 2. Shares in Global Emissions of CO$_2$ and World Population for Some Countries

Country	% emissions	% population
China	22	20
USA	20	5
EU	14	7
India	5	17
Japan	4	2
Other major[a]	9	6
Former Soviet Union[b]	9	4
Oil exporters[c]	11	10
Other countries	7	30

Source: Carbon Dioxide Information Analysis Center of the U.S. Department of Energy.

Note: CO$_2$ emissions from the burning of fossil fuel only. Numbers do not total 100 due to rounding.

a. Canada; South Africa; Korea, Rep.; Australia, Brazil.

b. Russian Federation, Ukraine, Kazakhstan, Uzbekistan, Belarus, Turkmenistan, Azerbaijan, Tajikistan, Kyrgyzstan, Armenia,
Georgia, Moldova, Mongolia.

c. OPEC, Mexico, Malasia, Oman, Trinidad and Tobago, Yemen, Brunei.

significantly if allocations were based on per capita equity. Just for India, the difference between grandfathering and per capita allocation would be 12 percentage points. If we considered one day limiting fossil carbon emissions to 4 billion metric tons (Gt) globally, the difference would be 0.5 Gt of carbon. This is almost 2 Gt of CO_2, and if the price of CO_2 were US\$50–\$100 per ton, it would be US\$100–US\$200 million per year.

Enclosure is a term used when a natural resource that is held in common or by no one is turned into private or state property. The term was coined in England, where common property or unclaimed land was literally open, and hedges surrounded private property. Hedges are cheap and self-perpetuating fences, and they characterize the British countryside, so one often has the feeling of driving through a green corridor. The 17th and 18th centuries were heavily marked by struggles originating in the enclosure of the commons. In the United States, the great move west was similarly one giant creation of personal property. The atmosphere is perhaps the biggest enclosure ever. In fact, it requires a huge stretch of the imagination to use the word "enclosure" for the atmosphere, because, of course, we cannot enclose it in a physical sense. However, what truly matters is not the physical but the legal and ethical. Enclosure has come to be synonymous with the creation or appropriation of property or property rights, often, but not necessarily, by private interests. Using the word helps us see the historic dimensions and analogies in terms of increased efficiency but concomitant equity problems. If emissions were limited to something like 15 Gt of CO_2 per year, and each ton had a shadow value of US\$100, the annual rental value would be over a thousand billion US\$. Naturally, it matters to India whether it receives 5 percent or 17 percent of such property. The values are bigger than anything that is likely to be paid as a result of climate negotiations.

If we view the opportunity of using the atmosphere to dispose of carbon dioxide and other climate gases as a natural resource, this resource becomes very valuable and will probably be regulated someday. Its value is so large that it will presumably take decades to agree on how to apportion rights to it. We can look to the partial enclosure of ocean resources as an illustration. The League of Nations first called for this in 1930 but could reach no agreement. In 1945, the United States unilaterally appropriated its continental shelf, and other countries soon followed suit. Formal negotiations took place in the United Nations between 1973 and 1982, finally resulting in the treaty known as the Law of the Sea, which entered into force in 1994, 64 years after the effort began. If it takes 30 years to negotiate the enclosure of the atmosphere, we could have a viable, all-inclusive, and binding agreement by the mid-2020s. This may be an optimistic scenario, but it gives a perspective on the current negotiations, to which we will return later.

Dealing with Countries That Do Not (Currently) Want a Climate Deal

In spite of the somewhat sobering time perspective and the large resource rents at stake, a case can be made for cautious optimism. This issue is clearly not as easy as the phase-out of ozone-depleting substances in the Montreal Protocol, which concerned a rather small number of countries and producers, and minor rents. Indeed, it may be much bigger and more complicated than the enclosure of the seas. Still, it need not be as complicated as global nuclear disarmament, the land conflicts of the Middle East, or the rights of immigrants from low-income countries in rich countries such as the United States and the European Union. Seen in the context of long-run economic growth, the costs are, though large, quite manageable.[10]

We have entered a phase in which powerful countries are struggling to avoid carrying an unduly large share of the total burden. This struggle could continue for another decade and has the potential to get acrimonious, but many of the major economic powers have made serious efforts in the climate area and significant pledges in the Copenhagen Accord, even with limited incentives to do so. These countries include China, India, the European Union, the United States, Japan, Canada, Australia, New Zealand, and some regional powers such as South Africa, the Republic of Korea, and Brazil. They may ultimately want to commit to some form of climate policy, particularly if stronger evidence emerges that the climate is changing. However, we can expect a tough battle concerning the fairness of shares. Both Kyoto and the Copenhagen Accord are part of this historic bargaining process.

These countries are a manageably small group of 11 major players (counting the European Union as one) that together account for just short of 75 percent of current global emissions. We are still very far from any agreement among them, but to avoid surprises as the negotiations progress, consider what would happen if only these countries agreed. Unfortunately, it is likely that the oil-exporting countries at least would represent a serious policy challenge. Climate policy would cause major economic loss in these countries. The costs would depend somewhat on the type of policy, but a tax in the consuming countries would significantly cut the large oil rents that have provided the economic backbone of oil-producing countries for decades. It is not difficult to imagine scenarios in which these exporting countries are economically ruined. Something similar might apply to fossil fuel exporters. Because the carbon content of the various fossil fuels varies significantly, correct carbon pricing would hit the exporters of coal, heavy tar sands, oil shale deposits, and the like much harder than it would the owners of conventional oilfields. Gas exporters would actually benefit in comparison.

The OPEC (Organization of Petroleum Exporting Countries) countries have been skeptical of climate change and tend to believe it is at least exaggerated to enable the OECD (Organisation for Co-operation and Development) countries to appropriate some of the oil rent. We can see many examples of this attitude in the *OPEC Bulletin* and similar publications. According to *Forbes,* "Saudi King Abdullah, whose country holds the world's largest oil reserves, vowed to continue to provide enough supplies, but called on leading consumer states to cut taxes on petroleum products" (*Forbes* 2005). These countries have argued that they should be compensated for climate policies that might reduce their income.[11] In fact, article 4.8 of the United Nations Framework Convention on Climate Change (UNFCCC) and articles 2.3 and 3.14 of the Kyoto Protocol state that they should be compensated for lost export revenues.

Table 2 includes OPEC and a number of major oil exporters that together account for 11 percent of carbon emissions worldwide and have a combined population of 10 percent. The former Soviet Union group also has vast fossil resources that are exported; they account for another 9 percent of global emissions, with an even lower percentage of global population (4 percent).

I return here to the earlier discussion of the importance of a very high coverage of countries in any global agreement. If the emissions from a group of countries currently represent a 20 percent share and those emissions continue to grow at, say, 5 percent or more, it will create a very serious threat to a climate agreement, even if, say, 70–80 percent of current emissions were covered or even reduced. Wei and colleagues (2010) analyze this situation as a dynamic strategic game; they note this possibility and demonstrate that it would be in the strategic interest of the fossil fuel-exporting countries to subsidize domestic consumption more if the "climate-conscious" importers tax it more.[12] Subsidizing domestic consumption in oil-exporting countries has a series of short-run advantages for the local policy maker. It helps keep up demand and use the production volumes produced; it generates some revenue (though less than international sales); it may attract some energy-intensive industries; and it helps distribute the rent locally (within the oil countries themselves). Finally, it will tend to weaken the effect of the climate tax that is hurting the economy of the exporters.

The domestic market in OPEC countries is already considerable—accounting for around 20 percent of OPEC's oil extraction—and the share is growing (Gately 2007). Net exports of some oil producers, such as Mexico, have fallen drastically because the domestic market grew so fast, largely because of the low domestic price. Virtually all developing-country fossil exporters have very heavily subsidized fuels on their domestic markets.[13]

Some say that a good short-term strategy is to remove irrational subsidies to fossil use. That is no doubt true in principle, but these subsidies are not only protected by strong lobbies, they may even have some rational basis in the struggle over rents between producers and consumers. In view of the large damages faced by many low-income countries with no culpability for the current climate problems, some people may find the notion that producers of oil or other fossil fuels should be compensated for climate policy to be atrocious.[14] However, the right to compensation is mentioned in the Kyoto Protocol and, considering the power the oil countries wield, it might be worth considering smart ways of unlocking collaboration rather than pursuing policies that could evoke stubborn responses such as local subsidies. One direction to explore is to involve oil-producing nations in the development of new solar alternatives. They have energy know-how and infrastructure for storage, handling, and so forth, and might be interested in collaborating on projects such as producing liquid fuels based on solar energy.

Technology Policy

Traditional analysis of climate economics assumes that the main market failure is the existence of external effects (such as carbon emissions) or unmanaged common property resources (in this case, the atmosphere). However, an additional market failure is very important: that of research and development (R&D) and the tenure security of intellectual property. Considering the gravity of climate change, strong incentives are needed for R&D to solve the problem.[15] There are numerous possible solutions, although none is perfect. One possibility is to drastically increase public funding for such R&D. Again, there is a problem of common actions for the countries involved, but an international treaty to stimulate R&D in new, climate-friendly technologies is likely to be much easier to implement than a treaty that aims to reduce fossil fuel use.

A research agreement is, however, far from enough. In the absence of a strong price signal, there is the risk that research will not be targeted to produce practical results for current or expected price levels. For this, we will need technology studies to demonstrate real-world actions that small industries can take to compete and survive. In the case of the energy sector, advantages to scale are very prominent, as are "learning by doing" and technical progress. A combination of these factors can create situations in which the barriers to commercialization are very high. Of course, policies such as feed-in tariffs or subsidies to production can be more effective than research grants. On the other hand, this approach presents a considerable challenge to policy makers, because we know that it is dangerous to pick winners and that subsidies can easily become self-perpetuating. The problems are compounded by the fact that the energy sector is characterized by agents with market power and the power to lobby.

The Copenhagen Accord

International policy making is much like domestic policy making except that an agreement among states, such as a climate treaty, must respect the sovereignty of the nation-states. There are, of course, limits to sovereignty and inequities in power. Smaller nations and nations with few resources can more easily be "persuaded" or coerced, but, on the whole, treaties cannot be designed just to tell countries what to do. They must make it compatible with national interest to join a treaty and comply with its provisions. Barrett (2010) says Kyoto provides insufficient incentives to countries to either participate or comply. Perhaps a more optimistic approach would be to form a portfolio of international treaties that together address various issues related to climate change. Treaties could deal with certain gases, for example, or technology, or adaptation, or international agreements for certain sectors of the economy (Barrett 2010; Stigson 2010).

The Copenhagen Accord appears to have suffered particularly from the high expectations that preceded it—a number of politicians and negotiators used the term "disappointment." However, it was neither a dramatic failure nor a great success but just another step on the rather long and arduous road. In interpreting the situation, it helps to keep in perspective the unusual characteristics that apply to climate change. Enclosure of the global atmosphere is a complicated process involving directly asymmetric costs and benefits to many generations of countries that are worlds apart in their economic and political conditions. The stakes are high, the uncertainties are many, and the number of conflicting perspectives concerning what would be fair and what actually needs to be done is daunting. Negotiations will take many years, not months, so it was utterly unrealistic to hope for a finished, binding agreement in Copenhagen.

Before we get to a binding agreement (if we ever do), we can expect many rounds of negotiation. Before we can negotiate any specific provisions or criteria, we will first have to hammer out the baselines and principles for the negotiations. In this light, the Copenhagen Accord is perhaps not so bad.[16] Some see it as a good starting point, although others are frustrated and note that the negotiations did not start in 2009 but in the 1990s. Kyoto was supposed to be the starting point, and some nations were aspiring for a second, more ambitious step now. Instead, we again have an agreement based on voluntary participation, and we all know that voluntary mechanisms are not ideal ways to provide public goods. A decisive element that would have been desirable was the notion of making the deal "binding" and the reductions of each country contingent on participation and ambitious reductions by other countries. This is the characteristic of the public good. Why make a big pledge of X if you can get away with a small pledge of x? The only reason would be if your own big and costly contribution were matched by equally big contributions from the other participants, so that the overall, collectively produced public good (in this case, climate stability) would be sufficiently large. Before Copenhagen, the European Union promised 20 percent if other countries did nothing and 30 percent if other countries were ambitious, but this seems to be the only example of this kind of contingent strategy. Had world political leaders been driven by a desire for maximum collective reductions in greenhouse gases, we would surely have seen more of such tactical bids.

On the other hand, the Copenhagen Accord is more ambitious in one truly decisive aspect: It undertakes to include at least the inner circle of major emitters, including not just the European Union, Japan, and other Kyoto members but also the United States, China, and India. This means that the parties to the Copenhagen Accord are so much more diverse in emission intensity and economic welfare that allocation and fairness become an order of magnitude more complex than in Kyoto. Maybe this was one of the reasons we did not get binding numerical targets.

By April 13, the Copenhagen Accord had been signed by 76 countries representing over 80 percent of world emissions. These pledges can be broadly classified into three categories: (1) reductions compared with 1990 (including, as for the United States, reductions compared with 2005 or base years that can easily be translated into reductions compared with 1990); (2) pledges to limit increases in carbon emissions below a certain figure; and (3) reductions in emission intensity. The first category includes the United States, the European Union, Japan, the Russian Federation, Australia, Ukraine, and some smaller countries, mainly formerly Soviet countries. Table 3 shows only countries with an emission share of more than 1 percent of the world total. These countries are, on the whole, slow-growing rich countries. The table also includes former Soviet countries that lost such a large share of industry after 1990 that they have an expected surplus of rights, even with big reductions.

TABLE 3. Copenhagen Accord Pledges: Reductions, Ceilings on Increase, and Reduced Intensities

Country	Share of world's total GHGs[a] (%)	CO_2 G tons per capita	Reduction by 2020 compared with 1990 (%)	Limited increase by 2020 compared with 1990 (%)	Reduction by 2020 in intensity (%)
China	16.64	4.7		40 to 45	
United States	15.78	19.0	4		
European Union	11.69	10.0	20 to 30		
Brazil	6.60	15.3		Increase <2 to 6	
Indonesia	4.73	9.3		Increase <22	
Russian Fed.	4.64	14.0	15 to 25		
India	4.32	1.7			20 to 25
Japan	3.14	10.6	25		
Canada	1.86	24.9		Increase <2,5	
Mexico	1.58	6.6		Increase <20	
Korea, Rep.	1.30	11.8		Increase <64	
Australia	1.30	27.4	−4 to 24		
Ukraine	1.14	10.5	20		
South Africa	0.98	9.0		Increase <48	

Source: Carbon Dioxide Information Analysis Center (CDIAC) of the U.S. Department of Energy.

Note: GHG = greenhouse gas.

a. CO_2 emissions from the burning of fossil fuel only.

The second category of countries includes fast-growing middle-income countries such as Brazil, Mexico, Korea, South Africa, and Indonesia. Their pledges range from a few percent for Brazil to 64 percent for Korea. Finally, we have India and China, which have the highest and perhaps most uncertain growth rates and which have chosen to formulate their pledges in terms of emission intensities. On the one hand, this approach alleviates the uncertainty for the country of unknown but potentially high growth rates; on the other hand, it makes it possible for a country to be seen as collaborative, while enabling it to defend its perceived right to a higher allocation per capita in the long run. Finally, many countries have made no numerical pledge at all or have not even joined. This includes most significant OPEC countries and most low-income developing countries.

It is impossible to state that a certain emission target for a group of countries for the year 2020 is or is not compatible with any particular long-term climate goal, say, for the year 2100. The ultimate concentrations and temperature response will depend not only on the inherently uncertain climate sensitivity parameters but also on what paths are followed after the year 2020. Chalmers provides an interactive online climate calculator (www.chalmers.se/ee/ccc2) the reader can use to test how various emission pathways for Annex 1 and non-Annex 1 countries will affect atmospheric concentration and temperature. If we assume that the first reductions are the most difficult because they imply a break with a trend, even small reductions now are a major achievement and will be followed by bigger reductions later. In that case, the accord's pledges could be seen as promising. On the other hand, if we assume (as we usually do) that marginal abatement costs are rising, the first reductions are the cheap and easy ones. From that perspective, the pledges do not look very impressive. Many observers take this approach and consider that we are far from being on a path to limit temperature rise to 2 degrees (Levin and Bradley 2010; Rogelj et al. 2010; Stigson 2010; UNEP 2010), despite the fact that this goal is mentioned or "reaffirmed" in the text of the accord. Rogelj and colleagues call the pledges "paltry" and say they may even lock the world into paths leading to more than 3 degrees of warming. They note that a 2 degree limit with the Copenhagen Accord as a starting point would require very dramatic cuts between 2020 and 2050, and they lament the fact that ambitious goals for 2050 were dropped from the accord at the very last moment. One might doubt the operative importance of goals for 2050, but just as temperature goals are important, visions of how to reach them are crucial. The advantage of discussing a vision for 2050 was also that fairness issues would seem more tractable in the long run (Guesnerie and Sterner 2009).

If the Copenhagen Accord was, indeed, a failure, there are many reasons for it and much blame. Some blame the UN procedure for being slow and bureaucratic; some countries and even individuals have been given a large share of the blame. We will not pursue this tack, although these factors were no doubt present and important. Rather, we will look at the broad perspective: Serious abatement works most effectively when property rights are fully allocated; that is, when an economic incentive exists for each agent who will otherwise pay the full cost of emissions. The details of that allocation are so valuable that the fight will continue for some time. Optimistically, we might envision successive waves of more and more serious abatement between 2020 and 2060, and a historical view of the years from 2000 to 2025 as a period when the world took stock of the issue and the options, and when property rights were defined, either through negotiation or conflict.

It is interesting to look at the structure of the Copenhagen Accord from the viewpoint of a strategic game. We do not normally expect the voluntary provision of public goods to give good results. Why would the pledges of individual countries— each on its own—contribute very much to a global public good? Why not a free ride? In this light, one would expect countries to volunteer almost nothing. In fact, the incentives might be worse than that because of the way people think about grandfathering. We could reason as follows:

- If the United States got away with not ratifying the Kyoto Protocol and now has 2005 as a baseline when the European Union and the other Kyoto countries have 1990 as their baseline; and
- if the pledges now are voluntary but will become almost mandatory around 2020 or 2025; then
- why make an ambitious pledge now? For 2012–2020, why not make a really loose pledge to get a good baseline for, say, 2025–2035?

There are definite signs that this has occurred. Rogelj and colleagues (2010) note that the Chinese target of reducing emission intensity by 40–45 percent is considered less ambitious by far than China's actual five-year plans and current investment plans for the energy sector. China's carbon emissions grew by 3 percent per year between 1990 and 2001; the growth rate then jumped to 13 percent per year between 2001 and 2006. It is complicated to judge Chinese emissions, and observers have cited poor accounting as an obstacle to trading. However, a good time to conduct a very detailed inventory of carbon emissions is just before you enter into negotiations with a counterpart that believes strongly in grandfathering.

It is cheap, however, to be overly critical of the Copenhagen Accord on this point. The slow, bureaucratic UN process was not delivering a binding accord. There is a definite need for a global agreement that includes many diverse countries and begins to deal with issues such as monitoring, reporting, and verification. Baselines must be established somehow, and there might be an incentive to underreport. Possibly this is counteracted by the strategic use of grandfathering, which creates an incentive to exaggerate emissions. We need to balance incentive compatibility and fairness issues. There are few alternatives that are not subject to the kind of strategic bias mentioned above. In Copenhagen, it could perhaps be claimed that the strategic incentive for free riding was somewhat balanced by some feeling of honor and some element of prestige for countries that took on serious commitments.

Domestic opinion is also very important, and we have been studying opinions in China, the United States, and Sweden in a unique survey (Carlsson et al. 2010). We find that a large majority in all three countries believe that the mean global temperature has increased over the past 100 years and that humans are responsible for the increase. (A somewhat smaller share of Americans believe these statements compared with Chinese and Swedes.) When we measure willingness to pay as a share of household income, it is the same for the Americans and Chinese but higher for the Swedes.

Green Growth

We are in a special period in history. The enclosure of the atmosphere is such a large creation of property and such a shift in developmental paradigm that it will take time to accomplish. One main obstacle is agreeing how to share costs. To overcome that obstacle, we must address certain dilemmas that affect the range of available policy options. Only when we have solved these issues can an international agreement be put in place.

- We are in a considerable hurry to start reducing emissions, but a global treaty implies large transfers of wealth and complex fairness issues that will take a long time to resolve, and their size hinges partly on the availability of new technologies.
- A global treaty would be easier to achieve if a sufficient number of clean technologies were available. However, there is no strong incentive to develop such

technologies before we have affirmed property rights or put a price signal in place, as would be the case under a binding global treaty.

- To demonstrate that reductions are possible, someone must go first. However, with the prevalence of grandfathering, proactive behavior not only goes unrewarded, it may actually be punished.

We need to discuss alternative paths. We need a policy that will make it easier to fulfill future national goals for any given country and that makes a global agreement more likely. This is where green growth comes in. Green growth is attractive to some businesses, to some trade unions, to some researchers, and to some environmentalists. Politically, people seem to accept stimuli for green cars and green fuels more easily than they accept higher fuel taxes, although the latter are likely to be considerably more efficient in reducing carbon emissions. Developing countries are attracted by the idea of green growth, particularly in the past few years—it fits nicely into the rather dismal state of the business cycle, after the demise of several banks and the near-demise of entire countries, such as Iceland and Greece. The strong threat of a slowdown in global growth makes the lure of green growth all the more attractive. The question is, what makes this a sustainable strategy?

Many environmentalists who believe costs for abatement are small compared with potential damages have been severely frustrated by the difficulty of reaching agreements. Some of them suggest we abandon the whole discourse on burden sharing and instead frame the issue positively and optimistically as "competing to be first into the solar age."

Even prominent heads of state have been enthused. In November 2008, UN Secretary General Ban Ki-moon, together with President Susilo Bambang Yudhoyono of Indonesia and prime ministers Donald F. Tusk of Poland and Fogh Rasmussen of Denmark, wrote an article for the *International Herald Tribune* entitled "Crisis Is Opportunity." They argue as follows:

> We do not need to await the arrival of new technologies, nor need we worry excessively about the costs of taking action. Studies show that the United States could cut carbon emissions significantly at low or near-zero cost, using existing know-how. For evidence, consider how Denmark has invested heavily in green growth. Since 1980, GDP increased 78 percent with only minimal increases in energy consumption. For businesses, such savings translate into profits. Poland has cut emissions by a third over the past 17 years, even as its economy boomed. Today, for example, European companies in the green tech sector enjoy substantial "first mover" advantages, accounting for one third of the world's burgeoning market in environmental technologies.

> With the right policies and financial incentives—within a global framework—we can steer economic growth in a low-carbon direction. With the right policies and the right incentives, we can be sure that developed and developing countries alike contribute to the cause of fighting global warming, each in their own way and without compromising every nation's right to development and the economic well-being of its citizens.

They go on to say that most forward-looking CEOs know this and, therefore, demand clear and consistent policies on climate change. Turning to the business sector, one of the most influential organizations is the World Business Council on

Sustainable Development (WBCSD). The title of its latest annual report is *The Green Race Is On*. The president's message begins this way:

> We hoped the December climate talks in Copenhagen would deliver a clear new framework to manage climate change. [They] did not. But, the year did deliver a new sense of the reality and urgency of the energy and climate agenda. *Business leaders realized that they must help lead society toward solutions, stepping into political and diplomatic arenas previously alien to them . . . .* At the same time, the Council's own Vision 2050 Project began to document the spectacular breadth of business opportunity inherent in pathways toward sustainability.

The message is that the Green Race is on among countries to transform to low-carbon economies and to become the leading suppliers of resource-efficient technologies and solutions. The countries that want to win must transform their home markets to build competencies and scale and thereby gain comparative advantage. The report conveys a sense of urgency and the risk of missing vital opportunities. Japan is portrayed as a leader in energy-efficient solutions because it correctly understood the opportunity provided by the energy crises of the 1970s. The European Union is considered the leader today, with a market share of 40 percent in green technologies and plans for a 300 percent increase in R&D for green technologies. Even so, there is concern that the European Union is not building its domestic green market fast enough. The Obama administration is portrayed as mobilizing U.S. innovation capacity to make the country a world leader in green technologies. Jeffrey Immelt, CEO of General Electric, is quoted as saying, "Let's not take this growth industry and give it to every other country in the world but the U.S." (*Scientific American*, March 3, 2010[17]). The WBCSD, however, considers that China may emerge as the winner because it has focused its next five-year plan very strategically toward these goals. And India is portrayed as a key supplier of low-cost solutions in response to domestic demand from its large and poor population.

The United Nations Environmental Programme (UNEP) has launched the Green Economy Initiative, which provides advisory services to help governments and corporations.[18] It recommends stimulus to green industries, such as renewable energy, improved and ecologically sustainable housing, and transport solutions.

These developments are encouraging and tempting for environmentalists and politicians alike, but we wonder whether this growth will be green enough. And, specifically, what policies make growth sustainable? A simple answer is that the increase in efficiency—in the use of ecologically sensitive inputs or waste products—must be more rapid than the increase in output. More miles driven by more cars can be sustainable only if the average emissions per mile go down faster than the miles go up.

This can be illustrated with the transport sector, which has many hundreds of studies on vehicle fuel demand (Dahl and Sterner 1991a, 1991b; Goodwin, Dargay and Hanly 2004; Graham and Gleister 2002, 2004; Hanly, Dargay, and Goodwin 2002). To simplify, we can say that the fuel demand function is surprisingly constant and can be approximated by the function:

$$G = Y^a P^b$$

Fuel demand has an income elasticity of *a,* which is roughly equal to unity, and a price elasticity of *b,* which roughly equals –0.7. This means that a 10 percent increase in income will inspire consumers, if they have the liberty afforded by democracy and market economics to choose to increase their spending on fuel by around 10 percent. In rapidly growing middle-income countries, the elasticity is sometimes above 1.0. The price elasticity is usually around –0.7, but this is a long-run equilibrium value. It does *not* mean that consumption will drop like a stone by 7 percent if the price goes up by 10 percent. Instead, it means that after a full set of adaptations has taken place, in the long run, the fuel demand will be 7 percent lower than it would have been otherwise. In the short-run perspective of a year, the fuel demand will only drop by maybe 1 or 2 percent, and even this will not be visible if there is, say, a 5 percent growth rate. The observer will simply see an increase of 4 percent, which for the econometrician comes "instead of" the expected 5 percent.

Now we are equipped to answer the grand question of how we can make growth sustainable. Suppose we want to reduce emissions of carbon dioxide by 2 percent at the same time we increase income by 4 percent per year. To do that, we would need tougher policies to compensate for the effects of growth. With constant taxes, even if they are high, emissions from the transport sector will increase 4 percent per annum. To combine growth in income and a fall in emissions, we need to have the price rise by 9 percent per year. This is a very strong policy instrument—it means prices double every eight years. Eventually, prices become so high that the elasticities are unlikely to be constant over such a broad range of data. One may eventually find that all kinds of alternatives are profitable, such as public transport and solar-powered cars. But that is the purpose of the exercise and, in principle, the elasticities sum up all these reactions.

For other sectors—such as residential and commercial buildings, industry, and so forth—similar mechanisms are at play, but the elasticities will be different; in some cases it may be more difficult to replace fossil fuels, in which case elasticities will be lower. Other sectors may experience rapid energy-saving technical progress or ready substitutes, so that elasticities are higher. They are not very likely to be much higher than –0.7, so overall fossil prices would need to rise by at least 10 percent per year to make economic growth of 4 percent feasible. The mechanism we have discussed here is the demand-side mechanism. Eventually, energy prices will be so high that fossil-free alternatives can compete and the price of energy does not need to rise.

Higher fuel prices are not very popular and tend to be attacked with whatever argument is at hand. It is sometimes said that higher fuel prices are inflationary. For an importing country, a price shock in imported fuel will have at least some temporary inflationary effect. However, an environmental tax reform in which fuel is taxed higher while some other factor is taxed less should not be inflationary. Budget deficits are also inflationary; if a fuel tax were to be used to eliminate a budget deficit, that would not have to be inflationary either.

Another often used argument is that fuel taxes hurt the poor. Some recent research on this subject suggests that in the very richest countries there could be a slight regressivity of the fuel tax itself, although the overall regressivity of a tax reform depends on how the revenue is used. It is possible to make an increased fuel tax reform very progressive. Most important, it is found that fuel taxes themselves are quite progressive in low-income countries (Sterner 2011).

Fuel taxes are only one example, albeit an important one. The real cost of the most efficient policy instrument—higher fuel taxes—is very limited. However, fuel taxes are not popular and are perceived as costly or difficult. Maybe if politicians were somehow obliged to raise fuel taxes (e.g., through an international agreement), people would eventually discover that the costs are not really so high. Ironically, other instruments—such as banning cars over a certain age or mandating new green cars that run on alternative fuels—are sometimes perceived as easier to implement. Again, there are political economy reasons for this; for instance, the car industry may be very positive about this type of instrument. One still needs to be a little wary in the balance between these instruments, because the green car type of policy is much more expensive in relation to gains in abatement, at least in the short run. If we want a growing economy that is truly green, we must encourage truly green technologies.

Discussion

It is clear that the costs of abatement are sufficiently high that we need to think of efficiency, and this implies both a unique price of carbon and a global agreement with close to total participation. Global participation requires dealing with ethical issues of fairness and distribution. These arguments can be used by those who are skeptical about climate action. They point to the difficulty of negotiating a big global deal. It is particularly hard if no positive and functioning examples of abatement or low-carbon growth exist. So we risk being caught in a Catch-22 dilemma: no local action before a global deal and no global deal because it is too complicated and there are no examples to follow. A unique price of carbon and a global agreement that is fair and efficient are clearly difficult to attain in the short run.

It is important to understand that this is a very long-run process and that different arguments apply to different stages in that process. Climate change will dominate discourse throughout this century. In the year 2040, we may be discussing how to deal with the next step because the actions after 2030 were not sufficient. We are still at the beginning, and many of the issues we are discussing are just first steps. The importance of cost-efficiency, a global treaty, and a unique price of carbon are topics for the later stages in climate negotiations, when we face the most difficult and expensive reductions in carbon intensity.

Costs are big, but not so big that we should do nothing. The costs of inaction in the form of damages are likely to be much bigger. Through successful policy, the costs would actually never be visible, because most of the "costs" are, in fact, minute modifications to long-run growth rates. Green tax reform does imply some loss in consumer surplus, but this is hardly noticeable to the individual—the main problems are political acceptability and the damage that can be done by lobbyists. Most of the costs of abatement will come later. In the immediate future, marginal costs of abatement will be low, hence the argument that we need global coordination. A unique global price of carbon is not quite so important in the first years. During this period, we should not judge abatement actions primarily by whether they are cost-efficient but by whether they lead the overall process of bargaining and negotiation forward. A good example is demonstrations of new technology that are likely to be copied or that can be used to argue for the feasibility of more stringent targets.

Even though the costs are small compared with the potential damage—and very small compared with the expected growth in the economy—they are sizable enough to require attention to cost-efficiency, particularly in the future, when the tougher reductions are undertaken. It will take time before we have a unique price of carbon in the world, because it is tied in with the difficult questions of who appropriates the rent and how the burdens are split. In the meantime, we must live with an array of prices or shadow prices and gradually work toward unifying them as property rights become defined. We must still reduce emissions, both to reduce pressure on the atmosphere and—perhaps most important—to learn. Today we are taking the first steps, such as experiments with green cars in the European Union and the United States, and clean development mechanism projects. Critics call these actions "symbolic." They are symbolic, but they are also learning experiences. Green growth is no panacea. It will require policy instruments, and in the long run it will not replace international treaties. But it is a start, and perhaps it can help facilitate those treaties by providing good examples of new technology.

Notes

1. See, for instance, http://www.guardian.co.uk/commentisfree/cif-green/2009/nov/28/africa-climate-change or http://www.bloomberg.com/apps/news?pid=newsarchive&sid=agSY4t VL.oOw. Similar views are expressed by Blaise Compaoré of Burkina Faso, http://www .afrik.com/article17747.html. For additional quotes from heads of state, see http://www .unep.org/climateneutral/Resources/Quotes/tabid/362/Default.aspx, http://allafrica.com/ stories/201009201379.html, http://www.ethjournal.com/index.php?option=com_content& view=article&id=2155:ethiopia-pushes-for-more-financing-to-mitigate-and-adopt-climate-change&catid=13:headlines&Itemid=19,Brazil, http://beta.worldbank.org/news/ low-carbon-growth-brazil, and http://www.hindustantimes.com/Copenhagen-accord-not-legally-binding-Basic-countries/Article1-501441.aspx.

2. Nuclear energy is essentially carbon free but presents some special problems, especially in an era of terrorism.

3. I use "taxed" for simplicity, but the effect would be the same with any other regulations, such as permits that raise the effective cost of using fossil fuel.

4. If the United States, China, the European Union, India, Japan, and other major countries representing up to 80 percent of emissions agreed, they could begin to exercise very strong formal and informal pressure on other countries.

5. The increasing carbon content will also have other effects; for example, increased acidification of the oceans will have important biological effects, such as changes in an organism's ability to grow a shell using calcium.

6. Ironically, this will probably lead to a new wave of oil drilling there, as if we had not learned anything.

7. Uncertainty regarding costs complicates the matter. There is, for instance, a low but still positive probability of truly catastrophic damage. Assuming some form of aversion to risk (and maybe to ambiguity), we are not only willing to pay to avoid the expected damages but also willing to pay a form of insurance premium to avoid even a small risk of very large damages.

8. Note that this initial allocation of rights is intended to make an instrument politically fair and acceptable. It should not influence where abatement is carried out; that should be decided by a comparison of marginal abatement costs.

9. The EU's internal burden-sharing agreement was more radical in its departure from pure grandfathering, because the EU total of minus 8 percent still allowed some countries—such as Portugal, Greece, and Spain—very substantial increases (27, 25, and 15 percent, respectively), while other countries took correspondingly larger cuts (Denmark and Germany each had cuts of 21 percent). This burden-sharing agreement was heavily influenced by such unique factors as German reunification and other internal EU politics.

10. According to the *Stern Review* (2006), the costs are on the order of 1 percent of GDP. In the context of decades of growth at a few percent per year, this is quite small.

11. See, for instance, http://findarticles.com/p/articles/mi_qn4182/is_20000920/ai_n10140573. Obviously, not all oil countries agree.

12. See Liski and Tahvonen (2004) for a similar analysis. Persson and colleagues (2007) offer an alternative view in which oil producers end up gaining from carbon taxation because the differences in carbon content of coal and oil imply that carbon taxation hurts coal much more than oil. See also Larsen and Shah (1992) for real data on fuel subsidies.

13. In December 2007, when international bulk prices for gasoline in Rotterdam were 105 U.S. cents per gallon, the retail consumer prices in some oil-producing countries were as follows: Iran 18.4; Libya, 19.8; Kuwait 41.9; Qatar 32.8; and Saudi Arabia 22.2.

14. In reality, the relations between oil producers and consumers are much more complicated. The former are cartels, as, to some extent, are the companies that produce and sell oil. They depend heavily on savings and military alliances with the United States, and their reaction to taxation is very complex. For example, their demand will shrink in response to falling oil prices, and this would counteract the effect they have by subsidizing domestic consumption.

15. An attribute of this problem is that potential solutions can be as different as carbon capture and storage, CCS, fusion, hybrid rice, the social engineering needed to make domestic fuel taxation politically acceptable, or the fertilization of the seas with iron shavings.

16. An experienced senior negotiator, Ambassador Bo Kjellén, commented that people tend to exaggerate. When negotiations appear to be going well, victory is proclaimed, but—as he pointed out—the results are often not quite as good as claimed. Often, victory has been achieved at the expense of hiding away some troubling details, which tend to come back and haunt implementation in future rounds of negotiation. On the other hand, when negotiations are said to have collapsed, it is also the case that much can be salvaged and the situation may not be as bad as it seems.

17. http://www.scientificamerican.com/article.cfm?id=arpa-e-keep-us-lead-in-clean-energy-revolution.

18. http://www.unep.org/greeneconomy.

References

Aldy, J. E., and R. N. Stavins, eds. 2010. *Post-Kyoto International Climate Policy: Implementing Architectures for Agreement*. Cambridge, MA: Cambridge University Press.

Azar, C., and S. Schneider. 2002. "Are the Economic Costs of Stabilising the Atmosphere Prohibitive?" *Ecological Economics* 42: 73–80.

Barrett, S. 2010. "A Portfolio System of Climate Treaties." In *Post-Kyoto International Climate Policy: Implementing Architectures for Agreement,* ed. J. E. Aldy and R. N. Stavins, 240–270. Cambridge, MA: Cambridge University Press.

Carlsson, F., M. Kataria, A. Krupnick, E. Lampi, Å. Löfgren, P. Qin, S. Chung, and T. Sterner. 2010. "Paying for Mitigation: A Multi-Country Study." Working Paper, Swopec WP number 447, University of Gothenburg.

Dahl, C., and T. Sterner. 1991a. "Analysing Gasoline Demand Elasticities: A Survey." *Energy Economics* 13: 203–10.

———. 1991b. "A Survey of Econometric Gasoline Demand Elasticities." *International Journal of Energy System* 11: 53–76.

Forbes. 2005. "OPEC Tells European Countries to Cut Oil Taxes." November 20. http://www .forbes.com/markets/feeds/afx/2005/11/20/afx2347009.html, accessed June 1, 2010.

Gately, Dermot. 2007. "What Oil Export Levels Should We Expect from OPEC?" *The Energy Journal* 28 (2): 151–73.

Goodwin, P., J. Dargay, and M. Hanly. 2004. "Elasticities of Road Traffic and Fuel Consumption with Respect to Price and Income: A Review." *Transport Reviews* 24 (3): 275–292.

Graham, D., and S. Glaister. 2002. "The Demand for Automobile Fuel: A Survey of Elasticities." *Journal of Transport Economics and Policy* 36: 1–26.

———. 2004. "Road Traffic Demand: A Review." *Transport Review* 24: 261–74.

Guesnerie, R., and T. Sterner. 2009. "Big Advantage of Discussing 2050." *Financial Times,* November 9. http://www.ft.com/cms/s/0/3bcad73e-cccd-11de-8e30-00144feabdc0.html.

Hanly, M., J. Dargay, and P. Goodwin. 2002. *Review of Income and Price Elasticities in the Demand for Road Traffic.* London: Department for Transport.

Hoel, M., and T. Sterner. 2007. "Discounting and Relative Prices." *Climatic Change* 84: 265–80.

IPCC. 2007. *Climate Change 2007: The Physical Science Basis,* ed. S. Solomon, D. Qin, M. Manning, Z. Chen, M. Marquis, K. B. Averyt, M. Tignor, and H. L. Miller. Contribution of Working Group I to the Fourth Assessment Report of the Intergovernmental Panel on Climate Change. Cambridge, U.K., and New York, NY: Cambridge University Press.

Larsen, B., and A. Shah. 1992. *World Fossil Fuel Subsidies and Global Carbon Emissions.* Policy Research Working Paper 1002. Washington, DC: World Bank.

Levin, K., and R. Bradley. 2010. "Comparability of Annex I Emission Reduction Pledges." http://www.wri.org/publication/comparability-of-annexi-emission-reduction-pledges.

Liski, M., and O. Tahvonen. 2004. "Can Carbon Tax Eat OPEC's Oil Rent?" *Journal of Environmental Economics and Management* 47 (1): 1–12.

Millennium Ecosystem Assessment. 2005. *Ecosystems and Human Well-Being: Synthesis.* Washington, DC: Island Press.

Persson, T. A., C. Azar, K. Lindgren, and D. J. A. Johansson. 2007. "Major Oil Exporters May Profit Rather Than Lose in a Carbon Constrained World." *Energy Policy* 35: 6346–53.

Rogelj, J., J. Nabel, C. Chen. W. Hare, K. Markmann, M. Meinshausen, M. Schaeffer, K. Macey, and N. Höhne. 2010. "Copenhagen Accord Pledges Are Paltry." *Nature.* http://www.nature.com/nature/journal/v464/n7292/full/4641126a.html.

Stern, N. H. 2006. *The Economics of Climate Change.* http://www.hmtreasury.gov.uk/independent_reviews/stern_review_economics_climate_change/stern_review_report.cfm.

Sterner, T. 2003. *Policy Instruments for Environmental and Natural Resource Management.* Washington, DC: RFF Press in collaboration with the World Bank and Sida.

Sterner, T., and U. M. Persson. 2008. *An Even Sterner Review: Introducing Relative Prices into the Discounting Debate.* Discussion Paper 07-37. Washington, DC: Resources for the Future.

———. 2011. *Fuel Taxes and the Poor: The Distributional Consequences of Gasoline Taxation and Their Consequences for Climate Policy.* Forthcoming from RFF Press.

Stigson, B. 2010. "The World in Transition Towards Sustainability—The Role of Business." Inauguration lecture, University of Gothenburg, May 4, 2010 (and personal communication).

Tyrole, J. 2009. *Politique Climatique: Une Nouvelle Architecture Internationa.* Paris: La Documentation Francaise.

UNEP. 2010. *How Close Are We to the Two Degree Limit?* Information note to the UNEP Governing Council/Global Ministerial Environment Forum.

Wei, J., M. Hennlock, D. Johansson, and T. Sterner. 2010. *The Fossil Endgame: Strategic Oil Price Discrimination and Carbon Taxation.* Working Paper. Washington, DC: Resources for the Future.

World Bank. 2010. *World Development Report 2010: Development and Climate Change.* Washington, DC: World Bank.

The World Business Council for Sustainable Development. 2009. *The Green Race Is On.* Annual Review for 2009. http://www.wbcsd.org/Plugins/DocSearch/details.asp?DocTypeId=25&ObjectId=MzgwNTc.

World Economic Crises: Commodity Prices and Environmental Scarcity as Missing Links

RAMÓN LÓPEZ

Two new structural factors affected the emergence and unusual depth of the financial crisis and world recession of 2008–09: (1) the emergence of highly populated countries—most prominently China and India, awakening from centuries of economic lethargy—as engines of world growth and massive providers of industrial goods; and (2) the increasing scarcity of certain natural resources that, for the first time in history, is beginning to be reckoned with in rich and poor countries. These structural changes have significantly tightened the links between world growth and commodity prices—growth has become more commodity-intensive, and the world commodity supply curve is becoming less elastic.

In this paper I focus on the likely effect of the financial crisis on the commodity supply flexibility in the developing world, the main provider of such goods. The impact of the world economic crisis is likely to exacerbate environmental scarcities in the developing world and may force further tightening of environmental policies over the long run in response to such degradation. This, in turn, may make the commodity supply curve even steeper in the future, thus reinforcing the sensitivity of commodity prices to world economic growth.

Given the great heterogeneity of developing countries in many respects, the effects of the crisis are likely to vary dramatically across countries and across different types of environmental resources. Naturally it is impossible to capture in one initial review even a small fraction of the variety of potential effects of the crisis on developing countries. This paper uses a taxonomical approach based on a number of key distinguishing conditions—policies, natural resources, and other country characteristics—that suggest potentially testable hypotheses about the direction and likely gravity of

Ramón López is Professor in the Agricultural and Resource Economics Department at the University of Maryland at College Park. Research assistance was provided by Asif Islam, a graduate student at the University of Maryland at College Park. Useful comments on an earlier version of this paper were made by Jon Strand and Michael Toman. Stefan Csordas provided some useful input. Partial funding was provided by the World Bank's research support budget. Responsibility for the content is the author's alone.

Annual World Bank Conference on Development Economics 2011, Global

the environmental effects of the crisis under a limited number of possible situations. Because it is too early to have empirical evidence about the impact of the most recent crisis, we refer to two previous crisis episodes—the 1995 Mexican peso crisis and the 1997–99 Asian crisis—as empirical references. I focus mainly on the potential effects on pollution, deforestation, and the extraction of natural resources, especially in fragile environments.

New Economic Order and the Great Recession

I first provide a retrospective analysis of the changing nature of the interdependences between rich ("the North") and poor countries ("the South") and then show how resource and environmental scarcity is a natural outcome of the patterns of growth arising from such interdependences.

Economic Growth in the North

For much of the 20th century, persistent economic growth was the privilege of an exclusive club comprising no more than a fifth of the world population, the currently rich countries or the North. As the North grew richer, it experienced continuous structural change, leading to an increasing "dematerialization" of its production (López and Stocking 2009). The structure of gross domestic product (GDP) in the North became increasingly focused on services and, in general, on activities that depend on human capital and technology, while the resource-based and most manufacturing sectors gradually shrank as a share of total output. Figures 1 and 1A show the intensity of this process over the past half-century in the United States as reflected by the persistent decline of the shares of commodity and manufacturing output in total GDP. Production of manufacturing, agriculture, forestry, fishing, and mining have dramatically reduced their combined participation in GDP from more than 40 percent in the early 1950s to less than 20 percent in the early 2000s, while the share of nonmaterial output (i.e., services) has increased from 50 percent to more than 70 percent over the same period.

Figure 1 illustrates the great contrast between the sharp dematerialization of production and the increasing materialization of consumption as shown by the continuous reduction of the share of services in household expenditures. In fact, the share of services in total consumer expenditures declined from about 30 percent to 25 percent over the past three decades. While some shifting in the structure of consumer demand away from certain commodities (such as food products) into services did take place, American consumers continued to expand their demands for industrial goods, especially durables, at a pace that often exceeded the growth of per capita income.

The slow but persistent increase of the share of material-based consumption in the advanced countries is dramatically illustrated and in part explained by the evolution of certain important material components of consumption, including average per capita house size and number of vehicles, as well as by the generation of household

FIGURE 1.
Services As Percentage of U.S. GDP and Average Share of Household Expenditures on Services

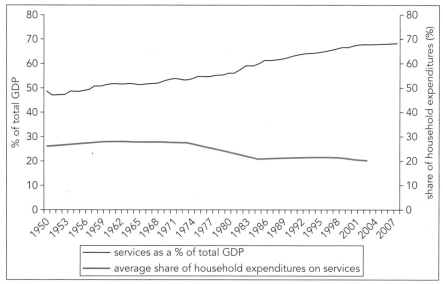

Sources: Data on GDP shares from the U.S. Bureau of Economic Analysis; data on household expenditure shares from the U.S. Bureau of Labor Statistics Report 2006.

Note: Service expenditures are considered expenditures on apparel services, health care, entertainment, personal care, reading and education, religion and charity, and miscellaneous. Production of services consists of utilities; wholesale trade; retail trade; transportation and warehousing; information; finance, insurance, real estate, rental, and leasing; professional and business services; educational services; health care and social assistance; arts, entertainment, recreation, accommodation, and food services; and other services, except government.

waste over time in the United States. As Figure 1B shows, over the past half-century, the average house size more than tripled, from 290 square feet per capita in the 1950s to almost 1,000 square feet in the early 2000s; the number of passenger vehicles increased from 3.2 to almost 8.5 vehicles for every 10 persons over the same period, while the average daily volume of municipal waste generation increased from 2.6 to 4.5 pounds per person. These statistics are highly indicative of the heavy biases of consumption toward material goods over what could be regarded as less tangible and less material-intensive forms of consumption, such as culture, education, leisure, and other services.

The sharp divergence between structural change in domestic production and in consumption has meant that the North has become increasingly reliant on the rest of the world (the South) as a supplier of primary commodities and, especially over the past three decades, of manufacturing goods as well (Ghertner and Fripp 2007). In fact, an examination of the evolution of trade flows clearly shows a rapid increase of net imports of primary products and industrial goods over time, which is consistent with the fact that consumption became ever-more reliant on material goods at the same time as production became increasingly less material. Figures 2 and 3 illustrate

FIGURE 1A.
Sector Composition of U.S. GDP

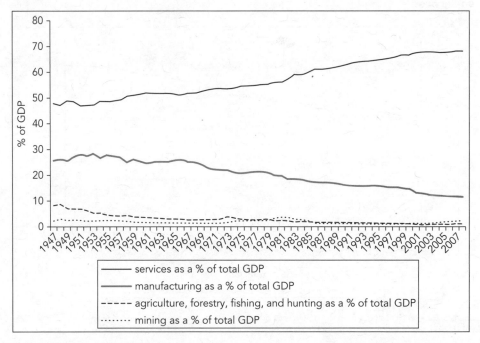

Source: U.S. Bureau of Economic Analysis.

this for the United States. Figure 2 shows the significant rise in imports of industrial goods in total U.S. imports. Figure 3 shows the large increases in the imports of manufacturing and industrial goods as a proportion of U.S. output. This is also true for most other commodities, including metals (Figure 3A). As these figures show, the increase in imports of industrial and commodity goods has been particularly steep over the past two decades.

Has the North Become Cleaner?

The large and increasing gap between the ever-more material-intensive consumption and decreasing material content of production has meant that the advanced countries have not become environmentally cleaner but simply better at dumping their pollution into the rest of the world. Nothing illustrates this phenomenon better than an analysis of the embodied pollutant emissions of international trade. A recent study by Weber and Matthews (2007) estimated the net pollutant balance of U.S. international trade for three major pollutants—sulfur dioxide (SO_2), nitrogen dioxide (NO_x), and carbon dioxide (CO_2)—over the period 1997 to 2004. The findings are startling: While the export content of the three pollutants remained practically constant over the period, the import content of all three increased dramatically. The SO_2 net import content doubled in just seven years between 1997 and 2004; NO_x increased by about 120

FIGURE 1B.
Evolution of Selected Material Components of U.S. Household Consumption and Consumer Waste Generation

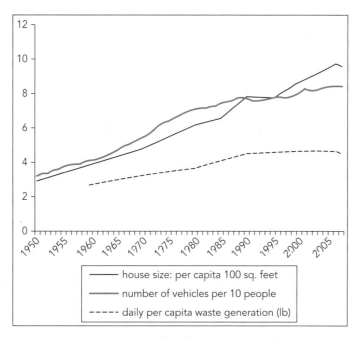

Sources: For house size: median and average square feet of floor area in new one-family houses completed by location (medians and averages computed from unrounded figures) and U.S. Census Bureau, Current Population Reports. From *Statistical Abstract of the United States* 2008; http://www.soflo.fau.edu/report/NAHBhousingfactsMarch 2006.pdf; http://www.nahb.org/fileUpload_details.aspx?contentID=80051.

For number of vehicles: U.S. Department of Energy, Fact #577: June 29, 2009, changes in vehicles per capita around the world.

For daily per capita waste generation: U.S. Environmental Protection Agency, *Municipal Solid Waste Generation, Recycling, and Disposal in the United States: Facts and Figures for 2008*

percent and the net import content of CO_2 more than doubled over the same period, from 600 to 1,300 million tons. In other words, the net trade balance of pollutants doubled or more than doubled for all gases in just seven years.

These increases are massive relative to total world emissions. For example, the CO_2 net trade increases of 700 million tons represented about 2.5 percent of total annual world emissions in 2007. The study also shows that most of the imbalance that emerges mainly from the large asymmetry between progressively less material-intensive production and more material-intensive consumption in the United States is increasingly supplied by China, Mexico, India, and other developing countries. That is, the United States is not becoming cleaner; it is becoming more effective in dumping pollution elsewhere, especially in the developing countries.

This massive dumping of pollution into the rest of the world through trade is true not only for the United States. A study by Helm, Smale, and Phillips (2007) provides data for the greenhouse gases (GHGs) associated with imports and exports of the United Kingdom over the 1992–2006 period. The authors show a pattern of

FIGURE 2.
Share of Industrial Imports over Total Imports in the United States

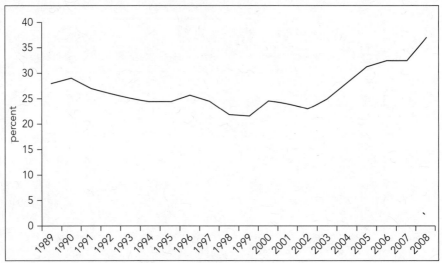

Source: U.S. Bureau of Economic Analysis.

Note: Categories include fuel and lubricants, paper and paper-based stocks, materials associated with nondurables, selected building materials, unfinished and finished metals associated with durables, and nonmetals associated with durables.

FIGURE 3.
Industrial and Manufacturing Imports over GDP in the United States

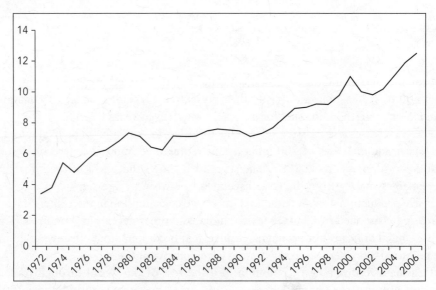

Source: Feenstra, Romalis, and Schott 2001, http://www.internationaldata.org.

Note: Categories include mineral fuels, lubricants and related materials, chemicals and related products, manufactured goods, machinery and transport equipment, and other miscellaneous manufactured articles.

FIGURE 3A.
Metal Imports As a Proportion of U.S. Domestic Production

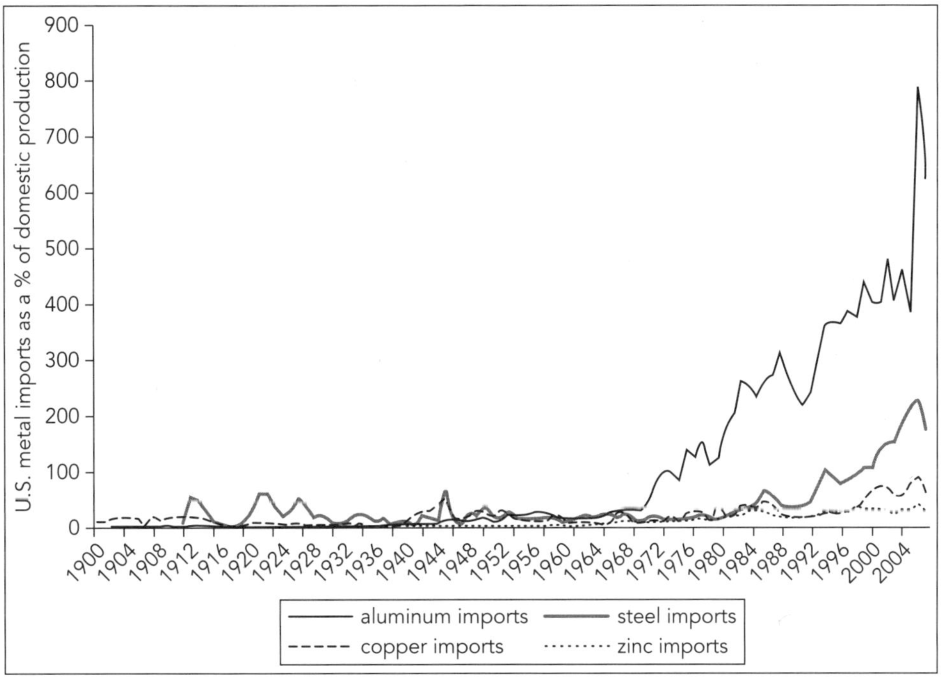

Source: U.S. Geological Survey.

trade balance emissions similar to that of the United States. While the GHG content of U.K. exports increased moderately—from about 150 million tons of CO_2-equivalent emissions per annum in the early 1990s to about 260 million tons per year in 2006 the GHG content of U.K. imports more than tripled over the same period, from 300 to 950 million tons of CO_2-equivalent emissions. So the trade gap of CO_2 emissions increased from 150 to 700 million tons per annum over the period or almost 400 percent (figure 4). As with the United States, the additional net demand for CO_2 emissions is mostly supplied by China, India, and a few other developing countries.

The importance of international trade of emissions is obvious if one compares territorial emissions with total residents' emissions, the latter measuring both territorial and foreign emissions necessary to meet the net import demand from the United Kingdom. Figure 4A shows that the U.K. residents increased world GHG emissions over the period 1992–2003 because the increases of their net imports of carbon more than offset the reduction of territorial emissions. If one considered only territorial emissions, one would conclude that the United Kingdom has decreased its carbon emissions by 15 percent; but this conclusion is reversed if we consider all emissions

FIGURE 4.
Greenhouse Gases Associated with U.K. Imports and Exports, 1992–2006

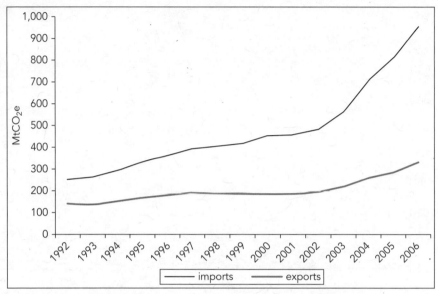

Source: Helm, Smale, and Phillips 2007.

FIGURE 4A.
Greenhouse Gas Emissions on a Consumption Basis for the United Kingdom, 1990–2003

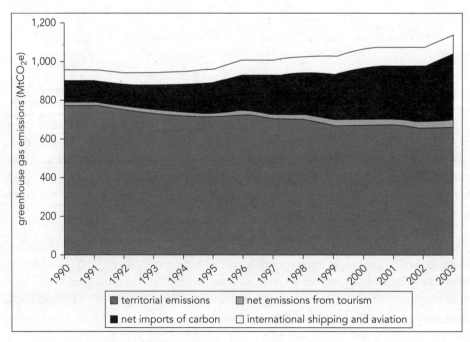

Source: Helm, Smale, and Phillips 2007.

caused by residents. Including the world emissions generated by U.K. residents through net imports, the country increased carbon emissions by almost 20 percent over the two decades.[1]

Economic Growth in the South

While the South was at times able to exhibit some modest growth, until the past three or four decades, most of these countries could not sustain such growth for prolonged periods and thus became mainly passive suppliers of primary commodities to the North. As the North increased its net demand for commodities, the South was an effective supplier. The South seemed to have almost boundless natural resources and imposed practically no effective environmental regulations limiting the heavy environmental damages entailed by their exploitation; this, combined with a slow expansion of its own domestic demand for commodities as a consequence of its relative stagnation, enabled the North to enjoy stable and low commodity prices (figure 5).

From colonial times, the North had established efficient commodity-producing enclaves in the South, keeping the markets in the North as their almost exclusive goal (de Janvry 1975). The increasing demand for commodities from the North was matched by the continuous exploration and new Northern investments in the expansion of these enclave economies in the South. In a context of resource abundance and no effective regulations limiting the environmental damages from resource extraction in the South, combined with continuous Northern investments in resource extraction

FIGURE 5.
Real Commodity Price Trends: Producer Price Index, All Commodities

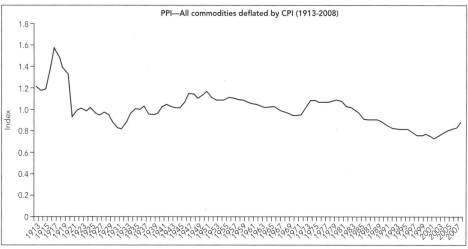

Source: U.S. Bureau of Labor Statistics.

Note: Components of the Producer Price Index (PPI) for all commodities include farm products; processed foods and feeds; textile products and apparel; hides, skins, leather, and related products; fuels and related products and power; chemicals and allied products; rubber and plastic products; lumber and wood products; pulp, paper, and allied products; metals and metal products; machinery and equipment; furniture and household durables; nonmetallic mineral products; transportation equipment; and miscellaneous products.

in the South, the supply curve of commodities was essentially flat for a long time (López and Stocking 2009). That is, the world commodity supply exhibited almost infinite price elasticity. This meant that the North could grow for many decades with the luxury of constant and even at times declining commodity prices, despite the fact that its consumption patterns were heavily dependent on material goods rather than services, which ultimately implied a high if indirect commodity component.

As has been well documented by several studies, the commodity production enclaves established in the South by Northern investments spilled over very little into the rest of the economies in the South, which meant that they played little role in promoting economic growth in the South (de Janvry 1975; Prebisch 1959; Weiskoff and Wolff 1977). The South remained essentially stagnant, thus exerting little pressure on commodity demand, which facilitated the stability of prices. This process continued well into the second half of the 20th century (Acemoglu, Johnson, and Robinson 2001; Khor 2000; Sokoloff and Engerman 2000).

The little giants. Things started to change in the 1970s with the emergence of a few countries in the South, mainly in Southeast Asia, that were able to grow rapidly for prolonged periods by relying on an export-oriented strategy. This was possible because of the increasing net demand for material goods in the advanced countries caused by the patterns of production and consumption prevailing in those economies.

The emergence of these "little giants" of manufacturing exports was both a consequence and a cause of the changes in the structures of production and consumption of the North. The North continued to deepen its relative specialization in clean, nonmaterial outputs, increasingly relying on the old South and on newly industrialized countries (NICs) as steady suppliers of primary commodities and industrial goods, respectively, to satisfy its ever-increasing consumer demand for material goods. While the NICs were able to grow very rapidly through a phenomenal increase in manufacturing exports to the North, their populations were too small to have an effect on the world demand for primary commodities, including energy, metals, and food commodities. Thus, the expansion of the NICs did not mean greater demand pressures on commodity prices, which remained essentially stable (see figure 5).

By the late 1980s, the world had achieved a remarkable equilibrium. The North and a few NICs were able to grow fast—the North on the basis of clean, service-oriented production that greatly facilitated its environmentally "sustainable" development at low cost, and the NICs by supplying the North with an increasing percentage of its growing industrial demands at low market prices, albeit at great domestic environmental costs. Meanwhile, the still languishing old South supplied raw materials, also at low prices but at the cost of a continuous erosion of natural resources and the environment.[2]

The real giants. The 1990s brought even more dramatic change. The emergence of the new industrial giants (NIGs)—China, India, and a few other large, initially poor countries that were able to grow at remarkably fast rates—was in part a consequence of drastic policy reforms in these countries. The new policies included pro-market reforms, privatization of state enterprises, export promotion through exchange rate policies and other incentives, and weak enforcement of environmental regulations, which meant the ability to grow with few environmental constraints. The success of these new policies was ensured by the rapidly growing consumer demands of the North for industrial goods and the slower expansion of its supply of material goods.

The NIGs were as effective as the NICs at supplying industrial goods but on a much greater scale. Like the NICs, they experienced more than two decades of unprecedented economic growth, fueled by industrial exports. Both the NICs and the NIGs based their development on the rapid expansion of industrial exports, made possible by undervalued exchange rates.[3] This, in turn, meant an enormous accumulation of foreign exchange, which was recycled into the North, especially the United States and parts of Europe, creating large current account deficits.[4] The financial resources flowing into the North made possible low interest rates and easy credit. In addition, the flow of capital into the North from both the NIGs and oil exporters contributed to a continuous appreciation of equities and real estate, which prolonged the economic boom and the financial bubble. This, in turn, fed a massive appetite in the North for more industrial imports from the emerging and prosperous NIGs.

Again, a remarkable and seemingly self-sustained equilibrium was created: The NIGs' massive financial assets, created by their industrial export success, fed the Northern boom, which, in turn, fueled the continuous expansion of the NIGs. The real annual GDP growth rates of China and India over the past three decades have been consistently above 8 percent, more than three times the growth rates in the advanced economies (table 1). More important, the NIGs became large contributors to world economic growth, adding an estimated US$350 billion to the annual growth of the world in the early 2000s. That is more than a third of the total annual growth of the world in those years, which is estimated at about $1.1 trillion. Table 2 shows that the participation of China and India, at about $200 billion, constituted almost

TABLE 1. Real GDP Growth Rate (%)

	China and India	Advanced economies	Rest of the world	World
1961–2007	6.8	3.4	2.7	3.4
1961–1990	5.6	4.2	2.7	3.9
1991–2009	8.4	2.5	3.3	2.9
1961–1969	3.9	5.4	5.3	5.3
1970–1979	4.4	4.0	3.1	3.8
1980–1989	8.2	3.3	2.5	3.2
1990–1999	8.9	2.5	2.6	2.8
2000–2007	9.2	2.3	4.4	3.1

Source: World Development Indicators, World Bank. Advanced Economy List: Australia, Austria, Belgium, Canada, Cyprus, Denmark, Finland, France, Germany, Greece, Hong Kong, SAR, China, Iceland, Ireland, Israel, Italy, Japan, Korea, Rep. Netherlands, New Zealand, Norway, Portugal, Singapore, Spain, Sweden, Switzerland, Taiwan, China, United Kingdom, United States.

TABLE 2. Annual Change in World Real GDP (US$ millions as of 2000)

Decade	China and India	Advanced economies	Rest of the world	World
1961–1969	5,154	366,333	120,100	491,587
1970–1979	12,198	514,740	47,150	574,088
1980–1989	36,740	472,160	94,735	603,635
1990–1999	86,310	519,200	116,040	721,550
2000–2007	201,375	618,875	274,525	1,094,775

Source: World Development Indicators, World Bank. Advanced Economy List: Australia, Austria, Belgium, Canada, Cyprus, Denmark, Finland, France, Germany, Greece, Hong Kong, SAR, China, Iceland, Ireland, Israel, Italy, Japan, Korea, Rep. Netherlands, New Zealand, Norway, Portugal, Singapore, Spain, Sweden, Switzerland, Taiwan, China, United Kingdom, United States.

20 percent of total annual growth in the world in the 2000–07 period, compared with only about 5 percent in the 1980s.

Environmental and Commodity Scarcity

The North-NIG boom equilibrium of the 1990s and early 2000s was different in one important way from the North-NIC equilibrium of the previous decades. The NIGs represent almost 50 percent of humanity, compared with the NICs, which represent 5 percent at most. Thus, the emergence of the NIGs brought about a dramatic expansion of the growth club, and a large segment of the South became an important and rapidly growing user of energy and primary commodities. Persistent economic growth was no longer exclusive to a small portion of humankind; for the first time in history, growth is benefiting more than two-thirds of the world population.

The startling and persistent growth of the NIGs brought about not only a drastic increase in the supply of industrial goods but also a dramatic increase in net NIG demands for energy, food, and other raw materials. At first, because the NIGs started from very low levels of consumption, their increased demand for these commodities had little consequence for world markets. However, after a decade or so of 8 percent to 10 percent growth rates, the enormous population size of the NIGs, combined with their rising incomes, caused their demand for commodities to increase to a sizable portion of total world demand. Figures 6 through 8 show the rapid increase in China's and India's level of consumption and their share of total world consumption of energy and certain other commodities over the past two decades. In fact, by 2006 their combined share of the world's total energy consumption had reached almost 20 percent and of agricultural commodities such as wheat, more than 25 percent. Figure 9 shows the increase in their carbon dioxide (CO_2) emissions over the past 25 years, which reached 25 percent of the world's total in 2006.

By the early 2000s, the NIG share of world commodity demand had become sufficiently large that it started having an effect on market prices. Fast NIG growth led to a run-up on commodities, with consequent drastic price increases. Continued

FIGURE 6.
China and India Energy Consumption and Share of World Consumption

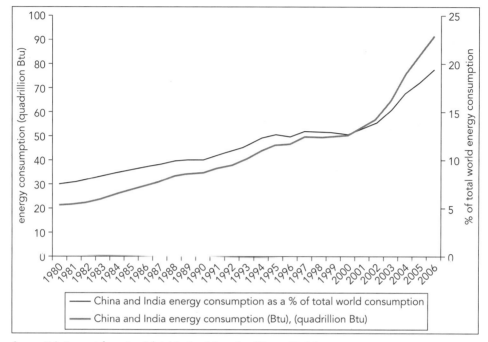

Source: U.S. Energy Information Administration, International Energy Statistics.

FIGURE 7.
China and India Petroleum Consumption and Share of World Consumption

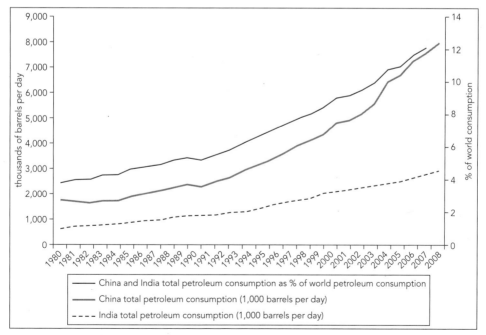

Source: U.S. Energy Information Administration, International Energy Statistics.

FIGURE 8.
China and India Wheat Consumption and Share of World Consumption

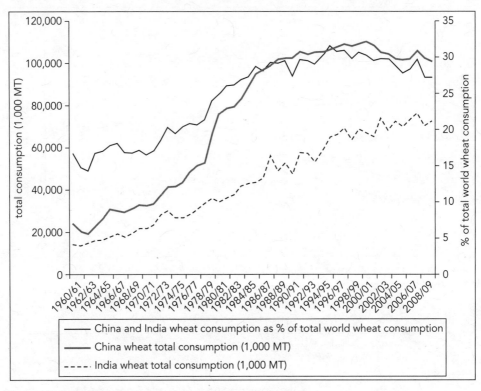

Source: U.S. Department of Agriculture, Foreign Agricultural Service (FAS).

Note: MT = metric tons.

rapid economic growth in the NIGs, triggered by the North's insatiable demand for material goods, helped precipitate the drastic increases in oil and other commodity prices that began in 2002.

Resource Scarcity

The increased connection between commodity demand and economic growth after the incorporation of the NIGs into the growth club has happened at a time when natural resources in the South are becoming less abundant and the severe environmental consequences of the frenetic expansion of natural resource extraction and use are beginning to be taken seriously in the South. Even if the underground availability of many raw materials may still be plentiful, there are growing signs that their supply must rely on increasingly expensive sources. Resource extraction and use have led to massive environmental costs affecting crucial ecosystems, including water quality, forests, and many other at-risk environments.[5]

Under increasing pressure from international nongovernmental organizations and parts of domestic civil society—including organizations in the communities suffering

FIGURE 9.
China and India Carbon Dioxide Emissions

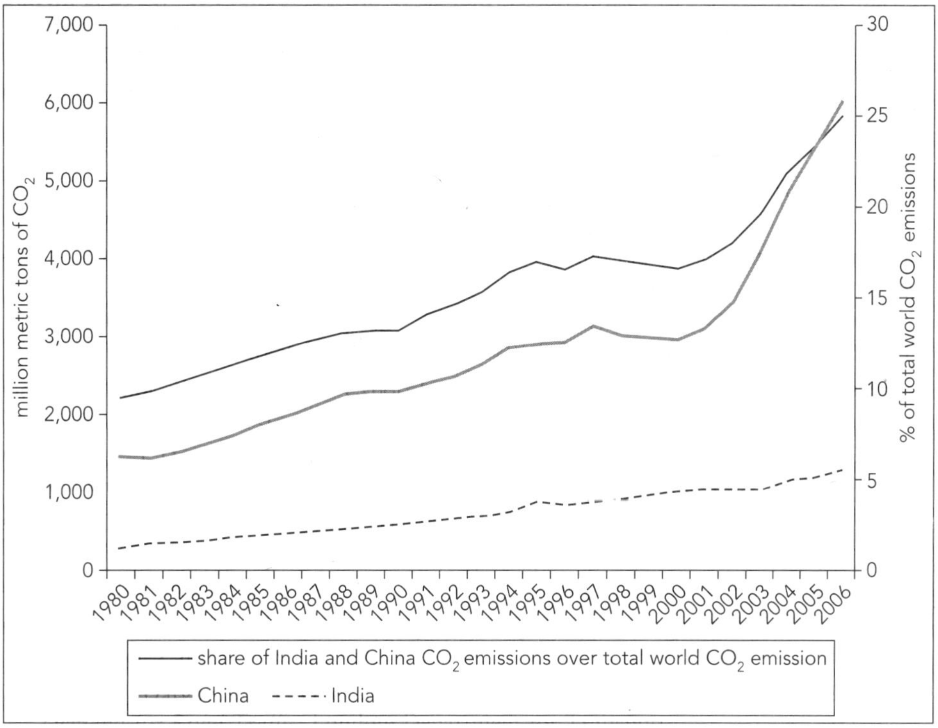

Source: U.S. Energy Information Administration, International Energy Statistics.

the environmental costs of resource extraction—developing-country governments are at last beginning to take some of these costs into consideration. More countries are enforcing at least some modest environmental regulations affecting the use of ecosystems that tend to be destroyed by the spillover effects of resource extraction. These restrictions ultimately make the extraction of commodities more costly, even where the resource is still plentiful.

Thus, perhaps for the first time in modern history, the long-run supply curve of resource commodities has become price-inelastic. This phenomenon, in conjunction with the increased commodity demand associated with world economic growth, explains the unusual response of commodity prices to fast world growth observed throughout the 2000s.

The effect of world economic growth on commodity demand is likely to be associated with the emergence of the NIGs for at least two reasons. First, the volume of new world output produced each year has increased dramatically compared with earlier periods, when growth was mainly restricted to a small portion of the world population. Second, because the NIGs are still much poorer than the advanced economies, their production structures are more material-dependent than those in the advanced countries.[6] They are at an earlier phase of development in which GDP mostly reflects material- and energy-intensive outputs. Thus, the volume of world output growth has become bigger and more commodity- and energy-intensive than in previous decades. The consequence of this has been that the commodity demand curve is shifting upward more rapidly at a time when world commodity supply has become less price-elastic. World economic growth and commodity prices are more intimately related than ever. Below I offer empirical evidence about this new phenomenon that has arisen, especially over the past decade.

The extraordinarily fast growth of the NIGs has been a key factor in making world economic growth much more environmentally demanding. But the expansion of the giants is merely a proximate cause of this increased environmental demand. The reason the NIGs can grow at an almost aberrant speed lies in the equally aberrant expansion of material consumption in the North.

Increasing Links between Growth and Commodity Price

As shown in figure 10, the boom times of the 2002–07 period were associated with very rapid increases in the prices of almost all commodities, including agriculture,

FIGURE 10.
Prices of Primary Commodities in the 21st Century

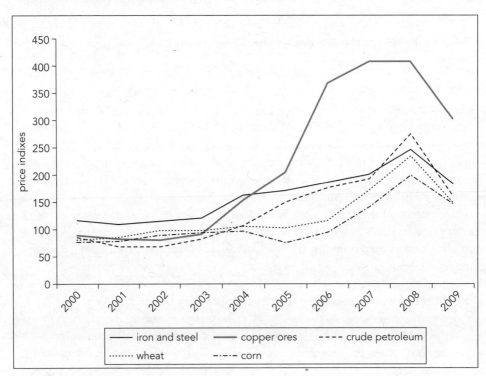

Source: United States Bureau of Labor Statistics.

oil, and minerals. While commodity price upturns of similar magnitudes have taken place in earlier eras, this is probably the first time in recent history that the increases were not associated with exogenous shocks such as war, cartelization, or political conflict. These increases appear to be purely endogenous, associated with the increased demand for commodities caused by fast world growth. This is consistent with the idea that world growth has recently become more dependent on commodities and that the world commodity supply has become less price-elastic.

The high degree of connection between commodity prices and economic growth in recent years is further confirmed by an in-depth look at the growth and commodity price data. Figure 11 shows the quarterly co-evolution of U.S. per capita GDP and world oil prices between the first quarter of 2000 and first quarter of 2010: the real price of oil moves in parallel with the evolution of U.S. per capita GDP. Both measures continuously and rapidly expanded between the last quarter of 2001 and the last quarter of 2007. The economic collapse between the first quarter of 2008 and the first quarter of 2009 was associated with an almost equal collapse of oil prices, and the economic recovery since the second quarter of 2009 has been concomitant with a vigorous recovery of oil prices.[7] The variations in world oil prices have been closely associated with similar trends in practically all other primary commodity prices, and the changes in U.S. GDP are closely correlated with world GDP changes. Thus, we have a dramatic positive correlation between world GDP growth and the prices of most primary commodities over the decade. The estimated correlation coefficient is 0.87 and highly significant; it is the highest of any 10-year period since 1952.

FIGURE 11.
Real Quarterly Oil Prices (Deflated by U.S. CPI) and Real Quarterly U.S. GDP per Capita, 2000–10

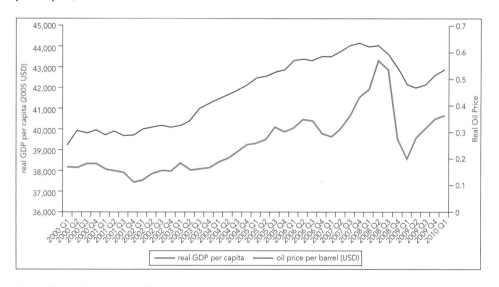

Source: Federal Reserve Bank of St. Louis.

Implications for Sustained Economic Growth

This closed link between economic growth and commodity prices is a new phenomenon that might mark a new structural condition with dramatic implications regarding the capacity of the world to support steady rates of economic growth in the future. Sustaining economic growth with rising commodity prices is difficult for several reasons. The reason I emphasize here is the connection between rising commodity prices and inflation.

Although the inflationary pressures of rising commodity prices may be small, even negligible, in the context of much slack affecting capital utilization (as has been the case in the past few quarters), this ceases to be the case when the slack subsides as economic growth continues. Once capacity utilization rises, the economy becomes increasingly susceptible to cost pressures from rising commodity prices—this occurred in the period from 2003 through 2008 (figure 5A).[8] Increasing cost pressures coming from the commodity component of the consumer price index (CPI)—which has a low direct weight but high indirect weight as a consequence of the dependence of consumer expenditures on material goods—eventually threaten the so-called core inflation targets. At this point, central banks are forced to intervene, leading to tight monetary policies and high interest rates.

In fact, core inflation started to increase by 2005, which eventually prompted the Federal Reserve to tighten monetary policy by raising the effective federal fund rate from 1 percent in early 2004 to more than 5 percent by mid-2007. In economies affected by extremely high levels of both private and public debt (as is the case of most advanced economies), even a modest increase in interest rates is likely to have a dramatic effect on fiscal deficits and household expenditures, which forces a deceleration of economic growth or even negative growth rates.[9] Much has been made of the idea that modern economies are less dependent on energy and other primary commodities than in the past. As a consequence, macroeconomists have been quick to dismiss any significant connection between inflation and commodity prices. However, while commodity prices have a low cost effect on the productive sector of advanced economies because of the increasing dematerialization of GDP, this is not the case for consumption. As noted earlier, consumers in rich countries have not embarked on a dematerializing of their consumption patterns in any significant way. Primary commodities are behind any material goods consumed, which implies that the dependence of consumption expenditures on commodities is still very high once we account for both the direct and indirect effects of commodity prices. This is reflected in consumer price indexes once commodity price changes make their way into the prices of the large material component of the consumer budget.

Can Technical Change Save the Day?

The increasing scarcity of natural resources could be partially offset by the development of resource-saving technologies. New technologies could soften the tight connection between world economic growth and commodity prices. Paradoxically, sustained high and, for a period, increasing energy and other commodity prices are needed as a key incentive for technical change to be oriented toward the generation of such technologies. The low and stable commodity prices prevailing over most of the 20th century directed research and development to produce new technologies that were generally capital- and energy-intensive as well as labor-saving. These new technologies were mostly intensive users of the cheapest factors of production: the environment and natural resources.[10] While some internalization of the true cost of the environment was implemented in the North, environmental compliance costs are extremely low, even in the wealthiest countries, and the low real prices of commodities during the 20th century reduced incentives to produce technologies that were not commodity-intensive.

The connection between commodity prices and the direction of technological change implies a classic coordination problem: Reducing the dependence of economic growth on natural resources and commodities requires high and temporarily increasing commodity prices as a signal to the private sector to invest more in the generation of resource- and environment-saving new technologies. However, increasing commodity prices make the world economies more vulnerable to inflation by causing greater cost pressures that central banks must combat via tighter monetary policies to prevent inflation. To prevent the increasing commodity prices from spilling over into generalized price increases, the monetary authority may face more pressures to raise interest rates in boom periods than when commodity prices were not very responsive to world growth. Interest rates jump when higher commodity prices threaten low inflation targets, and this reduces economic growth. Given the current strong connection between growth and commodity prices, the latter fall quite rapidly when world growth decelerates.

Thus, allowing commodity prices to increase to the extent needed to reduce the long-run dependence of world growth on commodities through the development of new resource-saving technologies would trigger inflation in the context of an accommodative monetary policy. This is unacceptable for the North, so monetary policy is used to counter the threat of inflation.[11] In principle this would not affect the relative price of commodities while arresting inflationary pressures; however, because of the extreme dependence of growth on easy credit, the tightening of money rapidly affects consumption, which in turn leads to slower or even negative growth. This in turn prevents commodity prices from remaining high and cancels the long-run incentives to generate commodity-saving technical change.

The Crisis and the Developing Countries

The impact of the crisis on the developing countries is likely to depend on certain key factors that will determine the intensity of the recession as well as the social and environmental effects. These factors are macroeconomic policies during the boom times before the crisis, the stringency of environmental regulatory regimes, domestic policies in response to the crisis, and country characteristics associated with factor endowments, population density, and poverty levels.

Macroeconomic Policies Before and After the Crisis

Most economic crises emerge after periods of fast economic growth. The current crisis is no exception, as most developing countries enjoyed several years of rapid growth, triggered in part by a great expansion of commodity exports. In addition, some countries—especially middle-income countries and the NIGs—greatly benefited from the rapid expansion of manufacturing exports. Also, part of the South was able to attract unprecedented levels of both financial and nonfinancial foreign investment. The export boom combined with capital inflows generated foreign exchange, which in many cases made the availability of foreign exchange nonbinding as a constraint to economic activity. The boom also contributed to rapid increases in tax revenues, which gave governments flexibility on the expenditure side. In most cases, the combination of export expansion, foreign capital inflows, and rapidly increasing fiscal expenditures led to high rates of economic growth.

Public savings. The extent to which a country was able to speed up growth during boom times depended not only on the positioning of the country to benefit from world expansion (e.g., types of export goods, attractiveness to foreign investors) but also on certain key policies. Among them, one is particularly important: the extent to which the government saved. Some countries were able to increase growth and even reduce poverty in the short run by spending most or all of the additional revenues on a myriad of programs and creating new social programs, many of which were poorly designed. In several cases, the government overshot expenditures by using the boom times as an opportunity to rapidly increase public debt.[12]

Other countries, knowing that the boom would eventually subside, adopted a more cautious approach: They saved a significant part of the increased revenues by paying off existing public debt, increasing foreign exchange reserves, and, in some cases, establishing sovereign investment funds. The accumulation of public savings during the boom times better positioned these countries to use countercyclical policies to face the subsequent crisis than those that did not save or even increased net public debt. They were able to implement fiscal stimulus policies like the United States, but they financed them not by increasing public debt (as in the United States) but by their own accumulated savings. Among countries that were able to increase public savings most during the boom times were Chile, Mexico, China, and the Republic of Korea.

Countries that save during boom times may be able to increase social benefits and implement countercyclical pro-employment expenditure policies during a crisis. They can allow themselves to use temporary deficit-financed fiscal policy to stimulate the economy. In contrast, countries that did not save (e.g., Greece) might be forced to use pro-cyclical policies, which often means cutting social services and reducing other expenditures. These countries become dependent on support from the International Monetary Fund (IMF), which often imposes restrictive policies that may be inconsistent with fiscal stimulus. The unemployment and poverty effects are likely to be magnified in these countries and mitigated in countries that save.

A crisis can have various effects on the poor and on natural resources, especially those that are open access or semi-open access, such as many tropical forests. Increased unemployment and poverty often lead to even greater pressures on such resources by subsistence producers, as these resources are the ultimate welfare refuge for the poor. In addition, governments that failed to save during the expansive phase may be forced to promote the commercial exploitation of natural resources—often at great environmental cost—in a desperate effort to reduce the impact of the crisis. Thus, the pressures on natural resources are likely to be more limited among countries that saved in boom times and can apply fiscal stimulus than among those that saved little.[13]

Exchange rates. A common effect of crises—especially in countries caught in a vulnerable position owing to their past policies—is that currencies are significantly devalued. Because most natural-resource-intensive products are tradable, exchange rate devaluation often induces an expansion of commodity exports that in turn causes more pressure on natural resources. It is hard to separate the effect of exchange rate devaluation from other factors that tend to change simultaneously with the exchange rate; thus, it is difficult to ascertain causality between exchange rate changes and natural resources. Several studies have documented a consistent correlation between exchange rate devaluation and increased pressure on natural resources. Kaimowitz, Thiele, and Pacheco (1999) show that in Bolivia episodes of exchange rate devaluation were linked to increased timber exports, putting additional strain on natural forests. Similarly, Sunderlin and colleagues (2000) show that exchange rate devaluation in Cameroon coincided with periods of increased pressure on forests. In most cases, exchange rate devaluation primarily mitigates declining world export prices, so the net effect on domestic commodity prices—the key factor affecting resource exploitation—is ambiguous.

Budget choices. It has been argued that the crisis presents an opportunity for modifying fiscal budget policies in a way that could be beneficial for the environment (Barbier 2009). There are two related issues to consider in this respect.

1. Environmentally perverse subsidies: Fuel, pesticide, water, and fertilizer subsidies, as well as a plethora of other expenditures, often constitute a heavy fiscal burden in developing countries. According to a recent study, annual fossil fuel subsidies in 20 developing countries reached US$220 billion, about 1.5 percent of GDP and more than 5 percent of total government expenditures (UNEP 2008). The fiscal burden of environmentally perverse subsidies in many countries may become even heavier in times of financial crises. This could, in principle, motivate their reduction or elimination, leading to important environmental improvement and a relief of the tight fiscal conditions. One could speculate that the incentives to remove environmentally perverse subsidies are even larger in countries that have failed to save during boom times and hence face worse fiscal conditions during the crisis. In contrast, countries that have saved typically do not face a fiscal situation dire enough to justify the removal of such subsidies. But even in countries that suffer great losses of fiscal revenues and have no savings, vested political interests may be too powerful to allow the government to effectively cut costly and environmentally perverse subsidies.

The evidence regarding the 1997 Asian crisis—the only one for which studies exist that include details of environmental subsidy expenditures—shows that most countries did not reduce perverse subsidies (Vincent et al. 2002; World Bank 1999). In Indonesia, for example, subsidies to gasoline more than doubled between the second quarter of 1997 and the last quarter of 1998, and total real budgetary outlays for input subsidies—including fertilizers and fuels—increased more than fourfold during the period (figures 12 and 13). While Indonesia might be aberrant in this respect, it appears that few countries in Asia significantly reduced subsidies during the crisis. Because the current crisis may be deeper and have greater fiscal impacts than previous crises, emphasis on subsidy removal (rather than merely on general fiscal restraint) by international financial institutions could be more effective.

2. Budgets and green fiscal stimulus: For the reasons discussed earlier, overall government expenditures are likely to be drastically reduced in crisis times, at least among countries that had overexpansive fiscal policies during the boom times. Budget choices are also likely to be affected. Governments tend to cut "discretionary expenditures" (i.e., those not protected by major interest lobbies), and environmental protection expenditures often fall into this category. Figure 14 and table 3 show a significant reduction in environmental expenditures in Indonesia after the Asian crisis. A study of the fiscal effects of the crisis in four countries (Malaysia, Korea, Thailand, and Indonesia) shows that environmental expenditures as a share of total government spending fell significantly in all but Malaysia, which retained the same

FIGURE 12.
Gasoline Subsidies in Indonesia

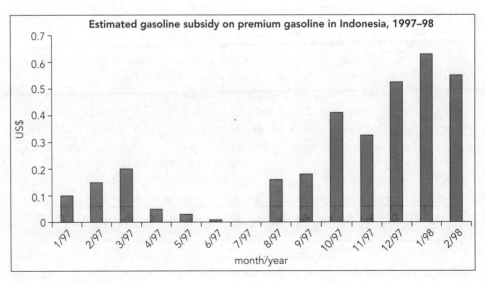

Source: World Bank 1999.

FIGURE 13.
Comparison of Government Spending on Environment and Input Subsidies
in Indonesia

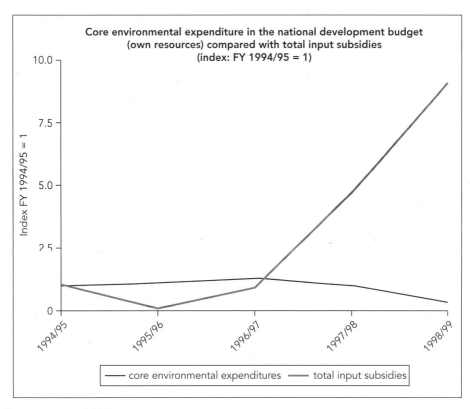

Source: Vincent et al. 2002.

low share (see table 4). Thus, the effect of the crisis on environmental protection expenditures was magnified by a reallocation of fiscal spending.

In previous crises, a precondition for IMF support to developing countries has been the reduction of fiscal deficits (IMF 2007). Countries that did not save enough to implement countercyclical fiscal policies with their own resources were not able to do so. In the past, most developing countries have been unable to introduce significant countercyclical fiscal policies and have cut environmental protection budgets (Vincent et al. 2002). Without such policy changes, most of the countries that did not save enough in the boom times (the majority) may not be able to access capital markets to finance fiscal stimulus of any significant magnitude.

Countries that can finance their own fiscal stimulus may be able to include a green component, although most of them seem to have priorities other than the environment at this point. An additional issue is whether green expenditures can compete with other public expenditures, such as infrastructure and other traditional programs, to create jobs.[14] Another issue is whether green expenditures can generate

FIGURE 14.
Government Spending in Indonesia

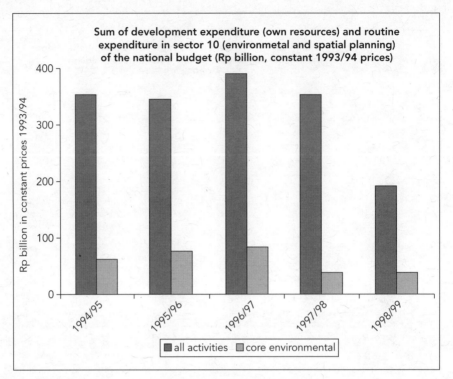

Source: Vincent et al. 2002.

TABLE 3. Government Spending on Environmental Activities in Indonesia

Expenditures on Environmental Activities in the Routine Budgets of the Industrial Zone and Environment Division, the Mining Inspectorate and the Environmental Agencies in Sector 10 (Rp million, constant 1993/94 prices)

Fiscal year	Industrial zone and environment division[a]	Mining inspectorate[a]	Environmental agencies, sector 10[b]
1994/95	858	457	3,330
1995/96	666	364	3,630
1996/97	704	415	5,406
1997/98	606	271	4,630
1998/99	163	56	4,167

Source: Vincent et al. 2002.

Note: a. Planned expenditures.
b. Actual expenditures.

a sufficiently powerful political and ideological constituency. When it comes to fiscal stimulus, traditional programs emphasizing infrastructure have powerful ideological support.[15]

A recent study by Khatiwada (2009) looked at the composition of the stimulus spending packages in 10 advanced countries and 12 developing countries. Among

TABLE 4. Environmental Expenditures in Asian Countries

Environmental Expenditures in Asian Countries Affected by the Financial Crisis[a]

	Share of Government Expenditure (%)	Share of GDP (%)
Indonesia		
1997	0.163	0.030
1998	0.079	0.017
Malaysia		
1997	0.067	0.015
1998	0.070	0.016
Thailand		
1997	1.19	0.22
1998	0.98	0.18
Korea, Rep.		
1997	1.56	0.27
1998	1.38	0.29

Source: Vincent et al. 2002.
a. definition of year varies across countries

the developing countries, only China, Malaysia, Mexico, Argentina, Chile, Korea, Thailand, and the Philippines implemented significant fiscal stimulus rescue packages of more than 2 percent of GDP. These are generally the countries that had accumulated enough of a fiscal surplus to finance significant rescue packages. China, which saved the most during the years before the crisis, was able to develop the largest fiscal stimulus package in the world: more than 13 percent of GDP (more than twice the size of the U.S. stimulus as a proportion of GDP).

An important finding is that the share of new social spending and tax cuts in the total fiscal stimulus in the developing countries was only 9.8 percent—much lower than the 45 percent among the advanced economies (Khatiwada 2009). In contrast, the stimulus aimed at particular sectors or firms was 43.5 percent in the developing countries, a much higher share than the 37 percent in the advanced countries studied. Most of these incentives were subsidies benefiting industrial sector firms, many of which are linked to the extraction or heavy consumption of natural resources. So while these subsidies are not directly environmentally perverse, they can be environmentally detrimental, especially given weak property rights and weak enforcement of environmental regulations.

In some countries the stimulus package includes an increase of subsidies that can be considered environmentally perverse. In Mexico, for example, about 15 percent of the total stimulus money was directed to increasing subsidies for gasoline and other fuels. In Indonesia a significant part of the stimulus was devoted to financing voluntary transmigration programs from Java into areas less affected by unemployment, roughly corresponding to frontier areas. Migration into these areas is likely to increase deforestation. Of all the developing countries, only China includes an important component explicitly directed to environmental protection but, as Strand

and Toman (2010) point out, the effectiveness of these expenditures appears quite limited.

This analysis has two implications. First, significant fiscal stimulus programs among developing countries exist mainly in countries that were able to finance such programs with their own resources: China, Malaysia, Mexico, Chile, and a few others. But fiscal stimulus is not necessarily accompanied by green stimulus, and it appears that some countries have expanded subsidies that are deemed environmentally perverse.

Regulatory Frameworks for Natural Resources and the Environment

Among developing countries, significant disparities exist in the scope of the regulatory framework and the extent to which it is enforced. A key issue is that countries with more effective environmental and natural resource regulations are able to impose binding constraints on pollution levels and natural resource degradation in normal circumstances, while countries without such effective regulation cannot impose binding constraints.

The pollution implications of the crisis can be opposite in the two cases. With more binding pollution constraints, a possible response to the crisis is de facto relaxation of enforcement as a means to reduce costs for firms and mitigate the employment effects of the crisis. In that case we would see two opposite effects: (1) the contracting output scale effect that reduces pollution and (2) the pollution intensity effect (i.e., the level of pollution per unit of output or consumption) that increases it.[16] The net effect is ambiguous, but it may be positive, despite the decline in economic activity and employment. In contrast, in countries without strongly binding pollution constraints, air and water pollution are likely to decline with economic activity, because the scale effect may not be countered by a pollution intensity effect from changing regulatory constraints. In this case, we have the scale effect of the crisis but not the pollution intensity effect.

Thus we have the following hypothesis: Crises can worsen pollution in countries that have more binding regulatory frameworks if the constraints are weakened, while they tend to reduce pollution in countries with a weak regulatory framework. A similar hypothesis can apply to natural resources, where the role of regulation is to limit overexploitation through, for example, open access to forests for timber harvesting. Empirical scrutiny of these hypotheses is complicated by the fact that countries rarely announce that they are relaxing environmental and natural resource constraints as a crisis response. Moreover, for local air pollution in particular, impacts occur as a result of changes in the composition of output and fuel use as well as via macroeconomic channels. The next three sections consider evidence bearing on these hypotheses, drawing on the experiences of the 1997 Asia-originated crisis and the 1995 Mexico-originated crisis. The goal is not to establish or refute the hypotheses but rather to provide enough evidence to underscore the importance of further study.

Pressures on forests and other natural resources. Forest and related ecosystems are affected by two forces that are likely to behave in opposite ways during a crisis.

The first force is pressure from the poor and from subsistence producers. Forests are generally the last social protection against poverty. An increase in poverty may mean more deforestation and more forest burning. The second force is pressure from commercial interests. Forest clearing by large commercial interests linked to agriculture, mining, or energy is likely to decline as the crisis reduces commodity prices and diminishes the rate of return for such operations.

While the net effect of the crisis on deforestation may be ambiguous, we can distinguish conditions under which the two factors are made weaker or stronger. The larger and poorer the country's population, the more likely subsistence forces of deforestation will dominate the for-profit motives; that is, the more likely the crisis will worsen deforestation and increase resource degradation. Studies using remote sensing and survey forest data have found that increasing poverty, especially in a context of high population density, intensifies forest pressures and increases deforestation (Barbier 2004; Deininger and Minten 2002). Similarly, a study by Kerr and others (2004) found that in Costa Rica poorer areas are cleared more rapidly than richer areas, suggesting that poverty increases deforestation. Also, Son (2003) shows that poverty is a cause of deforestation in Vietnam.

Middle-income countries with low population density. In countries where population density and poverty are low, the commercial interest effect may dominate. In middle-income countries, for example, it appears that crises in the past have reduced commercial resource extraction activities as well as agricultural expansion. A study by López and Galinato (2005) found that deforestation in Brazil (a middle-income country with relatively low population density and moderate poverty levels) falls significantly during economic slowdowns. The main reason is the contraction of commercial agriculture often associated with declining commodity prices.

Two main forces may reduce the impact of the crisis on the profitability of domestic resource extraction activities: (1) exchange rate devaluation and (2) government subsidies. Developing-country currencies may suffer significant devaluations in a crisis. Since most primary commodities are tradable, currency devaluation is an incentive to expand resource extraction, especially by commercial interests. However, because international commodity prices fall during a crisis as a consequence of reduced demand for commodities from the developed world, the net effect on domestic commodity prices is ambiguous. The World Bank (1999) cites a vast literature showing that currency devaluation can increase deforestation and environmentally damaging resource extraction.[17] However, its analysis of the 1997 Asian crisis also shows that the net effect in some countries was to negatively affect the profitability of logging and other commercial resource-extracting activities.

The reduction in the profitability of resource-extracting activities and the consequent amelioration of pressure on forests from commercial interests can be reversed by government subsidies and other distortive policies that compensate commercial or for-profit natural resource enterprises for the fall in commodity prices. Ironically, these undesirable government subsidies may be more feasible in cases where governments have been able to save during boom times, as they will have more financial resources to implement such policies.

Exchange rate devaluation and government subsidies that encourage resource-extraction activities may at least partially mitigate the effect of the crisis on deforestation, but these factors are rarely large enough to fully reverse the decrease in extractive commercial activities caused by economic slowdowns (López and Galinato 2005). The net effect of the crisis is likely to reduce deforestation and forest carbon emissions during times of crisis in middle-income countries with lower population densities, such as Peru, Brazil, and Chile. Brazil appears to have a pro-cyclical pattern of deforestation: The high-growth periods of 1977–88 and 1993–94 coincide with high forest losses, while deforestation has slowed during severe economic crises (Wunder 2005). One reason for the reduction in deforestation during economic crises is that public projects such as road building and dam construction are postponed and agricultural subsidies reduced as a consequence of the fiscal squeeze. This may be a typical pattern in middle-income developing countries where most of the resource degradation is associated with commercial exploitation and only a small part is due to subsistence activities by the poor.

Poor countries with high population density. Among the Asian countries on which we have focused, according to Chen and Ravallion (2010), poverty (poverty line: US$1.25 per day) affects a large portion of the population: India (44% of the rural population), China (26%), Indonesia (24%), the Philippines (23%), and Vietnam (21%). Some of these countries also have a very high population density, especially India (305 per square km), the Philippines (224), and Vietnam (219). One would think that in countries that combine high poverty levels with dense populations, the crisis could trigger significant additional pressures from subsistence households on rural natural resources, including forest habitats. Unfortunately, few aggregate studies on deforestation in Asia are based on real data; the commonly used data from the United Nations Food and Agriculture Organization are mostly based on interpolations. The case studies below support the hypothesis that forest pressures increase during crises in poor, highly populated countries.

Most empirical studies have concluded that the Asian crisis led to a drastic fall in economic activity in the urban economy, which has been partly compensated by increased activity in rural areas. This is a spontaneous response by those who become unemployed in urban areas and return to rural areas, where they can subsist as self-employed or temporary workers living with their extended families. It is also a response to government policies that encourage greater access to natural resources—including forest activities, mining, and fishing—during times of crisis. For example, the share of the primary sectors in total GDP significantly increased during the crisis in Indonesia, from 25 percent to 31 percent.

Indonesia is the most studied case and the country in which the impact of the crisis was strongest. According to Aswicahyono, Bird, and Hill (2009), Indonesia suffered a 13 percent fall in GDP in 1998, by far the largest decrease among the four East Asian countries directly affected by the crisis. The focus on Indonesia is also convenient because the magnitude of the current crisis is such that its impact on developing countries is likely to be greater than that of any previous crisis in modern times since the Great Depression. The impact of this crisis on the developing world is likely to be as bad as or perhaps even worse than Indonesia in 1998. For this reason, an analysis of the Indonesian experience might be relevant to evaluate the possible future effect of the current crisis on poor developing countries.

Dauvergne (1999) concludes that the 1997 crisis in Indonesia caused a large expansion of agriculture, associated with a significant increase in part-time agricultural workers. The same is true for mining; in 1997, the stock of existing contracts awarded by the government to mine gold, diamonds, coal, and nickel increased by 25 percent. The government also promoted the commercial fishing industry, and illegal fishing by poor households increased dramatically. Dauvergne documented that wildlife conservation suffered dramatically as a consequence of increased illegal hunting. Sunderlin and colleagues (2001) found that the crisis caused a large increase in forest clearing by commercial interests to expand exports of rubber and other tree crops. They also found a notable increase in forest clearing by smallholders. Pagiola (2001) reaches similar though more nuanced conclusions: Deforestation did not increase homogeneously in all regions in Indonesia, and in fact may have fallen in some areas during the crisis. Gaveau and colleagues (2009) use detailed survey data to show that the 1997–98 crisis caused a significant reversal in law enforcement efforts in the area studied (Bukit Barisan Selatan). The authors show how the weakening of environmental law enforcement in conjunction with increases in real domestic commodity prices caused significant losses of protected forests and biodiversity.

In Indonesia, the crisis appears to have caused a massive expansion of deforestation and resource extraction. Possible causes of this strong effect is that Indonesia, at the epicenter of the crisis, was affected by a particularly large devaluation of its currency (table 5), which allowed commercial resource-extractive activities to increase their relative profitability and increased pressures on forested areas by the large segment of the population that became subsistence producers.

The magnitude of the devaluation was such that it apparently offset the fall of international commodity prices, leading to an increase in domestic commodity prices and hence in the profitability of commodity resource extraction. The effects of the crisis on resource extraction in other Asian countries were not as severe (World Bank 1999). Pagiola (2001) found that pressure on forests did not significantly increase in

TABLE 5. Asian Financial Crisis Currency Depreciation

Asian Crisis - Forex Markets vs. US$		
Country	Depreciation	Period
Indonesia	–84%	July 97 to July 98
Thailand	–53%	July 97 to July 98
Korea, Rep.	–51%	July 97 to July 98
Malaysia	–47%	July 97 to July 98
Philippines	–40%	July 97 to July 98

Source: World Bank Crisis Talk, http://crisistalk.worldbank.org/2008/10/currency-deprec.html.

Thailand or the Philippines; however, the overall effect of the crisis on the Philippines was relatively mild (Datt and Hoogeveen 2003), so the finding that forest pressures did not increase might simply be due to the fact that the quantitative impact on forests was harder to identify.

In addition to world commodity prices and exchange rate devaluation, other factors affected the impact of the crisis on natural resources. A crucial factor is the public expenditure response. A study by Vincent and others (2002) showed that the 1997–98 crisis resulted in drastic cuts in environmental protection expenditures in all East Asian countries, with the single exception of Malaysia. Kittiprapas (2002) reports deep cuts in both social services and environmental protection in Thailand. In general, the cuts were much deeper in rural environmental expenditures than in urban ones. This means that the impact of the crisis was stronger for the mostly rural natural resources than for urban pollutants, not only because of the reverse migration tendencies mentioned earlier but because environmental enforcement may have weakened more in rural than urban areas.

Global pollutants: greenhouse gases. Currently, emissions of CO_2 and other greenhouse gases are not subject to regulation in developing countries. Consistent with the hypothesis presented above, these emissions are likely to fall with the reduction of economic activity caused by economic crises, although under some conditions it is possible that a recession may induce changes in emissions owing to shifts in the composition of fuel consumption if the crisis changes relative fuel prices.[18] However, in countries with open-access or semi-open-access forests, the crisis may trigger increased deforestation and forest burning, which are likely to increase nonindustrial carbon emissions. This mixed pattern of influences is reflected in the data.

Impacts on local air and water pollution. Table 6, reproduced from Esty and Porter (2001), is an index of environmental regulatory strength for 71 countries, of which about 50 are developing countries. The index is based on data for the late 1990s and is thus relevant for the time frame we are considering. The developing countries exhibit very large disparities in environmental regulatory effectiveness. For example, Uruguay is much closer to Japan than to the Philippines or the Dominican Republic in this respect. Among the countries we analyze below, Chile and Uruguay—and, to a lesser extent, Brazil—have the highest environmental effectiveness among developing countries; Korea, Malaysia, Thailand, and China have intermediate effectiveness; and Mexico, Argentina, India, the Philippines, República Bolivariana de Venezuela, Indonesia, and Paraguay are among those with the least effective environmental regulations. Note that while most of the highest ranked countries are also high-income countries, the ranking is not completely driven by per capita income, especially among developing countries. In fact, countries with similar per capita incomes (e.g., Uruguay, Malaysia, and Argentina) are ranked very differently in terms of environmental regulations.

The hypothesis is corroborated by some small case studies for water pollutants. For Indonesia, Afsah (1999) showed that while output of a large number of surveyed industrial plants declined by 18 percent during the 1997–98 crisis, water pollution

TABLE 6. Environmental Regulatory Regime Index by Country, Absolute Ranking

Environmental Regulatory Regime Index					
Rank	Country	Score	Rank	Country	Score
1	Finland	2.303	37	Korea, Rep.	−0.121
2	Sweden	1.772	38	Malaysia	−0.127
3	Singapore	1.771	39	Lithuania	−0.146
4	Netherlands	1.747	40	Slovak Republic	−0.177
5	Austria	1.641	41	Egypt, Arab Rep.	−0.224
6	Switzerland	1.631	42	Panama	−0.242
7	Germany	1.522	43	Mauritius	−0.290
8	France	1.464	44	China	−0.348
9	Denmark	1.384	45	Thailand	−0.389
10	Iceland	1.354	46	Colombia	−0.416
11	New Zealand	1.299	47	Bulgaria	−0.584
12	Canada	1.297	48	Mexico	−0.602
13	United Kingdom	1.185	49	Greece	−0.619
14	United States	1.184	50	Peru	−0.722
15	Belgium	1.159	51	Argentina	−0.732
16	Australia	1.083	52	Zimbabwe	−0.732
17	Japan	1.057	53	Bolivia	−0.743
18	Norway	1.045	54	Indonesia	−0.758
19	Ireland	0.546	55	India	−0.759
20	Italy	0.498	56	Vietnam	−0.770
21	Spain	0.437	57	Russian Federation	−0.895
22	Estonia	0.296	58	Sri Lanka	−0.936
23	Hungary	0.283	59	Philippines	−1.014
24	Slovenia	0.209	60	Dominican Republic	−1.014
25	Chile	0.177	61	Venezuela, RB	−1.079
26	Czech Republic	0.073	62	Nicaragua	−1.164
27	Uruguay	0.059	63	El Salvador	−1.215
28	Israel	0.021	64	Romania	−1.268
29	Poland	0.005	65	Ukraine	−1.297
30	Jordan	0.002	66	Honduras	−1.300
31	Portugal	−0.028	67	Nigeria	−1.314
32	South Africa	−0.029	68	Bangladesh	−1.331
33	Latvia	−0.036	69	Guatemala	−1.532
34	Jamaica	−0.037	70	Ecuador	−1.616
35	Brazil	−0.077	71	Paraguay	−1.743
36	Costa Rica	−0.078			

Source: Esty and Porter 2001.

from organic waste in industrial effluents as measured by the biochemical oxygen demand increased by 15 percent. Afsah documents how environmental inspections declined during the crisis, which reduced abatement efforts by industrial plants. Similarly, Caffera (2005) documents that the political will to enforce environmental regulations in Uruguay in the aftermath of the Mexican peso crisis was low. In fact, during the 1997–99 period, the reported violation rate was consistently above 40 percent, and the number of fines imposed was extraordinarily low. In China, firms facing financial difficulties have greater bargaining power with regulators and pay smaller environmental fees (Dasgupta et al. 2003). A study by Dauvergne (1999) shows a significant weakening of environmental enforcement in periods of slow growth in several East Asian countries.

Air pollution effects of the crisis. Air pollution concentration levels among countries vary significantly once we account for a per capita income norm. Table 7, also taken from Esty and Porter (2001), provides measures of the difference of SO_2 concentration between the actual and expected levels obtained using predictions based on regressing SO_2 concentrations on per capita GDP for a large sample of developing and advanced countries.[19] Table 7 shows areawide variation in this index as well. For example, India has concentrations below the per capita GDP norm, while China has concentrations well above the norm. Among the upper-middle-income countries, Chile has pollution levels below the norm, while Mexico and Brazil greatly exceed the norm. It is not clear whether the quality of the environmental regulatory framework explains the deviations from the norm, as there are other potentially important explanatory factors. For example, significant differences in the speed of economic growth may explain why China is above the norm while India is below it, although China is ranked higher in the regulatory quality index. Over the 1990s, China grew almost twice as fast as India. It is likely that countries that grow very fast face serious difficulties in controlling pollution, even if their regulatory framework is adequate.

In our sample of Latin American countries, those with the most effective environmental regulations—Chile, Uruguay, and, to some extent, Brazil—appear to have increased SO_2 emissions after the 1995 Mexican peso crisis. Their emissions continued to increase all the way into 1999, when the Asian crisis had subsided. Figure 15 shows the annual SO_2 emissions for these countries. Before the Mexican peso crisis, Chile had experienced negative rates of emission growth for almost five years, despite rapid economic growth, which indicates that its SO_2 controls were effective. However, starting in 1995 and continuing through 1999, emissions increased at a relatively fast pace. In 2000, once the effects of the two crises had passed, emissions began to decrease again. Emissions in Uruguay and Brazil followed a similar path.

Thus, the cases of Chile, Uruguay, and Brazil fit our hypothesis for countries that have effective regulations. During the crisis, the regulations are relaxed, possibly as a deliberate effort to mitigate unemployment. In these cases the pollution intensity effect may dominate the potential output scale effects of the crisis. The patterns of pollution growth in Paraguay and Argentina (countries with the least effective environmental regulation in the region) are quite different. In these countries the crises do not seem to have prompted significant increases in emissions.

The data for emissions in Asia show that SO_2 concentrations fell significantly in most countries of the region, especially in 1998 and 1999, when the crisis had its full impact (figures 16 and 17). Given the magnitude of the crisis in most of these

TABLE 7. Difference in Urban SO$_2$ Concentration between Actual and Expected Levels, Given per Capita GDP

Low-Income Countries (≤$6,500)		
Rank	Country	Residual
1	Ecuador	−28.49
2	Romania	−28.10
3	Thailand	−26.69
4	India	−26.49
5	Philippines	−12.81
6	Venezuela, RB	−6.84
7	Bulgaria	11.99
8	Egypt, Arab Rep.	21.64
9	China	51.25

* Not all data were available for all countries.

Middle-Income Countries ($6,500–$23,000)		
Rank	Country	Residual
1	Lithuania	−34.29
2	Latvia	−31.41
3	Argentina	−26.04
4	New Zealand	−15.54
5	Portugal	−12.63
6	Malaysia	−11.88
7	South Africa	−9.52
8	Spain	−8.72
9	Slovak Republic	−6.21
10	Chile	−2.89
11	Czech Republic	2.07
12	Singapore	3.26
13	Costa Rica	7.03
14	Hungary	10.30
15	Greece	11.60
16	Poland	22.43
17	Korea, Rep.	30.98
18	Brazil	40.29
19	Mexico	41.61
20	Russian Federation	63.80

High-Income Countries (≥$23,000)		
Rank	Country	Residual
1	Finland	−11.07
2	Sweden	−10.89
3	Iceland	−7.81
4	Norway	−7.16
5	Denmark	−7.02
6	Netherlands	−4.97
7	Germany	−2.60
8	France	−2.12
9	Switzerland	−1.85
10	Australia	−1.70
11	Austria	−1.31
12	Italy	−0.97
13	Canada	−0.75
14	Ireland	3.67
15	United States	5.09
16	United Kingdom	5.37
17	Belgium	6.91
18	Japan	9.49

Source: Esty and Porter 2001.

countries, it is possible that any potential pollution intensity effect in countries that had binding environmental regulations was dominated by a strong output contraction effect. In Korea, however, pollution concentrations continuously declined over the 1990s, and the effect of the crisis was a temporary interruption of the declining trend. This small and temporary change in trend in Korea contrasts with the more

FIGURE 15.
SO₂ Emissions, Latin America

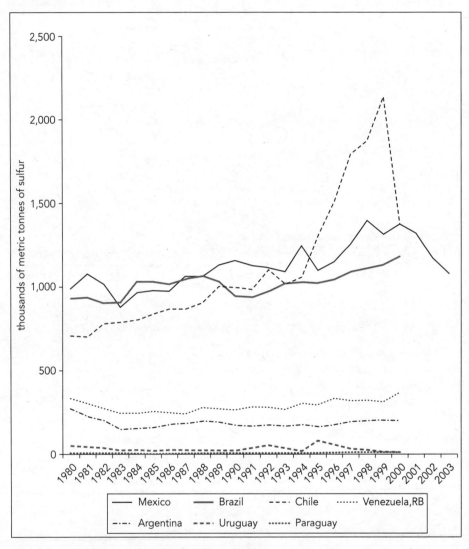

Source: Stern 2005, http://www.sterndavidi.com/datasite.html.

precipitous and longer-lasting reductions of pollution in most of the other Asian countries that generally had weaker environmental regulation. According to table 6, Korea had one of the highest ranking among Asian countries in the sample with respect to environmental regulatory effectiveness. One explanation would be that the output effect dominated in other countries, while in Korea there may have been an effect from less vigorous implementation of environmental standards.

Case studies and aggregate data suggest that one response to an economic crisis is to reduce environmental enforcement when such regulations are initially binding. Where this occurs, it could be a deliberate decision by governments aimed at mitigating the effects of the crisis on production and employment. However, it could also be that environmental budgets are cut during crises as part of a general reduction in discretionary government expenditures to offset shortfalls in public revenues. More research is needed to identify the strength of different explanations for the patterns observed. This is especially true in the area of local air pollutants. Some evidence seems to support our hypothesis for SO_2, but other explanations might be identified based on changes in patterns of output and energy use before and during the crises that are not driven by environmental regulatory practices.

Conclusion

Growing environmental scarcity is not an entirely new phenomenon, despite the fact that commodity prices only recently have started to reflect it. In part because commodity prices have not historically reflected environmental scarcity, ominous signs of it have been systematically and happily ignored by policy makers for several decades. During the 20th century the world supply of energy, agricultural goods, metals, and other primary commodities was amazingly responsive to rising commodity demand, but the supply of these commodities has been increasingly reliant on more and more fragile ecosystems. With some important exceptions, the key underlying scarcity was not the exhaustion of raw materials underground but the increasing damage to ever-more-fragile ecosystems, overuse and contamination of water resources, loss of

FIGURE 16.
SO_2 Emissions, China and India

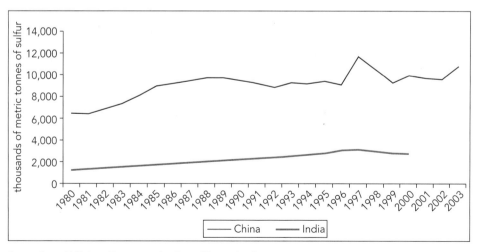

Source: Stern 2005, http://www.sterndavidi.com/datasite.html.

FIGURE 17.
SO$_2$ Emissions, East Asia

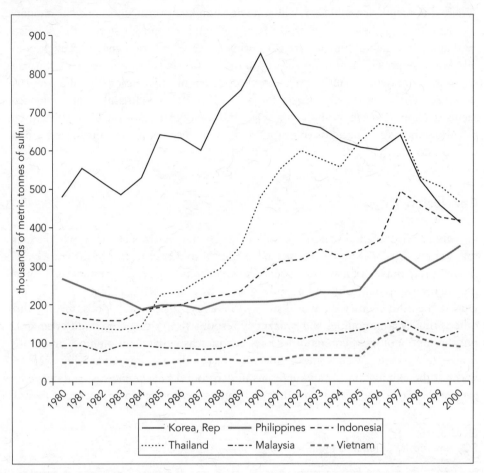

Source: Stern 2005, http://www.sterndavidi.com/datasite.html.

biodiversity, and the large emissions of climate change gases generated by the conversion of natural ecosystems to agriculture, petroleum exploitation, logging, mining, and other resource-extractive uses. Commodity supply appeared until recently to have been almost infinitely elastic, because these ever-increasing environmental costs have been ignored by producers, especially, but not only, in developing countries.

The growing scarcity is finally beginning to be at least partially addressed, precisely at the time when world economic growth has become more commodity-intensive as a consequence of the awakening of the sleeping giant countries to the growth process and the increasing materialization of consumption in advanced economies. The commodity supply curve has become steeper, and demand shifts upward more rapidly with economic growth. The result is obvious: Unlike the past, when growth was the privilege of a small and exclusive club, current rapid growth in the world leads to increasing commodity prices. And increasing commodity prices are not consistent with price stability, which forces monetary tightening when energy and other commodity prices rise in response to growth. This situation tends to suffocate world economic growth, making the world more prone to crisis.

The analysis of the natural environments in the South has shown that the impact of the 2008–09 crisis is likely to degrade environmental resources even more dramatically as a consequence of the efforts by some developing countries to mitigate the economic and social consequences of the crisis. This may exacerbate the underlying long-term environmental resource scarcity in the South and may further compromise the South's ability to respond to a growing demand for commodities when economic growth resumes. The environmental destruction the crisis might create in parts of the South could increase the damages so extensively that, once normal times return, governments will have even greater difficulty ignoring demands to implement serious environmental policies and will have to consider some further restrictions on resource extraction. All this may make the commodity supply curve even steeper in the future, which in turn may exacerbate the economic growth–commodity prices links over the medium term.

A key implication of this analysis is that sustaining positive rates of economic growth over the long run is likely to become more difficult in the future. The irony is that this is in part the result of the fact that economic growth has become more inclusive—potentially accessible for the first time in history to the majority of the world population. Sustaining such inclusive growth may require significant changes in the patterns of growth, especially in the advanced countries. The increasing dematerialization of production in the advanced economies will have to be matched by a similar dematerialization of their consumption expenditures.

We must remove the incentives to continuous expansion of the consumption of material goods, which is often supported by public policies that discriminate in favor of such consumption patterns (e.g., reduced taxes and more lenient environmental regulations benefiting huge sport utility vehicles and certain tax policies that encourage ever-increasing house size). A carbon tax and other consumption taxes that focus on material goods but exclude services would be steps in the right direction. A dematerialization of public expenditures by increasing the provision of public social goods—including education, health, environmental protection, crime prevention, science, and the arts—and a concomitant reduction in the government's provision of material goods (which are often a vehicle to subsidize the wealthier segments of society) would not only induce a lower material component of the aggregate demand but would also increase social equity.

Notes

1. The analysis of pollution content of international trade in the United States and United Kingdom reveals in all its depth the fallacy of the so-called environmental Kuznets curve analyses, which have purported to show that after becoming dirtier for an income

range, increasingly richer countries become environmentally cleaner. The problem is that the empirical studies "showing" this inverted U-shaped relation between wealth and pollution use only data on territorial emissions within the borders of the countries and exclude residents' emissions taking place elsewhere, where international trade is the key vehicle.

2. Interestingly, the North started a dramatic reversal of its territorial environmental degradation by the mid-1970s, which coincided with the emergence of the NICs as suppliers of dirty industrial goods at low costs. This process also coincides with the implementation of modern environmental regulation in the North. Perhaps increasingly stringent environmental regulation in the North was made politically acceptable precisely because of the rise of foreign suppliers of dirty industrial goods. López (2008) offers some evidence showing that one of the reasons the North has been able to enforce significant environmental regulation at a very low cost (estimated at less than 2 percent of GDP) is the emergence of the NICs and, later, other big industrial suppliers, which allowed the North to rapidly shift its production away from dirty industrial goods. This view is consistent with the econometric evidence provided by Levinson and Taylor (2008).

3. According to Rodrik (2007), not only have China and India had undervalued exchange rates over the past two decades, but the degree of undervaluation has consistently increased over the period. Most of the NICs also based their industrial export take-off on undervalued exchange rates, although, unlike the NIGs, some of them have recently allowed their real exchange rate to become less undervalued and even at times overvalued.

4. Germany and Japan—themselves large exporters of technologically sophisticated goods and services—were the exception. The large current account deficits that developed in the United States, the United Kingdom, and several other countries in the developed world did not happen in Japan and Germany.

5. With some important exceptions, the limits to the supply of primary commodities are not so much the scarcity of in-ground raw materials but rather the large and increasing environmental costs that their production entails (Simpson, Toman, and Ayres 2005). Resource extraction greatly affects water quality (mining, oil extraction), soils, and forests (e.g., mountaintop removal for coal extraction). For example, the United States could dramatically increase its oil production at the cost of unacceptable further environmental destruction by expanding offshore or Alaskan production. The enthusiasm of the "drill, baby, drill" advocates in the United States, which even affected the Obama administration, has cooled a bit since the massive disaster caused by offshore drilling in the Gulf of Mexico. Oil spills in developing countries such as Nigeria reached almost legendary status in the 1980s, with some estimates suggesting one *Exxon Valdéz*-type disaster every year.

6. In China, for example, the service sector represents less than 30 percent of GDP (Farrell and Grant 2005). Production was thus about 70 percent geared to energy-intensive and commodity-intensive industrial goods and other material goods.

7. It is remarkable that primary commodity prices so closely follow economic growth even over intervals as short as quarters. This suggests that traders have already incorporated a close growth-commodity price link into their expectations. As soon as the quarterly growth rates are announced, commodity prices are adjusted accordingly, without waiting for the actual demand effect to materialize.

8. In fact, the economy becomes vulnerable to *any* cost pressures, including labor costs. But the commodity cost push is more interesting and important because commodity prices tend, as we showed above, to respond rapidly to expanded growth, while wages respond mainly when there is full or nearly full employment. It is well known that full employment tends to be reached only after protracted periods of fast economic growth. In this new environment, commodity price cost pressures tend to manifest themselves well before wage cost pressures arise.

9. See López (2010) for a thorough study of the conditions that have led most advanced economies to these levels of debt. This study shows how the unprecedented concentration of wealth occurring over the past few decades is largely responsible for equally unprecedented levels of household debt-to-income ratios.

10. Partha Dasgupta has eloquently described the situation in which market prices do not reflect the growing scarcity of the environment and new technologies are thus likely to be rapacious in their use of natural resources (Dasgupta 2005).

11. The recent low interest rates are feasible in part as a consequence of the world crisis that reduced world output for several quarters and thus induced lower commodity prices.

12. Some of these countries also wasted the additional revenues through increased inefficiency, corruption, and satisfying political clienteles.

13. Extreme opposite examples in Latin America are Chile and República Bolivariana de Venezuela. Chile's net public liquid assets increased dramatically during the boom times. Net government foreign assets (foreign reserves plus sovereign fund holdings minus public debt) increased from less than 2 percent of GDP in 2000 to more than 30 percent by early 2009 (Chile, Central Bank). This increase was made possible primarily by the extraordinarily high prices of copper, Chile's main export commodity. In contrast, República Bolivariana de Venezuela saved little of the large oil revenues it enjoyed over several years, despite receiving three times more revenues than Chile during the 2000–06 period. By 2006 the financial position of the Venezuelan public sector was quite precarious, with net foreign public asset holdings equivalent to a negligible fraction of GDP (Venezuela, Central Bank).

14. A recent paper by Strand and Toman (2010) indicates that the near-term employment effects of many green investment programs are limited, especially those in renewable energy and energy-efficient heavy infrastructure, which are fairly capital-intensive.

15. Japan in the 1990s is a dramatic example of a massive, single-minded, and ineffective expansion of fiscal expenditures in infrastructure as a means to mitigate what has become a chronic crisis.

16. The potential also exists for changes in the composition of GDP caused by both the crisis and the relaxation of pollution controls.

17. Arcand, Guillaumont, and Jeanneney-Guillaumont (2008) econometrically corroborate this finding using a pooled sample of 101 countries over a 25-year period. Wunder (2005) also finds that real exchange rate devaluation significantly increases deforestation by promoting timber exports.

18. For example, if coal becomes cheaper relative to oil, the reduction of economic activity could be accompanied by an increase in carbon emissions, because burning coal is generally much dirtier than burning oil.

19. We use SO_2 as a key indicator of air pollution because it is a pollutant for which data are available in many countries. It is better measured than other pollutants, although the data often reflect estimates based on emissions factors per unit of production rather than physical measurements.

References

Acemoglu, D., S. Johnson, and J. A. Robinson. 2001. "The Colonial Origins of Comparative Development: An Empirical Investigation." *American Economic Review* 91: 1369–401.

Afsah, S. 1999. "Impact of Financial Crisis on Industrial Growth and Environmental Performance in Indonesia." Washington, DC: U.S.-Asia Environmental Partnership.

Arcand, J.-L., P. Guillaumont, and S. Jeanneney-Guillaumont. 2008. "Deforestation and the Real Exchange Rate." *Journal of Development Economics* 86 (2): 242–62.

Aswicahyono, H., K. Bird, and H. Hill. 2009. "Making Economic Policy in Weak, Democratic, Post-crisis States: An Indonesian Case Study." *World Development* 37 (2): 354–70.

Barbier, E. B. 2004, "Explaining Agricultural Land Expansion and Deforestation in Developing Countries." *American Journal of Agricultural Economics* 86 (5): 1347–53.

———. 2009. *A Global Green New Deal*. United Nations Environmental Programme, Economics and Trade Branch. Final Report, February.

Caffera, M. 2005. *Financial Assistance of Multilateral Aid Agencies to Enforce Environmental Regulations. Is It Effective?* Montevideo, Uruguay: Departamento de Economía, Universidad de Montevideo.

Chen, S., and M. Ravallion. 2010 "The Developing World Is Poorer Than We Thought, but No Less Successful in the Fight against Poverty." *The Quarterly Journal of Economics* 125 (4): 1577–625.

Dasgupta, P. 2005. "Sustainable Economic Development in the World of Today's Poor." In *Scarcity and Growth Revisited,* ed. D. Simpson, M. Toman, and R. Ayres. Washington, DC: Resources for the Future.

Dasgupta, S., H. Wang, N. Mamingi, and B. Laplante. 2003. "Incomplete Enforcement of Pollution Regulation: Bargaining Power of Chinese Factories." *Environmental and Resource Economics* 24: 245–62.

Datt, G., and H. Hoogeveen. 2003. "El Niño or El Peso? Crisis, Poverty and Income Distribution in the Philippines." *World Development* 31 (7): 1103–24.

Dauvergne, P. 1999. "The Environmental Implications of Asia's 1997 Financial Crisis." *IDS Bulletin* 30: 31–42.

Deininger, K., and B. Minten. 2002. "Determinants of Forest Cover and the Economics of Protection: An Application to Mexico." *American Journal of Agricultural Economics* 84 (4): 943–60.

de Janvry, A. 1975. "The Political Economy of Rural Development in Latin America: An Interpretation." *American Journal of Agricultural Economics* 57 (3): 490–99.

Esty, D., and M. E. Porter. 2001. *The Global Competitiveness Report 2001–2002*. New York: Oxford University Press.

Farrell, D., and A. Grant. 2005. "China's Looming Talent Shortage." *The McKinsey Quarterly* 4: 1–7.

Feenstra, R. C., J. Romalis, and P. L. Schott. 2001. "U.S. Imports, Exports and Tariff Data, 1989–2001." National Bureau of Economic Research (NBER) Working Paper 9387. Washington, DC: NBER.

Gaveau, D. L. A., M. Linkie, S. Suyadi, and N. Leader-Williams. 2009. "Three Decades of Deforestation in Southwest Sumatra: Effects of Coffee Prices, Law Enforcement, and Rural Poverty." *Biological Conservation* 142: 597–605.

Ghertner, D. A., and M. Fripp. 2007. "Trading Away Damage: Quantifying Environmental Leakage through Consumption-Based Life-Cycle Analysis." *Ecological Economics* 63: 563–77.

Helm, D., R. Smale, and J. Phillips. 2007. *Too Good to Be True? The UK's Climate Change Record*. Oxford, England: University of Oxford.

IMF (International Monetary Fund). 2007. *Structural Conditionality in IMF-Supported Programs*. Evaluation Report. Washington, DC: Independent Evaluation Office of the International Monetary Fund.

Kaimowitz, D., G. Thiele, and P. Pacheco. 1999. "The Effects of Structural Adjustment on Deforestation and Forest Degradation in Lowland Bolivia." *World Development* 27 (3): 505–20.

Kerr, S., A. S. P. Pfaff, R. Cavatassi, B. Davis, L. Lipper, A. Sanchez, and J. Timmins. 2004. *Effects of Poverty on Deforestation: Distinguishing Behavior from Location*. Ecological Society of America Working Paper No. 04-19, November. Washington, DC.

Khatiwada, S. 2009. *Stimulus Packages to Counter the Global Economic Crisis: A Review*. Discussion Paper 196/2009. Geneva, Switzerland: International Institute for Labour Studies.

Khor, M. 2000. *Globalization and the South: Some Critical Issues*. United Nations Conference on Trade and Development (UNCTAD) Discussion Paper No 147, April.

Kittiprapas, S. 2002. *Social Impacts of Financial and Economic Crisis in Thailand*. East Asian Development Network (EADN) Regional Project on the Social Impact of the Asian Financial Crisis.

Levison, A., and M. Scott Taylor. 2008. "Unmasking the Pollution Haven Effect." *International Economic Review* 49 (1): 223–54.

López, R. 2008. "Sustainable Economic Growth: The Ominous Potency of Structural Change." Keynote address presented at the third Conference on Sustainable Resource Use and Dynamics (SURED), Ascona, Switzerland, June.

——— 2010. "World Economic Crises in Times of Environmental Scarcity and Wealth Concentration." *Cepal Review* (in press).

López, R., and G. Galinato. 2005. "Trade Policies, Economic Growth, and the Direct Causes of Deforestation." *Land Economics* 81 (2): 145–69.

López, R., and A. Stocking. 2009. *Bringing Growth Theory Down to Earth*. Working Paper WP 09-01, Department of Agricultural and Resource Economics. College Park, MD: University of Maryland at College Park.

Pagiola, S. 2001. *Deforestation and Land Use Changes Induced by the East Asian Economic Crisis*. East Asia Environment and Social Development Unit (EASES) Discussion Paper, March. Washington, DC: World Bank.

Prebisch, R. 1959. "Commercial Policy in the Underdeveloped Countries." *American Economic Review* 49 (2): 251–73.

Rodrik, D. 2007. "The Real Exchange Rate and Economic Growth: Theory and Evidence." Unpublished manuscript, John F. Kennedy School of Government, Harvard University, July.

Simpson, David R., M. Toman, and R. Ayres. 2005. *Scarcity and Growth Revisited: Natural Resources and the Environment in the New Millennium*. Washington, DC: Resources for the Future.

Sokoloff, K. L., and S. L. Engerman. 2000. "History Lessons: Institutions, Factor Endowments, and Paths of Development in the New World." *Journal of Economic Perspectives* 14 (3): 217–32.

Son, V. T. 2003. "Food Production and Deforestation in the Northern Uplands: A Cartographic Approach." *Geoinformatics* 14 (1): 13–16.

Stern, D. I. 2005. "Global Sulfur Emissions from 1850 to 2000." *Chemosphere* 58: 163–75.

Strand, J., and M. Toman. 2010. *Green Stimulus, Economic Recovery, and Long-Term Sustainable Development*. Policy Research Working Paper 5163. Washington, DC: World Bank.

Sunderlin, W. D., A. Angelsen, D. P. Resosudarmo, and A. D. E. Rianto. 2001. "Economic Crisis, Small Farmer Well-Being, and Forest Cover Change in Indonesia." *World Development* 29 (5): 767–82.

Sunderlin, W. D., O. Ndoye, H. Bikie, N. Laporte, B. Mertens, and J. Pokam. 2000. "Economic Crisis, Small-Scale Agriculture, and Forest Cover Change in Southern Cameroon." *Environmental Conservation* 27 (3): 284–90.

UNEP (United Nations Environment Programme). 2008. "Reforming Energy Subsidies—Opportunities to Contribute to the Climate Change Agenda." Division of Technology, Industry and Economics, UNEP.

Vincent, J. R., J. Aden, G. Dore, M. Adriani, V. Rambe, and T. Walton. 2002. "Public Environmental Expenditures in Indonesia." *Bulletin of Indonesian Economic Studies* 38 (1): 61–74.

Weber, C., and H. Matthews. 2007. "Embodied Environmental Emissions in U.S. International Trade, 1997–2004." *Environmental Science and Technology* 41 (14): 4875–81.

Weiskoff, R., and E. Wolff. 1977. "Linkages and Leakages: Industrial Tracking in an Enclave Economy." *Economic Development and Cultural Change* 25 (4): 607–28.

World Bank. 1999. *Environmental Implications of the Economic Crisis and Adjustment in East Asia.* East Asia Environment and Social Development Departmental Discussion Paper 1. Washington, DC: World Bank.

Wunder, S. 2005. "Macroeconomic Change, Competitiveness and Timber Production: A Five Country Comparison." *World Development* 33 (1): 65–86.

Comment on "Voluntary Pledges and Green Growth in the Post-Copenhagen Climate" by Thomas Sterner and "World Economic Crises: Commodity Prices and Environmental Scarcity as Missing Links" by Ramón López

SIMON LEVIN

The central problem facing global society today is how to achieve a sustainable future (see Clark and Levin 2010). The Brundtland Commission, set up by the United Nations in 1983, was established to address "the accelerating deterioration of the human environment and natural resources and the consequences of that deterioration for economic and social development. . . . Believing that sustainable development, which implies meeting the needs of the present without compromising the ability of future generations to meet their own needs, should become a central guiding principle of the United Nations" (UN 1987).

Sterner writes that there is "no alternative to sustainability." Can we grow economically without compromising the options future generations have for enjoying the same quality of life as we do? (See Arrow et al. 2004.) The UN resolution notes "in view of the global character of major environmental problems, the common interest of all countries to pursue policies aimed at sustainable and environmentally sound development." Is sustainability, so defined, an achievable goal?

Climate change and other anthropogenic influences threaten the goal of sustainability and raise challenges, both scientific and political. The puzzle is that on many core environmental issues scientific consensus is strong, yet adequate action to address these issues has been lacking. Why? Much is still unknown scientifically, and much is unknowable. However, the primary limitations to implementing solutions to these problems are not scientific; in many cases, such as climate change, the science is clear and so are the steps that should be taken. The limitations involve the willingness of people and governments to accept the science and make the commitments to the public good that are essential to deal with the great challenges. The solutions to local resource management often require local cooperation (Ostrom 1990); how can we extend that cooperation to larger scales, to

Simon Levin is the George M. Moffett Professor of Biology at Princeton University.
The author gratefully acknowledges careful reading of this manuscript and helpful comments from Avinash Dixit, Carole Levin, Elinor Ostrom, and Daniel Rubenstein.
Annual World Bank Conference on Development Economics 2011, Global

address global environmental challenges? Ostrom (2010) argues that externalities occur at local, regional, and interregional levels, so solving climate change issues will require actions at multiple levels. Studying how cooperation can be fostered at diverse scales is an essential step toward reducing the threat of global warming. It is all well and good to advocate for "green growth," but as López (2010) points out, this requires cooperation that is vulnerable to cheating, as in all classic conflicts involving the commons.

The central issues, then, are issues of behavior and culture. How do we address intergenerational and intragenerational equity? How do we deal with public goods and common pool resources? How do we achieve cooperation in these contexts, and what are the roles of customs, norms, and institutions? If we need new institutions, how should they be designed? Market-based mechanisms will ultimately be needed, but conventional markets have failed to contain environmental damage because they do not adequately incorporate social costs (see Arrow 1963).

Many of the central ethical issues in sustainability involve discounting of one sort or another. Individuals and societies discount the future and similarly discount the interests of others. This raises questions of intergenerational and intragenerational equity (Solow 1991). How much should we leave to future generations? How should we discount the future (Weitzman 1998)? Indeed, much of the debate about the conclusions of the landmark 2006 *Review on the Economic Impacts of Climate Change*, led by Sir Nicholas Stern for the U.K. government, hinges on the choice of discount rate, or even whether a constant discount rate is appropriate (Arrow 2007; Dasgupta 2006; Nordhaus 2007; Tol and Yohe 2006; Weitzman 2007).

Intergenerational equity is only half the problem; we also need to address intragenerational equity and ask what accounts for the inequity in the distribution of wealth and why that inequity is increasing at multiple levels of aggregation.

Intergenerational Equity

In terms of the decisions a person must make in determining the temporal pattern of consumption of wealth, intergenerational equity has three dimensions: (1) How should one balance consumption and savings over my own lifetime? (2) How should one modify that calculation to account for one's offspring? (3) How should one regard others' offspring? Each dimension has its own discount rate (or suite of discount rates, given that different people's welfare will be discounted differently), and the general problem of allocation of resources must balance them all. The situation is basically no different when raised to the level of nations, just more complicated. The issue of other peoples' offspring is confounded with that of intragenerational equity (discussed in the next section).

The primary allocation problem is straightforward. One has a given wealth and a stream of expected income, and one must determine an optimal consumption path to maximize discounted future utility. This is the standard approach to intertemporal decision making and should take into account one's survival demographics and those of one's spouse. This is an inadequate solution, however, because we care for the welfare of our children as well, so the discounted future utility must be replaced by a total welfare function that combines one's own utility with the utility of heirs, discounted by a factor that represents the relative value of the heir's utility to the decision maker (Becker 1976). Because different individuals have different numbers of children the optimal allocation leads to a distribution of wealth in which inequity grows over time (Arrow and Levin 2009). Only the beginnings of such a theory exist at the level of individual decisions, and extensions to the level of societies are even less developed. Indeed, because of the difficulty in determining optimality, the optimization problem in such formulations is sometimes replaced by one that simply seeks sustainability (Arrow et al. 2004).

Intragenerational Equity

As nations become wealthier, measures of pollution and environmental degradation typically increase along with income and industrial production, but only up to a point, beyond which environmental quality begins to improve (Grossman and Krueger 1995; World Bank 1992). The shape of this relationship has been termed an "environmental Kuznets curve" because of its similarity to the relationship between income and inequality described by Kuznets (1955). The improvement in environmental quality at high levels of income might reflect increasing investment in environmental measures as well as simply a natural transition to less polluting activities such as banking, but it might also represent the ability of richer countries to export pollution by shifting industrial production to less developed nations (Arrow et al. 1995).

Alan Turing (1952), better known perhaps for his work in other fields, created a highly influential model of embryogenesis in which the differential diffusion rates of two chemical species, one an activator and the other an inhibitor, could lead to endogenous pattern formation, stable over time, in which the distributions of activator and inhibitor are nonuniform over space. In this situation, the production of industrial goods may be thought of as the activator, stimulating economic growth and pollution alike, while pollution plays the role of inhibitor. A Turing-like model based on these assumptions could give rise to and sustain an inequitable distribution of wealth and environmental quality in which there is a net flow of goods from poor to rich and, effectively, a net flow of the factors that drive pollution from rich to poor. But, as López (2010) points out, such an equilibrium can break down endogenously as new industrial giants such as China develop economically or exogenously as the result of global financial shocks like the one we have just experienced. The equilibrium in the simple model presented above breaks down because of changes in other, hidden variables.

As in intergenerational equity, a literature is developing on intragenerational equity; in particular, on how people deal with public goods and common pool resources (Dixit 2009; Ostrom 1990). However, we desperately need ways to extend that thinking to the level of international relations.

Cooperation and the Need for New Institutions

We live in a global commons in which individual agents act largely in their own self-interest and social costs are not adequately incorporated. This situation is exaggerated when the individual agents are nations and is the primary reason why an international consensus on climate change and other core environmental issues is so difficult to achieve. The task before us is to create global cooperation of a magnitude equal to the great challenge we face in achieving a sustainable future. Cooperation is relatively easily achieved in small groups held together by repeated interactions (Ostrom 1990). Building on the foundation provided by such small-group structures, larger societies have arisen, held together by shared customs and norms, and ultimately by the development of laws and institutions. To reach beyond these societies to meet the global challenges, we are likely to need new compacts and institutions that are polycentric (Ostrom 2010), deriving robustness from strong partnerships among smaller sets of nations. Sustained robustness in these institutions will require an adaptive capacity that flows from flexibility in the face of new information. It is not clear that we can succeed in this endeavor, but it is clear that we cannot afford to fail.

References

Arrow, Kenneth J. 1963. "Uncertainty and the Welfare Economics of Medical Care." *American Economic Review* 53 (5): 941–73.

———. 2007. "Global Climate Change: A Challenge to Policy." *Economist's Voice* 4 (3): 13–21.

Arrow, Kenneth J., Bert Bolin, Robert Costanza, Partha Dasgupta, Carl Folke, Crawford S. Holling, Bengt-Owe Jansson, Simon Levin, Karl-Göran Mäler, Charles Perrings, and David Pimentel. 1995. "Economic Growth, Carrying Capacity, and the Environment." *Science* 268: 520–21.

Arrow, Kenneth J., Partha Dasgupta, Lawrence Goulder, Gretchen Daily, Paul Ehrlich, Geoffrey Heal, Simon Levin, Karl-Göran Mäler, Stephen Schneider, David Starrett, and Brian Walker. 2004. "Are We Consuming Too Much?" *Journal of Economic Perspectives* 18 (3): 147–72.

Arrow, Kenneth J., and Simon A. Levin. 2009. "Intergenerational Resource Transfers with Random Offspring Numbers." *Proceedings of the National Academy of Sciences* 106 (33): 13702–06.

Becker, Gary S. 1976. "Altruism, Egoism and Genetic Fitness: Economics and Sociobiology." *Journal of Economic Literature* 14 (3): 817–26.

Clark, William C., and Simon A. Levin. 2010. *Toward a Science of Sustainability*. Working Paper No. 196. Cambridge, MA: Harvard University, Center for International Development.

Dasgupta, Partha. 2006. "Comments on the Stern Review of the Economics of Climate Change." http://www.econ.cam.ac.uk/faculty/dasgupta/STERN.pdf.

Dixit, Avinash. 2009. "Governance Institutions and Economic Activity." *American Economic Review* 99 (1): 5–24.

Grossman, Gene, and Alan Krueger. 1995. "Economic Growth and the Environment." *Quarterly Journal of Economics* 110 (2): 353–77.

Kuznets, Simon. 1955. "Economic Growth and Income Inequality." *American Economic Review* 45 (1): 1–28.

Nordhaus, William D. 2007. "A Review of the Stern Review on the Economics of Climate Change." *Journal of Economic Literature* 45 (3): 686–702.

Ostrom, Elinor. 1990. *Governing the Commons: The Evolution of Institutions for Collective Action.* Cambridge, England: Cambridge University Press.

———. 2010. "Polycentric Systems for Coping with Collective Action and Global Environmental Change." *Global Environmental Change* (in press). Online First, August 3, 2010, http://dx.doi.org/10.1016/j.gloenvcha.2010.07.004.

Solow, Robert. 1991. "Sustainability: An Economist's Perspective." J. Seward Johnson Lecture, Woods Hole Oceanographic Institution, Marine Policy Center, Woods Hole, MA, June 14.

Stern, Nicholas. 2006. *Stern Review on the Economics of Climate Change.* London: HM Treasury.

Tol, Richard S. J., and Gary Yohe. 2006. "A Review of the *Stern Review*." *World Economics* 7 (4): 233–50.

Turing, Alan M. (1952). "The Chemical Basis of Morphogenesis." *Philosophical Transactions of the Royal Society* B237 (641): 37–72.

UN (United Nations). 1987. *Report of the World Commission on Environment and Development* A/RES/42/187. New York: United Nations Press.

Weitzman, Martin L. 1998. *Gamma Discounting.* Harvard University Institute of Economic Research Working Paper 1843. Cambridge, MA.

———. 2007. "A Review of the *Stern Review on the Economics of Climate Change*." *Journal of Economic Literature* 45 (3): 703–24.

World Bank. 1992. *World Development Report 1992.* New York: Oxford University Press.

Postcrisis Debates on
Development Strategy

Does a Leapfrogging Growth Strategy Raise the Growth Rate? Some International Evidence

ZHI WANG, SHANG-JIN WEI, AND ANNA WONG

All countries want to grow fast on a sustained basis. In East Asia, many economies excel in this area. Following the example of Japan after World War II, the "four little dragons"   the Republic of Korea; Singapore; Taiwan, China; and Hong Kong SAR, China—are familiar success stories. Other economies in the region—including Malaysia, Thailand, and Indonesia—quickly followed, achieving higher growth rates than most other developing countries that had a comparable level of development in the 1960s. Since 2000, China, India, and Vietnam are the new growth miracles, achieving the same high growth rates as their neighbors for two to three decades in a row.[1] Naturally, this record invites admiration and scrutiny. What is the Asian growth model? Is it something that can be transplanted to Latin America, Africa, or elsewhere, with the same magical effect?

The triggers for growth records in these economies are complex, but at the risk of oversimplification, we suggest that two aspects of their growth model merit particular attention. First, almost all fast-growing emerging market economies since the 1970s have embraced trade openness. Trade barriers are taken down or progressively reduced, either at the start of the growth process or shortly thereafter. Trade liberalization does not have to take the narrow form of reducing tariff rates on imported goods, although that is often part of the process. It can take the form of demonopolizing and delicensing. The right to import and export used to be concentrated in a small number of firms by government regulations; trade liberalization broadens the set of firms that can directly participate in international trade. Even

Zhi Wang is Senior Economist in the Research Division, Office of Economics, United States International Trade Commission (USITC). Shang-Jin Wei is Director of the Chazen Institute, Professor of Finance and Economics and N.T. Wang Professor of Chinese Business and Economy at the Graduate School of Business, Columbia University. Anna Wong is a graduate student at the Department of Economics, University of Chicago. The views expressed here are those of the authors and do not represent the official views of the USITC or any other organization that the authors are or have been affiliated with. The authors thank an anonymous World Bank reviewer, participants at a session of the American Economic Association meeting, and Maria Porter and the International Economics Working Group at the University of Chicago for very helpful comments. All errors are the responsibility of the authors.

Annual World Bank Conference on Development Economics 2011, Global
© 2013 The International Bank for Reconstruction and Development/The World Bank

holding tariff rates constant, such democratization of trading rights can dramatically increase a country's trade openness. This was a significant part of the Chinese trade liberalization in the 1980s. Trade liberalization can also come in conjunction with reducing entry barriers or offering incentives for foreign firms to jump-start the domestic export industry. This may be particularly important for countries that have been isolated from the world market for a while. The Asian model is sometimes called an "outward-oriented strategy." This is not very accurate, since many Asian economies do not simultaneously embrace capital account openness, at least not to the same extent, in the areas of cross-border portfolio equity and portfolio debt flows.

The second aspect of the growth model is the use of government policies to promote high-tech and domestic value-added industries, presumably beyond what the economies would naturally develop if left to their own devices. This aspect can be labeled as a leapfrogging strategy. China, Singapore, and Malaysia all have various aggressive policies to promote certain high value-added sectors. Other countries in the region do not wish to fall behind. For example, the Philippine National Information Technology Council announced in 1997, "Within the first decade of the 21st century, the Philippines will be a knowledge center in the Asia Pacific region: the leader in IT education, in IT-assisted training, and in the application of information and knowledge to business, professional services, and the arts."[2]

Are these two aspects responsible for growth? The first—trade openness—has been subjected to extensive and intensive scholarly scrutiny. While there is notable skepticism (Rodriguez and Rodrik 2000), most economists agree that trade openness does seem to help promote economic growth. Following and extending the work by Frankel and Romer (1999), Feyrer (2009) pays attention to sorting out causality from correlation and shows that greater trade openness causally leads to a rise in income. Using changes in infant mortality and life expectancy as an alternative measure of well-being, Wei and Wu (2004) present evidence that trade openness helps improve social welfare by reducing infant mortality and raising life expectancy beyond increasing per capita income. On the basis of an overwhelming amount of evidence, we lean strongly toward the belief that trade openness has played a key role in the success stories in Asia and indeed in most high and sustained growth episodes in the world.

How about the second aspect of the growth model? Has a leapfrogging strategy played a key role? In comparison with the trade openness issue, far less scholarly work exists on the effectiveness of leapfrogging. In theory, if the production of sophisticated goods generates positive externalities via learning by doing, there generally would be an underinvestment among private economic agents relative to the socially optimal level. A leapfrogging strategy—a government-led industrial policy that tilts resource allocation to technologically sophisticated industries— could correct this market failure. The natural inference from this argument is that a country might benefit more from exporting sophisticated products than from exporting unsophisticated and low domestic value-added products, even if its current comparative advantage lies in producing the latter type of goods. Recent academic studies have reported evidence supporting such a comparative advantage defying development strategy.

Hausmann, Hwang, and Rodrik (2007) suggest that some export goods have higher spillover effects than others. They develop a measure of export sophistication and find a positive relationship between their measure and the country's subsequent economic growth rate. However, there is no shortage of skepticism toward the leap-frogging growth strategy. On the one hand, one might question the size of any such market failure in the real world. On the other hand, one might wonder whether a "government failure" if it were to pursue a leapfrogging strategy could overwhelm whatever benefits a country might derive from correcting the market failure. In a series of papers, including Lin (2009), World Bank chief economist Justin Lin advocates strongly for development strategies that follow a country's comparative advantage and against what he calls "comparative advantage defying strategies," which include a leapfrogging industrial policy. At the same time, Lin (2010) is open to the idea of a government role in helping private firms find "latent comparative advantage."[3]

In this paper, we test the validity of the leapfrogging hypothesis with fresh evidence from a cross-country data set. One bottleneck in testing this hypothesis is to identify which countries (regions) engage in such a growth strategy. We employ four different measures, including a new indicator based on the proportion of identifiable high-tech products in a country's exports.

Overall, it is difficult to find strong and robust evidence that a leapfrogging strategy contributes to a higher growth rate. In other words, the empirical investigation does not support the contention that a government intervention aimed at raising a country's technological sophistication beyond what is expected of its level of development produces a better growth result on a sustained basis.

Important caveats for our approach should be borne in mind when interpreting the results. Our measures of a country's leapfrogging strategy are based on its export data. To the extent that a country's export structure may not accurately capture its production structure, we may have missed some true leapfrogging strategies. In addition, the efficacy of a leapfrogging strategy could be more subtle than what we test. For example, it is conceptually possible that only when several policy instruments are implemented as a package can the positive effect of a leapfrogging strategy be detected. Because of these qualifications, we view this paper as a stepping-stone toward a more comprehensive examination of the leapfrogging strategy.

Statistical Specification and Leapfrogging Measurement

A key to this exercise is to assess whether a country pursues a leapfrogging strategy and, if so, the degree of leapfrogging. Ideally, we would compare a country's actual production structure with what would have been predicted on the basis of its factor endowment. This approach holds two challenges. First, data on production structure by an internationally comparable classification are not available for most countries, especially developing countries, for which evaluating the efficacy of a leapfrogging strategy is most pertinent. Second, even when internationally comparable production data are available, one gets only a relatively coarse classification, with fewer than 100 sectors. Many differences in economic structure do not reveal themselves at such an aggregate level. For example, many countries have electronics industries, but different types of electronic products may have very different levels of skill content. We address these challenges by looking at trade data instead. Generally speaking, a country's export structure closely resembles its production structure. Trade data are available for a much larger set of economies (more than 250 in the World Integrated Trade Solution [WITS] database). The most detailed and still internationally comparable level (6-digit Harmonized System[HS]) includes more than 5,000 products a country can export or import. To control for the "normal" amount of sophistication based on a country's factor endowment, we include a country's income and education levels as controls in a growth regression framework.

In the rest of the section, we first review two existing measures of export sophistication in the literature and propose two additional measures that may address some shortcomings of the existing measures. We then describe the data that we use to implement the measures. Finally, we conduct some simple "smell checks" to see how well these measures capture the countries that are commonly reported as having a leapfrogging industrial policy.

Regression Specification

We consider a growth regression specification of the following type:

$$LnGDPc_{it+k} - LnGDPc_{it} = \alpha_0 + \alpha_1 LnGDPc_{it} + \alpha_2 ExpSophis_{it} + X_{it}\Gamma + \omega_{it} \quad (1)$$

The left-hand variable measures the growth rate for country i from year t to year $t + k$. In most cases, we examine the growth performance for a country from 1992 to 2003. $LnGDPc_{it}$ denotes the natural log of per capita gross domestic product (GDP) for country i in year t, $ExpSophis_{it}$ denotes the level of economic sophistication measured using trade data, and X_{it} is a vector of other control variables. Coefficient α_2 measures the impact of leapfrogging policies.

Measures of Industrial Sophistication Based on Export Data

While it is difficult to directly measure a country's industrial sophistication, in part because the standard industrial classification is too coarse for this purpose, the literature has considered proxies based on the data on a country's export bundles. The idea is that, leaving aside nontradable goods, the structure of the export bundle should mimic that of production. One measure is the level of income implied in the export bundle, introduced in Hausmann, Hwang, and Rodrik (2007). This measure builds on the concept that the degree of sophistication in a country's exports can be inferred by the income level of each good's exporter. The second measure is the export dissimilarity index (EDI) introduced by Schott (2008) and adopted by Wang and Wei (2010), which gauges the distance between a country's export structure and that of high-income economies such as Japan, the United States, and the European Union (EU15). Both measures assume that higher-income countries, on average, produce more sophisticated products. One can avoid making this arbitrary assumption and focus on the degree of technological sophistication of the product itself by using a classification of high-tech advanced technology products (ATPs) from the Organisation for Economic Co-operation and Development (OECD) and the United States.

Income Implied in a Country's Export Bundle (EXPY)

This indicator of export sophistication is a measure of the typical income associated with a country's export basket. For every good, one can compute the "typical income" (PRODY) of the countries that export the good, or the weighted average of the income levels across the exporters of this good, with weights proportional to the value of the exports by countries. For any given exporter, one can look at its export basket and compute the weighted average of the typical income levels across all products in the basket, with the weights proportional to the value of each good in the basket. The key underlying assumption here is that advanced countries produce more sophisticated goods and poorer countries produce less sophisticated goods.

$$PRODY_i = \sum_k^n \frac{s_{ik}}{\sum_j s_{ij}} \cdot Y_k \qquad (2)$$

$$EXPY_k = \sum_i s_{ik} \cdot PRODY_i, \qquad (3)$$

where s_{ik} is the share of country k's exports in product i, Y_k is country k's per capita GDP.

This index has two major advantages. First, it does not require one to tediously sift through and classify goods as sophisticated goods or high-tech products. Second, it can be computed easily with data in trade flows and per capita GDP. But it also has several weaknesses. First, the key assumption underlying PRODY—that more advanced countries produce sophisticated goods—may not be true. Advanced countries often produce a larger set of goods than poor countries. Furthermore, larger countries produce a larger set of goods than smaller countries. This suggests that the PRODY index may overweight advanced and large countries. Second, the index may conceal diversity in the quality and type of goods in finer details within a product category. Third, the index fails to capture processing trade, in which a country imports sophisticated product parts to produce the final sophisticated product. This is the case in China, where a significant share of sophisticated exports is based on processing trade. We have constructed the following index in hopes of avoiding some of the pitfalls of the EXPY index.

Unit-Value-Adjusted Implied Income (Modified EXPY)

In this modified version of the EXPY index, we discount the PRODY of each good by the ratio of the unit value of the exporter to the mean unit value of the same goods in the G-3 countries (the United States, Japan, and the European Union):

$$PRODY_i = \sum_k^n \frac{s_{ik}}{\sum_j s_{ij}} Y_k \frac{v_{ik}}{v_{iG3}}. \tag{4}$$

The modified EXPY is computed similarly to the original EXPY index in equation (3).

The motivation for this modification is our belief that the unit value data add an additional layer of differentiation among goods of a different quality or variety. This approach takes account of the diversity within the 6-digit HS category. The assumption behind this modification is that unit value is a proxy for quality, and the G-3 countries export higher-quality goods.

Since we only have unit value of products at the 6-digit HS level around the world for 2005, we apply the same unit value discount factor to the PRODY during our whole sample period.

Distance to the Export Bundle by High-Income Countries

We define an index for a lack of sophistication by the dissimilarity between the structure of a country's or city's exports and that of the G-3 economies or the export dissimilarity index (EDI), as:

$$EDI_{rft} = 100\left(\sum_i abs\left(s_{irt} - s_{i,t}^{ref}\right)\right), \tag{5}$$

$$\text{where } s_{irt} = \frac{E_{irt}}{\sum_i E_{irt}}, \tag{6}$$

where s_{irt} is the share of HS product i at the 6-digit level in a country's or city's exports at year t, and $s_{i,t}^{ref}$ is the share of HS product i in the 6-digit level exports of the G-3 countries. The greater the value of the index, the more dissimilar the compared export structures. If the two export structures were identical, the value of the index would be zero; if the two export structures had no overlap, the value of the index would be 200. We regard an export structure as more sophisticated if the index takes a smaller value. Alternatively, one could use the similarity index proposed by Finger and Kreinin (1979) and used by Schott (2008) (except for the scale):

$$ESI_{rft} = 100\sum_i \min(s_{irtf}, s_{i,t}^{ref}). \tag{7}$$

This index is bounded by zero and 100. If a country's or city's export structure had no overlap with that of the G-3 countries, ESI would be zero; if the two export structures had a perfect overlap, the index would take the value of 100. It can be verified that there is a one-to-one linear mapping between ESI and EDI:

$$ESI_{rft} = \frac{200 - EDI_{rft}}{2}. \tag{8}$$

Share of Advanced Technology Products in Total Exports

Besides the measures already in the literature, we propose a new measure of the share of advanced technology products in a country's export bundle that does not require assuming that richer countries automatically export more sophisticated products:

$$ATPSH_{it} = 100 \frac{EXP_{it}^{ATP}}{EXP_{it}^{TOT}} \tag{9}$$

where EXP_{it}^{ATP} is exports of ATP of country i at time t, EXP_{it}^{TOT} is total exports of country i at time t. This measure of export sophistication requires us to specifically define "high-tech exports"; thus, it sacrifices EXPY's simplicity.

To compute this measure, one needs an expert definition of which product is high-tech. Two lists of expert definitions are well respected. One, developed by the U.S. Census Bureau, identified about 700 product categories as ATPs from about 20,000 10-digit HS codes used by the United States. The other, developed by the OECD, identified 195 high-tech product categories from 5-digit Standard International Trade Classification (SITC) codes. Because the HS classification is more detailed and comparable across countries at the 6-digit level, we concord both lists into 6-digit HS product categories. We convert the OECD product list to 328 6-digit HS codes on the basis of concordance between SITC (rev3) and HS (2002) published by the United Nations Statistical Division.

To condense the U.S. Census ATP list from the 10-digit HS to the 6-digit HS, we first calculate the ATP value share in both U.S. imports from the world at the HS-6 level based on U.S. trade statistics in 2006, bearing in mind that within each HS-6 heading, some of the U.S. Harmonized Tariff Schedule (HTS)–10 lines are considered to be ATPs and others are not. We choose two separate cutoff points. For a narrow ATP definition, we select the 6-digit HS categories in which the ATP share is 100 percent in total U.S. imports from the world according to the Census ATP list, which results in 92 HS-6 lines. For a wider ATP definition, we select the 6-digit HS categories in which the ATP share is at least 25 percent in total U.S. imports from the world, which results in 157 HS-6 lines. We use the 6-digit HS code in which all products are in the Census ATP list and also in the OECD high-tech product list as our narrow definition of ATP. For a wider ATP definition, we deem an HS-6 line as ATP if it is in the OECD high-tech product list or at least 25 percent of its value is ATP products in U.S. imports from the world according to the Census ATP list.

The recent literature documents significant variations within the same product. Although both developed and developing countries may export products under the same 6-digit HS code, their unit value usually varies significantly, largely reflecting the difference in quality between the exports. To allow for the possibility that a very large difference in unit values may signal different products misclassified in the same 6-digit category, we take unit value for all products from Japan, EU15, and the United States (G-3 for short) in our narrow ATP definition as reference; any products with a unit value below the G-3 unit value minus 5 times standard deviation will not be counted as ATP. This provides our third definition of ATP.

Data and Basic Facts

The EXPY measure requires data on trade flow and per capita GDP. We computed EXPY for both a short and a long sample. For the short sample, dating from 1992 to 2006, the data on country exports come from the United Nations COMTRADE database, downloaded from the World Integrated Trade Solution (WITS). The data from 1992 to 2006 are at the 6-digit HS (1988/1992 version), covering 5,016 product categories and 167 countries. For the long sample, dating from 1962 to 2000, the trade flow data are taken from the National Bureau of Economic Research (NBER)-UN data compiled by Feenstra and colleagues (2005), which can be downloaded from the NBER website. The data are at 4-digit SITC (rev 2), covering 700 to more than 1,000 product categories and 72 countries. The per capita GDP data on a purchasing power parity (PPP) basis are taken from the Penn World Table.

The modified EXPY measure also requires data on unit value. These data are obtained from Ferrantino, Feinberg, and Deason (2008), who obtained them from the UN COMTRADE database. The data are for the year 2005 only and are cleaned of products that do not have well-defined quantity units, have inconsistent reporting, have small value, or have unit value belonging to a 2.5 percent tail of the distribution of the product's unit values. In total, the resulting unit value data set covers 3,628 6-digit HS subheadings.

The other two export sophistication indexes—EDI and ATP share (narrow, broad)—are computed excluding HS chapters 1–27 (agricultural and mineral products), as well as raw materials and their simple transformations (mostly at the 4-digit level) in other HS chapters. A list of excluded products is reported in appendix table 1. Each country's ATP export share is computed by the country's ATP exports divided by its total manufacturing exports. Our sample of countries is listed in appendix table 2.

The other explanatory variables included in the growth regressions are human capital, per capita GDP, and institutional quality. The human capital variable in the cross-country regressions uses the average school year in the Barro-Lee education database. Per capita GDP is on a PPP basis and is taken from the Penn World Table. The institutional quality variable is proxied by the government effectiveness index downloaded from the World Bank and Transparency International websites.[4]

Do Leapfroggers Grow Faster? An Examination of Cross-Country Evidence

We now formally examine if a leapfrogging growth strategy produces a faster rate of economic growth in a robust and reliable way.

The Elusive Growth Effect of a Leapfrogging Strategy

Hausmann, Hwang, and Rodrik (2007) provide the most recent and best known paper to offer an empirical foundation for the proposition that a leapfrogging strategy as measured by a country's export sophistication delivers a faster economic growth rate. We begin our statistical analysis by taking a careful look at their specifications, with a view to checking the robustness of their conclusion. In particular, we follow their econometric strategy, regressing the economic growth rate across countries on a leapfrogging measure and other control variables that are typically included in empirical growth papers. After replicating their regressions with EXPY as the leap-frogging proxy, we use the alternative measures discussed above: modified EXP, the EDI indicator, and the ATP shares.

Table 1 shows our replication of the Hausmann and colleagues cross-section regressions for the short sample of 1992–2003 (corresponding to their table 8). The controls include human capital and a measure of institutional quality. Since the source of their rule of law index is not clearly stated, we use four other well-known institutional variables: corruption, government effectiveness, regulation quality, and Consumer Price Index (CPI) score. In the ordinary least squares (OLS) regressions, the coefficients on the first three institution measures are significant; in particular, the coefficient on regulation quality (0.013) is close to Hausmann and colleagues' coefficient on their rule of law index (0.011). Columns 1, 2, 7, and 8 in table 1 can be compared with the corresponding regression in Hausmann and colleagues' table 8; the coefficients on the initial per capita GDP and human capital variables are basically the same as theirs. While the coefficients on log initial EXPY have different magnitudes than Hausmann and colleagues' results for the same sample period of 1992–2003, they are all statistically significant (though not as strong, depending on the institutional variable) and are positive, like theirs. A possible explanation for the difference in the size of the coefficients is that trade data for the countries in the 1992–2003 sample have been revised. The bottom line from this replication exercise is that the Hausmann and colleagues results can be replicated.

In the next step, we replaced the EXPY variable with alternative measures of export sophistication—modified EXPY, EDI, and the ATP shares—and reestimated the regressions. The results for each of these variables are displayed in tables 2–5. In table 2, the coefficient on the modified EXPY is statistically insignificant in all but the first specification with only human capital as control, even as the direction of the coefficients and significance on initial per capita GDP, human capital, and institutional variables remains the same as in table 1. This remains true whether EDI or the broad definition of ATP is used as the export sophistication measure, as shown in tables 3 and 4. However, the coefficient on the ATP share using a more stringent

TABLE 1. Cross-National Growth Regressions Using EXPY as Proposed by Hausmann, Hwang, and Rodrik, 1992–2003

Dependent variable: growth rate of per capita GDP over 1992–2003

	(1)	(2)	(3)	(4)	(5)	(6)	(7)	(8)	(9)	(10)	(11)	(12)
	OLS	OLS	OLS	OLS	OLS	OLS	IV	IV	IV	IV	IV	IV
Log initial GDP/cap	-0.011 [0.005]*	-0.02 [0.007]**	-0.025 [0.007]**	-0.026 [0.006]**	-0.03 [0.007]**	-0.023 [0.007]**	-0.009 [0.006]	-0.017 [0.011]	-0.025 [0.012]*	-0.025 [0.010]*	-0.024 [0.011]*	-0.02 [0.012]
Log initial EXPY	0.036 [0.011]**	0.029 [0.011]*	0.025 [0.010]*	0.019 [0.010]	0.03 [0.010]**	0.027 [0.011]*	0.031 [0.014]*	0.023 [0.015]	0.023 [0.012]	0.016 [0.011]	0.025 [0.013]	0.023 [0.014]
Log human capital		0.033 [0.012]*	0.028 [0.012]*	0.026 [0.010]*	0.021 [0.010]*	0.029 [0.013]*		0.03 [0.017]	0.029 [0.015]*	0.024 [0.012]*	0.016 [0.012]	0.029 [0.016]
Corruption			0.008 [0.003]*						0.008 [0.004]			
Government effectiveness				0.013 [0.003]**						0.013 [0.004]**		
Regulation quality					0.021 [0.005]**						0.018 [0.006]**	
Cpi score						0.002 [0.001]						0.001 [0.002]
Constant	-0.193 [0.066]**	-0.114 [0.072]	-0.023 [0.065]	0.041 [0.074]	-0.029 [0.061]	-0.066 [0.070]	-0.168 [0.078]*	-0.079 [0.080]	-0.014 [0.064]	0.054 [0.069]	-0.019 [0.062]	-0.057 [0.072]
Observations	52	42	42	42	42	42	52	42	42	42	42	42
R-squared	0.24	0.35	0.41	0.5	0.53	0.38						
Hansen J							0.93	1.69	1.61	0.82	0.35	1.95
Chi-sq p-value							0.33	0.19	0.2	0.36	0.56	0.16

Note: Robust standard errors in brackets; instruments for IV regressions are log(population) and log(land).

* significant at 5%.

** significant at 1%.

TABLE 2. Alternative Measure of Export Sophistication — Unit-Value-Adjusted Implied Income in the Export Bundle: Modified EXPY, 1992–2003

	(1)	(2)	(3)	(4)	(5)	(6)	(7)	(8)	(9)	(10)	(11)	(12)
	— Dependent variable: growth rate of per capita GDP over 1992–2003											
	OLS	OLS	OLS	OLS	OLS	OLS	IV	IV	IV	IV	IV	IV
Log initial GDP/cap	-0.004	-0.016	-0.02	-0.023	-0.022	-0.018	-0.005	-0.017	-0.032	-0.034	-0.031	-0.022
	[0.004]	[0.006]*	[0.006]**	[0.006]**	[0.007]**	[0.006]**	[0.003]	[0.011]	[0.017]	[0.012]**	[0.013]*	[0.016]
Log initial modified EXPY	0.011	0.009	0.004	-0.001	0.004	0.006	0.012	0.01	0.006	-0.001	0.005	0.008
	[0.004]**	[0.006]	[0.006]	[0.006]	[0.007]	[0.006]	[0.004]**	[0.006]	[0.006]	[0.006]	[0.006]	[0.006]
Log human capital		0.033	0.03	0.027	0.025	0.031		0.035	0.041	0.038	0.033	0.035
		[0.014]*	[0.013]*	[0.011]*	[0.012]	[0.014]*		[0.023]	[0.024]	[0.016]*	[0.018]	[0.024]
Corruption			0.009						0.013			
			[0.003]*						[0.009]			
Government effectiveness				0.016						0.021		
				[0.004]**						[0.007]**		
Regulation quality					0.019						0.024	
					[0.007]*						[0.010]*	
Cpi score						0.002						0.002
						[0.002]						[0.003]
Constant	-0.024	0.037	0.123	0.195	0.144	0.077	-0.023	0.038	0.188	0.264	0.193	0.085
	[0.029]	[0.043]	[0.052]*	[0.061]**	[0.052]**	[0.050]	[0.029]	[0.048]	[0.125]	[0.103]*	[0.086]*	[0.089]
Observations	52	42	42	42	42	42	52	42	42	42	42	42
R-squared	0.17	0.28	0.34	0.45	0.4	0.3						
Hansen J							0.11	1.05	1.22	0.66	0.13	1.49
Chi-sq p-value							0.74	0.31	0.27	0.42	0.72	0.22

Note: Robust standard errors in brackets; instruments for IV regressions are log(population) and log(land).

* significant at 5%.

** significant at 1%.

213

TABLE 3. Cross-National Growth Regressions with ATP Share (Narrow Definition), 1992–2003

Dependent variable: growth rate of per capita GDP over 1992–2003

	(1)	(2)	(3)	(4)	(5)	(6)	(7)	(8)	(9)	(10)	(11)	(12)
	OLS	OLS	OLS	OLS	OLS	OLS	IV	IV	IV	IV	IV	IV
log initial GDP/cap	-0.002	-0.015	-0.021	-0.023	-0.022	-0.019	-0.008	-0.017	-0.033	-0.026	-0.03	-0.026
	[0.003]	[0.006]*	[0.007]**	[0.007]**	[0.007]*	[0.007]*	[0.006]	[0.015]	[0.019]	[0.014]	[0.020]	[0.020]
initial ATP share (narrow)	0.087	0.076	0.069	0.049	0.056	0.07	0.112	0.083	0.077	0.05	0.055	0.081
	[0.026]**	[0.027]**	[0.024]**	[0.027]	[0.023]*	[0.025]**	[0.034]**	[0.030]**	[0.022]**	[0.025]*	[0.022]*	[0.024]**
log human capital		0.036	0.03	0.027	0.026	0.031		0.041	0.042	0.03	0.035	0.039
		[0.014]*	[0.013]*	[0.011]*	[0.013]	[0.014]*		[0.032]	[0.023]	[0.018]	[0.023]	[0.026]
corruption			0.009						0.015			
			[0.003]**						[0.009]			
government effectiveness				0.014						0.015		
				[0.004]**						[0.008]*		
regulation quality					0.018						0.024	
					[0.006]**						[0.015]	
cpi score						0.003						0.004
						[0.002]						[0.004]
Constant	0.054	0.098	0.164	0.181	0.172	0.129	0.105	0.112	0.241	0.198	0.225	0.173
	[0.030]	[0.036]**	[0.045]**	[0.043]**	[0.042]**	[0.044]**	[0.056]	[0.071]	[0.119]*	[0.088]*	[0.124]	[0.111]
Observations	52	42	42	42	42	42	52	42	42	42	42	42
R-squared	0.13	0.32	0.41	0.49	0.44	0.36						
Hansen J							0	0.59	0.16	0.02	0.07	0.72
Chi-sq p-value							0.97	0.44	0.69	0.88	0.78	0.4

Note: Robust standard errors in brackets; instruments for IV regressions are log(population) and log(land).

* significant at 5%.

** significant at 1%.

TABLE 4. Cross-National Growth Regressions with ATP Share (Broad) as a Measure of Sophistication, 1992–2003

	(1)	(2)	(3)	(4)	(5)	(6)	(7)	(8)	(9)	(10)	(11)	(12)
						Dependent variable: growth rate of GDP per capita over 1992–2003					
	OLS	OLS	OLS	OLS	OLS	OLS	IV	IV	IV	IV	IV	IV
log initial GDP/cap	-0.002	-0.014	-0.021	-0.023	-0.023	-0.019	-0.007	-0.018	-0.033	-0.028	-0.03	-0.027
	[0.004]	[0.006]*	[0.007]**	[0.006]**	[0.007]**	[0.007]*	[0.006]	[0.014]	[0.017]	[0.013]*	[0.017]	[0.018]
initial ATP share (broad)	0.056	0.041	0.035	0.019	0.031	0.036	0.074	0.049	0.046	0.022	0.034	0.048
	[0.022]*	[0.026]	[0.023]	[0.023]	[0.020]	[0.024]	[0.028]**	[0.028]	[0.020]*	[0.020]	[0.020]	[0.022]*
log human capital		0.036	0.029	0.027	0.025	0.031		0.044	0.041	0.031	0.032	0.039
		[0.014]*	[0.013]*	[0.011]*	[0.013]	[0.014]*		[0.030]	[0.023]	[0.018]	[0.021]	[0.026]
corruption			0.01						0.015			
			[0.003]**						[0.008]			
government effectiveness				0.015						0.017		
				[0.004]**						[0.007]*		
regulation quality					0.019						0.024	
					[0.006]**						[0.012]	
cpi score						0.003						0.004
						[0.002]						[0.003]
Constant	0.055	0.097	0.164	0.183	0.178	0.129	0.054	0.118	0.244	0.212	0.222	0.18
	[0.032]	[0.036]*	[0.045]**	[0.041]**	[0.043]**	[0.044]**	[0.049]	[0.067]	[0.108]*	[0.082]**	[0.104]*	[0.101]
Observations	52	42	42	42	42	42	52	42	42	42	42	42
R-squared	0.09	0.26	0.36	0.46	0.41	0.31						
Hansen J							0.03	1.2	0.48	0.23	0.01	1.34
Chi-sq p-value							0.85	0.27	0.49	0.63	0.91	0.25

Note: Robust standard errors in brackets; instruments for IV regressions are log(population) and log(land).

* significant at 5%.

** significant at 1%.

TABLE 5. Cross-National Growth Regressions with EDI as a Measure of Leapfrogging, 1992–2003

	(1)	(2)	(3)	(4)	(5)	(6)	(7)	(8)	(9)	(10)	(11)	(12)
	OLS	OLS	OLS	OLS	OLS	OLS	IV	IV	IV	IV	IV	IV
log initial GDP/cap	-0.005	-0.017	-0.024	-0.026	-0.025	-0.021	-0.007	-0.02	-0.035	-0.034	-0.03	-0.031
	[0.004]	[0.007]*	[0.007]**	[0.006]**	[0.007]**	[0.007]**	[0.004]	[0.008]*	[0.010]**	[0.008]**	[0.011]**	[0.009]**
log initial EDI	-0.025	-0.011	-0.001	0.008	-0.007	-0.002	-0.029	-0.012	-0.011	0.002	-0.01	-0.011
	[0.012]*	[0.014]	[0.012]	[0.010]	[0.014]	[0.013]	[0.015]*	[0.017]	[0.014]	[0.011]	[0.015]	[0.015]
log human capital		0.038	0.029	0.027	0.026	0.03		0.044	0.043	0.036	0.031	0.044
		[0.014]**	[0.013]*	[0.011]*	[0.013]*	[0.014]*		[0.019]*	[0.017]*	[0.014]*	[0.016]	[0.018]*
corruption			0.012						0.016			
			[0.004]**						[0.005]**			
government effectiveness				0.018						0.021		
				[0.004]**						[0.005]**		
regulation quality					0.019						0.023	
					[0.007]**						[0.010]*	
cpi score						0.004						0.005
						[0.002]*						[0.002]*
Constant	0.213	0.174	0.195	0.165	0.233	0.162	0.248	0.197	0.318	0.246	0.286	0.264
	[0.081]*	[0.104]	[0.095]*	[0.083]	[0.108]*	[0.097]	[0.103]*	[0.122]	[0.114]**	[0.085]**	[0.130]*	[0.111]*
Observations	52	41	41	41	41	41	52	41	41	41	41	41
R-squared	0.09	0.23	0.37	0.48	0.36	0.31						
Hansen J							0.97	1.36	1.26	0.39	0.15	2.08
Chi-sq p-value							0.33	0.24	0.26	0.53	0.7	0.15

Note: Robust standard errors in brackets; instruments for IV regressions are log(population) and log(land).

* significant at 5%.

** significant at 1%.

colleagues' measure of sophistication by taking into account possible differences in unit values when computing the implied income in an export bundle makes the positive association disappear. It may be too early to conclude that pursuing a leapfrogging strategy will raise a country's growth rate.

Does Growth in Sophistication Lead to Growth in Income?

The level of a country's export sophistication may not capture policy incentives or other government actions. If a country pursues an education policy that generates an unusually large pool of scientists and engineers, its level of export sophistication may surpass what can be predicted solely on the basis of its income or endowment. A useful alternative empirical strategy is to look at the growth of a country's export sophistication. Holding the initial levels of export sophistication constant, would countries that have an unusually fast increase in sophistication also have an unusually high rate of economic growth?

In table 6, we rank the 49 countries in our sample by descending order on the pace of the growth of their export sophistication. As an intuitive "smell test," we pay particular attention to where Ireland and China fit, as both countries are often cited as examples of extensive government programs to promote industrial transformation toward high-tech industries. All five measures are able to capture China as having experienced a high level of change in its export sophistication. But only the modified EXPY variable is able to capture both China and Ireland as having undergone a significant change in export sophistication during the period. This strengthens our confidence in the relative adequacy of the modified EXPY against the original EXPY in capturing leapfrogging in industrial structure.

Table 7 shows the regression results with this specification for all five export sophistication measures and their changes over the 1992–2003 period. The initial GDP level, human capital, and institutional variables all have the correct signs. None of the export sophistication growth variables enter significantly into the regression. But the most conspicuous finding is connected to the initial export sophistication measures: all but the EXPY variable are insignificant with this specification. In contrast to the previous specification, the ATP share is no longer significant either. This again shows that when export sophistication is constructed in alternative ways, it no longer indicates a significant impact on growth. These results cast doubt on the view that leapfrogging leads to higher growth.

Panel Regressions with Instrumental Variables

The cross-section regressions assume that productivity growth is the same for all countries except for differences in the leapfrog policies. As an extension that relaxes this assumption, we turn to a panel analysis with separate country fixed effects. New challenges emerge with the panel analysis: One has to deal with

TABLE 6. Ranking Growth in Export Sophistication, 1992–2003

Ranking	Country	EXPY	Country	Modified EXPY	Country	ATP (narrow)	Country	ATP (broad)	Country	EDI
1	Hungary	3.14	Ireland	5.54	Malaysia	1.50	Malaysia	2.01	Australia	-2.32
2	Bangladesh	3.12	Hungary	4.44	Iceland	1.41	Hungary	1.93	Korea, Rep.	-1.70
3	Kenya	3.05	Madagascar	4.38	China	1.20	China	1.88	Oman	-1.56
4	Madagascar	2.78	Kenya	3.55	Singapore	1.09	Finland	1.31	Hungary	-1.50
5	Korea, Rep.	2.10	Ecuador	3.41	Netherlands	0.88	Singapore	1.10	Mexico	-1.46
6	Thailand	2.07	Indonesia	3.22	Hungary	0.56	Korea, Rep.	1.09	Kenya	-1.45
7	China	2.03	South Africa	3.12	Indonesia	0.50	Iceland	1.08	Greece	-1.42
8	Trinidad and Tobago	1.96	Bangladesh	3.04	Thailand	0.49	Netherlands	1.04	Thailand	-1.40
9	Paraguay	1.89	Singapore	3.01	Korea, Rep.	0.40	Indonesia	0.95	Indonesia	-1.38
10	Singapore	1.83	China	2.98	Mexico	0.33	Mexico	0.93	Turkey	-1.35
11	Turkey	1.82	Brunei	2.98	Portugal	0.33	Thailanc	0.70	Portugal	-1.28
12	Colombia	1.50	Turkey	2.91	St. Lucia	0.20	Greece	0.64	Ecuador	-1.09
13	Iceland	1.40	Malaysia	2.87	Tunisia	0.16	Croatia	0.61	China	-1.02
14	Malaysia	1.37	Thailand	2.61	Switzerland	0.15	Switzerland	0.59	India	-1.00
15	Cyprus	1.30	Korea, Rep.	2.29	Australia	0.15	Brazil	0.54	Spain	-0.98
16	Bolivia	1.24	Greece	2.05	Finland	0.15	Denmark	0.49	Saudi Arabia	-0.96
17	Portugal	1.24	Portugal	1.96	Bolivia	0.13	Portugal	0.45	Malaysia	-0.79
18	Croatia	1.16	Cyprus	1.94	Sweden	0.13	St. Lucia	0.42	Colombia	-0.73
19	Greece	1.15	Colombia	1.78	Greece	0.11	Australia	0.39	Sweden	-0.63
20	Finland	1.12	Tunisia	1.75	Kenya	0.09	New Zealand	0.39	Denmark	-0.59
21	India	1.08	Croatia	1.70	Croatia	0.09	Paraguay	0.30	Paraguay	-0.55
22	Ecuador	1.01	Mexico	1.67	India	0.08	Tunisia	0.26	New Zealand	-0.54
23	Mexico	0.99	Iceland	1.41	New Zealand	0.08	Sweden	0.24	Romania	-0.51

#	Country	Value	Country	Value	Country	Value	Country	Value	Value
24	Indonesia	0.90	Denmark	1.35	Romania	0.07	Iceland	0.21	-0.50
25	Sri Lanka	0.86	Cyprus	1.24	Kenya	0.05	St. Lucia	0.20	-0.48
26	South Africa	0.86	Romania	1.15	India	0.05	Brazil	0.15	-0.46
27	Switzerland	0.65	Algeria	1.06	Bolivia	0.04	Cyprus	0.14	-0.46
28	Australia	0.63	Saudi Arabia	1.06	Algeria	0.03	Japan	0.14	-0.43
29	New Zealand	0.54	Paraguay	1.04	Saudi Arabia	0.03	Tunisia	0.10	-0.42
30	Oman	0.52	Ecuador	0.98	Turkey	0.03	South Africa	0.08	-0.40
31	Ireland	0.31	Peru	0.93	Chile	0.01	Croatia	0.05	-0.39
32	Brazil	0.27	Chile	0.91	Spain	0.01	Sri Lanka	0.03	-0.37
33	Tunisia	0.27	Turkey	0.88	Peru	0.01	Canada	0.02	-0.36
34	Denmark	0.27	Bangladesh	0.80	Japan	0.00	Peru	0.02	-0.31
35	Japan	0.25	South Africa	0.67	Bangladesh	0.00	Singapore	0.01	-0.25
36	Sweden	0.25	Belize	0.66	Belize	0.00	Bolivia	0.01	-0.22
37	Netherlands	0.20	Trinidad and Tobago	0.24	Trinidad and Tobago	0.00	Algeria	0.00	-0.07
38	St. Lucia	0.20	Brunei	0.24	Canada	0.00	Brunei	0.00	-0.01
39	Spain	0.20	Jamaica	0.17	Brunei	0.00	Bangladesh	0.00	-0.01
40	Canada	0.17	Spain	0.11	Jamaica	-0.01	Netherlands	-0.01	0.00
41	Chile	0.07	Japan	0.09	Spain	-0.01	Chile	-0.02	0.00
42	Algeria	0.01	Colombia	-0.22	Ecuador	-0.02	Switzerland	-0.02	0.01
43	Brunei	-0.03	Madagascar	-0.37	Madagascar	-0.02	Belize	-0.03	0.02
44	Saudi Arabia	-0.07	Brazil	-0.42	Sri Lanka	-0.03	Trinidad and Tobago	-0.05	0.04
45	Jamaica	-0.25	Sri Lanka	-0.50	Cyprus	-0.04	Finland	-0.05	0.11
46	Macao	-0.40	Macao	-0.51	Colombia	-0.06	Madagascar	-0.08	0.14
47	Romania	-0.68	Ireland	-0.91	Ireland	-0.15	Jamaica	-0.10	0.16
48	Peru	-0.84	Canada	-2.74	South Africa	-0.24	Ireland	-0.13	0.34
49	Belize	-1.09	Oman	-3.17	Oman	-0.25	Macao	-0.23	0.48

Note: Robust standard errors in brackets; instruments for IV regressions are log(population) and log(land).

* significant at 5%.

** significant at 1%.

TABLE 7. Cross-National Growth Regressions, with Growth in Export Sophistication As Key Regressor

	Dependent variable: growth in real per capita GDP, 1992–2003				
	(1)	(2)	(3)	(4)	(5)
log initial per capita GDP	−0.028	−0.02	−0.02	−0.02	−0.02
	[0.005]**	[0.005]**	[0.005]**	[0.005]**	[0.005]**
human capital	0.016	0.021	0.022	0.019	0.023
	[0.010]	[0.011]	[0.010]*	[0.010]	[0.011]
regulation quality	0.018	0.015	0.015	0.016	0.018
	[0.006]**	[0.007]*	[0.006]*	[0.006]*	[0.007]*
log initial EXPY	0.032				
	[0.009]**				
growth in log EXPY	0.252				
	[0.240]				
log initial modified EXPY		0.005			
		[0.005]			
growth in log modified EXPY		0.081			
		[0.153]			
initial ATP share (narrow)			0.04		
			[0.031]		
growth in ATP share (narrow)			0.891		
			[0.567]		
initial ATP share (broad)				0.026	
				[0.023]	
growth in ATP share (broad)				0.731	
				[0.388]	
initial log EDI					−0.001
					[0.015]
growth in log EDI					−0.003
					[0.407]
Constant	−0.06	0.12	0.16	0.162	0.17
	[0.070]	[0.052]*	[0.033]**	[0.033]**	[0.095]
Observations	41	41	41	41	39
R-squared	0.51	0.36	0.44	0.43	0.33

Note: Robust standard errors in brackets.

* significant at 5%.

** significant at 1%.

definition is positively significant across all specifications. We will show in the next section that even this result is not robust.

To summarize, the positive association between a country's export sophistication and economic growth rate is not a strong and robust pattern of the data. In particular, alternative measures of export sophistication often produce statistically insignificant coefficients. For example, a reasonable adjustment to Hausmann and shorter time intervals and must have instrumental variables that have meaningful time-series variations.

We do not have clever instrumental variables. For lack of better ones, we experiment with the idea that the professional background and educational preparedness of a political leader may affect his or her choice of economic strategy and are therefore candidates for instrumental variables. The idea is imported from Dreher and colleagues (2009). After constructing a database of profession and education for more than 500 political leaders from 73 countries for the period 1970–2002, we found that pro-market reforms are more likely to be proposed and implemented by leaders who are former entrepreneurs or scientists. Educational background sometimes has an influence, but the effect is not robust. We follow the approach of Dreher and colleagues and, in fact, borrow their data set. One set of dummies codifies the educational background for chief executives: law, economics, politics, natural science, and other. Another set of dummies codifies the professions of chief executives before they took office: entrepreneur, white collar, blue collar, union executive, science, economics, law, military, politician, and other. We use this set of variables as instruments for export sophistication.

These instruments are not ideal. In the first-stage regressions (not reported), we cannot confirm the findings by Dreher and colleagues (2009) that former entrepreneurs or former scientists-turned-politicians do things differently in the context of a leapfrogging strategy. However, there is some evidence that leaders who are former blue collar workers or former labor union executives are more likely to pursue a leapfrogging strategy (when leapfrogging is measured by the criterion of EDI). There is also some evidence that lifetime politicians are more likely to pursue a leapfrogging strategy.

The Durbin-Wu-Hausmann chi-square test fails to reject the null that the OLS and the Instrumental Variable (IV) estimates are different (with a p-value of 0.50). This might imply that there is no significant endogeneity issue in the current context, and that an IV approach is not necessary. On the other hand, the F statistics (for the null that all regressors are jointly zero) is only 3.08. So we cannot rule out the possibility that these leader background variables are weak instruments.

For what it is worth, table 8 shows the second-stage growth regression results for the long sample of 1970–2000, using EXPY and EDI as measures of export sophistication. Unfortunately, we cannot use the ATP shares, as they are not available for early years. Panel A shows the results using EXPY as export sophistication. To compare with the analysis in Hausmann, Hwang, and Rodrik (2007), our sample starts a few years later (as opposed to their 1962–2000). Our OLS estimation closely replicates their estimates: the coefficient on initial GDP per capita is negative and significant at –0.001, the coefficient on initial EXPY is positive and significant at 0.02, and the coefficient on human capital is positive and significant at 0.01. In the fixed effects and IV specifications, neither of the coefficients on initial EXPY is significant, despite the improved Hansen-J statistics given our set of instruments. The R-squared of our regression for the OLS case is more than twice as large as theirs, despite the similarities in the estimates. Panel B shows the results for the same regression, replacing

TABLE 8. Long Sample, Panel Regressions with Fixed Effects

A. EXPY

5-year panels

	(1)	(2)	(3)
	OLS	FE	IV
log initial GDP/cap	–0.0103	–0.0479	–0.0113
	[0.0027]**	[0.0060]**	[0.0104]
log initial EXPY	0.0208	0.0027	0.0223
	[0.0055]**	[0.0091]	[0.0423]
log human capital	0.0116	–0.0102	0.0088
	[0.0027]**	[0.0065]	[0.0078]
Constant	–0.059	0.3688	–0.0573
	[0.0379]	[0.0788]**	[0.3033]
Observations	640	640	369
R-squared	0.39	0.47	
First-stage F stat			1.35
Hansen J-statistics (p-value)			0.186

B. EDI

5-year panels

	(1)	(2)	(3)
	OLS	FE	IV
log initial GDP/cap	–0.0065	–0.0517	–0.0097
	[0.0026]*	[0.0062]**	[0.0054]
log initial EDI	–0.0117	0.004	–0.0271
	[0.0071]	[0.0191]	[0.0180]
log human capital	0.0128	–0.0256	0.0081
	[0.0030]**	[0.0079]**	[0.0041]*
Constant	0.1555	0.4266	0.2709
	[0.0473]**	[0.1136]**	[0.1222]*
Observations	475	475	314
R-squared	0.43	0.59	
First-stage F stat			3.08
Hansen J-statistics (p-value)			0.089

Note: Robust standard errors in brackets; the instruments are professions and educational background of political leaders from Dreher and others 2009.

 * significant at 5%.

** significant at 1%.

EXPY with EDI. None of the export sophistication variables are significant, while the initial per capita GDP and human capital variables are both significant. We conclude that in the panel regressions, no strong and robust support exists for the notion that a leapfrogging strategy promotes growth (subject to the caveat that we may not have found powerful instruments).

Conclusion

Transforming an economy's economic structure ahead of its income level toward higher domestic value added and more sophisticated sectors is desirable in the abstract. Many governments have pursued policies to bring about such a transformation. There are examples of success—government policies that result in the expansion of a certain industry. However, any such policy promotion takes resources away from other industries, especially those that are consistent with the country's factor endowment and level of development. On balance, the effect is conceptually less clear. Given the popularity of leapfrogging strategies, it is important to evaluate empirically whether they work. Unfortunately, evaluation is difficult, because it is not straightforward to quantify the degree of leapfrogging an economy may exhibit. Typical data on production structures are not sufficiently refined, and most relevant policies are not easily quantifiable or comparable across countries.

One way to gauge the degree of leapfrogging is by inferring from a country's detailed export data. We pursue this strategy by developing a number of different ways to measure leapfrogging from revealed sophistication in a country's exports, while recognizing that any particular measure may have both advantages and shortcomings. It should be noted here that none of the measures is perfect. For example, the presence of processing trade—use of imported inputs in the production for exports—could introduce a bias in all such measures. Processing trade has a significant presence in some countries. For example, Koopman, Wang, and Wei (2008) estimated that the actual domestic value added is only about 50 percent of China's gross exports.

After a battery of analyses, a succinct summary of the findings is a lack of strong and robust support for the notion that a leapfrogging industrial policy can reliably raise economic growth. Again, there are individual success stories, but there are also failures. If leapfrogging is a policy gamble, no systematic evidence suggests that the odds are favorable.

We conclude by noting again two distinct aspects of a growth model that embraces the world market. The first aspect is export orientation—an investment environment with few policy impediments to firms participating in international trade. While we do not reproduce the vast quantity of analysis on this, we do not doubt its validity. The second aspect is leapfrogging—the use of policy instruments to engineer a faster industrial transformation than what may emerge naturally on the basis of an economy's stage of development and factor endowment. We cast some doubt on how effective such a strategy is empirically.

Important follow-up research remains to be done. First, part of the leapfrogging strategy works on the "import side," which our empirical strategy does not fully capture; for example, the use of tariff and other policies to reduce imports of high-tech or high value-added products to give domestically produced substitutes some space. One can imagine how such a strategy could backfire, but a systematic examination of the data would be useful. Second, while a leapfrogging strategy might not work in general, moderate and subtle versions of the strategy exist that aim not to defy comparative advantage generally but to explore latent comparative advantage—the economic structure a country would have evolved into naturally in the next stage. Is a pattern of latent comparative advantage identifiable and explorable on a systematic basis? We leave these topics for future research.

APPENDIX TABLE 1. HS Products Excluded from Export Data

HS Code	Description	HS Code	Description
01–24	Agricultural products	25–27	Mineral products
4103	Other raw hides and skins (fresh, o	8002	Tin waste and scrap.
4104	Tanned or crust hides and skins of	8101	Tungsten (wolfram) and articles the
4105	Tanned or crust skins of sheep or l	8102	Molybdenum and articles thereof, in
4106	Tanned or crust hides and skins of	8103	Tantalum and articles thereof, incl
4402	Wood charcoal (including shell or n	8104	Magnesium and articles thereof, inc
4403	Wood in the rough, whether or not s	8105	Cobalt mattes and other intermediate
7201	Pig iron and spiegeleisen in pigs,	8106	Bismuth and articles thereof, inclu
7202	Ferro-alloys.	8107	Cadmium and articles thereof, inclu
7204	Ferrous waste and scrap; remelting	8108	Titanium and articles thereof, incl
7404	Copper waste and scrap.	8109	Zirconium and articles thereof, inc
7501	Nickel mattes, nickel oxide sinters	8110	Antimony and articles thereof, incl
7502	Unwrought nickel.	8111	Manganese and articles thereof, inc
7503	Nickel waste and scrap.	8112	Beryllium, chromium, germanium, van
7601	Unwrought aluminum.	8113	Cermets and articles thereof, inclu
7602	Aluminum waste and scrap.	9701	Paintings, drawings and pastels, ex
7801	Unwrought lead.	9702	Original engravings, prints and lit
7802	Lead waste and scrap.	9703	Original sculptures and statuary, i
7901	Unwrought zinc.	9704	Postage or revenue stamps, stamp-po
7902	Zinc waste and scrap.	9705	Collections and collectors' pieces
8001	Unwrought tin.	9706	Antiques of an age exceeding one hundred years
530521	Coconut, abaca (Manila hemp or Musa	811252	Beryllium, chromium, germanium, van

APPENDIX TABLE 2. Countries (165) Included in the Sample Used in Cross-Country Regression

Code	Reporting country/ economy	# Year reported	Code	Reporting country/ economy	# Year reported	Code	Reporting country	# Year reported
ABW	Aruba	5	GBR	United Kingdom	14	NCL	New Caledonia	8
AIA	Anguilla	6	GEO	Georgia	11	NER	Niger	11
ALB	Albania	11	GHA	Ghana	10	NGA	Nigeria	8
AND	Andorra	12	GIN	Guinea	8	NIC	Nicaragua	14
ARG	Argentina	14	GMB	Gambia, The	12	NLD	Netherlands	15
ARM	Armenia	9	GRC	Greece	15	NOR	Norway	14
AUS	Australia	15	GRD	Grenada	14	NPL	Nepal	5
AUT	Austria	13	GRL	Greenland	13	NZL	New Zealand	15
AZE	Azerbaijan	11	GTM	Guatemala	14	OMN	Oman	15
BDI	Burundi	14	GUY	Guyana	10	PAK	Pakistan	4
BEL	Belgium	8	HKG	Hong Kong SAR, China	14	PAN	Panama	12
BEN	Benin	8	HND	Honduras	13	PER	Peru	14
BFA	Burkina Faso	10	HRV	Croatia	15	PHL	Philippines	11
BGD	Bangladesh	12	HTI	Haiti	6	PNG	Papua New Guinea	6
BGR	Bulgaria	11	HUN	Hungary	15	POL	Poland	13
BHR	Bahrain	7	IDN	Indonesia	15	PRT	Portugal	15
BHS	Bahamas, The	6	IND	India	15	PRY	Paraguay	15
BIH	Bosnia and Herzegovina	4	IRL	Ireland	15	PYF	French Polynesia	11
BLR	Belarus	9	IRN	Iran, Islamic Rep.	10	QAT	Qatar	7
BLZ	Belize	15	ISL	Iceland	15	ROM	Romania	15
BOL	Bolivia	15	ISR	Israel	12	RUS	Russian Federation	11
BRA	Brazil	15	ITA	Italy	13	RWA	Rwanda	10
BRB	Barbados	10	JAM	Jamaica	13	SAU	Saudi Arabia	14
BRN	Brunei	9	JOR	Jordan	12	SDN	Sudan	12
BTN	Bhutan	4	JPN	Japan	15	SEN	Senegal	11
BWA	Botswana	7	KAZ	Kazakhstan	7	SER	Yugoslavia	11
CAF	Central African Republic	13	KEN	Kenya	11	SGP	Singapore	15
CAN	Canada	15	KGZ	Kyrgyz Republic	9	SLV	El Salvador	13

(continued)

APPENDIX TABLE 2. (Continued)

Code	Reporting country/ economy	# Year reported	Code	Reporting country/ economy	# Year reported	Code	Reporting country	# Year reported
CHE	Switzerland	15	KHM	Cambodia	5	STP	São Tomé and Principe	8
CHL	Chile	15	KIR	Kiribati	6	SUR	Suriname	6
CHN	China	15	KNA	St. Kitts and Nevis	13	SVK	Slovak Republic	13
CIV	Côte d'Ivoire	12	KOR	Korea, Rep.	15	SVN	Slovenia	13
CMR	Cameroon	10	LBN	Lebanon	8	SWE	Sweden	15
COK	Cook Islands	4	LCA	St. Lucia	15	SWZ	Swaziland	6
COL	Colombia	15	LKA	Sri Lanka	9	SYC	Seychelles	11
COM	Comoros	10	LSO	Lesotho	5	SYR	Syrian Arab Republic	6
CPV	Cape Verde	10	LTU	Lithuania	13	TCA	Turks and Caicos Island	6
CRI	Costa Rica	13	LUX	Luxembourg	8	TGO	Togo	12
CUB	Cuba	8	LVA	Latvia	13	THA	Thailand	15
CYP	Cyprus	15	MAC	Macao	14	TTC	Trinidad and Tobago	15
CZE	Czech Republic	14	MAR	Morocco	14	TUN	Tunisia	15
DEU	Germany	15	MDA	Moldova	11	TUR	Turkey	15
DMA	Dominica	13	MDG	Madagascar	15	TWN	Taiwan, China	10
DNK	Denmark	15	MDV	Maldives	12	TZA	Tanzania	10
DZA	Algeria	15	MEX	Mexico	15	UGA	Uganda	13
ECU	Ecuador	15	MKD	Macedonia, FYR	13	UKR	Ukraine	11
EGY	Egypt, Arab Rep.	13	MLI	Mali	11	URY	Uruguay	13
ESP	Spain	15	MLT	Malta	13	USA	United States	15
EST	Estonia	12	MNG	Mongolia	11	VCT	St. Vincent and the Grena dines	14
ETH	Ethiopia (excludes Eritrea)	11	MOZ	Mozambique	7	VEN	Venezuela, RB	13
FIN	Finland	15	MSR	Montserrat	8	VNM	Vietnam	6
FJI	Fiji	6	MUS	Mauritius	14	WSM	Samoa	5
FRA	France	13	MWI	Malawi	13	ZAF	South Africa	15
FRO	Faeroe Islands	11	MYS	Malaysia	15	ZMB	Zambia	12
GAB	Gabon	13	NAM	Namibia	7	ZWE	Zimbabwe	6

Notes

1. Myanmar (Burma) has also consistently reported double-digit real gross domestic product growth rates every year since 2001, but international financial institutions and other observers are somewhat skeptical about the reliability of the statistics. Chinese official growth rates are also sometimes challenged for their veracity, although most scholars, economists of major international investment banks, and international financial institutions take the view that the officially released figures are reliable. Or, if there is a bias, the bias could be either positive or negative.

2. Republic of the Philippines National Information Technology Council, "I.T. Action Agenda for the 21st Century," October 1997, http://www.neda.gov.ph/IT21/default.htm.

3. See Harrison and Rodrìguez-Clare (2010) for an excellent review of potential justifications and pitfalls for industrial policies in developing countries.

4. http://www.worldbank.org/wbi/governance/govdata/ and http://ww1.transparency.org/surveys/index.html#cpi.

References

Dreher, Axel, Michael J. Lamla, Sarah M. Lein, and Frank Somogyi. 2009. "The Impact of Political Leaders' Profession and Education on Reforms." *Journal of Comparative Economics* 37 (1), 169–93.

Feenstra, Robert, Robert E. Lipsey, Haiyan Deng, Alyson C. Ma, and Hengyong Mo. 2005. *World Trade Flows: 1962–2000*. National Bureau of Economic Research (NBER) Working Paper 11040, January. Washington, DC.

Ferrantino, Michael, Robert M. Feinberg, and Lauren Deason. 2008. "Quality Competition, Pricing-to-Market and Non-Tariff Measures: A Unified Framework for the Analysis of Bilateral Unit Values," working paper, http://papers.ssrn.com/sol3/papers.cfm?abstract_id=1266183.

Feyrer, James. 2009. "Trade and Income—Exploiting Time Series in Geography." Working Paper, Dartmouth College.

Finger, J. Michael, and M. E. Kreinin, 1979, "A Measure of 'Export Similarity' and Its Possible Uses," *Economic Journal*, 89: 905–912.

Frankel, Jeffrey, and David Romer. 1999. "Does Trade Cause Growth?" *American Economic Review* 89 (3): 379–99.

Harrison, Ann, and Andrés Rodríguez-Clare. 2010. "Trade, Foreign Investment, and Industrial Policy for Developing Countries." In Dani Rodrik and Mark Rosenzweig, eds., *Handbook of Development Economics*, vol. 5, North-Holland.

Hausmann, Ricardo, David Hwang, and Dani Rodrik. 2007. "What You Export Matters." *Journal of Economic Growth* 12 (1): 1–25.

Koopman, Robert, Zhi Wang, and Shang-Jin Wei. 2008. *How Much of Chinese Exports Is Really Made in China? Assessing Domestic Value-Added When Processing Trade Is Pervasive*. NBER Working Paper No. 14109, June. Washington, DC.

Lin, Justin Yifu. 2009. *Marshall Lectures: Economic Development and Transition: Thought, Strategy, and Viability*. London: Cambridge University Press.

———. 2010. *New Structural Economics: A Framework for Rethinking Development*. Policy Research Working Paper5197. Washington, DC: World Bank.

Rodriguez, Francisco, and Dani Rodrik. 2000. "Trade Policy and Economic Growth: A Skeptic's Guide to the Cross-National Evidence." *NBER Macroeconomics Annual* 15: 261–325.

Schott, Peter. 2008. "The Relative Sophistication of Chinese Exports." *Economic Policy* 53: 5–49.

Wang, Zhi, and Shang-Jin Wei. 2010. "What Accounts for the Rising Sophistication of China's Exports?" In *The Growing Role of China in World Trade*, ed. Robert Feestra and Shang-Jin Wei. Chicago: University of Chicago Press.

Wei, Shang-Jin, and Yi Wu. 2004. *The Life and Death Implications of Globalization*. IMF working paper. Washington, DC: International Monetary Fund.

Comment on "Does a Leapfrogging Growth Strategy Raise the Growth Rate?" by Zhi Wang, Shang-Jin Wei, and Anna Wong

FRANJO ŠTIBLAR

The global financial crisis has consequences for the role of government in the economy. A neoclassical concept was prevalent in theory and practice during the past few decades—of government intervention as a "grabbing hand" rather than a welcome "helping hand." This view was embodied in the Washington Consensus, which promoted rapid privatization, market liberalization, and fiscal discipline. The neoliberal concepts that caused the global financial crisis excluded government almost entirely. In the wake of the crisis, government's role is being reaffirmed in economic theory, economic policy, economic/financial system building, and development models.

This discussion deals with the role of government in development.

- Adam Smith explicitly mentioned the role of government in creating an adequate infrastructure for successful market development, but neoliberals ignored this view because it did not fit well with their doctrine only of *l'état gendarme*. Neoliberals also ignored the moral sentiments in Smith's doctrine in their model of *homo oeconomicus* (rational economic man) as representative agent.
- What Justin Lin (2009) calls the "old structural economics" took into account the role of the state in active industrial policy as a way to accelerate growth; for example, in relaxing binding constraints in the fast follower strategy pursued in the East Asian model.
- The neoclassicists (neoliberals) denied any active role for state intervention in development.
- The "new structural economics" as presented by Justin Lin (2009) recognizes the role of the state but in a different form. The state should help provide infrastructure (both hard and soft) appropriate to the level of development in industrial structure, which in turn depends on the level of development of factor endowments, which change and improve over time.

Franjo Štiblar is a professor at the School of Law, University of Ljubljana, and researcher at the Economic Institute of the School of Law, Ljubljana, Slovenia.

Annual World Bank Conference on Development Economics 2011, Global

In the wake of the global financial crisis, economic strategies are changing, and the government's role in development models is moving away from the laissez-faire approach of neoliberals. However, differences exist as development economists and practitioners attempt to define appropriate government intervention.

The old structural economics prefers an active role for government (an active industrial policy) and advocates a fast follower strategy (FFS), or leapfrogging strategy, or a technology leverage competitive strategy (which opponents call "competitive advantage defying strategy"). The new structural economics (Lin 2009) prefers a more passive role for government—improving endowments to pursue a comparative advantage facilitating strategy. Proponents speak of latent comparative advantages (which opponents call "the fundamental view").

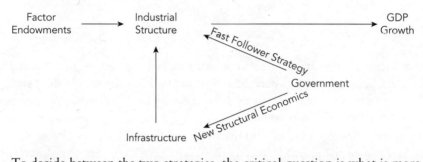

To decide between the two strategies, the critical question is what is more crucial for economic growth: the potentially positive effect of direct government intervention toward a more technologically sophisticated production structure or the potentially negative effect of such intervention in defying a comparative advantage strategy based on the availability of factor endowments?

This contribution focuses on empirical testing of both theories as they were presented at the 2010 ABCDE conference in Stockholm. In "Does a Leapfrogging Growth Strategy Raise Growth Rate?" Zhi Wang, Shang-Jin Wei, and Anna Wong tested the active development strategy. Parallel Session 4 on "Binding Constraints on Sustainable Growth and How to Loosen Them" included four papers with empirical evidence in favor of an active development policy. Both views discuss the Asian development model, sometimes regarded as a miracle. It is interesting to observe that this model contains some elements of the well-known Yugoslav development model of the 1960–80 period.

This comment proceeds with a discussion of both theories and their implications, followed by an overview of results from empirical testing and an evaluation of their relevance. After some brief conclusions, the comment ends with an extension of the current discussion in development economics into the wider framework of global rethinking of the role of government and economics in the aftermath of the global financial crisis.

Theory

The theoretical framework consists of presenting determinants of economic growth and two strategies of development strategies.

Determinants of Economic Growth

Different authors perceive different determinants of economic growth as relevant (see Lin 2009, chapter 5). Some see differences in physical capital, human capital, and productivity as most important. Others cite luck, geography, institutions, culture, and social capital. Rodrigues and Rodrik (2000) emphasize geography, institutions, and integration (trade). Bajt and Štiblar (2004) list five production factors—labor, capital, entrepreneurship, technology inventions, and natural resources—as well as population and technological progress as crucial determinants of potential economic growth.

Lin (2009) concludes that the most important factors are ideas, dominant social thought, government policies, and political leaders to implement them. He analyzes the role of development strategies in the transition from a socialist to a capitalist economy. His starting position is that continuous technological innovation and upgrading of industrial structure and corresponding institutional changes are driving forces of long-term economic growth in modern times. According to Lin, economic performance in developing countries depends largely on government strategy. If government plays a facilitating role, enabling firms to exploit the economy's comparative advantages, the economy will develop successfully.

Wang, Wei, and Wong analyze two determinants of economic growth related to global markets: openness to trade and trade liberalization. With regard to trade, Rodriguez and Rodrik (2000) reject the assertion that lower trade barriers lead to faster growth. Most of the research in the literature was focused on export and growth, not trade policies and growth.

New Structural Economics

The new structural economics is based on comparative advantage facilitating strategy.

Comparative advantage facilitating strategy. Lin (2009) develops the theory of new structural economics based on a comparative advantage facilitating (CAF) strategy. Government should upgrade the endowment structure before upgrading industry and technology. In his 2010 working paper, Lin presented the basic elements of the new structural economics:

- The economy's structure of factor endowments evolves during various stages of development. Different industrial structures are defined in earlier stages and require corresponding hard and soft infrastructure.
- A continuum exists in development rather than a sharp division between rich and poor.
- The market is an effective mechanism for resource allocation, but government industrial upgrading and improvements of hard and soft infrastructure are needed. Government needs to intervene to facilitate both, as it has externalities to firms' transaction costs.

According to Lin, factor endowment defines industrial structure, which needs to be supported by adequate infrastructure. Lin tested five hypotheses in favor of the new structural economics (2009, chapter 6):

1. Less developed countries that pursue comparative advantage defying (CAD) strategies will require various government interventions and distortions in their economies.
2. Overextended CAD strategies will lead to poor economic performance.
3. These countries will have volatile economies.
4. They will have less equitable income distribution.
5. Countries in transition will perform better if high-technology industries are supported using the fast follower strategy. This will facilitate the development of formerly suppressed labor-intensive industries.

Critique of the comparative advantage facilitating strategy. According to Hausmann, Hwang, and Rodrik (2007), the "fundamentalist" view of the world is that the endowments of production factors, along with the overall quality of institutions, determine the relative costs and the patterns of specialization. Attempts to reshape the production structure beyond the boundaries based on fundamentals will fail and hamper economic performance, in the opinion of new structuralists. But the authors assert that idiosyncratic elements in specialization should be taken into account. Specializing in some products rather than others will bring higher growth. Therefore, government policy has a potentially important positive role to play in reshaping the production structure, if it is appropriately targeted on the market failure in question. Specialization patterns are not entirely predictable. Countries that specialize in the types of goods that rich countries export are likely to grow faster.

According to Hausmann and colleagues (2007), cost-discovery externalities play a role in restricting entrepreneurship in new activities—where it matters most. Countries that export goods associated with higher productivity levels grow more rapidly, even after controlling for initial income per capita and time-invariant country statistics, such as population and area.

Growth is the result of transferring resources from lower to higher productivity activities identified by the entrepreneurial cost-discovery process. Demand for these goods in world markets is elastic, and companies in developing countries need to take advantage of this elasticity. Fostering an environment that promotes entrepreneurship and investment in new activities is critical to economic convergence. Such activities generate information spillovers for emulators. The requisite is to subsidize initial entrants in new activities.

In illustrating the use of the CAF strategy, the argument is that even in China, which claims to adopt CAF in practice, world equilibrium prices did not prevail, because government interventions have kept them artificially below the equilibrium market level owing to pressure on endowments alone. Social and environmental externalities are not fully internalized; therefore, factor prices remain below equilibrium level.

Leapfrogging

Leapfrogging is also called fast follower strategy (FFS). It means using policies to guide the industrial structural transformation to promote high-tech and high domestic value added (VA) ahead of a country's relatively abundant endowments. If the production of sophisticated goods generates positive externalities via learning by doing, there would be an underinvestment among private economic agents relative to the socially optimal level. Leapfrogging is government-led industrial policy that tilts resource allocation to technologically sophisticated industries and that can correct market failure. A country may benefit more from exporting sophisticated products with high domestic VA even if the current comparative advantage is to produce less sophisticated goods. For opponents, this is a comparative advantage defying development strategy; for proponents of fast follower strategy, it is a technology leverage competitive strategy.

According to Mathews (2010), FFSs are employed by countries that are ready to upgrade their industries and enter new industries. FFS works because globalization makes technologies more accessible through technology leverage, enabling countries to leverage their competitive advantage by purchasing equipment, licensing technology, contracting within global value chains, pursuing the time-honored route of skilled labor transfer (through inward foreign direct investment and migration of skilled labor), and pirating technology. Thus, they get around the binding constraint of technology access.

Hausmann, Hwang, and Rodrik (2007) suggest that some export goods have higher spillover effects than others. They develop a measure of export sophistication and find a positive relation to economic growth rate. The authors developed a model of "cost discovery." When cost discovery generates knowledge spillovers, specialization patterns become partly indeterminate and the mix of goods a country produces may have important implications for economic growth. The returns of pioneer investors' costs of discovery become socialized, while losses remain private. This knowledge externality implies that investment levels in cost discovery are suboptimal unless industry or government finds some way to internalize the externality. The more entrepreneurs that can be stimulated to engage in cost discovery in the modern sectors, the closer the economy can get to its productivity frontier. The authors focus on the spillover in cost information and are interested in the economic growth implications of different specialization patterns.

The Hausmann, Hwang, and Rodrik framework suggests a different binding constraint (sophistication of production industrial structure) on entrepreneurship than is considered in the literature of economic development: credit constraints, institutional weaknesses, and barriers to competition and entry.

Their strategy suggests more broadly that the type of goods in which a country specializes has important implications for its subsequent economic performance. The economy is better off producing goods that richer countries export (in a world with homogeneous goods, the problem is growth of output, not income). According to the standard model, pushing specialization up in the production scale would be bad for an economy's health, distorting production and creating efficiency losses. The authors' alternative interpretation is that a country's fundamentals generally allow it to produce more sophisticated goods than it currently produces. Countries can get stuck with lower income goods because entrepreneurship in cost discovery entails important externalities. If countries are able to overcome these externalities through policies that entice entrepreneurs into new activities, they can reap benefits in higher growth.

Mathews (2010) lists nine characteristics of the fast follower strategy:

1. It thrives in industries with growth potential, dominant technology, and mass production.
2. It favors capital-intensive industries in which leapfrogging captures latecomer advantages.
3. It strategizes around industrial dynamics, such as life cycles and pro-cyclicality.
4. It secures access to dominant technology, using links to leverage technology.
5. It covers the value chain quickly, building a cluster of complementary firms to promote diffusion of capabilities.
6. It seeks out emerging niche markets to avoid being stuck in a given technology or sector.
7. It promotes the domestic market as a platform for expansion.
8. It moves rapidly from imitation to innovation.
9. It repeats the process sequentially, in one industry after another, using characteristic institutional patterns of national economic learning.

To succeed, FFS needs the following conditions:

- Access to technology.
- Technology that moves relatively fast (but not too fast) through successive product or process cycles.
- The rise of global value chains as settings within which the fast follower can secure contracts for manufacturing or global value chains in services.

If these conditions hold for an industry, it is ripe for FFS. To succeed, it will need prior capabilities in mass production, financing, and technology leverage.

Critique of leapfrogging strategy. According to Lin (2009), the FFS/CAD leads to distortions in the form of inefficient resource allocation, suppressed working initiatives, rampant rent-seeking behavior, deteriorating income distribution, and poor economic performance. More haste, less speed increases the gap between developed and developing countries. Governments in most developing countries attempt to promote industries that go against their comparative advantages by creating various kinds of distortion to protect nonviable firms in priority industries (the so-called standard approach). In countries in transition, governments fail to recognize the original intention of many distortions. They attempt to eliminate those distortions without addressing firms' viability problem, causing economic performance to deteriorate in the transition process. On the other hand, governments in successful countries in transition adopt a pragmatic, dual-track approach: they encourage firms to enter sectors that were suppressed previously and give necessary support to firms in priority industries before viability issues emerge. China and Vietnam adopted such a gradual, dual-track approach.

Wang, Wei, and Wong (2010) assert that FFSs cause market failure and government failure. They believe that it is desirable to transform a country's economic structure ahead of its income level toward higher domestic VA and more sophisticated sectors. But any such policy promotion takes resources away from other industries, especially those consistent with the country's factor endowment and level of development.

On balance, the effect is conceptually less clear. The problem is to quantify the degree of leapfrogging an economy can support. However, data on production structure are not refined enough, and most relevant policies are not easily quantifiable or comparable across countries. One way to measure leapfrogging is to use export data.

Results of Empirical Tests

Several empirical test were made for both strategies, leapfrogging and comparative advantage facilitating strategy.

Testing of the Leapfrogging Strategy

Both critics and proponents have tested the leapfrogging strategy. We examine the critics' tests first.

Testing by critics. Wang, Wei, and Wong test the validity of the leapfrogging hypothesis with fresh evidence from a cross-country data set. They conclude that there is no strong and robust evidence that a leapfrogging strategy contributes to a higher growth rate. Leapfrogging can be measured, ideally, by comparing a country's actual production structure with what has been predicted on the basis of its factor endowments. However, data are not available or are relatively coarse, so differences in economic structure do not reveal themselves enough on the aggregate level. Therefore, export structure is used as an approximation of industrial structure. To control for a normal amount of sophistication based on factor endowments, a country's income and education level are included as controls.

Wang, Wei, and Wong use four indicators in their analysis:

1. EXPY (a country's export bundle) based on PRODY (income content of products, as used by Hausmann, Hwang, and Rodrik): level of income implied in the export bundle.
2. An export dissimilarity index (EDI) that measures the distance of a country's export structure from that of the high-income G-3 countries: Japan, the United States, and the EU15. An alternative is the export similarity index (ESI).

3. A modified EXPY to measure quality discounts the PRODY of each good by the ratio of the unit value of the exporter to the mean unit value of the same goods produced by the G-3.
4. The share of ATP (advanced technology products) in exports, narrow and broad.

Assumptions were that for the first three measures, the higher-income countries export more sophisticated products; the fourth measure is based on the degree of sophistication of the product itself.

Wang, Wei, and Wong assumed export structure to be the crucial explanatory variable for economic growth.

- EXPY requires data on trade flow and gross domestic product (GDP) per capita.
- Modified EXPY also requires data on unit value.
- EDI and ATP share use of harmonized system classification.

Other explanatory variables in the analysis include these:

- Human capital, measured by average years of schooling.
- GDP per capita, from the Penn World Tables.
- Institutional quality proxied by the government effectiveness index (World Bank); rule of law index (Hausmann, Hwang, and Rodrik 2007); various indicators of corruption; regulation quality; and the consumer price index score.

The authors followed a four-step estimation process:

1. The Hausmann, Hwang, and Rodrik specification was repeated. If the initial EXPY was statistically significant and positive but a different value resulted (perhaps due to the updated sample), the authors concluded that it could be replicated.
2. Three other export sophistication variables were included. They have the right direction, but were statistically not significant.
3. An alternative hypothesis was tested—whether growth instead of level of sophistication leads to growth in income. The authors rejected this hypothesis on the basis of empirical evidence.
4. Panel regressions were performed with instrumental variables.

In a panel analysis, preparedness of the political leader was used as an instrumental variable for export sophistication. Neither EXPY or EDI was found to be significant. Thus, the authors rejected the leapfrogging hypothesis.

Testing by proponents. The application of the FFS is discussed in three papers related to the role of big business, successive upgrading and industry entry, and absorptive capacities, and in an overview paper by Mathews (2010).

- Keun Lee, Young-Yoon Part, and Elias Sanidas (2010) identify big business versus the share of small and medium enterprises (SMEs) as binding constraints for middle- and high-income countries. They identify the positive role of big business, not the SMEs, in promoting economic growth for upper-middle- and high-income countries.

As the number of the largest companies in each country increases over time, the growth in real GDP increases and becomes more stable.

The merits of big business are in scale and scope economies, meaning that

$$\text{lower costs} \rightarrow \text{higher efficiency} \rightarrow \text{higher growth}$$

The authors draw the following policy implication regarding big business: middle-income countries that are latecomers should promote business groups as a useful vehicle to overcome business constraints on economic growth, as the Republic of Korea has done with Chaebols.

In the globalization process, a "big business revolution" is taking place with respect to networking and exports. Problems with testing the role of big business are lack of a common internationally comparable indicator of big business and endogeneity, or two-way causality. In testing the big business role in leapfrogging. Lee, Part, and Sanidas used data on the Global Fortune 500 and Business Weekly 1000. Econometric analysis consisted of pooled ordinary least squares, fixed-effect panel data, and two-stage residuals. Dependent variables were constant GDP per capita growth and variance of GDP per capita. Independent variables were as follows:

o Control variables: economy size, population growth, investment, human capital
o Crucial variable: number of big firms in the country
o Additional variable: share of SME employment

Lee and colleagues concluded that big firms have a significant positive effect on growth, with and without the United States and Japan included in the sample. The elasticity of the big business explanatory variable is 0.67 percent. The SME variable is not significant if it is included simultaneously with the big business variable, and the number of big firms is negatively associated with the higher variability of GDP per capita. Rich countries tend to have a larger number of big businesses than predicted by their size. Among developing countries, this holds only for China and Korea.

- Keun Lee and John Mathews (2010) discuss the role of successive upgrading and industry entry for sustained catch-up, using the experience of firms in Korea and Taiwan, China. They ask three questions:

  o On the country level, why has success been an exception to date?
  o On the firm level, how can successful latecomer firms be generated and sustained?
  o On both levels, how can innovative firms be generated to provide a solid basis for sustained national-level catch-up?

The authors tested the proposition that successful catch-up requires continuous upgrading in the same industry, as well as successive entries in new and promising industries over the course of industrial development. Otherwise, constant global relocation of productive activities by the multinational companies to new sites with lower wages makes current activities lower VA.

The authors find that latecomer firms are using diverse channels of knowledge access and learning, joint ventures, co-development with foreign specialized research and development (R&D) firms, individual scientists, reverse brain drains, overseas R&D outposts, strategic alliances, and international mergers and acquisitions.

- Moon Young Chung and Keun Lee (2010) study the link between foreign technology acquisition and indigenous R&D in Korea from 1970 to 1996. In upgrading in the same industry, firms acquire design capability for product differentiation and innovation.

  In Korea, support for upgrading came from cross-subsidizing R&D money among affiliates and through R&D consortiums with a government research institute. There was no formal transfer from incumbent firms, but leading firms hired or scouted engineers from each other.

  In Taiwan, China, there was more reliance on government, which developed parts and components and transferred the technology to private firms to produce them. Firms were more interdependent, with the forerunners relying on explicit technology transfer from Japan or from their own industry institutes.

  The study finds the missing link between the role of external knowledge inflow and in-house R&D: a series of learning processes ranging from acquisition of know-how, to know-how combined with patent licensing, to patents.

  Only after a firm has accumulated experience using imported know-how, continuously investing and gradually adopting a more capital-intensive production process, do gains in productivity come as the result of capital accumulation. Patent rights and know-how interact with accumulated learning experience to improve innovative capabilities and productivity.

  Patent rights show a positive effect only if the firm has built sufficient absorptive capacity. Firms with preexisting absorptive capacity show significant improvement in innovative capabilities and productivity as the result of R&D activities.

  Absorptive capacity is formed through the process of implementing, adapting, assimilating, and reorganizing foreign technology. Capacities formed at the earlier stages enable firms to be more effective and efficient in integrating advanced technology, whether imported or invented. It is the learning efforts of indigenous firms that make foreign knowledge inflow valuable and in-house R&D feasible. The innovative capability and the productivity gain in a latecomer firm do not come from single foreign technology acquisition but from a series of acquisitions, beginning with simple operational skills and advancing to product/process design technology protected by patents.

* * *

All fast follower and leapfrogging strategies have certain common characteristics:

- Upgrading: There is a radical separation from the past, backed by decisive investments in the form of public-private collaboration and interfirm risk sharing. For catch-up to occur, firms must be able to rapidly absorb new technology.

- Entries into new industries in the latecomer economies are made by the same firms (groups) that have accumulated certain absorption and execution capacities. In rich countries, entry is by new firms.
- Industry downturns and paradigm changes often serve as windows of opportunity for latecomers. Timing is critical for optimal entry.
- Entry modes for latecomers are often determined by gaining access to foreign knowledge. They are not a matter of choice, as in the developed world, but of historical circumstance.

Testing of Comparative Advantage Strategy

In applying the comparative advantage facilitating (CAF) strategy to China, Justin Lin (2009) showed its advantages. According to this strategy, the developing country government that plays the role of a facilitating state needs to proceed carefully. On one hand, it needs to build up and maintain competitive market institutions so that relative factor prices reflect changes in the relative abundance of factor endowments in the economy and guide enterprises to make appropriate choices. On the other hand, government needs to actively collect and disseminate information about new technologies and industries; promulgate industrial policy; coordinate the enterprises' investments; compensate for externalities; and strengthen legal, financial, and social institutions to facilitate the ability of enterprises to upgrade industry and technology.

Conclusions

The overall problems in the methodology of empirical testing growth strategies are as follows:

- The choice of proper indicator: the choice of proper observables for unobservable concepts as growth determinants
- The problem of using proper econometric methods:
  - Cross-country estimations; proper control variables for differences in country characteristics
  - Endogeneity—two-way causality and how to eliminate it
  - Choice of the proper instrument for Instrumental Variable estimation

Regarding fast forward and leapfrogging strategies, problems include the following:

- Extreme changes in exchange rates during the observation period
- Number of countries limited by the Global Fortune 500 and Business Week 1000 lists

The leapfrogging test study does not find strong and robust support for the leapfrogging hypothesis. The questionable assumption is that of one-to-one correspondence between the structure of exports and the structure of production, especially in larger, relatively less open economies, in which most of the production goes to the domestic market and exports are not a priority.

There are also problems with cross-country estimation of growth models, missing factors, and binding constraints. Another issue is the construction of variables of the technological content of exports. Measures of technical sophistication of export products can be direct and indirect.

In their study, Wang, Wei, and Wong rejected the leapfrogging hypothesis, but they were able to replicate Hausmann and colleagues' estimation results, finding a significant but weaker positive effect.

In promoting the FFS description of the East Asian development model, several authors, including Lee and Mathews (2010), obtained significant positive results for the effect of active policy factors such as advanced technology products, the presence of big business, and the role of upgrading industries.

The critical fact is that there is no one-to-one correspondence among the following elements in a causal chain:

EXPORT STRUCTURE → INDUSTRIAL STRUCTURE → GROWTH → WELFARE
(size, openness)　　　　　　(other growth factors)　(Y distribution)

Extensions and Wider Implications

Advocates of the new structural economics assert that it is not based on neoclassical theory. Lin (2010) provides seven insights citing differences between the two in areas such as fiscal and monetary policy, trade, the financial sector, and foreign direct investment. In general, Lin supports the role of government, but he is not a neoclassicist. He advocates a gradual approach to transition; Washington Consensus neoliberals (neoclassicists) favor shock therapy.

What is lacking in this approach (and in the Wang, Wei, and Wong paper) is consideration of the changing conditions and framework caused by the global financial crisis, started in 2008, as evidenced by the steeper drop in trade than in economic growth and the decline of imbalances. The crisis resulted from the improper dominance of the neoclassical approach of neoliberal economics in the creation of the economic (and especially the financial) system and the application of economic policies. The reality of the crisis invalidated some proposed economic laws of liberal economics, notably the hypothesis of ultra-rationality, as reflected in theories about *homo oeconomicus,* perfect competition, and representative agent. In development theory, one should take that failure into account and not base it explicitly on neoclassical foundations, as if nothing had happened. The current crisis was caused by a neoliberal, neoclassical approach, and solutions are based on Keynesian types of intervention. This should be recognized in economic growth theory too.

The fact is that active industrial policy is practiced around the world, including in China and the United States. The new structural economics opposes industrial policy and supports only adjustments to hard and soft infrastructure, which is defined by the development of factor endowments (following comparative advantage theory, in the case of exports). In contrast, the fast follower strategy focuses on relaxing binding constraints through active industrial policy for a specific country or level of development. Leapfrogging is FFS in the industrialization of developing countries, leading to technology leverage competitive advantages.

Preservation of comparative advantages means leaving the developing countries in their underdeveloped and dependent role in the world, and maintaining industrial countries in the lead forever. The argument that the comparative advantage of a developing country (workforce, natural resources) should determine its industrial structure—which means producing less sophisticated products with lower VA and more labor-intensive and natural-resource-intensive products—leaves them lagging behind developed countries forever. It is an illusion to think that a developing country can catch up by accumulating capital in the initial period, then using it later to support more capital-intensive production with higher value added.[1]

This strategy has a fundamental shortcoming. The missing fact in the argument is that the industrial countries are not willing to wait (stagnate) in the process of capital accumulation to be bypassed by developing countries. They accumulate and invest capital themselves, and because of their higher development level and more sophisticated production, they accumulate more capital than developing countries, so the gap between industrial and developing countries continues to widen rather than diminish. Without an active industrial policy, developing countries are bound to remain less developed in the long run by this comparative advantage facilitating (CAF) strategy. They will continue to be exploited by industrial countries.

The CAF strategy has three main arguments:

1. Government, through its intervention, distorts relative factor prices. But is not China (the main proponent and executor of the CAF strategy) doing exactly that regarding prices of labor, capital, environmental pollution, entrepreneurship, and natural resources—depressing them under market equilibrium level and leaving social and environmental externalities and world markets noninternalized?

2. Government should build markets as its major role in development. But certain preconditions to building markets need to be met. First, the rule of law should be established and fully operational; otherwise, "crooks" will misuse the market structure for their personal interest rather than the collective national interest. Second, market building is not enough if there are no conditions to establish perfect competition. Market failures exist, such as hereditary and acquired advantages and an unequal starting position in the system, which can lead to socially unfair—that is, suboptimal—market results; for example, the rich getting richer at the expense of the poor, as in the past 30 to 40 years of neoliberal policies and prevailing social thought, as indicated by increased income and wealth disparity measured by the Gini index. Government intervention is needed to correct market failures. Government cannot remain passive, as the CAF strategy would promote to a certain extent.

3. In his historic overview, Lin (2009) includes all Asian development success stories in one bundle—the Asian development model. But they are not all of the same

nature; for instance, it would be a mistake to lump together the strategies pursued by Japan and China.

＊

Recently, after the major collapse of the world economy was narrowly averted by the massive and unprecedented fiscal and monetary stimulus, neoliberals are returning to "business as usual." They act as if no financial crisis occurred and no crucial government intervention was necessary to prevent the collapse of the system. This is happening in economic policy, in the treatment of the financial system, in defining the role of economics as a science, and in long-term economic development theory. Ideological blindness and a lack of self-criticism are apparent.

Economic theory is valid only as long as its scientific laws are repeatedly proven in real-life economies. The Washington Consensus approach was soundly rebuked with respect to short-term economic policy—and the Keynesian approach was reaffirmed—by the financial crisis and the need to solve it by stimulus. With respect to long-term economic development, the success of industrial policy in producing the East Asian development model ("the miracle") calls into question the neoliberal laissez-faire approach and the use of a passive comparative advantage strategy. The East Asian countries used an active FFS to loosen constraints on growth.

The role of government in development can also be seen in a wider context. While solving general problems such as AIDS, ecological damage, starvation, and water shortages can be postponed, financial intervention and solutions to banking crises were immediately undertaken by all countries, regardless of ideological differences, to shore up trust in the markets. According to Žižek (2010), global capitalism has four antagonisms:

1. Ecological catastrophe
2. Incompatibility of private and intellectual property
3. Social and ethical consequences of new scientific technologies in biogenetics
4. New forms of apartheid

The first three work against the "common":

- Common culture (language, education, public infrastructure)
- Common outer nature (ecology)
- Common internal nature (biogenetic inheritance of humanity)

The fourth concerns the antagonism between included and excluded people—which is not a question of survival but of justice. Active government policies are required, at the very least, to mitigate the emerging conflict between included and excluded people in the world.

Note

1. This argument resembles Karl Marx's advocacy, in his famous tables, of faster development of production of the means of production than consumer goods as growth strategy.

Because of a conflict of growth between investors and the population at large, this strategy led to the defeat of socialist economic systems (Bajt and Štiblar 2004).

References

Bajt, A., and F. Štiblar. 2004. *Ekonomija (Economy)*, GV Ljubljana, Ljubljana.

Chung, Moon Young, and Keun Lee. 2010. "Linking Foreign Technology Acquisition and Indigenous R&D in Korea, 1970–1996." World Bank ABCDE Conference, Stockholm, May/June.

Hausmann, Ricardo, Jason Hwang, and Dani Rodrik. 2007. "What You Export Matters." *Journal of Economic Growth* 12:1, 1–25.

Lee, Keun, and John Mathews. 2010. "Successive Upgrading and Industry Entry for Sustained Catch-Up: The Experience of Firms from Korea and Taiwan." World Bank ABCDE Conference, Stockholm, May/June.

Lee, Keun, Young-Yoon Part, and Elias Sanidas. 2010. "Finding a Binding Constraint on Growth by a Country Panel Analysis: Big Business and National Economic Growth." World Bank ABCDE Conference, Stockholm, May/June.

Lin, Justin Yifu. 2009. *Economic Development and Transition: Thought, Strategy and Viability.* Cambridge, UK: Cambridge University Press.

———. 2010. *New Structural Economics*. Policy Research Working Paper 5197. Washington, DC: World Bank.

Mathews, A. 2010. "Loosening the Constraints on Sustainable Growth: Fast Follower Strategy." World Bank ABCDE Conference, Stockholm, May/June.

Rodriguez, Francisco, and Dani Rodrik. 2000. "Trade Policy and Economic Growth: A Skeptic's Guide to the Cross-National Evidence." *NBER Macroeconomics Annual* 15: 261–338.

The Political Economy of
Fragile States

State Fragility, Governance Indicators, and the Risk of Civil Conflict

JAMES D. FEARON

The term "fragile state" may be the most successful and influential development policy euphemism of the past 10 years. It has been embraced as an important operational concept by the World Bank, the Organisation for Economic Co-operation and Development's Development Assistance Committee, the United Kingdom's Department for International Development, and the U.S. Agency for International Development, among many other government and nongovernment donor agencies.

"Fragile state" is a delicate way of saying that a country has weak or dysfunctional institutions or is poorly governed. The term is also used to suggest the possibility or actuality of significant political violence—something that, for many years, aid agencies viewed as none of their business.[1] Fragile states are thought to be at risk of becoming "failed" or "collapsed," with terrible consequences for economic welfare and development.

Implicit in the concept of fragile states is a theory of economic development that has become increasingly influential, after years of project and program lending that has often had disappointing results. The theory is that economic growth requires, above all, good policies and capable government institutions to implement them. Violent conflict may be caused by bad policies and institutions and may in turn cause bad policies, the destruction of institutions, and more poverty. Fragile states are thought to be at risk of being stuck in a "conflict trap" (Collier et al. 2003). One of the central questions for development aid is whether aid can do anything to improve policies and institutions in a fragile state and, if so, what kind of aid. Indeed, another dimension of the term "fragility" suggests something that needs to be taken care of, for example, by providing more aid. But one could argue—and some have—that there is little point in providing aid if a government is riddled with corruption and led by elites who are not much interested in development.

James Fearon is the Theodore and Franceis Geballe Professor at the Department of Political Science, Stanford University.
Annual World Bank Conference on Development Economics 2011, Global
© 2013 The International Bank for Reconstruction and Development/The World Bank

At a conceptual level, the idea of a fragile state remains murky. What exactly are "weak institutions" and how do we recognize and measure them? But despite the conceptual or theoretical vagueness, aid agencies have managed to produce operational criteria for identifying fragility. In most cases, states are considered fragile if they score below a threshold value on governance indicators that are produced by expert ratings. For example, the World Bank designates a state as fragile if its aggregate score falls in the bottom 40 percent of the Bank's Country Policy and Institutional Assessment (CPIA), a set of governance indicators based on annual surveys completed by Bank officials working in particular regions and countries.[2]

There is almost no research on the question of whether these expert-based governance indicators actually forecast a country's performance over the next 5 or 10 years. If aid allocation and style decisions are going to be conditioned to a significant degree on these indicators, we might like to know whether perceptions-based measures of somewhat unclear concepts actually are picking up anything relevant to performance and outcomes. For example, is it true that fragile states as designated by governance indicators are at greater risk of violent conflict?

In this paper, I consider whether low values on governance indicators such as the CPIA index, the World Governance Indicators (WGI; Kaufmann, Kraay, and Mastruzzi 2009), and the International Country Risk Guide (ICRG) predict an elevated risk of civil violence in subsequent years. The existence of a bivariate relationship would not be surprising, as it is well known that governance indicators of all sorts are strongly related to per capita income levels and well documented that civil war is much more common in poor countries. What is less obvious is whether, controlling for a country's level of economic development, expert-based perceptions of the quality of governance have value for forecasting subsequent conflict experience.

I find that they do. A country that was judged in one year to have worse governance than expected given its income level has a significantly greater risk of civil war outbreak in the next 5 to 10 years. This is true for all three sets of governance indicators considered here, and it does not matter much which indicator one chooses—"government effectiveness" (WGI), "investment profile" (ICRG), "corruption," and "rule of law" all work. Results are weakest for the Bank's CPIA indicator.

These results may also have relevance for current debates on the causes of civil war. Are the poorest countries more likely to have a civil war because of direct labor market effects that make joining an armed group relatively attractive in a poor country? Or does low income proxy for weak governance, which raises civil war risk either because more people are frustrated and unhappy with the lack of services or because the state's weak administrative and coercive capabilities create better opportunities for rebel groups? I find that when one controls for governance quality, level of income has little or no predictive power for civil war onset. But when one controls for income, measures of governance quality do predict future conflict experience. These findings support the idea of low income as proxy for poor governance, although I will discuss a few other studies that can be interpreted as finding evidence of a direct causal effect from low income to conflict risk.

In terms of policy implications, the results lend support to the view that aid in conflict-affected countries must do more than try to raise incomes through project lending. If capable government is the root of the problem of conflict and development is more than a poverty trap, interventions may require an integrated approach that draws from the UN's peace-building and state-building experience and other peacekeeping operations.

In the next section, I briefly review some of relevant literature on causes and correlates of civil war, focusing on the question of how to interpret the robust finding that low income associates with much higher risk of violent conflict. In the following section, I introduce the three sets of governance indicators and consider how they are related to each other and how they vary across countries. I also discuss challenges to drawing inferences about the causal effect of "good governance" or "good institutions" using these expert-perceptions-based measures. I then examine the relationship between governance indicators and conflict onset, and offer conclusions.

Correlates and Causes of Civil War

Since the end of the Cold War, a moderately large literature has developed that uses cross-national data to study the correlates of large-scale civil violence, usually for the 65 years since the end of World War II. The typical design is an annual panel for roughly 160 countries (microstates are often omitted for lack of data or other reasons) with 35 to 45 observations per country. Researchers have formulated the dependent variable in several ways, considering (1) onset, or the start of episodes of violent conflict; (2) duration, or the length of conflicts conditional on one occurring; and (3) conflict incidence, which is a mixture of onset and duration.[3] I will focus on conflict onset.

The following are some of the more interesting and relatively robust results from the literature on onset. For the period since World War II (or since the early 1960s), the countries most prone to *major civil war* have been distinguished by low income, large populations, mountainous terrain, and possibly by oil production, a high share of politically excluded ethnic minorities, and (perhaps) greater gender inequality. Recent independence and recent changes in degree of democracy augur a higher risk of major conflict onset in the next few years. For all conflicts, including *low-intensity conflicts,* these same factors are statistically associated with conflict outbreak, as are higher levels of ethnic fractionalization. Factors that show no very consistent relationship with a propensity for violent civil conflict include income inequality (as measured by Gini coefficients) and level of democracy, although there is some indication that countries with anocracy (partial democracy) are at greater risk.[4]

For the most part, these findings from cross-national statistical models should be viewed as more descriptive than structural or causal. They have been of great value for making clear which political, economic, and demographic factors are associated with higher civil war propensity in the past 60 years; which factors are not; and which are associated with onset when you control for other factors. But for many covariates found to be statistically and substantively significant in these models, the argument for interpreting the estimated coefficients as causal effects is speculative. Most of the factors mentioned above—such as income, ethnic diversity, and mountainous terrain—vary little or not at all over time within countries. This means that many of the results are based on comparisons in rates of conflict outbreak across countries, and we may have substantial reason to worry that the observed associations are spurious correlations rather than estimates of causal effects. It could be, for example, that low income does not directly cause higher conflict risk but happens to be correlated with some third, unmeasured factor that does cause conflict. In some cases, it could be that the mere expectation of conflict for unmeasured reasons influences one of our presumed causal factors, such as income or perceived ethnic diversity, again leading to spurious correlations. So caution is necessary in interpreting cross-national patterns.

For the several factors that vary a lot over time within countries—such as recent independence or change in governing arrangements—we can ask whether change in the factor is reliably followed by a higher risk of conflict outbreak (this is called a fixed-effects analysis). Recent independence, a change in governing arrangements, and the onset of partial democracy all tend to predict the outbreak of conflict and so may have a stronger claim on being (or marking) causal effects.

In the literature up to this point, opportunities for natural experiments to allow cleaner identification of causal effects have been rare. Miguel, Satyanath, and Sergenti (2004) cleverly used exogenous variation in rainfall in Sub-Saharan Africa to estimate the effect of changes in income on civil conflict propensity; but Bruckner and Ciccone (2010b) examined the same data and reached a quite different conclusion. A few papers use variation in international commodity prices in a similar fashion (Besley and Persson 2009; Bruckner and Ciccone 2010a). But even these papers are of limited value for understanding why an effect is observed (e.g., what is the causal mechanism connecting changes in income to civil war propensity) and thus whether and how it might generalize. Thus, arguments about causes of civil conflict have generally taken the form of attempts to pose a theoretical framework or interpretation that has the potential to make sense of the complicated pattern of associations observed in the cross-national data.

In early versions of their influential paper "Greed and Grievance in Civil War," Collier and Hoeffler (2004) compared the strong association they found between civil war onset and measures of dependence on primary commodity exports and low education levels with the weak association of onset with measures of ethnic diversity, income inequality, and democracy. They argued that this finding suggested that rebel groups are primarily motivated by opportunities for profit rather than by a desire to right perceived wrongs. They suggested that aspiring "grievance-based" rebellions might face a more severe collective action problem than would "greed-based" or "loot-seeking" rebellions. In this initial formulation, the implicit assumption was that the causes of civil war would be located in the *motivations* of rebel groups.

Later versions of the paper converged (at least on this point) with the interpretation in Fearon and Laitin (2003), who wrote, "Surely ethnic antagonisms, nationalist sentiments, and grievances often motivate rebels and their supporters. But such broad factors are too common to distinguish the cases where civil war breaks out" (p. 76). The idea is that grievances that could potentially motivate a rebellion are regrettably common (and reasonable) in much of the world, so that more of the explanation for cross-national variation in civil war propensities is likely to be found in variation in factors that affect the viability of or *opportunity* for rebellion.

Very few civil wars since 1945 have been, or have emerged out of, popular revolutions characterized by mass protests and mass action—the French Revolution model. Instead, the vast majority of violent civil conflicts in this period have been fought as guerrilla wars or militia-based conflicts, typically by small rebel groups that often number in the hundreds, especially in their early years. Fearon and Laitin (2003) suggested that "because insurgency can be successfully practiced by small numbers of rebels under the right conditions, civil war may require only a small number with intense grievances to get going" (p. 76).

The prevalence of small-scale guerrilla or militia-based wars does not rule out the possibility that variation in the level of broad social grievances across countries could be an important explanation for civil war risk. In principle, it could be that social support from many sympathetic people is necessary for a small rebel band to operate successfully. However, if this is the case, it seems to apply mainly to rebellions in countries where the central state is relatively capable. Where states are less capable, rebel groups often seem able to operate without broad or deep social support, or they can coerce it.[5]

Fearon and Laitin (2003) give mainly "opportunity" interpretations for the patterns of correlation summarized above. For example, when a colony gains independence, its central government receives a negative shock to its capability to deter and fight rebels, if and when the colonial army leaves. Likewise, political instability may signal weakness at the center, as may anocracy (Hegre et al. 2001). Large populations are thought to make rebellion generally more feasible by making the governance problem harder for the center; it is harder to develop reliable chains of principals and agents to monitor what is going on at the local level. (India is much harder to govern than, say, Mauritius.) Rough terrain is thought to be associated with better opportunities for rebel groups to hide and less historical development of central administrative structures throughout a region.

Along similar lines, Collier and Hoeffler (2004) found strong results for a variable measuring the share of primary commodity exports in gross domestic product (GDP). In the 2004 version, they interpreted this as an indicator of greater financing opportunities for would-be rebel groups, principally through extortion of producers. They also found some evidence that having a large minority diaspora in the United States is associated with greater likelihood of war renewal, which they interpret as evidence that diaspora funding provides opportunities for rebel groups to return to war.

As noted above, lower per capita income is strongly related to a higher propensity to have civil wars and conflicts across countries, although there is not much evidence that economic growth or decline within countries over time strongly predicts change in conflict risk. This is perhaps the most robust pattern emerging from the cross-national statistical literature (Hegre and Sambanis 2006). Two main causal interpretations of the pattern have been advanced. Collier and Hoeffler (2004) stressed a *labor market* explanation: low income, they hypothesize, means lots of underemployed youth who find the opportunity costs of joining a rebel band to be small. Fearon and Laitin (2003), by contrast, stressed a *state capabilities* explanation.

In this view, per capita income is largely a proxy for state administrative, military, and police competence, and thus the ability to deter or defeat nascent insurgencies.[6]

The state capabilities explanation is arguably more consistent with the lack of a robust within-country relationship between income and civil war: One would not expect a lockstep relationship between state capabilities and income, whereas short-run income changes should affect labor market conditions. The labor market explanation might be more consistent with Miguel, Satyanath, and Sergenti (2004), who found that exogenous variation in rainfall is related to civil war onset in Sub-Saharan Africa. They argue that a direct causal effect of income on civil war propensity can be identified using the variation in income related to variation in rainfall, on the assumption that the only way rainfall variation affects civil war propensity is through income. As they note, it is possible that heavy rainfall might provide a negative shock to state capabilities by making roads less passable. But it is perhaps more likely that the effects would go through labor market channels.

A major barrier to assessing the relative importance of state capabilities versus labor market explanations has been the absence of good direct measures of state capabilities. One cannot simply use the size of a state's military or police force, for example, as these are endogenous to conflict. Iceland may have a very small army and police force, but the state's competence is such that if faced with a potential insurgent threat, it could probably scale up quickly and perform effectively.

Below I pit several expert-perceptions-based measures of state capacities or governance against income in models of civil conflict onset. These measures are far from perfect, but they appear to be the best available. Moreover, they are increasingly used by donors to make aid allocation decisions, so it is of independent interest to see whether they have diagnostic value.

Governance Indicators

This section introduces the three sets of governance indicators to be used in the analysis, and discusses potential threats to causal inference when using these indicators as explanatory variables for conflict risk.

The ICRG series, which starts in 1984, is produced and sold by Political Risk Services; the variables are derived from expert surveys of business and political conditions in about 140 countries. The WGI project began in the 1990s at the World Bank. Kaufmann and Kraay assembled a large set of expert-based governance ratings produced each year by think tanks, academic research groups, nongovernment organizations (NGOs), international organizations, and businesses, and divided them into sets that they say correspond to six dimensions of governance: government effectiveness, voice, political instability, rule of law, corruption, and regulatory quality.[7] They used techniques akin to factor analysis to extract a common dimension in each area. This has yielded a panel for 212 countries and territories for 1996 to the present (not including 1997, 1999, and 2001).

Each year since 1977, World Bank staff have coded Bank client countries on 16 or more dimensions concerning the quality of policies and institutions. These codings are then aggregated to a summary measure called the Country Policy and Institutional Assessment, which is used for various purposes, including decisions about aid allocation. The aggregate index ranges from 1 to 6, with higher scores indicating a better policy and governance environment from the Bank's perspective. Unfortunately, the CPIA index is produced only for aid recipient countries, so we have nearly complete series for only 85 countries.

To my knowledge, this paper is the first to exploit these data for an analysis of civil war onset. An earlier version for the ICRG data, for 1982 only, has been used as a measure of governance or good institutions in a number of studies of the determinants of economic growth, including influential papers by Acemoglu, Johnson, and Robinson (2001); Knack and Keefer (1995); and Mauro (1995). But the longer time series employed here appear not to have been used even in that much larger literature on growth.

Measurement and Inferential Issues Raised by Expert-Based Governance Measures

Whether we seek to explain growth or civil war onset, expert-survey-based measures of good institutions and good governance face a number of problems. First, it is not completely clear what the expert ratings are measuring. This is partly due to lack of clarity about what we are trying to measure. Just what are "good governance" and "good institutions"? Many people have strong intuitions here, having experienced the relative efficiency, competence, and corruption of public services and officials in various countries. In theoretical terms, the tradition associated with North and Thomas (1973) identifies good institutions as formal and informal political institutions that render unlikely the expropriation of private wealth and investments by political elites. In work on state capabilities and civil war, the focus tends to be on the efficiency and competence of the police, armed forces, and judiciary (rule of law, in part).

But the competence of public management, expropriation risk and contract enforcement, and rule of law are not easily observed and measured. Ideally, we would like to have objective indicators for these constructs, but even if we did, concepts such as efficiency, competence, and expropriation risk seem to be latent variables that would have to be inferred from diverse observations of different things.

This fact makes expert surveys a natural approach for measuring the quality of governance and good institutions, but it also makes it hard to know exactly what the experts are doing. For example, are they really making judgments about the quality of governance and particular institutions, or are they answering the general question "How do you think things are going these days in country X (perhaps implicitly compared with other countries in the same region)?" Answers to the latter might partly measure quality of governance or institutions but could also include considerations that we would not associate conceptually with governance and institutions. In sum, there are reasons to be concerned about both the validity and reliability of the expert-survey-based measures of governance, but it is not obvious what a better approach would be.[8]

The second major problem in trying to use governance indicators to assess the causes of economic growth or civil war onset is endogeneity. If an indicator is well correlated with contemporaneous growth or civil war onset, we cannot infer causality, because it could be that the observation of growth is leading the experts to think that governance is good or that the observation of civil war leads them to infer that governance or institutions are bad.

When one has only a single observation of governance quality for a set of countries and a single observation of level or growth of income or conflict performance, the only feasible solution is to find an instrument for governance—an exogenous variable that affects growth or conflict *only* through its effect on governance. Such variables are very hard to find, and the exclusion restriction is not testable.[9]

With data from time t on governance and from time $t+1$ on growth or conflict, we can ask whether the former predicts the latter, controlling for other possible determinants of growth or conflict. An important advantage of this design is that it cannot be that observation of the outcome (growth or conflict in time $t+1$) caused the experts to code better governance or institutions in time t, because the outcome had not yet happened when they made those judgments. So, if we have enough years of data on governance and growth or conflict, we can ask whether expert assessments of governance actually *predict* subsequent conflict or growth experience.

If the answer is yes, this still does not settle the question of causality—it could be that omitted variables are causing both expert assessments of quality of governance at time t and conflict or growth performance subsequently. In particular, as we will see below, all the WGI and ICRG indicators are highly correlated with per capita income. This is as it should be, if it is true that income is a proxy for state capabilities and that good governance and good institutions cause economic growth over the long term. But it raises the question of how to separate out the causal impact of governance on conflict or growth versus that of other determinants of high income.

The approach we take is to control for prior income levels, thus asking about the relationship between what we might call "surprisingly good governance" and civil war onset. A country has surprisingly good governance when experts gave it high ratings compared with other countries at the same level of per capita income. The attempt to identify the causal impact of governance quality on conflict then comes from seeing whether surprisingly good or bad governance in one period predicts subsequent conflict onset. The strategy will be effective to the extent that whatever determines surprisingly good or bad governance in one period influences subsequent conflict risk primarily through governance and institutions rather than via some other path.

With the ICRG and CPIA indicators, we have long enough time series and enough variation over time within countries to go a step further. We can consider models with country fixed effects, thus controlling for all manner of unobserved time-invariant country characteristics.

The core strategy here is potentially subject to the concerns that normally arise for "policy regressions," in which the researcher tries to infer something about the causal effect of a policy choice by measuring different policies across cases and putting them on the right-hand side in a regression model (Rodrik 2005). Surprisingly good governance (SGG) is at least partly a policy choice by a leadership or political regime. We will *underestimate* the positive impact of good governance if leaders tend to choose better governance when, for other unmeasured reasons, they expect that the risk of civil conflict is high. In that case, SGG will be partly correlated with unobserved factors that favor conflict, so that our estimates of the pacifying effects of SGG will be biased downward. On the other hand, what if leaders are better able to implement SGG in country years when, for reasons completely unrelated to governance, conflict is unlikely? To this extent, we would tend to *overestimate* the causal impact of good governance on conflict risk. I find it difficult to think of plausible examples—perhaps certain cultural trends arise wholly independent of governance but can enable better governance, and these directly determine civil war propensity. However, in principle the risk is there.

The efficacy of the approach depends on what explains variation in SGG. If, or to the extent that, leaders and state bureaucracies "get their acts together" for reasons that are largely independent of other, independent causes of civil strife, the results below suggest that good governance and institutions are important factors in reducing a country's conflict risk. For instance, governance and institutions may improve when an old leader dies and the new one is more capable or is politically situated so that he or she can implement better policies and develop better institutions. Or governance may be fairly steady, but income varies owing to international shocks and other vagaries of economic growth, in which case SGG will appropriately estimate a causal effect. I find these possibilities more plausible than alternative arguments that imply that this approach leads to overestimation of the governance effect, but more work is obviously needed on the determinants of surprisingly good governance.

The issues raised so far bear on the question of what can be inferred about a causal relationship between governance quality and subsequent conflict risk. If a causal relationship exists, questions remain about the nature of the mechanism. For assessing the state capabilities and labor market interpretations discussed earlier, it is important to determine whether governance and institutions affect conflict directly (e.g., by lowering the military prospects of a viable rebel organization) or indirectly (e.g., by improving the economy and thus affecting the labor supply for would-be rebels). A blunt way to address this issue is by controlling for current economic growth; in effect, to compare countries that have similar levels of previous income and similar current growth performance but different previous quality of governance. Adding current growth has little impact on the estimates for the governance measures in any of the models.[10]

WGI, ICRG, and CPIA Governance Indicators

The WGI project produces indicators for six dimensions of governance: government effectiveness, voice and accountability, political instability, rule of law, corruption, and regulatory quality. ICRG produces a large set of indicators that have varied somewhat over the years. In this paper I consider four ICRG indicators that have the longest history and correspond most closely to the WGI categories: investment profile, corruption, rule of law (or law and order), and bureaucratic quality. The correspondence with the WGI indicators is clear except for investment profile. ICRG intends this measure as a general indicator of business climate and political risks to business in a country year. It is the successor of the "expropriation risk" and "observance of contracts" variables from the 1982 ICRG data used in a number of growth studies.

Because they are derived from a factor-analysis-like technique, the WGI indicators all have mean zero and standard deviation of 1, with higher values indicating better-quality governance on that dimension.[11] For ICRG, corruption and rule of law are on a 1-to-6 scale. Investment profile ranges from 1 to 12, and bureaucratic quality from 1 to 4. Higher values are better.

The World Bank's CPIA indicator ranges from 1 to 6, with higher values indicating better governance. The scale is an average of a large number of components, which since 1997 have been grouped into four equally weighted clusters: economic management, structural policies, policies for social inclusion/equity, and public sector management and institutions.

For our purposes, a major liability of the CPIA index is that it is coded only for countries that receive International Development Association loans, and that countries can "graduate from" or enter this category depending on their economic and government performance. As a result, the CPIA sample is truncated by including relatively poor countries, and there is a built-in selection bias that works against identifying the impact of governance on conflict (or growth) outcomes. Namely, countries that perform well are more likely to exit the CPIA sample, and countries that perform poorly may enter it.

Table 1 shows correlations among the different ICRG and WGI governance indicators and (the log of) per capita income. Note the generally high correlations between income and the governance measures, and the strong associations among the governance measures.[12] There is not much indication that correlations across the

TABLE 1. Income and Governance Indicator Correlations

				WGI					ICRG		
	mcome	ge	voice	pol. stab.	corr.	rol	reg. qual.	ip	corr.	rol	bq
govt eff.	79										
voice	58	75									
pol. stab.	67	79	71								
corruption	74	94	72	77							
rule of law	77	95	79	83	94						
reg. qual.	75	94	79	75	88	91					
inv. prof.	72	82	73	73	79	83	88				
corruption	61	85	74	67	88	84	78	65			
rule of law	69	73	50	72	75	78	66	61	65		
bur. qual.	77	89	77	66	82	85	83	72	76	63	
CPIA	51	78	58	47	62	67	82	73	51	39	62

Note: The first six row entries are for the WGI indicators "government effectiveness" ("ge"), "voice," "political stability," "rule of law" ("rol"), and "regulatory quality." The next four are the ICRG indicators "investment profile" ("ip"), "corruption," "law and order" ("rol"), and "bureaucratic quality" ("bq"). The last row is the CPIA aggregate indicator.

TABLE 2. Correlation between WGI and ICRG, Netting Out Income

ICRG	WGI					
	ge	voice	pol. stab.	rol	corruption	reg. qual.
ip	38	36	33	40	35	47
corruption	60	51	41	61	66	52
rol	42	14	42	55	46	33
bq	67	54	27	58	53	57
CPIA	61	41	24	51	47	64

Note: The row entries are the ICRG indicators "investment profile" (ip), "corruption," "rule of law" (rol), and "bureaucratic quality" (bq), followed by the CPIA indicator. The columns are the WGI indicators as described in the notes to table 1.

ICRG and WGI indicators are higher within the same dimension—for example, rule of law—in the two different data sets.

Table 2 shows the correlations among the residuals of the WGI, ICRG, and CPIA indicators after regressing each of them on log per capita income. They remain substantial, which is encouraging—it suggests that raters' perceptions of quality of governance or institutions are not completely determined by level of economic development. Instead, there appears to be some level of agreement about surprisingly good or bad governance. However, there is not much indication that agreement is markedly higher within categories (e.g., corruption, rule of law) than across them. This suggests that these various dimensions of governance quality tend in practice to align very closely or that the expert raters have in mind some general notion of "the country has its act together" rather than being able to actually separate out dimensions of performance.

One other descriptive statistic about these indicators is worth presenting before moving to the analysis. Table 3 shows the percentage of variation for each indicator that is due to variation across countries as opposed to over time within countries. Almost all of the variation in the WGI indicators is across countries, which makes sense given that the time period is just over a decade and state capabilities should not be expected to change a great deal from year to year. There is much more within-country variation for the longer ICRG and CPIA series, especially for the ICRG investment profile indicator. This will allow us to consider a fixed-effects model with the ICRG and CPIA data.

Governance Measures and Civil War Onset

Several of the most striking cross-national patterns in civil war onset might be explained by an interpretation that puts state capabilities at the center of the story. In this view, low per capita income is strongly related to conflict onset, because it is a proxy for the central state's capability to deter and suppress armed challengers, and possibly also to provide public services. A set of alternative interpretations argues that there is a direct effect of low income on civil war propensity through some labor

TABLE 3. Percentage Within Versus Between Country Variation in Governance Indicators

Variable	Between %	Within %
log(income)	85	15
ACD war onset	6	94
WGI: 1996–2008		
ge	96	4
voice	97	3
pol. stab.	91	9
corruption	96	4
rol	96	4
reg. qual.	94	6
ICRG: 1984–2006		
ip	41	59
corruption	71	29
rol	72	28
bq	82	18
CPIA: 1977–2008		
CPIA	58	42

Note: See table 1 for abbreviations used here.

market channel. For instance, many have argued that poverty makes joining a rebel group relatively more attractive for young men.

In this section, I present logistic regression models in which the dependent variable is 1 if a civil war or lower-level conflict began in the country and period of time in question, and zero if not. For the ICRG and CPIA governance indicators, we can exploit the longer time series by constructing country-year panels, lagging the governance measures by two years to avoid contamination of the expert judgments with observation of civil war onset (or incipient war). For the WGI measures, I use a straight cross-section, using the first available WGI variables (for 1996) as predictors for whether a civil war began between 1997 and 2008.[13]

The civil war and conflict measures used here are derived from the Uppsala Conflict Data Program/Peace Research Institute Oslo Armed Conflict Database (ACD), which codes for each country and year since 1945 whether a violent conflict that directly killed at least 25 people occurred between a named, nonstate armed group and government forces.[14] I work with a version of the data used in the preparation of the 2011 *World Development Report* (WDR) that has (rough) estimates of annual battle deaths for each conflict. Following the WDR's categorization scheme, I will distinguish between *major conflicts,* or civil wars that are estimated to have killed at least 1,000 persons, on average, per year over the duration of the conflict, and *all conflicts,* which are estimated to have met the low threshold requirement at least 25 battle deaths each year. Because the ACD codings do not distinguish discrete episodes of conflict (they simply identify whether a particular armed conflict occurred in each country year), we need additional criteria to demarcate episodes, which is necessary to code onsets. Following the standard convention used for the WDR, a new conflict episode is considered to have begun if it is preceded by at least two years of peace between the named armed group and the state.[15]

Table 4 shows the distribution of civil war and all conflict onsets by region and decade since the 1960s. We see a substantial drop in new conflicts in the past decade, especially for major civil wars, and even relative to the years before the conflict-prone 1990s. Sub-Saharan Africa and Asia have seen the most conflict, in terms of both onset and average country years of war (the latter are not shown here).

The statistical models below also include typical covariates for civil conflict regressions. Most important, for the reasons discussed above, is the log of per capita income (lagged one year). The measure I use is based on Penn World Table 6.3 but has been extended using World Bank and Maddison growth rates where necessary to get the most complete possible coverage.[16] I also include

- log of country population (lagged one year);
- log of the percentage of the country judged to be mountainous;
- dummy marking country years in which at least one-third of GDP came from oil or gas production (based on a variable in the World Development Indicators, with missing cases filled in by country-specific data);
- measure of recent political instability, which is 1 if there was any change in the Polity measure of degree of democracy in the previous year;
- measure of anocracy (partial democracy), which is 1 if in the previous year Polity rated the country as between –5 and 5 on its –10 to 10 democracy scale;
- commonly used measure of ethnolinguistic fractionalization (ELF), based on data from a 1960 Soviet ethnographic atlas but with some missing countries filled in using country-specific sources (Fearon and Laitin 2003); and
- variable that is 1 if there was a civil war (or conflict) going on in the previous year. Note that because the dependent variable is onset rather than incidence, the latter is *not* a lagged dependent variable. Rather, "prior war" is included as a control because the odds of a new civil war starting are likely to be influenced by whether the country already has a civil war in progress.

ICRG

Tables 5 and 6 show the results for the four ICRG governance indicators considered here: investment profile (a general measure of business climate), corruption, rule of law, and bureaucratic quality. For ease of comparison, the variables have been scaled to range between zero and 1.[17]

In table 5 the dependent variable is major conflicts, of which there were only 20 in the set of country years for which we have ICRG data (about 140 countries from 1984 to 2008). We find that all four governance measures have estimated coefficients that correspond to large substantive effects, with all but bureaucratic quality statistically significant (investment profile and rule of law strongly so). For investment profile, moving from the 75th to the 25th percentile is estimated to be associated with

TABLE 4. Civil War and All Conflict Onsets by Region and Decade

	Civil war onsets						All conflict onsets					
	60s	70s	80s	90s	00s	Total	60s	70s	80s	90s	00s	Total
Asia	3	8	3	3	1	18	8	13	9	23	10	63
E. Eur/FSU	0	0	0	10	0	10	0	0	1	21	6	28
L. Am/Carib	2	4	1	0	0	7	8	6	6	3	2	25
MENA	2	5	5	3	2	17	5	10	9	10	5	39
SSA	6	7	3	7	1	24	14	17	13	32	18	94
West	0	0	0	0	0	0	0	1	2	2	0	5
World	13	24	12	23	4	76	35	47	40	91	41	254

Note: "E. Eur/FSU" stands for Eastern Europe/former Soviet Union; "L. Am/Carib" for Latin America and the Caribbean; MENA for the Middle East and North Africa; SSA for Sub-Saharan Africa; and "West" for Western Europe, the U.S, Canada, Australia, New Zealand, and Japan.

TABLE 5. ICRG Governance and Civil War Onset (Major Conflicts)

	Model 1	Model 2	Model 3	Model 4	Model 5
investment profile$_{t-2}$		−5.99***			
		(1.41)			
control of corruption$_{t-2}$			−1.94†		
			(1.14)		
rule of law$_{t-2}$				−3.53***	
				(1.02)	
bureaucratic qualityg$_{t-2}$					−0.91
					(1.25)
log(gdp$_{t-1}$)	−0.13	0.33	0.04	0.23	0.04
	(0.23)	(0.24)	(0.25)	(0.24)	(0.34)
log(pop$_{t-1}$)	0.23	0.30	0.21	0.27	0.25
	(0.20)	(0.19)	(0.20)	(0.21)	(0.20)
log(% mountains)	0.11	0.04	0.14	0.13	0.10
	(0.17)	(0.17)	(0.18)	(0.18)	(0.17)
oil producer	1.34**	1.09*	1.18*	1.14*	1.23*
	(0.46)	(0.46)	(0.51)	(0.47)	(0.49)
political instability$_{t-1}$	−0.02	−0.06	0.02	−0.11	−0.03
	(0.58)	(0.54)	(0.58)	(0.59)	(0.59)
anocracy$_{t-1}$	1.08*	1.05*	1.06*	1.08*	1.08*
	(0.50)	(0.45)	(0.49)	(0.47)	(0.49)
ELF	0.92	1.55†	0.99	0.93	1.07
	(0.87)	(0.88)	(0.87)	(0.85)	(0.88)
prior war	−0.06	−0.52	−0.13	−0.45	−0.13
	(0.70)	(0.76)	(0.69)	(0.69)	(0.68)
constant	−7.55**	−9.25***	−7.92**	−9.10**	−8.73**
	(2.83)	(2.62)	(2.86)	(3.07)	(3.12)
N	2,777	2,777	2,776	2,776	2,776

SEs clustered by country.

Note: ELF = ethnolinguistic fractionalization.

†Significant at p < .10; *p < .05; **p < .01; ***p < .001.

an increase in annual civil war odds of a factor of 5.9. Moving from the 75th to the 25th percentile on rule of law and corruption is associated with increasing the annual onset odds of 4.6 and 1.9, respectively. Note that the estimates for investment profile and rule of law are remarkably large in substantive terms. By comparison, in typical conflict models, the estimate of the effect of income implies that a country at the 25th percentile has about twice the annual odds of a country at the 75th percentile.

Model 1 of table 5 is the same as model 2 but restricted to the country years that have ICRG data and data for the other variables. It shows that almost all the usual covariates of civil war are more weakly related in this sample than in typical analyses, which usually span 1945 to 1999 or 2008, and cover a larger set of countries. Still, in all cases, the signs are consistent with what we find in larger and more

TABLE 6. ICRG Governance and Conflict Onset (All ACD Conflicts)

	Model 1	Model 2	Model 3	Model 4	Model S
ip_{t-2}		−3.19***			
		(0.78)			
$corrupt_{t-2}$			−1.09†		
			(0.62)		
rol_{t-2}				−1.21*	
				(0.54)	
bq_{t-2}					−1.14†
					(0.64)
$\log(gdp_{t-1})$	−0.45**	−0.17	−0.37*	−0.33†	−0.23
	(0.17)	(0.15)	(0.18)	(0.20)	(0.19)
$\log(pop_{t-1})$	0.30**	0.35***	0.28**	0.32**	0.34**
	(0.10)	(0.10)	(0.10)	(0.11)	(0.11)
log(% mountains)	0.12	0.09	0.13	0.13	0.10
	(0.12)	(0.12)	(0.13)	(0.13)	(0.12)
oil producer	0.91**	0.72*	0.83*	0.81*	0.75*
	(0.33)	(0.32)	(0.35)	(0.34)	(0.34)
pol instability$_{t-1}$	0.12	0.10	0.12	0.07	0.11
	(0.25)	(0.26)	(0.26)	(0.26)	(0.26)
anocracy$_{t-1}$	−0.04	0.03	−0.06	−0.01	−0.03
	(0.31)	(0.30)	(0.31)	(0.30)	(0.31)
ELF	1.23*	1.58***	1.24*	1.24*	1.40**
	(0.52)	(0.47)	(0.52)	(0.52)	(0.51)
por war	0.53	0.27	0.49	0.40	0.44
	(0.34)	(0.34)	(0.33)	(0.34)	(0.36)
constant	−3.71*	−5.02**	−3.77*	−4.19*	−5.45**
	(1.75)	(1.59)	(1.81)	(1.91)	(1.84)
N	2,777	2,777	2,776	2,776	2,776
SEs clustered by country.					

Note: ip = investment profile; corrupt = control of corruption; rol = rule of law; bq = bureaucratic quality; ELF = ethnolinguistic fractionalization.

†Significant at $p < .10$; *$p < .05$; **$p < .01$; ***$p < .001$.

complete samples. Note that the coefficient on income takes its usual negative sign, although it is not statistically significant. One reason is that the ICRG measures are generally missing for low-income/high-conflict countries (presumably, investors don't need to be told that Afghanistan has a poor investment profile). If we consider the full post-1983 sample, the coefficient on income more than doubles and the p value drops to .14. Another reason is that there are few conflict events when we use this relatively high-threshold criterion for major civil war. So although the lack of data limits the importance of the findings, it is interesting that the estimated coefficients for per capita income actually turn positive (though not significantly different from zero) when we add the governance indicators in models 2–4. This is consistent with the hypothesis that income matters because it proxies for state capabilities.[18]

Table 6 is the same as table 5, except it covers all ACD conflicts. Here, all four ICRG governance indicators are significantly negatively related to conflict onset, with the strongest effects again being for investment profile and rule of law. Low income is significantly negatively related to conflict onset in this subsample (model 1), and while the signs remain negative when governance indicators are added, the estimated coefficients for income shrink toward zero and in several cases are no longer statistically significant. This outcome favors the interpretation that income is in large part a proxy for state capabilities and administrative or policy competence.

Could it be that surprisingly good governance causes more rapid economic growth in the next few years and lowers conflict risk through the economy rather than by a direct effect of greater state capabilities? When I add the current economic growth rate to the models in tables 5 and 6, the results are nearly identical for all conflicts and very close for major civil wars; for the latter, the estimated coefficients on the governance variables diminish slightly, but investment profile and rule of law remain strongly significant.

Table 7 repeats the exercise for all conflicts, but uses conditional fixed-effects logit, thus controlling for all unmeasured (but temporally stable) country characteristics. Remarkably, given the small number of countries in the sample and the relative lack of temporal variation in governance quality, all four of the ICRG indicators get negative coefficients (though corruption is essentially zero), and the estimates for investment profile and rule of law are statistically significant ($p = .002$ and $.091$, respectively). Per capita income may take the "wrong" sign and is never close to significant.

Thus, within countries over time, civil war onset has been somewhat more likely when investment profile, corruption, and rule of law were judged worse in recently preceding years. This result supports a causal interpretation of the relationship between governance quality and conflict onset more than the previous models, because identification is based on within-country comparisons (and because it is somewhat remarkable to find anything, given the lack of within-country variation in governance indicators).[19]

One might still worry that a two-year lag is not enough to rule out the possibility that expert raters are coding on the basis of indications of incipient civil war more than on the quality of governance or institutions. I have constructed a panel with three waves—for the 1980s, 1990s, and 2000s—asking whether average ICRG ratings in one decade forecast conflict in the next decade, controlling for prior conflict experience and lagged income levels. I find that the results are quite similar: ICRG indicators forecast conflict outbreak even in the next decade.

WGI

The WGI series is only for 1996 to 2008, and some of the early years are missing. It also has very little over-time variation within countries, and the method of its construction raises some questions about whether and how best to treat it as panel data.

However, because 14 years have passed since the first set of WGI indicators was constructed, we can ask whether expert-based assessments of different dimensions of governance quality in 1996 or 1998 actually forecast conflict experience in the next

TABLE 7. ICRG Governance and All Conflict Onsets, Country Fixed Effects

	Model 1	Model 2	Model 3	Model 4
ip_{t-2}	−2.735**			
	(0.896)			
$corrupt_{t-2}$		−0.227		
		(0.918)		
rol_{t-2}			−1.359[†]	
			(0.805)	
bq_{t-2}				−0.946
				(0.861)
$log(income)_{t-1}$	0.287	−0.166	0.015	−0.024
	(0.541)	(0.505)	(0.512)	(0.517)
$log(pop_{t-1})$	0.517	−0.352	0.104	−0.429
	(0.948)	(0.901)	(0.923)	(0.894)
oil	0.528	0.441	0.383	0.239
	(0.964)	(0.976)	(0.965)	(0.982)
political instability$_{t-1}$	0.184	0.163	0.155	0.161
	(0.324)	(0.325)	(0.326)	(0.325)
anocracy$_{t-1}$	−0.088	−0.131	−0.169	−0.126
	(0.398)	(0.396)	(0.399)	(0.398)
democracy$_{t-1}$	−0.587	−0.721	−0.746	−0.687
	(0.478)	(0.488)	(0.487)	(0.487)
prior war	−1.414**	−1.271	−1.342**	−
	(0.359)	(0.355)	(0.362)	(0.357)
N (N countries)	956(44)	955(44)	955(44)	955(44)
Country fixed effects	yes	yes	yes	yes

Note: ip = investment profile; corrupt = control of corruption; rol = rule of law; bq = bureaucratic quality; ELF = ethnolinguistic fractionalization.

[†]Significant at $p < .10$; *$p < .05$; **$p < .01$; ***$p < .001$.

decade, controlling for initial level of income and prior conflict experience. Using the ACD civil war variable, only 10 countries had onsets between 1997 and 2009. Using all ACD conflicts, 37 countries had a total of 63 onsets. I control for income level in 1996, along with prior conflict experience and ethnic fractionalization. Thus, the question is whether perceptions of surprisingly good governance relative to income level and conflict history can still forecast civil peace.

Table 8 shows that the perceptions of government effectiveness, political stability, and rule of law in 1996 are indeed significantly related to major conflict outbreak over the next 13 years. The result might not be too surprising with regard to political stability, which is based on expert surveys intended to capture "perceptions of the likelihood that the government will be destabilized or overthrown by unconstitutional or violent means" (Kaufmann, Kraay, and Mastruzzi 2009, 6). But the results are also present for government effectiveness and rule of law, and the estimated coefficients are negative and substantively large for corruption and regulatory

TABLE 8. WGI Governance in 1996 and ACD Civil War Onset, 1997–2008

	Model 1	Model 2	Model 3	Model 4	Model 5	Model 6	Model 7
gov't effec. 1996		−0.97[†]					
		(0.58)					
voice 1996			−0.52				
			(0.44)				
pol. stab. 1996				−0.97*			
				(0.44)			
rule of law 1996					−1.40*		
					(0.60)		
corruption 1996						−0.96	
						(0.66)	
reg. qual. 1996							−0.73
							(0.45)
onsets pre- 1997	0.50*	0.46*	0.43[†]	0.24	0.38	0.40[†]	0.45*
	(0.22)	(0.23)	(0.23)	(0.27)	(0.23)	(0.23)	(0.23)
log(income) 1996	−0.42	0.11	−0.20	0.08	0.24	−0.02	−0.02
	(0.34)	(0.47)	(0.38)	(0.42)	(0.45)	(0.45)	(0.41)
ELF	−0.71	−0.63	−0.46	−0.59	−0.60	−0.62	−0.60
	(1.29)	(1.28)	(1.32)	(1.30)	(1.32)	(1.28)	(1.30)
constant	0.60	−4.16	−1.51	−3.95	−5.57	−3.11	−2.95
	(2.98)	(4.17)	(3.48)	(3.81)	(4.09)	(4.02)	(3.69)
N	156	156	156	156	156	156	156

Note: DV = ACD civil war onset after 1996. Logit, with standard errors in parentheses.

[†]Significant at $p < .10$; *$p < .05$; **$p < .01$; ***$p < .001$.

quality as well. It is evident that adding governance measures tends to turn the sign on the estimate for income slightly positive or close to zero, again consistent with the hypothesis that income normally proxies for governance or state capabilities. The pattern continues to hold if we add region fixed effects (although the significance of government effectiveness weakens a bit), or measures of oil production or population in 1996.

Table 9 repeats the exercise with the dependent variable of all ACD conflicts. The results are marginally weaker, and here we see less tendency for the inclusion of governance measures to reduce the estimated coefficients for income.[20]

I have run the same models using the WGI indicators from 1998 and the dependent variable as onsets after 1998. The results are similar. This lowers the likelihood that the results are a fluke from one year of WGI data (which, as we have seen, are highly stable over time anyway). I have also added average growth rate of GDP per capita after 1996, again finding little change for the governance indicators.

Not much evidence exists that different dimensions of governance as measured by WGI show notably stronger or weaker relationships to subsequent conflict risk. Political stability, which is supposed to be an expert appraisal of conflict risk, is the most strongly related, while voice and accountability, which is based on assessments

TABLE 9. WGI Governance in 1996 and All ACD Conflict Onsets, 1997–2008

	Model 1	Model 2	Model 3	Model 4	Model 5	Model 6	Model 7
govt effect. 1996		−0.62					
		(0.41)					
voice 1996			−0.47				
			(0.30)				
pol. stab 1996				−0.93**			
				(0.30)			
rule of law 1996					−0.67[†]		
					(0.38)		
corruption 1996						−0.12	
						(0.41)	
reg. qual. 1996							−0.45
							(0.33)
log(# onsets pre- 1997 + 1)	1.26***	1.19***	1.15**	0.72[†]	1.12**	1.22***	1.17**
	(0.35)	(0.35)	(0.35)	(0.39)	(0.35)	(0.37)	(0.35)
log(income) 1996	−0.55*	−0.24	−0.40	−0.23	−0.27	−0.51[†]	−0.34
	(0.23)	(0.31)	(0.25)	(0.27)	(0.28)	(0.29)	(0.28)
ELF	1.30	1.39	1.53[†]	1.58[†]	1.41	1.30	1.43
	(0.87)	(0.88)	(0.89)	(0.91)	(0.88)	(0.87)	(0.88)
constant	1.72	−1.13	0.18	−1.18	−0.89	1.29	−0.22
	(2.07)	(2.76)	(2.29)	(2.37)	(2.56)	(2.56)	(2.54)
N	156	156	156	156	156	156	156

Note: DV = at least one ACD conflict onset after 1996. Logit, with standard errors in parentheses.

[†]Significant at p < .10; *p < .05; **p < .01; ***p < .001.

of democracy, is the weakest. (This is consistent with the standard finding in the conflict literature that measures of democracy are largely unrelated to onset risk when one compares countries at similar levels of economic development.) After political stability, the most predictive factors are rule of law and government effectiveness. Kaufmann, Kraay, and Mastruzzi (2009, 6) define the latter as "capturing perceptions of the quality of public services, the quality of the civil service and the degree of its independence from political pressures, the quality of policy formulation and implementation, and the credibility of the government's commitment to such policies." But overall, just as we saw that these several "dimensions" of governance are highly correlated, these regression results do not allow us to draw strong conclusions about which dimension of governance is most important for increasing the odds of civil peace.

The identification strategy here is plausible insofar as the following argument is plausible: once we control for 1996 income, prior conflict experience, and other factors, variation in countries' quality of governance as measured by expert ratings in 1996 is essentially random with respect to unmeasured other determinants of subsequent civil war risk. I find it difficult to think of omitted variables entirely distinct from governance or institutions that would plausibly affect both rater perceptions of governance quality and conflict performance over the subsequent 10 years. But the possibility exists.

The identification strategy here will not do a good job of estimating the long-run impact of good governance or state capabilities, since some part of these may be incorporated in per capita income in 1996. Depending on how we think about what causal effect we are trying to estimate—relatively short-run or long-run impact of governance on civil war odds—we will underestimate the long-run impact of governance quality if we are omitting an indirect effect through level of economic development.

CPIA

Table 10 replicates the model presented above for the ICRG indicators but using one- and two-year lags of the CPIA index as the governance measure. The estimated coefficients for the lagged CPIA index are negative and are significantly related to

TABLE 10. CPIA Governance and All ACD Conflict Onsets

	Model 1	Model 2	Model 3	Model 4
$cpia_{t-1}$		$-0.31^\dagger$		-0.08
		(0.16)		(0.17)
$cpia_{t-2}$			$-0.31^\dagger$	
			(0.18)	
$log(gdp_{t-1})$	-0.48^{**}	-0.37^*	-0.33^*	0.01
	(0.16)	(0.16)	(0.16)	(0.42)
$log(pop_{t-1})$	0.27^*	0.31^{**}	0.31^{**}	0.27
	(0.11)	(0.11)	(0.10)	(0.65)
$log(\%\ mountains)$	0.17^*	0.18^*	0.18^*	
	(0.08)	(0.08)	(0.09)	
oil producer	0.69^t	0.58	$0.65^\dagger$	0.91
	(0.37)	(0.37)	(0.37)	(0.77)
pol instability$_{t-1}$	0.03	-0.01	-0.00	0.11
	(0.25)	(0.25)	(0.27)	(0.29)
anocracy$_{t-1}$	-0.04	-0.06	-0.08	0.11
	(0.27)	(0.27)	(0.28)	(0.37)
democracy$_{t-1}$	-0.01	0.04	-0.04	0.09
	(0.34)	(0.35)	(0.35)	(0.43)
ELF	1.22^*	1.23^{**}	1.32^{**}	
	(0.49)	(0.47)	(0.45)	
pnor war	-0.16	-0.26	-0.14	-1.89^{***}
	(0.29)	(0.27)	(0.29)	(0.35)
constant	-3.09^*	-3.26^*	-3.62^*	
	(1.55)	(1.54)	(1.45)	
N	3120	3120	3063	1652(61)
Country fixed effects?	No	No	No	Yes

Note: SEs clustered by country.

†Significant at $p < .10$; $^*p < .05$; $^{**}p < .01$; $^{***}p < .001$.

conflict risk despite the truncated sample (no non-aid-receiving countries) and the selection bias issues. The substantive magnitude of the estimates is smaller than for the WGI and ICRG indicators, however; moving from the 75th to the 25th percentile on the CPIA index is associated here with about a 40 percent increase in the annual odds of conflict onset. Results are even weaker with fixed effects and looking only at major conflicts. The estimates hardly change when we use the two-year lag instead of the one-year lag, which suggests little coding of CPIA on civil war in progress. There is less indication here that the CPIA measure successfully competes with income.

Conclusions

Even when we compare countries at similar levels of per capita income, those judged as having worse governance have subsequently been at greater risk of the outbreak of significant civil conflict or war. And if we compare countries rated similarly on governance measures, variation in income appears less strongly or not at all related to conflict risk. For the ICRG measures of investment climate and rule of law—which have the longest time series and thus the most within-country variation—there is evidence that worsening governance in a country is associated with higher subsequent conflict risk, with the magnitude of the estimates similar to those derived from the pooled time-series cross-section.

In addition, it does not seem to matter much which dimension of governance we consider. There may be a weak tendency for measures of government effectiveness, investment climate, and rule of law to perform better than measures of corruption or bureaucratic quality; and measures of democracy (often viewed as an important dimension of good governance) do not forecast lower conflict risk across a broad range of income categories.[21] But overall, apart from democracy, the various expert-ratings-based governance measures are strongly correlated with each other, even after removing a common dimension associated with per capita income. So it is difficult to say whether particular dimensions are more or less important; whether expert raters are basically reporting on a single common dimension regardless of the labels they use; or whether good governance and institutions constitute a syndrome in which "all good things [need to] go together."

These results have implications for research on development and on civil war. For example, they may affect performance-based allocation (PBA), the practice of the World Bank and most other multilateral donors of conditioning aid allocation on an assessment of the quality of a country's institutional and policy frameworks. The Bank began using PBA in 1977, and increased the weight it put on assessment of governance in its allocation formulas in the late 1990s (Winters 2010). One motivation for increased attention to governance in PBA was cross-national statistical research suggesting that aid promoted growth in better-governed developing countries but not in badly governed countries (Burnside and Dollar 2000). These results have not proved to be robust (Easterly, Levine, and Roodman 2004), and the debate continues on whether and when aid promotes economic growth.

Even if it turns out that aid is more productive in better-governed countries, PBA could not meet its objectives if donors' subjective, expert-ratings-based indicators of good governance are not good measures of the relevant latent variable. It is thus encouraging that governance measures that are closely related to those used to allocate aid do seem to have value for forecasting events that are plausibly related to poor governance, namely, civil conflict. It is discouraging that the Bank's CPIA index is the least clearly related to the propensity for future conflict, although this may be due to limitations in the CPIA sample rather than the measure being less valid than the ICRG and WGI measures.

A common criticism of PBA is that people in the worst governed, most fragile states are most in need of aid projects, even if that aid might be less efficiently deployed. The results here could be used to support this position, since they suggest that PBA is directing aid away from countries at highest risk of civil conflict. However, it is not clear that increased development aid lowers civil war risk; indeed, it is possible that it increases risk, on average, and perhaps especially in poorly governed countries. A more compelling concern would be whether PBA is directing aid money away from postconflict countries, where there may be a window of opportunity for improved governance and plausibly high social and economic returns to investments that would make an immediate reversion to conflict more costly for elites.

Civil conflict is only one objective indicator of poor governance or fragility. Future research should examine whether other objective indicators of government performance—for example, the amount and quality of public goods supplied in education, health, and other services—are related to the subjective measures produced by expert surveys. The intuition that what we call "governance" or "institutions" is a critical determinant of foreign aid and economic development outcomes is a strong one, but it is disturbing that major policy decisions are driven by expert-based ratings when it is hard to know what they are actually measuring.

The results also have implications for debates about the causes of civil conflict and war. They tend to support the view that low income is strongly related to conflict risk because it is a proxy for low state capabilities rather than because of a direct labor market effect. Income growth or decline within a country is not much related to subsequent changes in conflict propensity, whereas changes in perceived quality of governance appear to be related (at least for the ICRG measures). It is interesting, but also unfortunate in a way, that no one dimension of governance appears markedly more important than the others. If this had been the case, the results might have supported greater focus in aid policies on improving corruption, or rule of law, or bureaucratic quality, or whatever came up most strongly related to reduction in conflict risk. Instead, we find that at least for our current measures of good governance or institutions, all good things go together and all of them appear related to lower conflict risk to a slightly different extent. This could suggest that good performance on all of these various dimensions is a by-product or function of some underlying political configuration or bargain, the nature of which remains unclear and should be the subject of investigation (see Besley and Persson 2009; North, Wallis, and Weingast 2009).

Notes

1. In the mid-1980s, there was more civil war in developing countries than there is now but essentially no discussion of the problems conflict posed for development.

2. The Bank also designates states as fragile if they have had a peacekeeping operation in the previous three years.

3. For examples of onset studies, see Hegre et al. (2001), Sambanis (2001), Fearon and Laitin (2003), Collier and Hoeffler (2004), and Hegre and Sambanis (2006); for duration, Balch-Lindsay and Enterline (2000), Collier, Hoeffler, and Soderbom (2004), Cunningham (2006), and Fearon (2004); for incidence, Montalvo and Querol (2005) and Besley and Persson (2009).

4. See Fearon (2010) for a detailed review and a replication of these results using conflict data used in this paper.

5. See Weinstein (2007). Drawing on an exhaustive reading of micro-level accounts of particular civil wars, Kalyvas (2006) provides myriad examples of how the relative local strength of rebel and government forces shaped local support for the rebels versus the government, more than the other way around.

6. Both papers mention the alternative stressed by the other as a possibility. Fearon (2008) develops a model of individual decisions to join a rebel movement, noting that the standard opportunity cost argument neglects the fact that while there may be less to lose by joining a rebel band in a poor country, there is also less to gain. Unless one assumes a specific sort of preference (increasing relative risk aversion), the propensity to join a rebel group will be independent of per capita income in the country. An alternative explanation, stressed in that paper, is that in more modern economies it may be more difficult for rebel groups to extract wealth using typical guerrilla-group methods, given that much of it is virtual wealth held in bank accounts, human capital, and businesses that are more mobile than are farmers in poor countries.

7. Kaufmann, Kraay, and Mastruzzi (2009, 6) describe these six areas as follows: "(1) Voice and Accountability (VA) capturing perceptions of the extent to which a country's citizens are able to participate in selecting their government, as well as freedom of expression, freedom of association, and a free media. (2) Political Stability and Absence of Violence (PV) capturing perceptions of the likelihood that the government will be destabilized or overthrown by unconstitutional or violent means, including politically motivated violence and terrorism. (3) Government Effectiveness (GE) capturing perceptions of the quality of public services, the quality of the civil service and the degree of its independence from political pressures, the quality of policy formulation and implementation, and the credibility of the government's commitment to such policies. (4) Regulatory Quality (RQ) capturing perceptions of the ability of the government to formulate and implement sound policies and regulations that permit and promote private sector development. (5) Rule of Law (RL) capturing perceptions of the extent to which agents have confidence in and abide by the rules of society, and in particular the quality of contract enforcement, property rights, the police, and the courts, as well as the likelihood of crime and violence. (6) Control of Corruption (CC) capturing perceptions of the extent to which public power is exercised for private gain, including both petty and grand forms of corruption, as well as capture of the state by elites and private interests."

8. An advantage of Kaufmann, Kraay, and Mastruzzi's (2009) approach is that because they draw on a large number of different expert-based measures, their measures may have greater reliability than any one source.

9. For studies of institutions and governance as causes of economic growth, Mauro (1995) used ethnic fractionalization as an instrument for corruption as measured by

expert surveys; however, it is implausible that the only path through which ethnic fractionalization would be related to economic growth is corruption. Acemoglu, Johnson, and Robinson (2001) famously used settler mortality in colonies hundreds of years ago as an instrument for 1983 expropriation risk (ICRG). Knack and Keefer (1995) did not really address the endogeneity issue.

10. This is a blunt instrument, because clearly civil conflict causes lower growth, which tends to inflate the estimates for the effect of current growth and so potentially bias the estimates for governance downward, given that governance may be related to subsequent growth. (In fact, it is not much related to subsequent growth except for the WGI measures and income growth in the 2000s, but that's an issue for another paper.)

11. One problem with this approach is that a country's rating may change from one year to the next not because anything changed in the country but because other countries changed; these measures have more validity as a ranking within a given year than as a time-series measure.

12. This is in a very small part mechanical, since ICRG indicators are one of the many inputs into the WGI indicators.

13. Results are similar if we start the conflict measurement in 1998 or 2000, and if we use the 1998 WGI measures instead of the 1996 measures.

14. http://www.prio.no/CSCWlDatasets/Armed-Conflict/UCDP-PRIO1

15. See Fearon (2010) for a more detailed discussion of conflict coding rules and the implications of different choices. Results presented here appear not to be very sensitive to the details of the conflict coding rules; for example, they are very similar if I use an updated version of the civil war list in Fearon and Laitin (2003) instead of the ACD codings.

16. List-wise deletion is often a big problem in conflict regressions, because countries that are prone to civil war often do not have economic data.

17. Means for investment profile, corruption, rule of law, and bureaucratic quality are, respectively, .57, .52, .61, and .53. Standard deviations are .21, .23, .25, and .30.

18. This effect is stronger if we consider models that drop other covariates; for example, leaving only prior war, income, population, and ethnic fractionalization.

19. Looking only at major conflicts, there are too few countries (only 17) with a major onset in the ICRG subsample to get anything reliable out of fixed effects. However, the coefficient for investment profile is negative and very close to significant at .10. As in the pooled analysis, adding current growth rate does not change the results for the governance measures.

20. I log the number of prior onsets (plus one) because some countries have many prior low-level onsets and the distribution is quite skewed. Also, because some countries have multiple onsets after 1996, a negative binomial model could be used instead of logit with whether a country had at least one onset as the dependent variable; results are quite similar.

21. There is some evidence—in the data used here and in other studies (Hegre and Nome 2010)—that higher levels of democracy correlate with lower conflict risk among wealthier countries.

References

Acemoglu, Daron, Simon Johnson, and James A. Robinson. 2001. "The Colonial Origins of Comparative Development: An Empirical Investigation." *American Economic Review* 91 (5): 1369–401.

Balch-Lindsay, Dylan, and Andrew J. Enterline. 2000. "Killing Time: The World Politics of Civil War Duration, 1820–1992." *International Studies Quarterly* 4: 615–642.

Besley, Timothy, and Torsten Persson. 2009. *Pillars of Prosperity*. Princeton, NJ: Princeton University Press, forthcoming.

Bruckner, Markus, and Antonio Ciccone. 2010a. "International Commodity Prices, Growth, and the Outbreak of Civil War in Sub-Saharan Africa." *The Economic Journal,* 120 (544): 519–34.

———. 2010b. "Transitory Economic Shocks and Civil Conflict." Unpublished paper, Universitat Pompeu Fabra, Barcelona.

Burnside, Craig, and David Dollar. 2000. "Aid, Policies, and Growth." *American Economic Review* 90(4): 847–868.

Collier, Paul, and Anke Hoeffler. 2004. "Greed and Grievance in Civil War." *Oxford Economic Papers* 56: 563–595.

Collier, Paul, Anke Hoeffler, and Mans Soderbom. 2004. "On the Duration of Civil War." *Journal of Peace Research* 41: 253–273.

Collier, Paul, V. L. Elliott, Havard Hegre, Anke Hoeffler, Marta Reynal-Querol, and Nicholas Sambanis. 2003. *Breaking the Conflict Trap: Civil War and Development Policy.* Washington, DC: World Bank and Oxford University Press.

Cunningham, David E. 2006. "Veto Players and Civil War Duration." *American Journal of Political Science* 50(4): 875–892.

Easterly, William, Ross Levine, and David Roodman. 2004. "Aid, Policies, and Growth: Comment." *American Economic Review* 94(3): 774–780.

Fearon, James D. 2004. "Why Do Some Civil Wars Last So Much Longer Than Others?" *Journal of Peace Research* 4l(3): 275–30l.

———. 2008. "Economic Development, Insurgency, and Civil War." In *Institutions and Economic Performance,* ed. Elhanan Helpman. Cambridge, MA: Harvard University Press.

———. 2010. "Governance and Civil War Onset." Background paper prepared for the World Bank's 2011 World Development Report.

Fearon, James D., and David D. Laitin. 2003. "Ethnicity, Insurgency, and Civil War." *American Political Science Review* 97(1): 75–90.

Hegre, Havard, and Martin Nome. 2010. "Democracy, Development, and Armed Conflict." Paper presented at the 2010 Annual Meetings of the American Political Science Association, Washington, DC, September 2–5.

Hegre, Havard, and Nicholas Sambanis. 2006. "Sensitivity Analysis of the Empirical Literature on Civil War Onset." *Journal of Conflict Resolution* 50(4): 508–535.

Hegre, Havard, Tanja Ellingsen, Scott Gates, and Nils Petter Gleditsch. 200l. "Toward a Democratic Civil Peace? Democracy, Political Change, and Civil War 1816–1992." *American Political Science Review* 95(1): 33–48.

Kalyvas, Stathis N. 2006. *The Logic of Violence in Civil War.* New York: Cambridge University Press.

Kaufmann, Daniel, Aart Kraay, and Massimo Mastruzzi. 2009. "Governance Matters VIII: Aggregate and Individual Governance Indicators, 1996–2008." World Bank, Development Research Group, Policy Research Working Paper 4978, Washington, DC.

Knack, Stephen, and Philip Keefer. 1995. "Institutions and Economic Performance: Cross-Country Tests Using Alternative Institutional Measures." *Economics and Politics* 7(3): 207–227.

Mauro, Paolo. 1995. "Corruption and Growth." *Quarterly Journal of Economics* 110(3): 681–712.

Miguel, Edward, Shanker Satyanath, and Ernest Sergenti. 2004. "Economic Growth and Civil Conflict: An Instrumental Variables Approach." *Journal of Political Economy* 112 (4): 725–53.

Montalvo, Jose, and Marta Reynal Querol. 2005. "Ethnic Polarization, Potential Conflict, and Civil War." *American Economic Review* 95 (3): 796–816.

North, Douglass C., and Robert Paul Thomas. 1973. *The Rise of the Western World: A New Economic History*. New York: Cambridge University Press.

North, Douglass C., John Joseph Wallis, and Barry R. Weingast. 2009. *Violence and Social Orders: A Conceptual Framework for Interpreting Recorded Human History*. New York: Cambridge University Press.

Rodrik, Dani. 2005. "Why We Learn Nothing from Regressing Economic Growth on Policies." Unpublished paper, Kennedy School of Government, Harvard University, Cambridge, MA.

Sambanis, Nicolas. 2001. "Do Ethnic and Non-Ethnic Civil Wars Have the Same Causes? A Theoretical and Empirical Inquiry (Part 1)." *Journal of Conflict Resolution* 45 (3): 259–82.

Weinstein, Jeremy M. 2007. *Inside Rebellion: The Politics of Insurgent Violence*. New York: Cambridge University Press.

Winters, Matthew S. 2010. "Choosing to Target: What Types of Countries Get Different Types of World Bank Projects." *World Politics* 62 (3): 422–58.

Comment on "State Fragility, Governance Indicators, and the Risk of Civil Conflict" by James D. Fearon

LOUISE ANTEN

Fragile States and the Paradox of Weak Governance

Is weak governance an independent cause of conflict? That is the question James Fearon addresses in his paper, and his work is most welcome to all of us who participate in the policy debates on how to deal with fragile states. His conclusion is that low values on various governance indicators do forecast subsequent conflict onset when one controls for a country's level of economic development. A country with worse governance indicators than one would expect given its income level has a significantly greater risk of civil war outbreak in the next 5 or 10 years. The policy implication is that conflict prevention cannot limit itself to development aid aiming to raise incomes. It suggests that governance issues also have to be addressed directly. Yet the findings also show that political instability—defined as a change toward either more autocracy or more democracy—significantly raises the risk of civil war onset. So if bad governance raises the risk of conflict and changes in governance also imply increased conflict risk, how can fragile states emerge from fragility?[1]

Reflections on Fearon's Paper

Since I am not an expert in the methodologies used by Fearon, I leave the expert debate on the validity of his results to others. I will assume here that his results are valid and explore some policy implications. However, I would like to raise one issue that is relevant to these policy implications. Fearon uses the concept of "surprisingly good governance" to control for income levels. In his definition, countries have surprisingly good governance when they have high ratings for governance compared

Louise Anten was Head of the Conflict Research Unit of the Netherlands Institute of International Relations "Clingendael" until August 2010, when she rejoined the Netherlands Ministry of Foreign Affairs.

Annual World Bank Conference on Development Economics 2011, Global

with those of other countries at the same level of per capita income. But this strategy raises questions. Why has this governance not yet led to the economic level that should statistically have been its effect? Could other factors explain both the lack of effect on economic development and the conflict-proneness of the country? Fearon promises more on this research strategy and potential threats, and more on the determinants of surprisingly good or bad governance. I look forward to his reflections.

Findings from a Policy Perspective

One important finding in the paper is that the factors most strongly related to increased risk of civil war onset are new states, per capita income, and any change in governing arrangements, whether in an autocratic or democratic direction. Autocratizing change is slightly more prone to be followed by war than democratizing change. The likelihood that democratic reform leads to civil conflict does not vary much across levels of development. The risk is slightly lower as one moves up the income scale, but not significantly so. The level of democracy itself is not significantly related to the outbreak of conflict.[2]

The second policy-relevant finding is that low values on various governance indicators do forecast subsequent conflict onset when a country's level of economic development is controlled for. The various dimensions of good governance used in the three sets of indicators—the World Governance Indicators (WGI) produced by Kaufmann, Kraay, and Mastruzzi[3]; the International Country Risk Guide (ICRG) indicators; and the World Bank's aggregate Country Policy Institutional Assessment (CPIA)—are strongly interrelated, and no strong conclusion can be drawn about what dimension of governance is most important for increasing the odds of civil peace.

Fearon presents an interesting discussion on the role of horizontal inequalities, which is notoriously difficult to establish mainly because of the difficulty of measuring inequality across groups. The findings are somewhat inconclusive. On the one hand, ethnic fractionalization is significantly related to civil war onset in most but not all of the models Fearon uses. On the other hand, he finds that ethnic fractionalization is almost completely unrelated to surprisingly good governance. These findings warrant more research into the role of horizontal inequalities and do not yet discredit the view that ethnic diversity may act as a conflict factor when it is politicized and used to exclude groups from access to economic and political power (as I argue in Anten 2009).

Policy Implications

The first policy implication is rather straightforward, but it is important to mark it, since the debates about fragile state policies often take place among the development, diplomatic, and security communities: Conflict policy cannot limit itself to development aid that focuses on raising incomes. The defining role of governance in causing conflict warrants specific attention to governance. This goes for countries that have never experienced civil war and even more for postconflict situations, since previous war is an added risk factor.

The next question is how to address weak governance, considering the paradox described above, which is familiar to policy makers in fragile countries and in the international community. If weak governance increases the risk of conflict and so do changes in government arrangements, how can a country emerge from fragility?

The second policy implication I propose is that any policy aiming to improve governance in order to reduce fragility has to include a security component, since the policy raises the risk of conflict or relapse into conflict. A country-specific analysis could shed more light on the "greed and grievance" and "opportunity for violence" structures in that country, as well as on the actors involved. This could point the way to complementary actions in the domain of security (e.g., armed violence reduction, security sector reform) that could mitigate the risks of, and possibly prevent, the outbreak of conflict.

The third cluster of policy implications goes to the heart of the matter of governance reform. In practice, ways out of the paradox cited above have been sought at two levels: at the level of the governance approaches to be followed, and at the level of the governance aims to be pursued.

Studies focusing on the approaches to be followed hold on to the conviction that, in the end, a substantive democracy is the only governance system that protects societies against fragility and conflict. Democracy may not be perfect, but it is still, as Winston Churchill said, "the worst form of government except for all the others that have been tried." Thus it should be the ultimate aim of peace-building and state-building approaches. In working out approaches to achieve this aim, two dilemmas are often encountered. One concerns the sequencing of elections and is particularly relevant for postconflict situations. The other concerns constitution-building: which institutions would result in the highest level of democracy in the given country and how these institutions should be designed.

Sisk (2009) reviewed the dilemmas surrounding electoral processes after civil war. His overview aligns with Fearon's findings that a change in government arrangements—in this case, toward democratization—increases the risk of instability, at least in the short term. The explanation for this phenomenon is that in the absence of a democratic culture and well-functioning institutions, including institutions that check violence, electoral competition is likely to exacerbate divisions in society to an unmanageable level. On the other hand, electoral processes in postconflict situations may be necessary to validate peace agreements and provide sorely needed legitimacy for postwar governance. In some cases (e.g., South Africa in 1984), electoral processes have been the critical turning point that ended an uncertain and turbulent transition period. Many efforts have been made to define the minimal conditions necessary for "good" elections in fragile settings. I have not seen a definitive answer, but most people stress a minimum level of security and rule of law, sufficient engagement of popular (including subnational) levels, and a functioning election infrastructure.

The dilemma in constitution-building originates in the fact that democracy comes in many forms—the defining criterion is not so much a set of specific rules but rather the outcome of those rules as applied in the specific country. For example, the rules can stipulate that every citizen has a vote, but we all know cases in which that vote does not lead to an actual say in how the country is ruled. So democracy ensues (or does not) from the interplay between the formal and informal rules, the way the rules are applied in practice, and context factors such as the level of institutionalization. In this view democracy is defined as consisting of substantial civil and political rights, legal equality, rule of law, institutional checks on elected officials, real pluralism, and civilian control over the military and state security apparatus. Thus defined, it comes close to good governance as defined by the sets of indicators used by Fearon. The challenge in any given country is to know what political system would produce the best democracy or best governance: a proportional or majority system, presidential or parliamentary, centralized or federalized, and so on. Experience has taught us that there is no "best package" and that the population is more likely to accept a system that is designed in a participatory way. The dilemma is that this process can easily take a few years in a weakly organized and fragmented society—one that has an urgent need for an adapted, effective, and legitimate political system, so trade-offs must be made.

Linked to the issue of constitution-building is the question of how best to build on existing formal and informal institutions. In many fragile states, informal institutions provide most of the governance; these institutions must be carefully integrated into the new systems if the latter are to be effective. The goal is to create effective "hybrid orders" that combine old and new institutions. Building on constructive societal values (such as participation, consensus-building, sharing, rejection of personal enrichment), rules and institutions can increase the legitimacy and effectiveness of the hybrid order. Such an approach must be country-specific.

The second way out of the paradox is more radical—it questions the feasibility of the basic goal of strengthening governance or state-building in fragile states. Spurred by persistent failures to reform governance in fragile states such as Sudan and the Democratic Republic of Congo (DRC), some authors question whether the basic conditions for governance reform exist in these states. De Waal (2009) and Eriksen (2009) suggest that we not analyze fragile states for what they are not but rather for what they are: political orders responding to their own rules that are not likely to develop into neoliberal Weberian states.

De Waal introduces the concept of the "political marketplace" to analyze how governance actually works in countries where state institutions are subordinate to strong patronage networks. The basic characteristic of a political marketplace is that political loyalty is for sale to the highest bidder. Provincial elites seek to extract from the national elites the best price for their allegiance, using the tools at their disposal, such as votes, economic cooperation, and violence. The national elites—especially those in government—likewise have their economic and military tools. The various factions bargain and eventually strike a deal. However, whenever market conditions change, the deal is up for renegotiation, so the system is inherently unstable. The market could temporarily stabilize if each faction got a stake in proportion to its power base; in other words, if all major stakeholders were co-opted in a full buy-in. In some countries (e.g., the Democratic Republic of Congo, Sudan, and Afghanistan), the political marketplace is plainly dysfunctional; it does not manage to reach enduring bargains or contain violence. In other countries the marketplace functions in a mostly nonviolent way behind the façade of formal democratic and bureaucratic institutions. However, the political marketplace system is fundamentally at odds with good governance and development, because it requires leaders to spend public capital to maintain their loyalty base (in a nepotist, arbitrary, and corrupt manner) rather than on public development.

The fundamental question is whether it is possible in robust political marketplace orders to work on peace-building and state-building with the aim of achieving democracy, even if we follow the best integrated strategies. De Waal warns that mandating integrated peace operations in these countries with the task of democratization would lead to a mission without end: the foreign troops would need to remain forever to enforce democratization. In the case of the Democratic Republic of Congo, Eriksen argues that not only must the means (policies, strategies) of the standard approach to state-building and good governance be adapted to the context but the ends as well. The conditions for successful state-building are largely absent in the Democratic Republic of Congo: The interests of the regime and power are not compatible with state-building, regime survival does not depend on strengthening the state (and may even be threatened by it), and the regime has alternative strategies for political survival. Many actors (the state, companies, warlords) profit from dealing in and with the weak state. The price for peace in the Democratic Republic of Congo, at least in the short term, could be the reproduction of state weakness.

Entrenched political marketplaces survive as long as they have access to substantial rentier income—from oil and minerals and also from aid—which provides the lifeline for the patronage networks. As long as external interventions do not consistently create incentives for leaders to reform and consistently sanction misbehavior, it is unlikely that the political order will change. Historically, the international community has not been able to take such a united stance long enough to effect such change.

Concluding Remarks

If we turn back to the original paradox and its policy implications, what can we conclude?

First, Fearon's findings lend support to an integrated approach toward fragile states that aims to achieve better governance (e.g., rule of law, government effectiveness, less corruption), including better economic governance, while trying to contain the risk of conflict through a security component. This approach must deal with the inherent paradox that strengthening governance might create conflict; it requires carefully crafted strategies tailored to country-specific contexts. The key components are building on existing institutions, encouraging participation, engaging all stakeholders, linking in subnational governance, taking an incremental approach, and

making a long-term commitment. In the most fragile states, however—those characterized by an entrenched political marketplace and supported by rentier income—it
might be wise to set more modest and realistic ambitions, at least for the short and
medium terms. Preserving stability could be a modest goal. Politically, stability might
be best served by a full buy-in that co-opted all major stakeholders in a governance
arrangement. If such political orders are to be reformed, it will take a long-term exercise in which external interventions cooperate to create the right incentives.

Notes

1. This comment is based on an incomplete draft paper by James Fearon that includes
   material to be used for his paper for the 2010 Annual Bank Conference on Development Economics. The author apologizes for any mismatch between this comment and
   the final paper presented at the conference by James Fearon.
2. Collier (2008) finds that in countries with an income of less than US$2,500 per capita per
   annum, a higher level of democracy is related to a greater chance of conflict onset, while
   above that income level the chance of conflict is lower.
3. http://info.worldbank.org/governance/wgi/index.asp.

References

Anten, Louise. 2009. *Strengthening Governance in Post-conflict Fragile States.* Issues paper.
   The Hague: Netherlands Institute of International Relations "Clingendael."

Collier, Paul. 2008. "Fragile States." In *Democracy and Development,* ed. Bernard Berendsen.
   Amsterdam: KIT Publishers.

De Waal, Alex. 2009. "Mission Without End? Peacekeeping in the African Political Marketplace." *International Affairs* 85 (1): 99–113.

Eriksen, Stein Sundstöl. 2009. "The Liberal Peace Is Neither: Peacebuilding, Statebuilding and
   the Reproduction of Conflict in the Democratic Republic of Congo." *International Peacekeeping* 16 (5): 652–66.

Sisk, Timothy D. 2009. "Pathways of the Political: Electoral Processes after Civil War." In *The
   Dilemmas of Statebuilding, Confronting the Contradictions of Postwar Peace Operations,*
   ed. Roland Paris and Timothy D. Sisk. London and New York: Routledge.

New Ways of Measuring
Welfare

Subjective Well-Being, Income, Economic Development, and Growth

DANIEL W. SACKS, BETSEY STEVENSON, AND JUSTIN WOLFERS

Does economic growth improve the human lot?[1] Using several data sets that collectively cover 140 countries and represent nearly all the world's population, we study the relationship between subjective well-being and income, identifying three stylized facts. First, we show that in a given country, richer persons report higher levels of life satisfaction. Second, we show that richer countries, on average, have higher levels of life satisfaction. Third, analyzing the time series of countries that we observe repeatedly, we show that as countries grow, their citizens report higher levels of satisfaction. An important finding is that the magnitude of the relationship between satisfaction and income is roughly the same across all three comparisons, which suggests that absolute income plays a large role in determining subjective well-being.

These results overturn the conventional wisdom that there is no relationship between growth and subjective well-being. In a series of influential papers, Easterlin (1973, 1995, 2005a, 2005b) has argued that economists' emphasis on growth is misguided, because he finds no statistically significant evidence of a link between a country's gross domestic product (GDP) and the subjective well-being of its citizens, despite the fact that Easterlin and others (e.g., Layard 1980) have found that richer persons in a given country report higher levels of well-being. Researchers have reconciled these discordant findings—called the Easterlin Paradox—by positing that well-being is determined by relative, rather than absolute, income. In this view, people want only to keep up with the Joneses. The Easterlin Paradox suggests that focusing on economic growth is futile; when everyone grows richer, no one becomes happier. A related concern—voiced, for example, by Di Tella and MacCulloch (2010)—is that subjective well-being adapts to circumstance. If this argument is correct, it implies that long-run growth makes people no better off, because their aspirations and expectations grow with their incomes. A third concern is that even if well-being rises with

Daniel W. Sacks: Wharton, University of Pennsylvania. Betsey Stevenson: Wharton School, University of Pennsylvania, CESifo and NBER. Justin Wolfers: Wharton School, University of Pennsylvania, Brookings Institution, CEPR, CESifo, IZA, and NBER.

Annual World Bank Conference on Development Economics 2011, Global
© 2013 The International Bank for Reconstruction and Development/The World Bank

income for the very poor, a person eventually reaches a satiation point above which additional income has no effect on well-being (Layard 2005). However, in this paper, we present evidence that well-being rises with absolute income, period. Our evidence suggests that relative income, adaptation, and satiation are of only secondary importance.

Subjective well-being is multifaceted; it includes both how happy people are at a point in time and how satisfied they are with their lives as a whole (Diener 2006). To begin, we briefly discuss relevant background information on the measurement of subjective well-being. Throughout the paper, we focus on life satisfaction—the variable that is most often measured and the one that has been the focus of much of the existing literature (although many economists have referred to life satisfaction questions as measuring "happiness"). Although life satisfaction is the focus of this paper, we consider a variety of alternative measures of subjective well-being and show that they also rise with income.

We demonstrate that richer people are more satisfied with their lives and that this finding holds across 140 countries and several data sets. The relationship between income and satisfaction is remarkably similar in all countries: Our graphical analysis suggests that subjective well-being rises with the log of income. This functional form implies that a 20 percent rise in income has the same impact on well-being, regardless of the initial level of income: Going from $500 to $600 of income per year yields the same impact on well-being as going from $50,000 to $60,000. This specification is appealing on theoretical grounds because a standard assumption in economics is that the marginal impact of a dollar of income is diminishing. Indeed, estimating well-being as a function of log income fits the data much better than the simple linear function of income emphasized by previous authors, and this holds whether we are making comparisons across individuals, among countries, or over time. Thus, all our formal analyses involve the log of income rather than its level, although we present scatter plots and nonparametric fitted values to allow readers to assess the functional form for themselves.

After this discussion, we turn to the cross-country evidence. Using larger data sets than previous authors have examined, we find an economically and statistically significant relationship between average levels of satisfaction in a country and the log of GDP per capita. The data also show no evidence of a satiation point: The same linear-log satisfaction-income gradient we observe for poor and middle-income countries holds equally well for rich countries; it does not flatten at high income.

Whereas Easterlin (1974) argued that the relationship between well-being and income seen within countries was stronger than the relationship seen between countries, and that this provided evidence for the importance of relative income, our evidence undermines the empirical foundation for this claim. Instead, we show that the relationship between income and well-being is similar both within and between countries, thereby suggesting that absolute income plays a strong role in determining well-being, and relative income is a less important influence than previously believed.

We then turn to the time-series evidence. While the within- and between-country comparisons cast doubt on the Easterlin Paradox, they do not by themselves tell us whether economic growth translates into gains in subjective well-being. This question has challenged researchers for some time because of a lack of consistent time-series data on subjective well-being. We analyze the time-series movements in subjective well-being using two sources of comparable repeated cross-national cross-sections. Each data set spans two decades and covers dozens of countries.

In analyzing the time-series data, we can subject the relative income hypothesis to a test: If notions of the good life change as the incomes of one's fellow citizens grow, we should see only a modest relationship between growth in satisfaction and growth in average income relative to our point-in-time estimates. We present economically and statistically significant evidence of a positive relationship between economic growth and rising satisfaction over time, although limited data mean that these estimates are less precise than those from the within- or between-country regressions. The magnitude of the estimated gradient between satisfaction and income in the time series is similar to the magnitude of the within- and between-country gradients. These results suggest that raising the income of all does indeed raise the well-being of all.

Finally, we turn to alternative measures of subjective well-being, showing that they too rise with a country's income. We find that happiness is positively related to per capita GDP across a sample of 69 countries. We then show that additional, affect-specific measures of subjective well-being—such as whether a person felt enjoyment or love, or did not feel pain—are all higher in countries with higher per capita GDP. Our finding that subjective well-being rises with income is therefore not confined to an unusual data set or a particular indicator of subjective well-being.

Taken together, these new stylized facts suggest that subjective well-being, however measured, rises with income. Other recent papers have noted this as well. Deaton (2008) finds that people in richer countries have both higher levels of subjective well-being and better health. Stevenson and Wolfers (2008), performing an analysis parallel to this one—although using slightly different methods[2]—report similar findings to those described here and discuss in detail why previous researchers failed to identify the strong link between subjective well-being and income.

Background on Subjective Well-Being

Subjective well-being has many facets. Some surveys, such as the World Values Survey, ask respondents about their life satisfaction: "All things considered, how satisfied are you with your life these days?" The Gallup World Poll includes a variant of this question in which respondents are shown a picture and told, "Here is a ladder representing the ladder of life. Let's suppose the top of the ladder represents the best possible life for you; and the bottom, the worst possible life for you. On which step [between 0 and 10] of the ladder do you feel you personally stand at the present time?" This question, which we refer to as the satisfaction ladder, is a form of Cantril's Self-Anchoring Striving Scale (Cantril 1965). Other surveys ask about happiness directly: "Taking all things together, how would you say things are these days—would you say you're very happy, fairly happy, or not too happy?" Gallup also asks a battery of more specific questions, ranging from "Were you proud of something you did yesterday?" to "Did you experience a lot of pain yesterday?" Whereas the satisfaction question invites subjects to assess the entirety of their well-being, the more specific questions hone in on affect; they measure feelings rather than assessments (Diener 2006). In this paper, we will largely focus on life satisfaction, although we do examine the relationship between income and particular components of well-being.

We focus on satisfaction rather than other measures of subjective well-being, such as happiness, for two reasons. First, we would like to use as many data sets as possible to assess the relationship between subjective well-being and income, and life satisfaction and the satisfaction ladder are used more than any other measures. Second, the previous literature documenting the Easterlin Paradox (including Easterlin 1974, 1995, 2005a, 2005b, 2009) has largely focused on life satisfaction questions, even though researchers have tended to refer to their work as analyses of "happiness." Thus, we focus our attention on analyzing similar questions for direct comparability with the previous literature. However, we also assess the income-happiness link in detail, along with other, more affective, measures of well-being—and the results are similar to the income-satisfaction link.

Subjective well-being data are useful only if the questions succeed in measuring what they intend to measure. Economists have traditionally been skeptical of subjective data because they lack any objective anchor and because some types of subjective data, such as contingent valuations, suffer from severe biases (e.g., Diamond and Hausman 1994). These objections apply to subjective well-being data, but a variety of evidence points to a robust correlation between answers to subjective well-being questions and alternative measures of personal well-being. For example, self-reported well-being is correlated with physical measures such as heart rate and electrical activity in the brain, as well as sociability and a propensity to laugh and smile (Diener 1984). Self-reported well-being is also correlated with independently ascertained reports from friends and with health and sleep quality (Diener, Lucas, and Scollon 2006; Kahneman and Krueger 2006). Measures of subjective well-being also tend to be relatively stable over time, and they have a high test-retest correlation (Diener and Tov 2007). If people answered subjective well-being questions without rhyme or reason, we would not see these correlations across questions and people and over time. Individual subjective well-being data are likely based on actual well-being.

Subjective well-being data lack a natural scale and are reported differently across data sets. For example, happiness questions often ask respondents to choose a level of happiness from "very happy" to "very unhappy," with one or two nominal values in between. Life satisfaction can be measured on a similar scale or on a ladder of life with 10 or 11 rungs. To compare answers across surveys, we convert all subjective well-being data into normalized variables, subtracting the sample mean and dividing by the sample standard deviation. Whenever we report the subjective well-being–income gradient, therefore, we are effectively reporting the average number of standard deviation changes in subjective well-being associated with a one unit change in income (or log income). This rescaling has the disadvantage of assuming that the difference between any two levels of life satisfaction is equal, although in fact the difference between the fifth and sixth rungs on the ladder of life may be very different from the difference between the ninth and tenth rungs. There are many alternative ways to standardize the scale of subjective well-being; Stevenson and Wolfers (2008) use an ordered probit and show that the results we discuss here are robust to alternative approaches.[3]

Within-country estimates of the satisfaction-income gradient. We begin our study of life satisfaction and income by comparing the reported satisfaction of relatively rich and less rich persons in a given country at a point in time. Many authors have found a positive and strong within-country relationship between subjective well-being, measured in various ways, and income. For example, Robert Frank argues for the importance of income as follows: "When we plot average happiness versus average income for clusters of people in a given country at a given time . . . rich people are in fact a lot happier than poor people. It's actually an astonishingly large difference. There's no one single change you can imagine that would make your life improve on the happiness scale as much as to move from the bottom 5 percent on the income scale to the top 5 percent" (Frank 2005, 67). We confirm this relationship and, taking advantage of the enormous size of many of our data sets, estimate precisely the magnitude of the within-country satisfaction-income gradient.

We assess the relationship between satisfaction and income by estimating lowess regressions of satisfaction against the log of household income. Lowess regression effectively estimates a separate bivariate regression around each point in the data set, but weights nearby points most heavily (Dinardo and Tobias 2001). Traditional regression analysis imposes a linear relationship, while the lowess procedure allows researchers to study the functional form of the relationship between two variables, such as life satisfaction and the log of income.

In figure 1, we plot the lowess estimate of the relationship between the satisfaction ladder score and the log of household income for each of the 25 largest countries in the world (estimated separately), using data from the Gallup World Poll.[4] (Analyzing income per equivalent household yields similar conclusions.) Satisfaction scores are shown as both raw (0–10) scores on the left axis and in their standardized form (obtained by subtracting the whole sample mean and dividing by the standard deviation) on the right axis. To ease comparison with subsequent figures, the standardized satisfaction scale and the income scale are kept approximately constant in the various charts throughout this paper.

Figure 1 reveals the well-known finding that richer citizens of a given country are more satisfied with their life. For most countries, this plot reveals that satisfaction rises linearly with the log of income (as the horizontal axis is on a log scale). Moreover, the gradient is similar across countries, with the estimated line for each country looking like parallel shifts of each other. In spite of the enormous differences among these countries, the relationship between income and life satisfaction is remarkably similar. Finally, we note that this figure provides no evidence of satiation. While some have argued that, above a certain point, income has no impact on well-being, in these countries we see that the curve is just as steep at high levels of income as at low levels.

FIGURE 1.
Relationship between Well-Being and Income, within Individual Countries,
Gallup World Poll

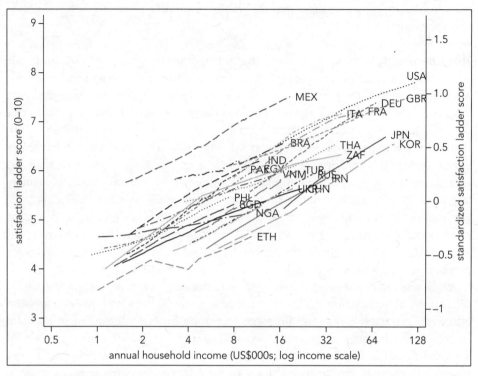

Source: Gallup World Poll.

Note: The figure shows, for the 25 largest countries, the lowess fit between individual satisfaction ladder scores and the log of household income, measured in the Gallup World Poll. The satisfaction data are shown both on their raw (0–10) scale on the left axis and as standardized variables on the right axis. We plot the lowess fit between the 10th and 90th percentiles of each country's income distribution. Satisfaction is assessed using the ladder of life question.

While these 25 countries account for the majority of the world's population, Gallup polled individuals in 132 countries, making this poll the widest survey of subjective well-being ever undertaken. We summarize and quantify the relationship between well-being and income by pooling data from all the countries in our data sets and estimating regressions of the following form:

$$Standardized\ satisfaction_{ic} = +_{countries}\ \alpha_c + \beta^{individual}\ ln(Income_{ic}) + X_{ic}\delta + \varepsilon_{ic}, \quad (1)$$

where i indexes individuals; c indexes countries; *Income* is self-reported household income; and X is a vector of individual-level controls including sex, a quartic in age, and their interaction. We include a country-specific intercept, α_c, which adjusts for differences in average satisfaction and income across countries, thereby ensuring that the estimation results are driven by differences between rich and poor within each country. We denote the coefficient of interest $\beta^{individual}$ because it isolates the well-being–income gradient obtained when comparing individuals within a country. In contrast to much of the literature, we focus on the relationship between subjective well-being and the log (rather than level) of income. Our graphical evidence supports this focus, since we observe that the satisfaction-income gradient is approximately linear-log.[5]

Table 1 presents the results, estimated separately in a variety of data sets. We begin by showing results from the 126 countries in the Gallup World Poll with valid income data. Next, we present results from the first four waves of the World Values Survey, which spans 1980–2004 and asks respondents to assess their life satisfaction on a 1–10 scale; we pool all waves and include wave fixed effects to account for changes through time and changes in surveys between waves. Stevenson and Wolfers (2008) document that for several countries in this survey the sampling frames are not nationally representative, so we drop these observations from all of our analyses. Finally, we also analyze the 2002 Pew Global Attitudes Survey, which covers 44 countries at all levels of development and uses the same ladder of life question as Gallup.

The first column of table 1 reports the regression results without any controls (beyond country fixed effects), and the estimated satisfaction-income gradient ranges from 0.216 in the World Values Survey to 0.281 in the Pew Global Attitudes Survey. In the second column we add controls for age and sex, but our results remain similar.[6] Within a given country, at a point in time, people with higher income tend to report greater life satisfaction.

We would like to compare the estimates from equation (1) to estimates of the cross-country subjective well-being–income gradient, but to do so we need to have a comparable concept of income changes. While differences in income between individuals within a country reflect both transitory and permanent differences (and each has different implications for subjective well-being), income differences between countries are likely to be much more persistent and close to entirely permanent.

How much of the cross-sectional variation in income within a country represents variation in permanent income? Standard estimates for the United States suggest

TABLE 1. Within-Country Satisfaction-Income Gradient

Dependent variable: Standardized life satisfaction	Without controls	With controls	Permanent income adjusted	Instrumental variables	Sample size
Gallup World Poll: Ladder question	0.236*** (0.014)	0.232*** (0.014)	0.422	0.449 *** (0.027)	171,900 (126 countries)
World Values Survey: Life satisfaction	0.216*** (0.017)	0.227*** (0.037)	0.413	0.26*** (0.035)	116,527 (61 countries)
Pew Global Attitudes Survey: Ladder question	0.281*** (0.027)	0.283*** (0.027)	0.515	0.393*** (0.033)	32,463 (43 countries)

Note: The table reports the coefficient on the log of household income, obtained from regressing standardized life satisfaction against the log of household income and country fixed effects using the indicated data set. Additional controls include a quartic in age, interacted with sex, plus indicators for age and sex missing. Our permanent income adjustment is to scale up our estimates by 1/0.55; see the text for the explanation. We instrument for income using a full set of country × education fixed effects. We report robust standard errors, clustered at the country level, in parentheses. For further details on the standardization of satisfaction and the exact wording of satisfaction questions, see the text.

***, **, and * denote statistically significant at 1 percent, 5 percent, and 10 percent, respectively.

that around two-fifths to one-half of the cross-sectional variation in annual income comes from permanent income (Gottschalk and Moffit 1994; Haider 2001).[7] Our survey asks about monthly income, suggesting that the transitory share is larger; to be conservative, we simply choose the upper end of these estimates. We also need to convert the variation in transitory income into its permanent income equivalent. If each extra dollar of transitory income persists for only one year, people would be indifferent between one extra dollar of transitory income and a rise in permanent income of about 5 cents (assuming a 5 percent discount rate). Estimates of the transitory component of annual income suggest that it does not all dissipate in one year; indeed, the autoregressive process estimated by Haider (2001) suggests that the permanent income equivalent of a $1 rise in transitory income would be about twice the one-year value, or 10 cents. Consequently a $1 increase in income in the cross-section represents, on average, a 50 cent rise in permanent income plus a 50 cent rise in transitory income, and this transitory income is valued equivalently to a rise in permanent income of about 5 cents. This implies that to interpret our estimated well-being–income gradient in terms of a $1 rise in permanent income, our cross-sectional estimates should be scaled up by about 80 percent (1/0.55). We report the adjusted estimates in the third column of table 1, and they tend to be slightly larger than 0.4.

We can also address this concern empirically by using an instrumental variables strategy designed to isolate variation in income that is likely permanent. Specifically, we use a full set of country × education fixed effects as instruments for permanent income. The instrumental variables estimates of $\beta^{individual}$—reported in the fourth column of table 1—are larger than the ordinary least squares (OLS) estimates, and in the Pew and Gallup data, they are close to the estimates we obtain after making the permanent income adjustment. Education, however, is very likely an imperfect instrument for permanent income. While education is correlated with permanent income, it likely also directly affects satisfaction, leading to upward bias on the instrumental variables estimates of $\beta^{individual}$. Our reading of the within-country evidence, therefore, is that the life satisfaction–log permanent income gradient falls between 0.3 and 0.5.

We should not push these adjustments too hard, however. While it seems straightforward to think that permanent rather than transitory income determines subjective well-being, direct evidence suggests the opposite: Subjective well-being and the business cycle move quite closely together. Stevenson and Wolfers (2008) report that the output gap strongly predicts subjective well-being, at least in the United States. Wolfers (2003) shows this also holds in Europe and across states in the United States.

International comparisons of satisfaction and income. The within-country relationship between income and life satisfaction is well known and admits at least two interpretations. The first interpretation is that greater earning capacity makes people satisfied with their lives: It purchases health care; allows people to enjoy their leisure time with fancier food and TVs; and affords them freedom from financial stress. A second interpretation, however, is that people care less about money than about having money relative to some reference point (Easterlin 1973). One reference point is their neighbor's income; others are a country's or the world's average income. Or perhaps people use their own previous income as a reference point. Under this view, people are stuck on a "hedonic treadmill": as they grow richer, their expectations adapt to their circumstances, and they end up no more satisfied than they were before (Brickman and Campbell 1990). On the other hand, on an "aspiration treadmill," even as higher income yields greater well-being, people may eventually report no higher well-being than they previously reported, because their expectations have grown with their income and well-being.

To sort out these interpretations, we turn to national data. If all that matters for satisfaction is my income relative to my neighbor's income, or relative to mean national income, people in countries with high average income should be no more satisfied than people in poorer countries. Alternatively, to the extent that national differences in income reflect long-lasting differences, people should adapt to them (if adaptation is important), so adaptation predicts that the cross-country satisfaction-income gradient should be small. On the other hand, if absolute income matters (or if the relevant reference point is mean global income), we would expect richer countries to be more satisfied. Thus, we now assess the satisfaction-income gradient across countries.

Our measure of average income in a country is GDP per capita, measured at purchasing power parity to adjust for international differences in price levels. These data come from the World Bank's World Development Indicators database; where we are missing data, we turn first to the Penn World Tables (version 6.2) and then to the *CIA Factbook*. For earlier years for which data are unavailable, we turn to Maddison (2007).

Figure 2 plots average (standardized) life satisfaction data drawn from each of the first four waves of the World Values Survey against GDP per capita (shown on a log scale). The figure shows both the OLS regression line and a nonparametric (lowess) fit. As previously noted, some of these observations were not based on nationally representative surveys (typically missing groups that might be expected to have low satisfaction), so we plot these with squares rather than circles; they clearly lie far from the regression line (which we calculate by excluding them).[8]

The early waves of the survey, which contain mostly wealthy nations, provide suggestive but not overwhelming evidence for a positive link between the log of GDP per capita and subjective well-being. A researcher who mistakenly included the nonrepresentative countries and who plotted satisfaction against the level rather than the log of income could (erroneously) fail to find a statistically significant relationship between GDP per capita and subjective well-being. Successive waves of the survey included more middle- and low-income countries, and the relationship between income and well-being is clearer in the later waves. The four waves span 25 years and 79 distinct countries, with income ranging from less than $1,000 to more than $32,000 (in 2000 international dollars). This figure shows a clearly positive and approximately linear-log relationship between life satisfaction and GDP.

Other data sets employing alternative measures of satisfaction show a similar positive relationship. Figure 3 plots the relationship between the satisfaction ladder

FIGURE 2.
Life Satisfaction and Real GDP per Capita, World Values Survey

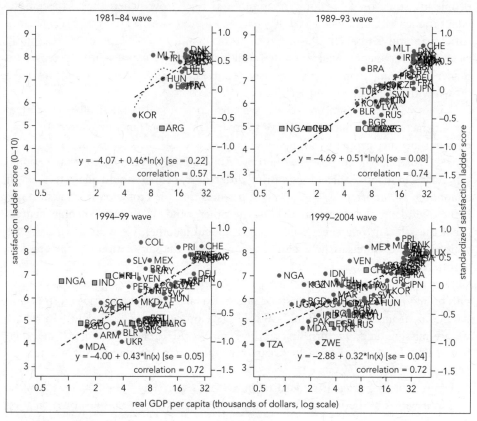

Source: World Values Survey.

Note: Respondents are asked, "All things considered, how satisfied are you with your life as a whole these days?"; respondents then choose a number from 1 (completely dissatisfied) to 10 (completely satisfied). Data are aggregated by first standardizing individual-level data to have mean zero and unit standard deviation, then taking country-year averages of the standardized values. The left axis gives the raw average satisfaction, and the right axis gives the standardized satisfaction. Dashed lines are fitted from an OLS regression; dotted lines are fitted from lowess regressions. These lines and the reported regressions are fitted only from the nationally representative samples. The units on the regression coefficients refer to the normalized scale. Real GDP per capita is at purchasing power parity in constant 2000 international dollars. Sample includes 20 (1981–84), 42 (1989–93), 52 (1984–99), or 69 countries (1999–2004) from the World Values Survey. Observations represented by hollow squares are drawn from countries in which the World Values Survey sample is not nationally representative. For details, see Stevenson and Wolfers (2008, appendix B).

scores estimated from the Pew Global Attitudes Survey and GDP per capita. The Pew data show the same pattern as the World Values Survey data: Richer countries exhibit higher levels of satisfaction. The nonparametric fit confirms the visual impression that there are no important nonlinearities: Satisfaction grows with log income at about the same rate whether we focus on rich countries or poor countries. This figure provides no evidence that the satisfaction–log income gradient diminishes as income grows, suggesting that no country is rich enough to have hit a satiation point, if such a point exists.

FIGURE 3.
Life Satisfaction and Real GDP per Capita, Pew Global Attitudes Survey 2002

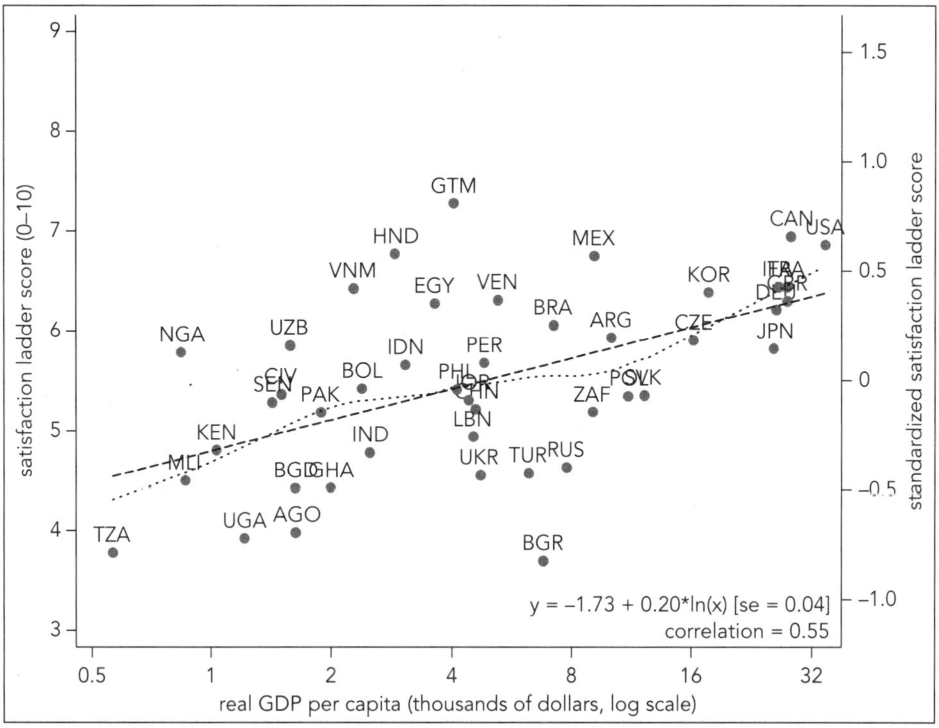

Source: Pew Global Attitudes Survey 2002.

Note: Respondents are shown a picture of a ladder with 10 steps and asked, "Here is a ladder representing the 'ladder of life.' Let's suppose the top of the ladder represents the best possible life for you; and the bottom, the worst possible life for you. On which step of the ladder do you feel you personally stand at the present time?" Data are aggregated by first standardizing individual-level data to have mean zero and unit standard deviation, then taking country-year averages of the standardized values. The left axis gives the raw average satisfaction, and the right axis gives the standardized satisfaction score. Dashed lines are fitted from an OLS regression; dotted lines are fitted from lowess regressions. Regression coefficients are in terms of the standardized scaling. Real GDP per capita is at purchasing power parity in constant 2000 international dollars. Sample includes 44 developed and developing countries.

Although the Pew and World Values Survey results provide strong evidence for the cross-country link between satisfaction and income, neither survey has quite the global coverage of the Gallup World Poll. In figure 4, we plot the satisfaction ladder scores against per capita GDP for 131 countries included in this poll (we exclude Palestine, because we were unable to find reliable GDP data). Every part of the GDP distribution is well represented. This figure confirms our strong impression that richer countries have higher levels of life satisfaction than poorer countries and that this relationship is approximately linear-log. Indeed, the correlation between average satisfaction scores in a country and its log of GDP per capita is above 0.8.

Because average well-being is rising in the log of average income, our results suggest that transferring a given amount of money from rich to poor countries could raise life satisfaction, because $100 is a larger percentage of income in poor countries than in rich countries. The linear-log relationship revealed by the nonparametric fits

FIGURE 4.
Life Satisfaction and Real GDP per Capita, Gallup World Poll

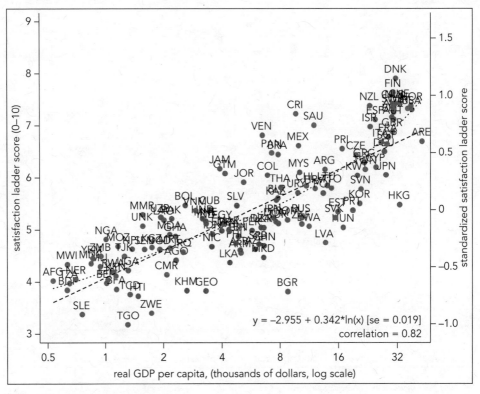

Source: Gallup World Poll.

Note: Respondents are shown a picture of a ladder with 10 steps and asked, "Here is a ladder representing the 'ladder of life.' Let's suppose the top of the ladder represents the best possible life for you; and the bottom, the worst possible life for you. On which step of the ladder do you feel you personally stand at the present time?" Data are aggregated by first standardizing individual-level data to have mean zero and unit standard deviation, then taking country-year averages of the standardized values. Dashed lines are fitted from an OLS regression; dotted lines are fitted from a lowess regressions. The units on the regression coefficients refer to the normalized scale. Real GDP per capita is at purchasing power parity in constant 2000 international dollars. Sample includes 131 developed and developing countries.

also provides evidence against satiation: The relationship between well-being and income does not diminish at high levels of income, except to the extent implied by the log functional form. If anything, the lowess curve appears to tick upward even more sharply at high levels of GDP.

We quantify the magnitude of the satisfaction-income link by running similar regressions to equation (1) but analyzing the satisfaction of individuals i in country c as a function of the log of average per capita income in their country instead of individual income (consequently, we also drop the country fixed effects):

$$Standardized\ satisfaction_{ic} = \alpha + \beta^{aggregate} \ln(GDP\ per\ capita_c) + X_{ic}\delta + \varepsilon_{ic} \quad (2)$$

Alternatively, we aggregate our satisfaction data up into national averages, and run:

$$\overline{Standardized\ satisfaction_c} = \alpha + \beta^{aggregate}\ \ln(GDP\ per\ capita_c) + \varepsilon_c \qquad (3)$$

We are interested in $\beta^{aggregate}$, which says by how much average satisfaction in a country increases (in standard deviations) when the log of average per capita income in a country is higher.

These results, summarized in table 2, confirm the impression given by the graphical analysis: All three of our data sets show a statistically significant and positive relationship between satisfaction and the log of GDP. These results suggest that absolute income plays an important role in explaining the relationship between satisfaction and income. The magnitude of the relationship is similar whether we estimate it in the individual-level data or the national averages, and whether or not we adjust for the differential age and sex composition of respondents. The coefficients on the log of average income vary somewhat but are centered on 0.3 to 0.4.

This range is striking for its resemblance to the within-country satisfaction-income gradient. To emphasize the similarity, figure 5 plots data from the Gallup World Poll. Each point in the figure is a separate country, and for each country we have plotted both a dot representing the average satisfaction and income in that country, and an arrow whose slope represents the slope of the satisfaction-income gradient when comparing people within that country. As we look across the 126 countries with valid household income data, we find that no country has a statistically significantly negative relationship between satisfaction and income; the bulk of the lines point in similar directions and have a similar slope. These slopes are roughly parallel to

TABLE 2. Cross-Country Regressions of Life Satisfaction on Log GDP per Capita

Dependent variable: Standardized life satisfaction	Microdata		National data	Sample size
	Without controls	With controls		
Gallup World Poll:	0.357***	0.378***	0.342***	291,383
Ladder question	(0.019)	(0.019)	(0.019)	(131 countries)
World Values Survey:	0.360***	0.364***	0.370***	234,093
Life satisfaction	(0.034)	(0.034)	(0.036)	(79 countries)
Pew Global Attitudes Survey:	0.214***	0.231***	0.204***	37,974
Ladder question	(0.039)	(0.038)	(0.037)	(44 countries)

Note: The table reports the coefficient on the log of per capita GDP, obtained from regressing standardized life satisfaction against the log of GDP, using individual data with and without controls, and using national-level data without controls, in the indicated data set. In the national-level regressions, we take the within-country average of standardized life satisfaction as the dependent variable. GDP per capita is at purchasing power parity. The additional controls include a quartic in age, interacted with sex, plus indicators for age and sex missing. We report robust standard errors, clustered at the country level, in parentheses. For further details on the standardization of satisfaction, the exact wording of satisfaction questions, and the sources for GDP per capita, see the text.

*** denote statistically significant at 1 percent, 5 percent, and 10 percent, respectively.

FIGURE 5.
Within-Country and Between-Country Estimates of the Life Satisfaction–Income Gradient, Gallup World Poll

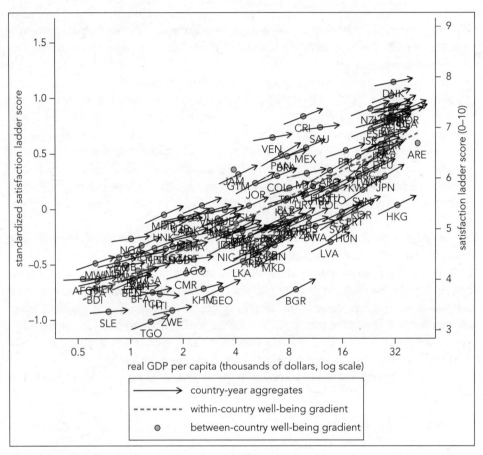

Source: Gallup World Poll.

Note: Each solid circle plots life satisfaction against GDP per capita for one of 131 developed and developing countries. The slope of the arrow represents the satisfaction-income gradient estimated for that country from a country-specific regression of individual standardized satisfaction on the log of their annual real household income, controlling for gender, a quartic in age, and their interaction. Usable household income data were unavailable for 18 countries. The dashed line represents the between-country satisfaction-income gradient estimated from an OLS regression of the satisfaction index on the log of real GDP per capita. GDP per capita is at purchasing power parity in constant 2000 international dollars.

the dashed line, which shows that the slope one obtains when comparing individuals within a country is similar to that obtained when making comparisons between country averages.

Thus, our estimates of the satisfaction-income gradient are similar whether estimated within or between countries. Recall that the Easterlin Paradox rested on the belief that the well-being–income gradient observed within countries is larger than that seen between countries. Earlier estimates of a statistically insignificant cross-country relationship between average satisfaction and average income reflected the fact that previous researchers were looking at small samples of fairly homogeneous countries. It was the juxtaposition of this statistically insignificant finding with evidence of a statistically significant well-being–income relationship that led Easterlin to declare the data paradoxical. But the historical absence of evidence for a proposition—that richer countries are happier—should not have been confused as being evidence of its absence. And indeed, with our larger data sets, we find statistically significant evidence that high-income countries are happier than their low-income counterparts. Instead, a claim about the importance of relative income comparisons should rest on the quantitative magnitudes of the estimated well-being–income gradients.

Indeed, the similarity of the within- and between-country gradients has an important interpretation that we can express more formally. Suppose that:

$$Satisfaction_{ic} = \alpha + \beta^{absolute} \ln(Income_{ic}) + \beta^{relative} \ln \frac{Income_{ic}}{Income_c}$$

$$= \alpha + (\beta^{absolute} + \beta^{relative}) \ln Income_{ic} - \beta^{relative} \ln \overline{Income_c} \qquad (4)$$

where $\beta^{absolute}$ and $\beta^{relative}$ measure the importance of absolute and relative income in determining life satisfaction. Equation (1) estimates regressions of this form, regressing standardized satisfaction scores on $\ln(Income_{ic})$ yielding a coefficient $\beta^{individual}$, and country fixed effects controlling for the influence of $\ln \overline{Income_c}$. Thus, our table 1 estimates of the within-country satisfaction-income gradient $\beta^{individual}$ is the sum of the absolute and relative income effects: $\beta^{individual} = \beta^{absolute} + \beta^{relative}$.

Next, taking country averages of equation (4) yields:

$$\overline{Satisfaction_c} = \alpha + \beta^{absolute} \ln \overline{Income_c} - (\beta^{absolute} + \beta^{relative}) MLD_c \qquad (5)$$

where MLD_c (which equals $\ln \overline{Income} - \overline{\ln Income}$) is the mean log deviation, a measure of a country's income inequality. This equation is very similar to the cross-country estimates of equation (3) shown in table 2. Indeed, if we had estimated $\beta^{aggregate}$ conditional on the mean log deviation, our estimate of $\beta^{aggregate}$ would give an exact estimate of $\beta^{absolute}$. Stevenson and Wolfers (2010) show that the covariance between MLD_c and $\ln(GDP_c)$ is small, so whether or not one controls for the mean log deviation has only a minimal impact on our estimate of $\beta^{aggregate}$. Our estimate of $\beta^{aggregate}$ is, therefore, approximately $\beta^{aggregate}$.

Consequently, the importance of relative income in determining life satisfaction, $\beta^{relative}$, is equal to the difference $\beta^{individual} - \beta^{aggregate}$. Since we estimate that the between-country gradient ($\beta^{aggregate}$) is similar to or slightly larger than the within-country gradient ($\beta^{individual}$), we conclude that relative income plays at best a minor role in determining life satisfaction.

An alternative explanation of reference-dependent preferences is based on adaptation. In this view, what matters for satisfaction is income relative to expectations, and these expectations adapt in light of recent experience. Thus, economic growth simply speeds up the pace of the hedonic treadmill, as we all run faster just to stay in place. This implies that variation in income that has persisted long enough for expectations to adapt should be unrelated to satisfaction. The differences in log GDP per capita shown in figures 3–5 are extremely persistent, and across the 131 countries in the Gallup World Poll, the correlation between the log GDP per capita in 2006 shown in figure 4 and its value in 1980 is 0.93. Consequently, this theory suggests that these persistent cross-country differences in GDP per capita should have little explanatory power for satisfaction. The data clearly falsify this hypothesis, too.

Satisfaction and economic growth. So far, we have shown that richer people report higher life satisfaction than poorer people in a given country, and that, on average, citizens of rich countries are more satisfied with their lives than are citizens of poor countries. These comparisons suggest that absolute income plays an important role in determining well-being, but they do not directly address our central question: does economic growth improve subjective well-being?

We answer this question by turning to the time-series evidence on life satisfaction and GDP, which allows us to assess whether countries that experience economic growth also experience growth in subjective well-being. Estimating the time-series relationship between GDP and subjective well-being is difficult, because sufficiently comparable data are rarely available. For example, the General Social Survey in the United States and the Life in Nation surveys in Japan both surveyed subjective well-being over a long horizon, but both are afflicted by important changes in the wording and ordering of questions that, if not recognized, can lead to serious interpretation errors. Nevertheless, many scholars have found that the United States has not gotten any happier over the past 35 years, despite becoming wealthier, and Stevenson and Wolfers (2009) note a somewhat puzzling decline in female happiness. In contrast, Japan, which was once thought to have experienced little increase in happiness over the postwar period, has in fact experienced significant happiness gains that are similar in magnitude to what one would expect given the cross-sectional and cross-country relationships between subjective well-being and income. However, these happiness gains become apparent only once changes in the survey over time are taken into account (Stevenson and Wolfers 2008); the failure to take account of these changes had led many previous scholars astray (including Easterlin 1995, 2005a).

We draw on two long-running data sets to examine the relationship between subjective well-being and economic growth: the World Values Survey and the Eurobarometer. We analyze the first four waves of the World Values Survey, which span 1980 to 2004 and cover 79 distinct countries. Because the World Values Survey added many countries in later waves, however, it is not possible to make many comparisons of a given country.[9] The Eurobarometer survey has the advantage that it has been surveying people in member nations of the European Union virtually continuously since 1973; however, it has the disadvantage of covering only relatively homogeneous countries. Unlike the other surveys, the Eurobarometer ascertains life satisfaction on a 4-point scale.[10]

Nine countries were included in the original Eurobarometer sample. Analyzing data through 1989, Easterlin (1995) concluded that the data failed to show any relationship between life satisfaction and economic growth. In figure 6, we present

FIGURE 6.
Changes in Life Satisfaction and Economic Growth in Europe, Eurobarometer

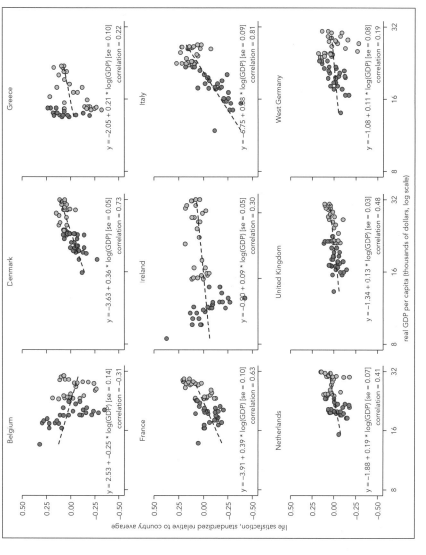

Source: Eurobarometer.

Note: Solid circles represent separate observations from each round of the Eurobarometer survey from 1973 to 1989; these were the data analyzed in Easterlin (1995). Open circles extend the sample from 1990 to 2002 using the Eurobarometer Trendfile, then through to 2007 using biannual Eurobarometer reports. Each panel shows data for one of the nine countries analyzed by Easterlin (1995). Data are aggregated by first standardizing individual-level data to have mean zero and unit standard deviation, then taking country-year averages of the standardized values. Dashed lines are fitted from the reported OLS regression; Newey-West standard errors (se) are reported, accounting for first-order autocorrelation. The life satisfaction question asks, "On the whole, are you very satisfied, fairly satisfied, not very satisfied or not at all satisfied with the life you lead?" GDP per capita is at purchasing power parity in constant 2000 international dollars.

299

scatter plots of life satisfaction and the log of GDP per capita for the nine countries Easterlin analyzed. In the figure, dark circles represent the original data he analyzed; hollow circles denote data that have subsequently become available through to 2007. The dark circles by themselves do not always show a strong relationship; however, over the full sample, eight of the nine countries show a positive relationship between life satisfaction and growth, and six of the nine slopes are statistically significantly positive. The slopes range from –0.25 in Belgium to 0.68 in Ireland. This reanalysis not only suggests a positive relationship between income and growth but also hints at the difficulty of isolating this relationship when data are scarce.

The positive relationship between life satisfaction and economic growth is not confined to European countries. In figure 7, we turn to the World Values Survey and plot changes in life satisfaction against cumulative changes in real GDP. This survey covers more countries at very different levels of development, which allows us to see whether populations become more satisfied as their countries transition from low to moderate income and from moderate to high income. To keep the comparisons clean, figure 7 excludes countries in which the sampling frame changed.

Each of the six graphs compares a different pair of waves. The top row compares short differences (the waves are separated by about five years), while the bottom row shows longer differences (10–20 years). All six graphs indicate a positive association between changes in subjective well-being and changes in income; the estimated gradients range from 0.22 between waves I and III to 0.71 between waves I and II. The figure shows that life satisfaction is more sensitive to short-run changes in income than to long-run changes, suggesting that business cycle variation may be driving some of the association. An alternative interpretation is that over time people adapt to their new circumstances or their aspirations change, so that even though their material welfare is increasing, their subjective well-being gains from these increases recede over time.

Figure 7 also reveals some potentially interesting (or problematic) outliers. The Republic of Korea, for example, often falls outside the GDP change scale but had only a modest change in subjective well-being; Hungary experienced very little growth but had a serious decline in life satisfaction. In regression results reported below, we include these outliers, but it is clear that excluding them could change our estimates.

The comparisons in figure 7 are particularly valuable because they are all between common pairs of waves, so they automatically adjust for the various changes in the survey—both question order and survey techniques—that occurred between waves. Stevenson and Wolfers (2008) document that these World Values Survey data are strongly influenced by methodological changes, so this control is important. Indeed, the influence of the changes is large enough to render naïve comparisons of raw survey averages through time to be problematic (Easterlin and Angelescu 2009; Easterlin and Sawangfa 2008).

To distill the information from these figures into a single estimate of the intertemporal relationship between satisfaction and economic growth, we estimate panel regressions of the following form:

$$Satisfaction_{tc} = \beta^{time\ series}\ \ln(GDP_{tc}) + \Sigma_{c\in\ countries}\ \alpha_c + \Sigma_{t\in\ waves}\ \mu_c + \epsilon_{tc} \qquad (6)$$

FIGURE 7.
Changes in Life Satisfaction and Economic Growth, World Values Survey

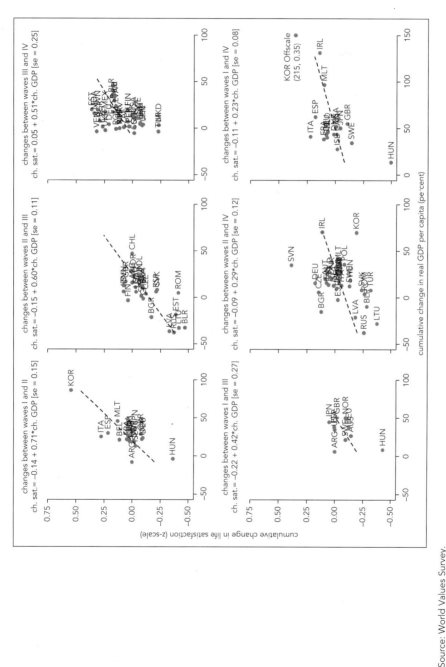

Source: World Values Survey.

Note: We restrict the sample in each graph to countries in which the World Values Survey sample did not change sampling frames between the given waves. Each point gives the change in life satisfaction and real GDP for a given country and a given pair of waves. Data are aggregated by first standardizing individual-level data to have mean zero and unit standard deviation, then taking country-year averages of the standardized values. The dashed lines give the OLS fit. Graphs in the first row show 19, 10, and 17 comparable short first differences, and those in the second row show 25, 32, and 33 long first differences. GDP per capita is at purchasing power parity in constant 2000 international dollars.

TABLE 3. Time-Series Regressions of Life Satisfaction on GDP per Capita

Dependent variable: Standardized life satisfaction	World Values Survey (WVS): All countries	WVS: Transition countries	WVS: Nontransition countries	Eurobarometer: All countries
Panel A: Panel regressions				
ln(GDP)	0.505***	0.628**	0.407***	0.17**
	(0.109)	(0.239)	(0.116)	(0.074)
N	166 observations	31 observations	135 observations	776 observations
	79 countries	10 countries	66 countries	31 countries
Panel B: Long differences				
ln(GDP)	0.47***	0.694*	0.35**	0.278*
	(0.128)	(0.387)	(0.163)	(0.164)
N	66 differences	10 differences	46 differences	30 differences

Note: The table reports the coefficient on the log of GDP per capita. In the panel regressions, we regress standardized life satisfaction against the log of GDP per capita as well as wave and country fixed effects. In the long differences, we regress the change in standardized satisfaction against the change in log GDP per capita, after adjusting satisfaction and log GDP for wave and country fixed effects. Long differences in the World Values Survey are taken between the first and last time we see a country; in the Eurobarometer, between decadal averages. We report robust standard errors, clustered at the country level, in parentheses. For further details on the standardization of satisfaction, the exact wording of satisfaction questions, the sources for GDP per capita, the procedure used to compute long differences, and the definition of transition countries, see the text.

***, **, and * denote statistically significant at 1 percent, 5 percent and 10 percent, respectively.

where the time fixed effects μ_c control for changes in question order between waves, and the country fixed effects α_c ensure that only within-country changes through time drive the comparisons.

Panel A of table 3 shows the results of estimating equation (6) using the World Values Survey and the Eurobarometer. We find a substantial and statistically significant relationship between life satisfaction and economic growth. The estimates are not particularly precise, however, and they differ considerably between the two data sets. The satisfaction-income gradient is 0.51 in the World Values Survey and 0.17 in the Eurobarometer. In neither data set can we reject the hypothesis that the true $\beta^{time\ series}$ lies between 0.3 and 0.4, the central estimate from the cross-country regressions. We can, however, reject the null hypothesis that $\beta^{time\ series} = 0$, which is the outcome suggested by the view that relative rather than absolute income determines well-being.

To assess whether these regressions are driven by outliers, figure 8 shows the variation underlying our World Values Survey panel regression estimates, while figure 9 illustrates the variation underlying our Eurobarometer results. Our panel regressions reflect variation in satisfaction and log GDP per capita, stripped of country and wave fixed effects. Thus, the vertical axis shows residual satisfaction defined by

$$\widetilde{Satisfaction}_{ct} = \overline{Satisfaction}_{ct} - E[\overline{Satisfaction}_{ct} \mid country\ and\ wave\ effects],$$

FIGURE 8.
Life Satisfaction and Log GDP, Relative to Country and Year Fixed Effects,
World Values Survey

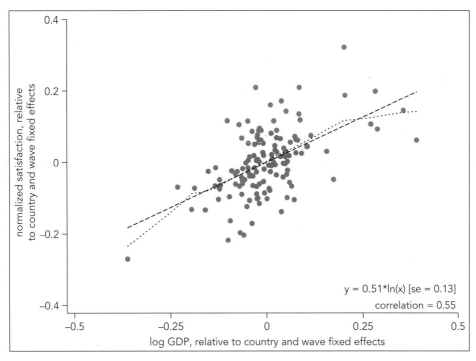

Source: World Values Survey.

Note: We plot residuals from a regression of log GDP or normalized average satisfaction against country and wave fixed effects, using all four waves of the World Values Survey and excluding countries for which the sampling frame is not nationally representative. Data were aggregated by first standardizing individual-level data to have mean zero and unit standard deviation, then taking country-year averages of the standardized values. The dashed line gives the OLS fit, and the dotted line is fitted from lowess regression. For details, see the text.

which is obtained as the residual from a regression of satisfaction on country and wave fixed effects. Likewise, the horizontal axis shows residual log GDP,

$$\ln(\widetilde{GDP}_{ct}) = \ln(GDP_{ct}) - E[\ln(GDP_{ct}) \,|\, country \ and \ wave \ effects],$$

which is obtained from a similar regression in which log GDP is the dependent variable. As can be seen, when a country is experiencing relatively high levels of GDP (relative to its country average and the estimated wave fixed effects), it also experiences high levels of satisfaction. By construction, our panel data regression coefficient in panel A of table 3, $\hat{\beta}^{time \ series}$, is exactly equal to the slope of the dashed bivariate regression line shown in each figure. These figures confirm that the results in table 3 are not driven by a few outliers; the points fit the regression line well, and the correlation is quite strong. The data in figure 9 paint a somewhat noisier picture for the Eurobarometer panel, although roughly similar conclusions hold.

FIGURE 9.
Life Satisfaction and Log GDP, Relative to Country and Year Fixed Effects, Eurobarometer

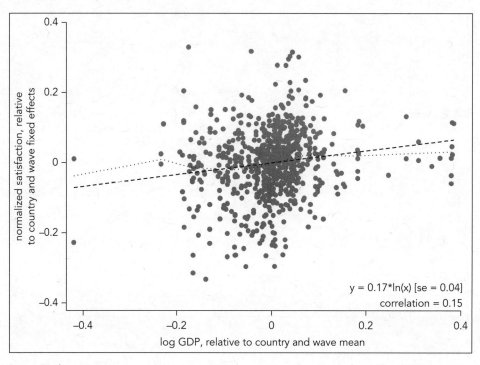

Source: Eurobarometer.

Note: We plot residuals from a regression of log GDP or normalized average satisfaction against country and wave fixed effects. Data were first aggregated by first standardizing individual-level data to have mean zero and unit standard deviation, then taking country-year averages of the standardized values. The dashed line gives the OLS fit, and the dotted line is fitted from lowess regression.

In obtaining these estimates, however, we have drawn on all the variation in GDP in our sample, including possibly high-frequency changes to which people do not have a chance to adapt. If adaptation occurs slowly, it would be better to focus on long-run changes in GDP. Indeed, Easterlin and Angelescu (2009) argue that only long-run economic growth can be used to assess the relationship between growth and well-being.

So far, only the data plotted on the bottom row of figure 7 speak to this point, showing that even 10-year changes in GDP continue to influence life satisfaction. However, each of these comparisons is limited to the sets of countries that are common to a pair of waves. Instead, we can assess long differences for all countries by comparing changes in $Satisfaction_{ct}$ and $\ln(\widetilde{GDP}_{ct})$ between the first and last time we observe a country in the World Values Survey.

We plot these variables against each other in figure 10 for each of the 56 countries in the World Values Survey that we observe multiple times. The average difference in time between the first and last observations is about 11 years. (This number is

FIGURE 10.
Long Differences in Life Satisfaction and Log GDP, World Values Survey

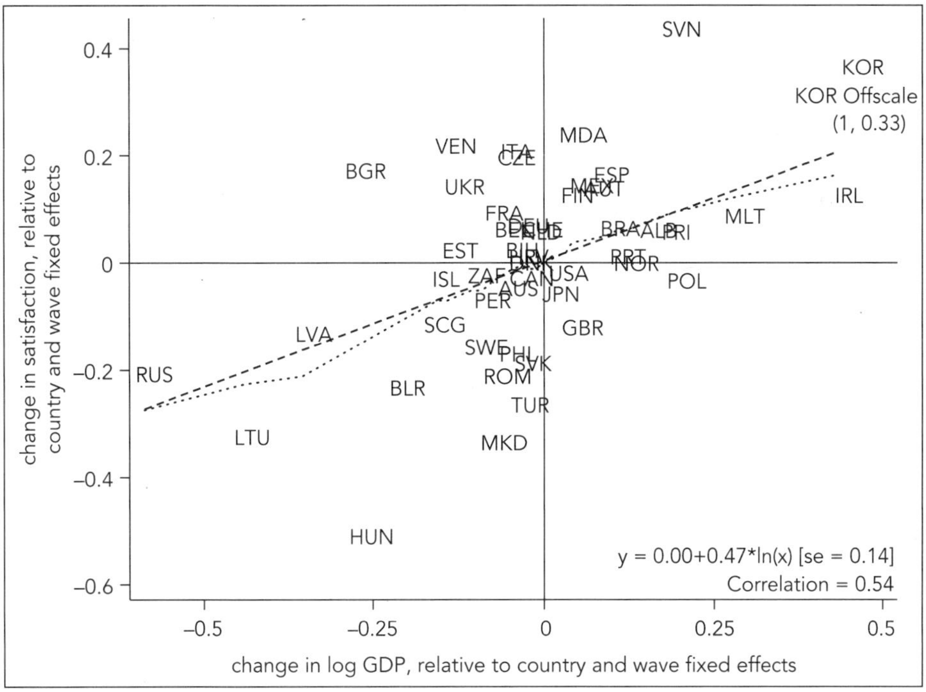

Source: World Values Survey.

Note: The vertical axis shows the long difference $Satisfaction_{c,last} - Satisfaction_{c,first}$, and the horizontal axis shows the long difference $\ln(\widetilde{GDP})_{c,last} - \ln(\widetilde{GDP})_{c,first}$, where the subscripts denote the first and last time each country was observed in the four waves of the World Values Survey. The variables $Satisfaction_{ct}$ and $\ln(\widetilde{GDP})_{ct}$ reflect the residuals estimated after regressing $Satisfaction_{ct}$ and $\ln(GDP)_{ct}$ (respectively) on country and wave fixed effects. We use all four waves of the World Values Survey and exclude countries for which the sampling frame is not nationally representative. Data are aggregated by first standardizing individual-level data to have mean zero and unit standard deviation, then taking country-year averages of the standardized values. The dashed line gives the OLS fit, and the dotted line is fitted from lowess regression. For details, see the text.

comparable with Easterlin and Sawangfa's notion of the "long run"—they require data spanning at least 10 years—but somewhat lower than Easterlin and Angelescu's 12-year requirement.) The majority of countries are located in the northeast and southwest quadrants; therefore, their GDP and satisfaction move together (relative to wave fixed effects). A notable number of countries, however, lie in the northwest and southeast; their life satisfaction and GDP move in opposite directions. Even so, the correlation between these variables is positive and remarkably strong, given that we are analyzing first differences.

In panel B of table 3, we report the estimate of the relationship between well-being and growth obtained from regressing these long differences in $Satisfaction_{ct}$ against long differences in $\ln(\widetilde{GDP_{ct}})$. We bootstrap our standard errors to account for the uncertainty in generating residual satisfaction and GDP.[11] The coefficient is 0.47 and statistically significantly different from zero, and with these long differences, once again, we cannot reject the hypothesis that the true $\beta^{time\,series}$ lies between 0.3 and 0.4.

Using these same data (although including the observations from the unrepresentative national samples and not adjusting for wave fixed effects), Easterlin and Sawangfa argue that "the positive association between the change in life satisfaction and that in GDP per capita reported by Stevenson and Wolfers rests almost entirely on the positively correlated V-shaped movement of the two variables during the post-1990 collapse and recovery in the transition countries" (2008, 13). To investigate this claim, we separately estimate our panel regressions and long differences for the sample of transition countries only and for all other World Values Survey nations. Although breaking the sample apart like this reduces our statistical precision, the key inferences remain the same in both samples: The influence of GDP growth on satisfaction is positive and statistically significantly different from zero. We cannot reject that these coefficients lie between 0.3 to 0.4 and, if anything, the World Values Survey yields estimates of the time-series satisfaction-income gradient that is somewhat larger. The critique leveled by Easterlin and Sawangfa seems, quite simply, wrong.

Figure 10 provides further evidence for why estimating the relationship between subjective well-being and long-run growth has challenged researchers. Many countries do not fit the general trend that growth in satisfaction is correlated with GDP growth. Bulgaria, Estonia, Ukraine, and República Bolivariana de Venezuela all experienced considerable declines in income with no accompanying decline in well-being. Furthermore, a researcher who is worried about outliers could easily drop a handful of influential countries from the sample—for example, Hungary, Korea, the Russian Federation, and Slovenia. Removing these countries clearly does not eliminate the positive correlation between these long differences, but it substantially reduces the statistical power of the regression, because these extreme cases involve so much of the variation in $\Delta \ln(\widetilde{GDP}_{ct})$. When we exclude these countries from our regression of long differences, our estimate of $\beta^{time\ series}$ remains positive and comparable to other estimates at 0.26, but the standard error grows to 0.15.

We repeat this exercise using the Eurobarometer data. The advantage of these data is that they include many observations for each country, which we can combine to reduce the influence of measurement error. Thus, we construct long differences in the Eurobarometer by taking averages of $Satisfaction_{ct}$ and $\ln(\widetilde{GDP}_{ct})$ for each country in each of the decades 1973–82, 1983–92, 1993–02, and 2003–07. We then construct decadal differences in satisfaction and GDP by comparing adjacent decades and plot these decadal differences in figure 11. Each point represents a single decadal difference in satisfaction and GDP for a given country. Many countries experienced sluggish income growth but no relative slowdown in subjective well-being. Most of these countries are in Western Europe. For a majority of countries, however, GDP and satisfaction move in the same direction, although the correlation is much weaker than in our previous estimates. The estimated satisfaction-income gradient resulting from these long differences, also reported in the right-hand column of table 3, summarizes the results from this figure. We find a marginally statistically significant gradient of 0.28.

Overall, we find a positive but somewhat less precise relationship between growth in subjective well-being and growth in GDP. When we use all the time-series variation in GDP, we find a well-being–income gradient that is similar to the within-country

FIGURE 11.
Decadal Differences in Life Satisfaction and Log GDP, Eurobarometer

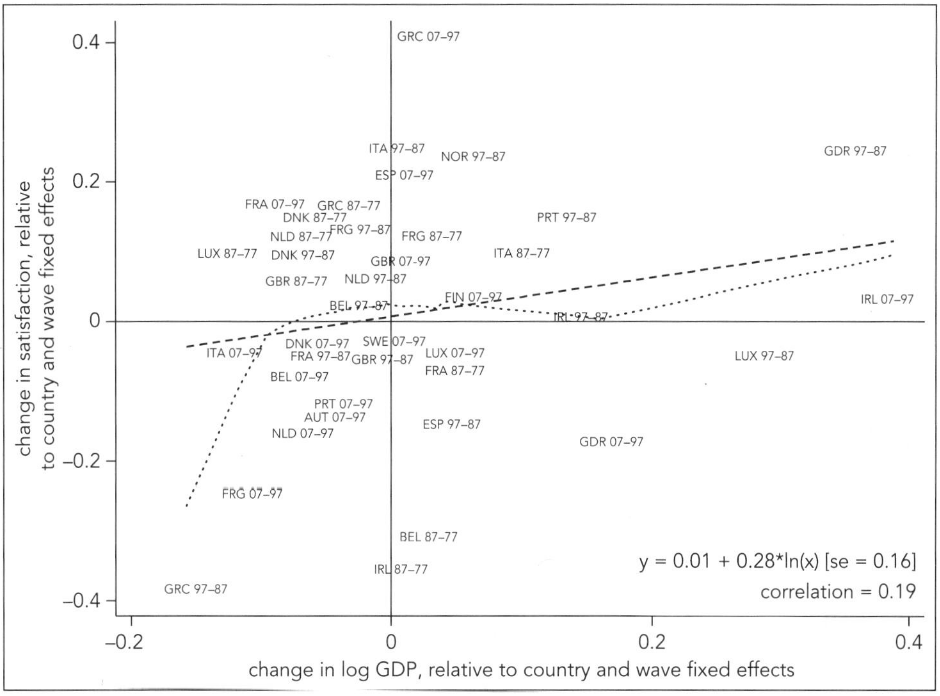

Source: Eurobarometer.

Note: Eurobarometer 1973–2007; sources for GDP per capita described in text. The vertical axis shows the long differences $Satisfaction_{c,d} - Satisfaction_{c,d-1}$, and the horizontal axis shows the long difference $\ln\widetilde{(GDP)}_{c,d} - \ln\widetilde{(GDP)}_{c,d-1}$, where $Satisfaction_{c,d}$ and $\ln\widetilde{(GDP)}_{c,d}$ are, respectively, decadal averages of $Satisfaction_{c,t}$ and $\log\widetilde{(GDP)}_{c,t}$, taken over the decades 1973–82, 1983–92, 1993–2002, and the partial decade 2003–07. The variables $Satisfaction_{c,t}$ and $\ln\widetilde{(GDP)}_{ct}$ reflect the residuals estimated after regressing $Satisfaction_{ct}$ and $\ln(GDP)_{ct}$ (respectively) on country and wave fixed effects. Data are aggregated by first standardizing individual-level data to have mean zero and unit standard deviation, then taking country-year averages of the standardized values. The dashed line gives the OLS fit, and the dotted line is fitted from lowess regression. For details, see the text.

and cross-sectional gradients. When we estimate longer differences, the precision of the relationship falls but the point estimate is similar in magnitude. This remains true whether we exclude potentially problematic "transition" economies from the sample or not; whether we limit our attention to long-run changes in income or not; and whether we analyze data from the World Values Survey or the Eurobarometer. None of our estimates using the full variation in GDP allows us to reject the hypothesis that $\beta^{time\ series}$ lies between 0.3 and 0.4, the range of our estimates of the static relationship between well-being and income.

Alternative measures of subjective well-being. Thus far, we have shown that there is a positive, statistically significant, and quantitatively important relationship between life satisfaction and income, and that this satisfaction-income gradient is similar in magnitude whether one analyzes individuals in a given country, countries at a point in time, or a given country over time. But life satisfaction is not the only measure of subjective well-being, so we consider the relationships between various other measures of subjective well-being and income. For brevity (and for reasons of data availability), we will focus on cross-country comparisons of these alternative indicators.

In figure 12 we begin by studying happiness, showing the cross-sectional relationship between happiness and the log of GDP per capita, using data from the fourth wave of the World Values Survey. We follow the same graphing conventions as in previous charts, showing the national averages as both their average on their original 4-point scale and as standardized values (on the right axis). We also show both the regression line (where the dependent variable is the standardized measure of happiness) and the nonparametric fit; this regression line shows a

FIGURE 12.
Happiness and GDP: World Values Survey, 1999–2004

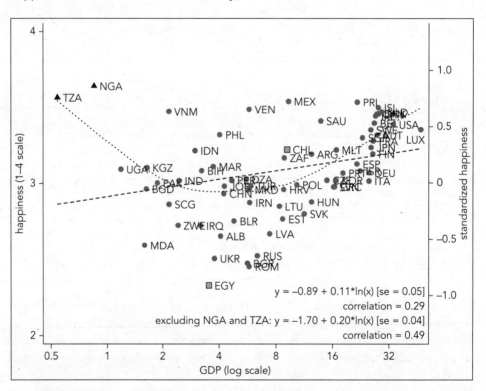

Source: World Values Survey, 1999–2004.

Note: World Values Survey 1999–2004 and authors' regressions. Sources for GDP per capita are described in the text. The happiness question asks, "Taking all things together, would you say you are: 'very happy,' 'quite happy,' 'not very happy,' [or] 'not at all happy'?" Data are aggregated into country averages by first standardizing individual-level data to have mean zero and standard deviation one, then taking the within-country average of individual happiness. The dashed line plots fitted values from the reported OLS regression (including Tanzania and Nigeria); the dotted line gives fitted values from a lowess regression. The regression coefficients are on the standardized scale. Both regressions are based on nationally representative samples. Observations represented by hollow squares are drawn from countries in which the World Values Survey sample is not nationally representative. See Stevenson and Wolfers (2008, appendix B) for details. Sample includes 69 developed and developing countries.

positive and statistically significant relationship between happiness and per capita GDP, although the estimated happiness-income gradient is not as large as the satisfaction-income gradient we estimate in table 2. The presence of two extreme outliers, Tanzania and Nigeria, skews the regression estimates considerably. These countries are particularly puzzling because they are the poorest in the sample, but they report among the highest levels of happiness. They also have much lower average life satisfaction; indeed, Tanzania is the least satisfied of any country in our sample. Perhaps there is a banal explanation for this puzzle: Survey documentation suggests that there were difficulties translating the happiness question in Tanzania. Stevenson and Wolfers (2008) discuss the happiness-income link more fully and find very similar results to the satisfaction-income link: Happiness increases at any aggregation of the data, and the magnitude of the link is not much affected by the degree of aggregation.

We turn now to alternative and more specific measures of subjective well-being. The Gallup World Poll asks respondents about many facets of their emotional health and daily experience. For several experiences—such as enjoyment, physical pain, worry, sadness, boredom, depression, anger, and love—the Gallup poll asks, "Did you experience [feeling] during a lot of the day yesterday?" These questions sketch a psychological profile of hundreds of thousands of people spanning the world's income distribution. In figure 13, we present scatter plots of the probability that a person in a given country experienced various emotions yesterday against GDP per capita. The figure suggests that citizens of richer countries are more likely to experience positive emotions and less likely to experience negative emotions. Enjoyment is very highly correlated with GDP, while love is moderately correlated. Physical pain, depression, sadness, and anger all decline moderately with GDP.[12] Worry increases slightly with GDP, although there is not a strong pattern.

The Gallup poll also probes respondents for an array of sentiments about their day yesterday, asking whether they felt well rested, were treated with respect, chose how to spend their time, smiled or laughed a lot, were proud of something they did, or ate good-tasting food. The daily experience questions, which uniformly measure positive experiences, paint a picture that is consistent with our analysis thus far. Figure 14 shows the percentage of people in each country that felt a certain way in the previous day. People in richer countries are more likely to report feeling better rested and respected, smiling more, and eating good-tasting foods than people in poorer countries, although they are no more likely to take pride in what they did or to have learned something interesting.

These data point to a more nuanced relationship between well-being and income. While they provide no reason to doubt that well-being rises with income, they also suggest that certain facets of well-being respond less to income than others. These data hint at the possibility of understanding which emotions and experiences translate into the part of life satisfaction that is sensitive to changes in income.

FIGURE 13.
Cross-Country Measures of Recalled Feelings and GDP, Gallup World Poll

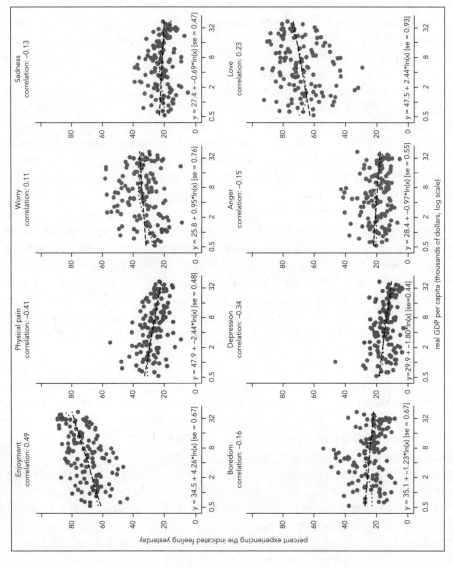

Source: Gallup World Poll 2006. Sources for GDP per capita described in the text.

Note: Respondents were asked, "Did you experience [feeling] during a lot of the day yesterday?" GDP per capita is at purchasing power parity in constant 2000 international dollars. Each observation represents 1 of up to 130 developed and developing countries in the sample (questions were not asked in Iraq). Dashed lines are fitted from ordinary least squares regressions of the percentage agreeing with the statement on log real GDP per capita; dotted lines are fitted from lowess estimations.

FIGURE 14.
Cross-Country Measures of Daily Experience and GDP, Gallup World Poll

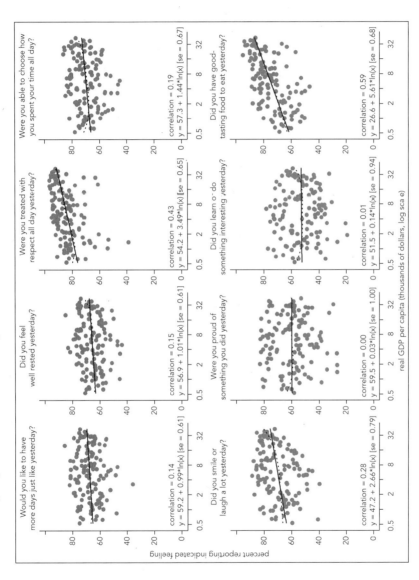

Source: Gallup World Poll 2006. Sources for GDP per capita described in the text.

Note: Questions were prefaced as follows: "Now, please think about yesterday, from the morning until the end of the day. Think about where you were, what you were doing, who you were with, and how you felt." Each observation represents 1 of up to 130 developed and developing countries in the sample (questions were not asked in Iraq). Dashed lines are fitted from OLS regressions of the percentage agreeing with the statement on log real GDP per capita; dotted lines are fitted from lowess estimations. GDP per capita is at purchasing power parity in constant 2000 international dollars.

Conclusions

This paper revisits the stylized facts on the relationship between subjective well-being and income. We find that in a given country, rich people are more satisfied with their lives than poorer people, and we find that richer countries have significantly higher levels of average life satisfaction. Studying the time-series relationship between satisfaction and income, we find that economic growth is associated with increases in life satisfaction.

The key innovation is this paper is to focus explicitly on the magnitude of the subjective well-being–income gradient (rather than its statistical significance), while also bringing the greatest quantity of data to bear on these questions. We show that the within-country, between-country, and over-time estimates all point to a quantitatively similar relationship between subjective well-being and income. This relationship is robust: We find it not only at different levels of aggregation but using different data sets. We also find that income is positively associated with other measures of subjective well-being, including happiness and other upbeat emotions.

The fact that life satisfaction and other measures of subjective well-being rise with income has significant implications for development economists. First, and most important, these findings cast doubt on the Easterlin Paradox and various theories suggesting that there is no long-term relationship between well-being and income growth. Absolute income appears to play a central role in determining subjective well-being. This conclusion suggests that economists' traditional interest in economic growth has not been misplaced. Second, our results suggest that differences in subjective well-being over time or across places likely reflect meaningful differences in actual well-being.

Subjective well-being data, therefore, permit cross-country well-being comparisons without reliance on price indexes. As Deaton (2010) notes, if we wish to use some kind of dollar-a-day threshold to count poverty, we need price indexes that account for differences in quality and quantity of consumption in different countries. In theory, constructing these indexes is straightforward, provided one is ready to assume identical homothetic preferences across countries. In practice, however, a central challenge to creating price indexes is that many countries consume very different sets of goods—there is no price of smoked bonga in some countries. As countries grow richer, previously unavailable goods start being traded as very expensive specialty items. Paradoxically, as a country grows richer, its poverty count can grow because its prices are revised upward, devaluing income.[13]

As Deaton suggests, many changes in purchasing power parity (PPP) adjustments simply involve better data and should not be ignored. But it can be difficult to know how much of the change in the poverty count reflects actual changes in global poverty and how much reflects updated measurement methods. In light of these difficulties, Deaton says, "Why don't we just ask people?" Using data from 87 countries spanning 2006–08, Deaton computes average life satisfaction for the world. "For the world as a whole," he writes, "2007 was a better year than 2006; in 2008, more households reported being in difficulty and being dissatisfied with their lives, and these reports were worse still in 2009" (Deaton 2010, 30).

Deaton notes that these comparisons are valid only if life satisfaction responds to absolute rather than relative well-being. If people assess their lives relative to contemporary standards, then as countries and the world grow richer, reported satisfaction may not change. However, our analysis suggests an important role for absolute income in determining life satisfaction; therefore, we conclude that subjective well-being data are likely to be useful in assessing trends in global well-being.

We have focused on establishing the magnitude of the relationship between subjective well-being and income rather than disentangling causality from correlation. The causal effect of income on individual or national subjective well-being, and the mechanisms by which income raises subjective well-being, remain open and important questions.

Notes

1. This paper revisits—and, we hope, clarifies and simplifies—many of the findings originally described in Stevenson and Wolfers (2008).

2. Some of the results in this paper differ from results in the earlier study, because we consider a simpler and more transparent scaling of subjective well-being, and we use more recent data from the Gallup World Poll.

3. In Stevenson and Wolfers (2008), we estimated well-being aggregates as the coefficients from an ordered probit of well-being on country fixed effects, which yielded very similar estimates. The most important difference is that the ordered probit scales differences relative to the standard deviation of well-being conditional on country dummies, while the simpler normalization in this paper scales differences relative to the (larger) unconditional standard deviation of well-being. Given that country fixed effects account for about 20 percent of the variation in well-being (that is, R^2 0.2 in an OLS regression of satisfaction on country fixed effects), this simpler normalization will tend to yield estimates of the well-being–income gradient that are about nine-tenths as large ($\sqrt{1 - R^2} \approx 0.9$).

4. We are using a more recent version of the Gallup World Poll than Stevenson and Wolfers (2008), incorporating data made available through October 13, 2008.

5. Throughout the paper, therefore, when we refer to the subjective well-being–income gradient, we mean the SWB-log income gradient.

6. These estimates are slightly smaller than those found in Stevenson and Wolfers (2008), which is partly due to the different normalization of satisfaction scores and partly due to the more recent vintage of the Gallup data analyzed here.

7. While our calculations will use these U.S. estimates as if they are representative of the entire world, we really need similar studies for countries at different levels of development.

8. For more details about the World Values sampling frame and which country-years include nationally representative samples, see appendix B in Stevenson and Wolfers (2008).

9. As noted earlier, some of the country samples in earlier waves of the World Values Survey are not directly comparable with later waves, as their survey frames were (intentionally) not nationally representative. Our analysis focuses on nationally representative samples.

10. For the analysis, we keep West Germany and East Germany as separate countries. For details on the Eurobarometer and our data procedures, see Stevenson and Wolfers (2008).

11. We bootstrap the two-step procedure as follows. For each bootstrap iteration, we first compute the residuals as described and then regress $\widetilde{Satisfaction}_{ct}$ $\widetilde{Satisfaction}_{ct}$ against

$\ln(\widetilde{GDP}_{ct})\ln(\widetilde{GDP}_{ic})$. We perform 1,000 iterations and take the standard deviation of the distribution of computed gradients as our estimated standard error (after making a degrees-of-freedom adjustment).

12. See Krueger, Stevenson, and Wolfers (2010) for a more thorough exploration of the relationship between experiencing pain and income.

13. As Deaton notes, adjusting for this difficulty is straightforward in theory: weight goods by whether they are considered luxury items. This task may be quite difficult, however, because it requires making judgments about many thousands of goods for each country in the world.

References

Brickman, P., and D. T. Campbell. 1990. "Hedonic Relativism and Planning the Good Society." In *Adaptation Level Theory: A Symposium,* ed. M. H. Appley. New York: Academic Press.

Cantril, Hadley. 1965. *The Pattern of Human Concerns.* New Brunswick, NJ: Rutgers University Press.

Deaton, Angus. 2008. "Income, Health and Well-Being around the World: Evidence from the Gallup World Poll." *Journal of Economic Perspectives* 22(2): 53–72.

———. 2010. "Price Indexes, Inequality, and the Measurement of World Poverty." *American Economic Review* 100(1): 5–34.

Di Tella, Rafael, and Robert MacCulloch. 2010. "Happiness Adaption to Income beyond 'Basic Needs.'" In *International Differences in Well-Being,* ed. Ed Diener, John Helliwell, and Daniel Kahneman. New York: Oxford University Press.

Diamond, Peter A., and Jerry A. Hausman. 1994. "Contingent Valuation: Is Some Number Better than No Number?" *Journal of Economic Perspectives* 8(4): 45–64.

Diener, Ed. 1984. "Subjective Well-Being." *Psychological Bulletin* 95(3): 542–575.

———. 2006."Guidelines for National Indicators of Subjective Well-Being and Ill-Being." *Journal of Happiness Studies* 7(4): 397–404.

Diener, Ed, Richard E. Lucas, and Christie Napa Scollon. 2006. "Beyond the Hedonic Treadmill: Revising the Adaptation Theory of Well-Being." *American Psychologist* 61(4): 305–314.

Diener, Ed, and William Tov. 2007. "Culture and Subjective Well-Being." In *Handbook of Cultural Psychology,* ed. Shinobu Kitayama and Dov Cohen. New York: Guilford.

Dinardo, John, and Justin L. Tobias. 2001. "Nonparametric Density and Regression Estimation." *Journal of Economic Perspectives* 15(4): 11–28.

Easterlin, Richard A. 1973. "Does Money Buy Happiness?" *The Public Interest* 30: 3–10.

———. 1974. "Does Economic Growth Improve the Human Lot? Some Empirical Evidence." In *Nations and Households in Economic Growth: Essays in Honor of Moses Abramowitz,* ed. Paul A. David and Melvin W. Reder. London: Academic Press.

———. 1995. "Will Raising the Incomes of All Increase the Happiness of All?" *Journal of Economic Behavior and Organization* 27(1): 35–48.

———. 2005a. "Feeding the Illusion of Growth and Happiness: A Reply to Hagerty and Veenhoven." *Social Indicators Research* 74(3): 429–433.

———. 2005b. "Diminishing Marginal Utility of Income? Caveat Emptor." *Social Indicators Research* 70(3): 243–255.

————. 2009. "Lost in Transition: Life Satisfaction on the Road to Capitalism." *Journal of Economic Behavior and Organization* 71(1): 130–145.

Easterlin, Richard A., and Laura Angelescu. 2009. *Happiness and Growth the World Over: Time Series Evidence on the Happiness-Income Paradox.* IZA Discussion Paper No. 4060.

Easterlin, Richard A., and Onnicha Sawangfa. 2008. *Happiness and Economic Growth: Does the Cross Section Predict Time Trends? Evidence from Developing Countries.* IZA Discussion Paper No. 4000.

Frank, Robert H. 2005. "Does Absolute Income Matter?" In *Economics and Happiness: Framing the Analysis,* ed. Pier Luigi Port and Luigino Bruni. Oxford: Oxford University Press.

Gottschalk, Peter, and Robert Moffit. 1994. "The Growth of Earnings Instability in the U.S. Labor Market." *Brookings Papers on Economic Activity* 1994(2): 217–254.

Haider, Steven J. 2001. "Earnings Instability and Earnings Inequality of Males in the United States: 1967–1991." *Journal of Labor Economics* 19(4): 799–836.

Kahneman, Daniel, and Alan B. Krueger. 2006. "Developments in the Measurement of Subjective Well-Being." *Journal of Economic Perspectives* 20(1): 3–24.

Kahneman, Daniel, Alan B. Krueger, David Schkade, Norbert Schwarz, and Arthur A. Stone. 2006. "Would You Be Happier If You Were Richer? A Focusing Illusion." *Science* 312(5782): 1908–1910.

Kruger, Alan, Betsey Stevenson, and Justin Wolfers. 2010. "A World of Pain." Mimeo, University of Pennsylvania.

Layard, Richard. 1980. "Human Satisfaction and Public Policy." *Economic Journal* 90(363): 737–750.

————. 2005. *Happiness: Lessons from a New Science.* London: Penguin.

Maddison, Angus. 2007. "Historical Statistics for the World Economic: 1–2003 AD." www .ggdc.net/maddison/Historical_Statistics/horizontal-file_03-2007.xls.

Stevenson, Betsey, and Justin Wolfers. 2008. "Economic Growth and Subjective Well-Being: Reassessing the Easterlin Paradox." *Brookings Papers on Economic Activity* 2008(1): 1–87.

————. 2009. "The Paradox of Declining Female Happiness." *American Economic Journal: Economic Policy* 1(2): 190–225.

————. 2010. "Inequality and Subjective Well-Being." Working paper.

Wolfers, Justin. 2003. "Is Business Cycle Volatility Costly? Evidence from Surveys of Subjective Well-Being" *International Finance* 6(1): 1–26.

Happiness Measures as a Guide to Development Policy? Promise and Potential Pitfalls

CAROL GRAHAM

The study of happiness was of great interest to early economists and philosophers such as Adam Smith and Jeremy Bentham, but as quantitative methods in economics called for more parsimonious definitions of welfare and utility became synonymous with income, happiness fell out of fashion. More than a century later, economists seem to have circled back around: Research on happiness has gone from the fringes of the profession to the mainstream. There is a renewed debate over the relationship between happiness and income, and economists are using happiness surveys to study a host of questions, ranging from the happiness effects of health, marriage, leisure time, and institutional and environmental arrangements to the unhappiness effects of unemployment, divorce, commuting time, and inflation.

Happiness surveys depart from traditional approaches in their reliance on expressed versus revealed preferences. Put more simply, happiness economics relies on data based on what people say as opposed to what they do (via consumption choices). While not without flaws, these data are uniquely suited to answering questions that standard revealed preference approaches do not answer well, such as the welfare effects of institutional arrangements that people are powerless to change. How can a poor peasant in Bolivia, for example, who is made unhappy by inequality or macroeconomic volatility, reveal his or her preferences, short of emigrating or protesting? Happiness surveys can also be used to explain behaviors that do not reflect optimal choices but rather norms, addiction, or self-control problems. Seemingly perverse savings or schooling choices by very poor people with limited education and information, and public health problems such as obesity and smoking come to mind.

As a result of the burgeoning research on happiness and the kinds of questions it addresses, a number of efforts are under way to develop national-level well-being

The author is senior fellow and Charles Robinson Chair at the Brookings Institution and Professor at the University of Maryland, College Park. She would like to thank an anonymous reviewer for very helpful comments on an early version of this paper. The paper draws heavily on her recently published book, *Happiness around the World: The Paradox of Happy Peasants and Miserable Millionaires* (Oxford University Press, 2010).

Annual World Bank Conference on Development Economics 2011, Global
© 2013 The International Bank for Reconstruction and Development/The World Bank

measures. The objective is to develop metrics that can be compared within and across countries and ultimately used as complements to traditional income and gross domestic product (GDP) data. Recently, the Sarkozy Commission, chaired by two Nobel Prize–winning economists and sponsored by the president of France, called for an international effort to develop and use such measures to assess human well-being and progress.

Surely this research is relevant to developing economies. And finding a definition of well-being that is broader than income seems to be an exercise that can contribute to our understanding of the development process, both across and within countries. Beyond that, should we be using happiness measures as a guide to development policies? Should happiness be an objective of these policies? The pursuit of happiness is written into the U.S. Constitution. Should it be part of the charter of the international financial institutions?

This paper addresses these questions, first reviewing what we know about the determinants of happiness across and within countries of different development levels, and then raising the challenge that adaptation poses for the use of these measures as comparative indicators. In conclusion, I discuss the potential for applying these measures to policy and identify a number of questions that must be resolved before doing so.

Happiness around the World: How Do Developed and Developing Countries Compare?

Most of the early studies of happiness focused on the developed economies, and primarily on the United States and Europe, and assumed that the developing economies were different because of their much higher levels of poverty. My research over the past decade has focused on the study of happiness around the world, with a focus on the developing economies. What is remarkable about my findings is the remarkable consistency in the determinants of happiness across the two contexts, regardless of the differences in income levels.

Study Methodology

In happiness surveys, people are asked, "Generally speaking, how happy are you with your life?" or "How satisfied are you with your life?" Possible answers are on a 4- to 7-point scale. These questions measure reported happiness, but they do not define happiness. We do not know when people answer these questions if they are thinking about happiness as contentment today or in the context of their overall lives and opportunities. I discuss the importance of this issue later in the paper, but generally I am using "happiness" as shorthand for reported well-being rather than as defined in a particular manner.

Different surveys use different happiness questions, at times interchangeably. Answers to happiness and life satisfaction questions, for example, correlate quite closely (Blanchflower and Oswald 2004; Graham and Pettinato 2002).[1] Still, the specific question can affect the results. For example, respondents' income level seems to matter more to their answers to life satisfaction questions than it does to their answers to questions focused on the innate character component of happiness (affect) as gauged by questions such as "How many times did you smile yesterday?"

Happiness questions are also particularly vulnerable to order bias. People will respond differently to an open-ended happiness question at the beginning of a survey than to one that is framed or biased by the questions posed beforehand, such as those about whether their income is sufficient or about the quality of their job. Bias in answers to happiness surveys can also result from unobserved personality traits. A naturally curmudgeonly person, for example, will tend to answer all sorts of questions in a manner that is more negative than the average. (These concerns can be addressed via econometric techniques if and when we have panel data.) Related concerns about unobservable variables are common to all economic disciplines and not unique to the study of happiness. For example, a naturally cheerful person may respond to policy measures differently or put more than average effort into his or her job.

Despite the potential pitfalls, cross-sections of large samples of respondents across countries and over time find remarkably consistent patterns in the determinants of happiness. Psychologists, meanwhile, find validation in the way people answer these surveys on the basis of physiological measures of happiness, such as frontal movements in the brain and the number of "genuine" (Duchenne) smiles (Diener and Seligman 2004).

The data in happiness surveys are analyzed via standard econometric techniques, with an error term that captures the unobserved characteristics and error described above.[2] Because the answers to happiness surveys are ordinal rather than cardinal, they are best analyzed via ordered logistic (logit) or probability (probit) equations. These equations depart from standard regression equations, which explore a continuous relationship between variables (e.g., happiness and income). Instead, they explore the probability that a person will place him- or herself in a particular category, typically ranging from unhappy to very happy. These regressions typically yield lower R-squares than economists are used to, reflecting the extent to which emotions and other components of true well-being (in addition to any number of other unobservables) are driving the results, as opposed to the variables that we are able to measure, such as income, education, and employment status.

While it is impossible to measure the precise effects of independent variables on true well-being, happiness researchers have used the coefficients on these variables as a basis for assigning relative weights to them.[3] For example, they have estimated how much income a typical person in the United States or Britain would need to produce the same change in stated happiness that comes from the well-being loss resulting from divorce ($100,000) or job loss ($60,000) (Blanchflower and Oswald 2004). Because of the low R-squares in these equations, as so much of happiness is explained by individual-specific character traits, these figures should be interpreted in relative terms (e.g., how much the average person values employment relative to marriage) rather than as precise estimates of willingness to pay.

Happiness within Countries

My research around the world builds on the extensive studies of happiness in the advanced economies and finds a remarkable consistency in the determinants of happiness across countries of all different levels of development. On average, stable marriage, good health, friendships, and enough income are good for happiness (how much income varies among countries), and unemployment, divorce, and economic instability are bad for happiness. We cannot always establish the direction of causality—at least when we are relying on cross-section data—and it may be that happier people are more likely to have friends or to get married rather than the other way around. The same goes for health and higher levels of income. Some evidence suggests that the causality runs in both directions for many of these variables. Several studies suggest that happier people are healthier, more optimistic, invest more in their future, and perform better in the labor market, among other things.

Age and happiness have a remarkably consistent U-shaped relationship, with the turning point in the mid- to late forties, when happiness increases with age as long as health and partnerships stay sound. I have studied this relationship in countries as diverse as Uzbekistan and United Kingdom, and Chile and Afghanistan, and it holds in all of them, with modest differences in the turning point. Among other things, this relationship reflects an alignment of expectations and reality as people "grow up."

On the other hand, my findings on gender are mixed. Women are typically happier than men in the United States and Europe, while there is no difference in Latin America. Men are happier than women in the Russian Federation, while in Afghanistan the few women we were able to interview were happier, on average, than men. (However, they were, no doubt, outliers and primarily urban and educated; we were unable to measure the happiness of women who were afraid to respond to our interviewers. Our priors are that they would be less happy than the average, but we have no way of testing that.) The differences in these findings may reflect differences in the satisfaction of gender rights in these places, among other things.

Context also mediates the relationship between happiness and religion. In places where religion is a moderate force—such as Europe, the United States, and Latin America—respondents with faith are happier, on average, than others. The direction of causality is unclear: It may be that happier people are more likely to have faith. There are some indications, though, that religiosity per se (and broadly defined) has positive effects on happiness. A recent study in Europe finds that even atheists are happier when they live in neighborhoods where there are more religious people around them, likely because of the positive social externalities that come from religious organizations (Clark and Lelkes 2009). In places where religion is a more divisive force, such as Afghanistan and Central Asia, there is no consistent relationship between faith and happiness (Graham 2010).

Participating in politics and in civic associations is associated with higher levels of happiness (Helliwell, Harris, and Huang 2008). Indeed, one study based on research in Swiss cantons finds a happiness effect from political participation (voting in referendums) that is above and beyond that of the public goods and freedom democracy provides (Frey and Stutzer 2002). My own research in Latin America finds that happier people are more likely to be satisfied with democracy and with market policies (Graham and Pettinato 2002).

Happiness across Countries: The Easterlin Paradox Revisited

In the mid-1970s, Richard Easterlin, the first modern economist to study happiness, uncovered a seeming paradox: Average happiness levels did not increase over time as countries grew wealthier, nor was there a clear relationship between average per capita GDP and average happiness levels across countries, once they achieved a certain minimum level of per capita income. This now well-known puzzle is called the Easterlin paradox.

In recent years there has been a renewed debate about whether or not the Easterlin paradox holds. Studies by Betsey Stevenson and Justin Wolfers (2008), and by Angus Deaton (2008), based on new data from the Gallup World Poll, find a consistent log-linear, cross-country relationship between income and happiness, directly challenging Easterlin's findings. These new findings have resulted in a heated and at times even acrimonious debate among economists.

Ironically, both sides of the debate may be correct. One reason for this is substantive: On the one hand, it makes sense that people in richer countries are happier than those in destitute ones; on the other, many things other than income contribute to people's happiness, regardless of their level of income. Many of these things—such as freedom, stable employment, and good health—are easier to come by in wealthier countries. Still, there is plenty of variance in their availability, even across countries with comparable income levels.

The other reason is methodological. The later studies use new data from the Gallup World Poll that include many more (unweighted) observations from small, poor countries in Africa and from the transition economies than Easterlin's original and more recent studies. The transition countries in particular have relatively low levels of happiness, in part because of the painful structural changes that accompanied the collapse of centrally planned economies. And some of the Sub-Saharan African countries have had flat or even negative rates of growth over time. Thus, rather than a story of higher levels of income pulling up happiness at the top, we may be looking at falling or volatile income trajectories pulling down happiness at the bottom.

Differences also exist in the questions used to measure happiness. Easterlin's work is based on the World Values survey, the U.S. General Social Survey, and the Eurobarometro survey, among others. All of these use open-ended happiness or life satisfaction questions ("Generally speaking, how happy are you with your life?" "Generally speaking, how satisfied are you with your life?") with possible answers ranging from "not at all" to "very" on a 4- or 5-point scale. The Gallup World Poll uses Cantril's best-possible-life question: "Please imagine a ladder with steps from zero to ten. If the higher the step, the better the life, on which step of the ladder do you personally feel you stand?"

Both sets of questions are reasonable gauges of happiness, broadly defined, and both correlate in a similar manner with the usual variables used to study happiness.

At the same time, there is some variance in the findings based on different questions. The best-possible-life question is more framed than the open-ended happiness questions, providing respondents with a relative component when they are asked to assess their lives. Mario Picon, Soumya Chattopadhyay, and I tested the questions against each other in the Gallup World Poll for Latin America, a region for which we had both sets of questions in the same survey (Graham, Chattopadhyay and Picon 2010b). We found that the answers to the best-possible-life question correlate more closely with income, both across and within countries, than open-ended happiness questions. The difference is greater across countries than within them, suggesting the extent to which unobservables across countries—including cultural differences—influence answers to open-ended happiness questions more than they do answers to more highly framed best-possible-life questions.

The objectives driving the particular study will dictate which happiness question is most appropriate. If the objective is to find a measure of reported well-being that has the most consistency across countries, a more highly framed question may be more appropriate. If the objective is to see how happiness varies across countries and cultures, a more open-ended question is more appropriate. Depending on which question is used, the happiness-income relationship may vary.

Two recent studies—one based on worldwide data and another on detailed data for the United States—provide strong support for the basic direction of our findings. They also highlight the various dimensions of happiness. Ed Diener (2010), in a study based on the Gallup World Poll (136,000 respondents in 132 nations), find that income is strongly correlated with how people evaluate their lives on the ladder-of-life question but only moderately correlated with day-to-day positive feelings, like smiling yesterday.

Daniel Kahneman and Angus Deaton (2010), in a study of 450,000 respondents to a Gallup daily survey of U.S. respondents from 2008 through 2009, also used the ladder question as well as questions about emotional experiences the previous day. They found that hedonic well-being (the emotional quality of a person's everyday experience) correlated less closely with income than did life evaluation (the thoughts people have about their life as measured by the ladder-of-life question). Both questions correlated closely with income in a log-linear manner at the bottom end of the income ladder, but the correlation between hedonic well-being and income tapered off at about $75,000 per year, while the correlation between life evaluation and income did not. Thus, more money does not necessarily buy more happiness, but less money is associated with emotional pain. Their findings highlight the importance of the distinction between the judgments people make when they think about their life and the feelings they experience as they live it. The former are sensitive to socioeconomic status; the latter, to circumstances that provoke positive and negative emotions, such as spending time with friends or caring for a sick relative.

Thus, it is possible to come to different conclusions about the Easterlin paradox simply by using a different methodology; that is, a different sample of countries or different happiness questions. The substantive question of what beyond income makes people happy is an additional and more complicated part of the story. This is illustrated in figure 1, from my research with Stefano Pettinato and based on an

FIGURE 1.
Happiness and Income per Capita, 1990s

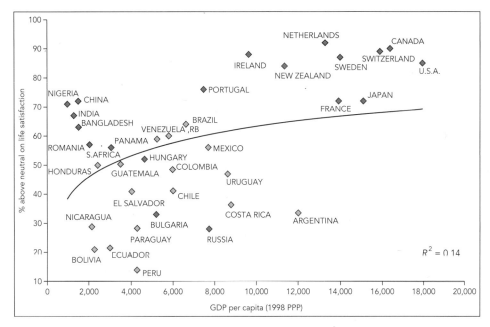

Source: Graham and Pettinato 2002.

open-ended happiness question and a very simple linear specification of income. While the richer countries are, on average, happier than the poorer ones, there is no clear income and happiness relationship within each set of countries, making it impossible to draw a clear conclusion about the Easterlin paradox.

The figure makes the point that wealthier countries are, on average, happier than destitute ones, but after that the story is more complicated. Country-level averages are influenced by, among other things, cultural differences in the way people answer surveys, and these cannot be controlled for in the cross-country comparisons the way they are when we assess happiness across large samples of individuals within and across countries.

Cross-country comparisons are also influenced by factors that are difficult or impossible to measure, such as the nature of public goods. Some cross-country studies find, for example, that countries with higher levels of social capital and more democracy are happier, on average. And these variables correlate closely but not perfectly with income. While at some level we can isolate their specific effects, cross-country comparisons in this arena are rife with endogeneity problems.

Unhappy Growth, Happy Peasants, and Frustrated Achievers

We know that within societies wealthier people are happier than the average, but after that the income-happiness relationship becomes more complicated. At the macroeconomic level, the relationship between happiness and income may be affected as much by the pace and nature of income change as it is by absolute levels. Both the behavioral economics and happiness literature highlight the extent to which people adapt very quickly to income gains and disproportionately value income losses.

Using the Gallup World Poll in 122 countries, Eduardo Lora (2008) and collaborators find that countries with higher levels of per capita GDP have, on average, higher levels of happiness. But controlling for levels, they find that individuals in countries with positive growth rates have lower happiness levels. When they split the sample into above- and below-median growth rates, the unhappy growth effect holds only for countries that are growing at rates above the median (table 1). In related work, Lora and I have called this the "paradox of unhappy growth" (Graham and Lora 2009).[4]

Deaton (2008) and Stevenson and Wolfers (2008) also find evidence of an unhappy growth effect using the Gallup World Poll. Stevenson and Wolfers find insignificant effects of growth in general but strong negative effects for the first stages of growth in "miracle economies" such as Ireland and the Republic of Korea during their takeoff stages. The negative effect becomes insignificant in later stages. Deaton finds that including region dummies makes a major difference in the results, with the results being driven by Africa and Russia, which were both growing fast at the time. It is important to distinguish between levels and change effects: Happiness levels in Russia are lower than income levels would predict, while in some—but not all—African countries, such as Nigeria, happiness levels are higher than income

TABLE 1. The Paradox of Unhappy Growth

The relationship among satisfaction, income per capita, and economic growth

	122 countries	
	GDP per capita	Economic growth
Life satisfaction	0.788***	−0.082***
Standard of living	0.108***	−0.018***
Health satisfaction	0.017*	−0.017***
Job satisfaction	0.077***	−0.006
Housing satisfaction	0.084***	−0.006

Source: Lora 2008.

Note: OLS regression; dependent variable is average life satisfaction per country; growth rates are averaged over the past five years. $N = 122$. The coefficients on GDP per capita are marginal effects; how much does the satisfaction of two countries differ when one has two times the income of another? The coefficients on growth imply how much an additional percentage point of growth affects life satisfaction. The life satisfaction variable is on a zero to 10 scale; all others are the percentage of respondents who are satisfied.

* statistically significant at the 10 percent level.

** at the 5 percent level.

*** at the 1 percent level.

levels would predict. People in both Russia and Africa seemed to be unusually unhappy at times of rapid growth, for any number of plausible reasons. It is also possible that the unhappiness started before the growth and not after it.

Soumya Chattopadhyay and I (2008b), using Latinobarometro data, also find hints of an unhappy—or at least irrelevant—growth effect. In contrast with the above studies, we use individual rather than average country happiness on the lefthand side, with the usual sociodemographic and economic controls (including individual income) and clustering the standard errors at the country level. When we include the current GDP growth rate in the equation as well as the lagged growth rate from the previous year (controlling for levels), we find that the effects of growth rates and lagged growth rates are, for the most part, negative but insignificant (table 2).

Another way of interpreting these findings, noted by both Justin Wolfers and Charles Kenny, is that past income still matters to well-being but is less important than current income.[5] Thus, countries that started from lower income levels in past years (remember, the growth rate is an average of the past five years) had lower happiness in those years than those with higher incomes. So the unhappy "growth" effect may be due to the starting point rather than to the effects of growth. In short, it is better to have had high levels of income for a long time than to start at lower levels and increase them quickly.

The difficulty in disentangling these two interpretations is that both levels and change effects are likely at play. The unhappy growth paradox focuses on the change effect, while the Wolfers and Kenny interpretation focuses on levels. Stevenson and Wolfers' own work (with Sacks, 2010) finds that short-term changes seem to have a more marked impact on subjective well-being than long-term trends.

To the extent the findings are driven by the change effect, a number of factors are easily identifiable, such as the insecurity attached to rapidly changing reward structures and macroeconomic volatility, and the frustration that rapidly increasing inequality tends to generate. The findings show that people are better able to adapt to the gains that accompany rapid growth than to the potential losses and uncertainty that are also associated with it. They suggest that people are often more content in low-growth equilibrium than in a process of change that results in gains but also includes instability and unequal rewards.

The within-country income and happiness story also reflects this paradox. I have described the micro-level version as the "paradox of happy peasants and frustrated achievers." It is typically not the poorest people who are most frustrated or unhappy with their conditions or the services to which they have access. Stefano Pettinato and I found, based on research in Peru and Russia, that a majority of very poor and destitute respondents reported high or relatively high levels of well-being, while much wealthier people, with more mobility and opportunities, reported much greater frustration with their economic and other situations (Graham and Pettinato 2002). The poor respondents may have a higher natural level of cheerfulness, or they may have scaled their expectations downward. The upwardly mobile respondents, meanwhile, have constantly rising expectations (or are naturally more curmudgeon-like). A third explanation is possible: that more driven and frustrated people are more likely to

TABLE 2. Happiness and Growth in Latin America

Dependent variable: happy

age	−0.0240	−0.0230	−0.0230	−0.0220
	(4.40)**	(4.34)**	(4.23)**	(4.29)**
age2	0.0000	0.0000	0.0000	0.0000
	(3.53)**	(3.88)**	(3.72)**	(3.76)**
gender	0.0330	0.0070	0.0070	0.0070
	−1.5500	−0.4800	−0.5200	−0.4800
married	0.0790	0.0910	0.0940	0.0930
	−1.7800	(2.40)*	(2.56)*	(2.60)**
edu	−0.0410	−0.0260	−0.0280	−0.0260
	−1.5300	−1.1800	−1.2900	−1.2800
edu2	0.0010	0.0010	0.0010	0.0010
	−0.8800	−0.7000	−0.7900	−0.7600
socecon	0.2110	0.2160	0.2150	0.2170
	(5.22)**	(5.76)**	(5.77)**	(5.78)**
subinc	0.2900	0.2900	0.2940	0.2920
	(8.78)**	(8.02)**	(8.36)**	(8.41)**
ceconcur	0.2340	0.2260	0.2360	0.2370
	(9.04)**	(9.50)**	(7.66)**	(8.92)**
unemp	−0.1810	−0.1760	−0.1900	−0.1880
	(2.05)*	(3.45)**	(3.59)**	(3.69)**
poum	0.1800	0.1890	0.1830	0.1840
	(4.48)**	(5.42)**	(5.56)**	(5.59)**
domlang	0.5380	0.4810	0.4840	0.4810
	(2.73)**	(2.48)*	(2.48)*	(2.48)*
vcrime	−0.1160	−0.1060	−0.1060	−0.1080
	(2.30)*	(2.98)**	(2.89)**	(3.08)**
els	0.0900			
	(5.48)**			
growth_gdp	0.0170	−0.0090	−0.0040	−0.0060
	−0.5300	−1.1100	−0.6000	−0.7700
gini	−0.0170	−0.0270	−0.0240	−0.0240
	−0.7000	−1.2400	−1.1200	−1.1900
gdpgrl1			−0.0190	−0.0180
			−1.4000	−0.9900
gdpvol2				0.0030
				−0.1400
Observations	34,808	67,308	67,308	67,308

Source: Graham and Chattopadhyay 2008b.

Notes: Absolute value of z statistics in parentheses.

 * significant at 5%.

** significant at 1%.

Regressions clustered at a country level.

seek to escape situations of static poverty (via channels such as migration), but even when they achieve a better situation, they remain more driven and frustrated than the average. Some combination of the three explanations could be at play.

The poor, some of whom rely on subsistence agriculture rather than earnings, have little to lose and have likely adapted to constant insecurity. Recent research on job satisfaction shows that reported job insecurity is actually higher among formal sector workers with more stable jobs than it is among informal sector workers. The latter either have adapted to higher levels of income and employment insecurity or have selected into jobs with less stability but more freedom (Graham and Lora 2009).

Other studies find analogous results in China, where urban migrants are materially better off than they were in their premigration stage yet report higher levels of frustration with their material situation. Upon migrating, their reference norm quickly shifted to match that of other urban residents rather than of their previous peers in rural areas (Knight and Gunatilaka 2007; Whyte and Hun 2006). Meanwhile, very poor rural migrants are much more likely to use their situation the year before as a reference point than to use comparisons with their neighbors, not least because they have less of an informational base on which to make those comparisons (Davey, Chen, and Lau 2009).

People seem to adapt much more quickly to income gains than to status gains (DiTella and MacCulloch 2006). In the context of frustrated achievers in very volatile emerging markets, where currencies are often shifting in value and social welfare systems and the rewards for particular skill and education sets are in flux, income gains may seem especially ephemeral.[6]

Crises bring about significant losses and uncertainty, and their unhappiness effects dwarf those of unhappy growth. Not surprisingly, they result in movements in happiness of an unusual magnitude. While national average happiness levels typically do not move much, they surely do at times of crisis, although they eventually adapt back. Our research on crises in Russia, Argentina, and the United States suggests that the unhappiness effects of crises are as much due to the uncertainty they generate as to the actual drops in income level they cause, because people have a much harder time adapting to uncertainty than to one-time shocks (Graham and Chattopadhyay 2008a; Graham, Chattopadhyay, and Picon 2010a; Graham and Sukhtankar 2004).

The Adaptation Conundrum

Although my research as well as that of others has established that the standard determinants of happiness demonstrate fairly stable patterns worldwide, the same research throws a monkey wrench into the equation because of the remarkable human capacity to adapt to both prosperity and adversity. Thus, many people living in conditions of prosperity report being miserable, while many others living in contexts of remarkable adversity report being very happy (Graham, forthcoming).

People in Afghanistan are as happy as Latin Americans, and report smiling as often—above the world average. Kenyans are as satisfied with their health care as

Americans. My research with Eduardo Lora finds that cross-country patterns in health satisfaction are better explained by cultural norms of health than by objective indicators such as life expectancy or infant mortality. In Latin America, Guatemalans are more satisfied with their health care than are Chileans, even though objective health standards in Guatemala are near Sub-Saharan African levels, while those in Chile are on par with Organisation for Economic Co-operation and Development standards (Graham and Lora 2009).

Crime makes people unhappy, but it matters less when there is more of it; the same goes for both corruption and obesity. Soumya Chattopadhyay and I find that crime and corruption have negative effects on reported happiness across Latin America, but those effects are mitigated by how common the phenomena are (Graham and Chattopadhyay 2008b).

In each case, we created a variable for each respondent's unexplained probability of being a victim of crime or corruption—a probability that was not explained by the usual variables such as age, income, gender, or rural versus urban. We found that this unexplained probability—a proxy for higher crime and corruption norms—mitigated the negative well-being effects of crime and corruption victimization (table 3). In places where crime and corruption are common occurrences, the well-being effects are lower, most likely because people have come to expect these phenomena and there is less stigma associated with being victimized. Our findings also hold for Africa and Afghanistan (Graham 2010).

Andrew Felton and I find that obese people in the United States are less happy than the average, but the effects are much stronger in low-obesity, high-skilled professional cohorts than in high-obesity, low-skilled cohorts or in regions where obesity is the norm (Graham 2008) (figure 2). Again, some combination of reduced stigma and adaptation is likely at play. In contrast, in Russia, where obesity is still seen as a sign of prosperity, the obese are, on average, happier than the nonobese, despite the health consequences. Similarly, several studies of the unemployed find that the unhappiness effects associated with the condition are mitigated by higher levels of unemployment and therefore less stigma (Clark and Oswald 1994; Eggers, Gaddy, and Graham 2006; Stutzer and Lalive 2004). An extreme analog of these findings is recent work showing that suicide rates are higher in happier states in the United States, suggesting that stigma is associated with being unhappy when the norm is to be happy (Daly et al. 2010).

Freedom and democracy make people happy, but they matter less when these goods are less common. Cross-country research by Helliwell, Harris, and Huang (2008) finds that the coefficient on freedom (on happiness) is higher in countries with higher average levels of freedom, while the coefficient on corruption is lower in countries that have more corruption. The bottom line is that people can adapt to tremendous adversity and retain their natural cheerfulness, while they can also have virtually everything—including good health—and be miserable.

One thing people have a hard time adapting to is uncertainty. For example, my newest research—with Soumya Chattopadhyay and Mario Picon, based on a new Gallup survey of approximately 1,000 Americans a day from January 2008 to the present—shows that average happiness in the United States declined significantly as

TABLE 3. The Effects of Crime and Corruption on Happiness in Latin America

Explanatory variables	Dependent variable: happy				Explanatory variables	Dependent variable: happy			
age	-0.0230 (0.000)**	-0.0200 (0.000)**	-0.0210 (0.000)**	-0.0180 (0.005)**	age	-0.0230 (0.000)**	-0.0210 (0.000)**	-0.0230 (0.000)**	-0.0190 (0.003)**
age2	0.0000 (0.000)**	0.0000 (0.000)**	0.0000 (0.000)**	0.0000 -0.051	age2	0.0000 (0.000)**	0.0000 (0.000)**	0.0000 (0.000)**	0.0000 (0.035)*
gender	0.0070 -0.614	0.0210 (0.050)*	0.0400 (0.050)*	0.0240 -0.199	gender	0.0100 -0.473	0.0410 (0.014)*	0.0500 (0.014)*	0.0470 -0.075
married	0.0850 (0.000)**	0.0600 (0.001)*	0.0630 (0.104)**	0.0620 -0.104	married	0.0840 (0.000)*	0.0620 (0.001)**	0.0710 (0.001)**	0.0690 (0.030)*
edu	-0.0220 (0.000)**	-0.0260 (0.000)**	-0.0280 (0.000)**	-0.0240 -0.385	edu	-0.0240 (0.000)**	-0.0350 (0.000)**	-0.0400 (0.000)**	-0.0380 -0.129
edu2	0.0010 -0.077	0.0010 (0.038)*	0.0010 (0.024)*	0.0010 -0.451	edu2	0.0010 -0.053	0.0010 (0.002)**	0.0010 (0.006)**	0.0020 -0.263
socecon	0.2110 (0.000)**	0.2140 (0.000)**	0.2280 (0.000)**	0.2280 (0.000)**	socecon	0.2120 (0.000)**	0.2270 (0.000)**	0.2360 (0.000)**	0.2400 (0.000)**
subinc	0.2870 (0.000)**	0.3030 (0.000)**	0.3060 (0.000)**	0.3140 (0.000)**	subinc	0.2910 (0.000)**	0.3150 (0.000)**	0.3120 (0.000)**	0.3280 (0.000)**
ceconcur	0.2190 (0.000)**	0.1970 (0.000)**	0.2350 (0.000)**	0.2180 (0.000)**	ceconcur	0.2170 (0.000)**	0.1840 (0.000)**	0.2310 (0.000)**	0.2120 (0.000)**
unemp	-0.1770 (0.000)**	-0.2170 (0.000)**	-0.1990 (0.000)**	-0.2300 (0.002)**	unemp	-0.1680 (0.000)**	-0.2000 (0.000)**	-0.1890 (0.000)**	-0.2190 (0.001)**
poum	0.1750 (0.000)**	0.1410 (0.000)**	0.1470 (0.000)**	0.1530 (0.000)**	poum	0.1760 (0.000)**	0.1580 (0.000)**	0.1690 (0.000)**	0.1730 (0.000)**

(continued)

TABLE 3. (*Continued*)

Explanatory variables	Dependent variable: happy			
domlang	0.5950	0.6520	0.6360	0.5490
	(0.000)**	(0.000)**	(0.000)**	(0.006)**
vcrime	-0.0960	-0.5360	-1.0770	-0.8930
	(0.000)**	(0.000)**	(0.000)**	-0.239
crresid		0.4460	1.0170	0.8020
		(0.000)**	(0.000)**	-0.286
els			0.1000	
			(0.000)**	
vcrimel1 (1 year lag)			-1.4710	-1.8190
			(10.77)**	-1.67
vcrimel2 (2 year lag)			1.8550	1.6760
			(15.52)**	-1.47
Control for gini	No	No	No	Yes
Control for GDP growth rate	No	No	No	Yes
Control for lagged GDP growth rates	No	No	No	Yes

Explanatory variables	Dependent variable: happy			
domlang	0.5970	0.6680	0.6450	0.5880
	(0.000)**	(0.000)**	(0.000)**	(0.001)**
vcorr	-0.1570	-0.9160	-0.9070	-1.1420
	(0.000)**	(0.000)**	(0.000)**	(0.017)*
corrresid		0.8090	0.8330	1.0340
		(0.000)*	(0.000)**	(0.027)*
els			0.0970	
			(0.000)**	
Control for gini	No	No	No	Yes
Control for GDP growth rate	No	No	No	Yes
Control for lagged GDP growth rates	No	No	No	Yes

Source: Graham and Chattopadhyay 2008b.

Notes: Absolute value of z statistics in parentheses.

* significant at 5%.

** significant at 1%.

FIGURE 2.
Obesity and Unhappiness

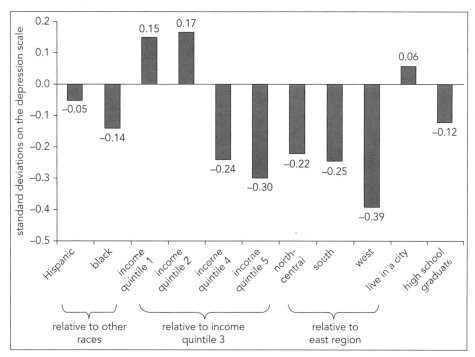

Source: Graham 2008.

the Dow fell with the onset of the crisis. Happiness declined 11 percent, from 6.94 (on an 11-point scale) before the onset of the crisis to a low of 6.19 on November 16, 2008. But when the market bottomed out and some semblance of stability was restored in late March 2009, average happiness recovered much faster than the Dow. By June 2009 it was higher than its precrisis level—7.15 on June 21—even though living standards and reported satisfaction with those standards remained markedly lower than they were before the crisis. Happiness levels remained that high at least through 2009. Once the period of uncertainty ended, people seemed to be able to return to previous happiness levels, while making do with less income or wealth (Graham, Chattopadhyay, and Picon 2010a). (See figure 3.)

We can point to analogous findings in the health arena. Eduardo Lora, Lucas Higuera, and I compared the life and health satisfaction effects of various health conditions, based on Gallup data for Latin America for 2007, a data set that also included respondents' scores on an indicator of self-reported health, the Euro-Quality Five Dimensions Index (EQ5D), which correlates very closely with objective indicators of health. We found that problems with mobility or self-care had very small, if any, lasting effects on life and health satisfaction, while those associated with uncertainty, such as pain and anxiety, had much stronger effects (table 4). While direction of causality likely plays a role (more anxious people are more likely to report unhappiness), our

FIGURE 3.
Happiness and Crisis in the United States

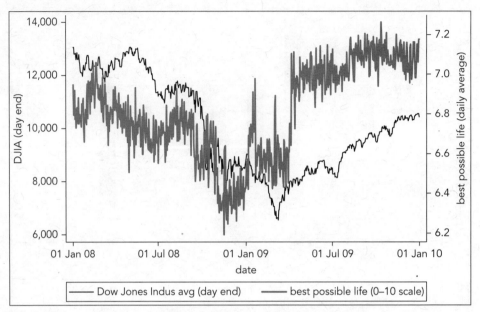

Source: Graham, Chattopadhyay, and Picon 2010a. Based on data from Gallup Daily Poll.

TABLE 4. Life and Health Satisfaction Costs of Various Conditions

	Health satisfaction 0–10		Life satisfaction 0–10	
	(1)	(2)	(3)	(4)
EQ5D index	5.188***		1.436***	
Mobility moderate		−0.460***		0.086
Mobility extreme		−0.032		0.091
Self-care moderate		−0.142		0.157
Self-care extreme		−0.236		0.281
Usual activities moderate		−0.690***		−0.230*
Usual activities extreme		−1.136*		−0.498
Pain moderate		−1.016***		−0.135
Pain extreme		−2.143***		−0.477**
Anxiety moderate		−0.480***		−0.303***
Anxiety extreme		−0.883***		−0.786***
Observations	8,249	8,249	8,250	8,250
Countries	17	17	17	17

Source: Graham, Higuera, and Lora 2009.

Notes: Results presented in this table are excerpts from columns 3, 4, 7, and 8 in appendix 1, where full regression results are presented.

***p<0.01.

**p<0.05.

*p<0.1.

findings suggest that people are better able to adapt to the unpleasant certainty of mobility and other physical conditions than to the uncertainty surrounding unpredictable pain and anxiety. Our research is supported by that of others on conditions such as uncontrolled epilepsy (Graham, Higuera, and Lora 2009).

In general, people seem to be better at adapting to unpleasant certainty than to uncertainty. It is surely a good thing that most Americans have been able to adapt to the economic costs of the crisis and return to their natural happiness levels, and even better that the average person in Afghanistan can maintain cheerfulness and hope despite the situation in that country. While this capacity to adapt may be a good thing from the perspective of individual psychological welfare, it may also result in collective tolerance for conditions that would be unacceptable by most people's standards. This may help explain why different societies tolerate such different norms of health, crime, and governance, both within and across countries. Without understanding these norm differences, it is difficult to craft policies to improve health, living conditions, and governance structures.

The capacity to adapt and the mediating role of norms and expectations pose all sorts of measurement and comparison challenges, especially in the study of the relationship between happiness and income. Can we really compare the happiness levels of a poor peasant in India (who reports being very happy, owing to low expectations or a naturally cheery character or both) with those of a successful and very wealthy chief executive officer (CEO) (who reports being miserable, owing to his or her relative ranking in comparison with other CEOs or to a naturally curmudgeonly character)?

At one level, the capacity to adapt suggests that all happiness is relative. At another, it suggests that some unhappiness might be necessary to achieve economic and other kinds of progress. Examples come to mind of migrants who leave their home countries and families to create better futures for their children and revolutionaries who sacrifice their lives for the greater public good. This leads to more difficult questions. One is whether outside observers, such as development practitioners, should tell poor peasants in India how miserable they are according to objective income measures to encourage them to seek a "better" life. A related question is whether we should worry more about addressing the millionaire's misery or increasing the peasant's happiness.

Challenges for Policy

Happiness surveys have provided us with a new and powerful tool to study and better understand the determinants of human welfare and well-being across and within countries, and across time as countries undergo the sometimes unsettling process of economic development. The findings from these surveys are relevant to a host of questions that policy makers care about, and they can inform policy decisions. The consistency in the relationship of the key variables that correlate with happiness across countries of all different levels of development allows us to test for variance in the effects of all sorts of contextual variables, ranging from macroeconomic and institutional regimes to the environment to changes in policy regimes.

Although these surveys and their results provide us with a great many opportunities to broaden our understanding of human welfare and our ability to craft policies to enhance it, a number of unanswered questions must be resolved—or at least further discussed—before we can think about happiness as a benchmark for progress or as an objective of development policy. Among these are the adaptation conundrum, the definition of happiness, intertemporal trade-offs, and cardinality versus ordinality.

The adaptation conundrum may be the most difficult question to resolve. On the one hand, it is a marvelous thing that people can adapt to all sorts of adversity and maintain their natural cheerfulness and psychological welfare. On the other, as noted above, adaptability may result in collective tolerance for a bad equilibrium. The seeming variance in this tolerance across societies suggests that happiness is relative. If that is the case, how can we use it as a benchmark for progress? But the within-country findings suggest that happiness is not all relative: Clear patterns exist across income, age, and employment cohorts, among others. We do not yet have a complete answer to this question.

One issue is whether the happy peasants are more or less able to change their situation. Are our frustrated achievers unhappy because the process of change is painful, or were they unhappy and more likely to seek change in the first place? Are migrants who report being unhappy today unhappy because their expectations have gone up and their reference norms for income have changed or because they have left their family behind to find longer term fulfillment (and happiness) in providing their children with an opportunity to lead better lives? While we cannot answer these questions at this juncture, they must be addressed, both because they can help resolve the question of how best to use happiness research in the policy arena and because they are fundamental to development.

The happy peasant and frustrated achiever (or miserable millionaire) paradox raises the related question of the appropriate definition of happiness. What makes happiness surveys such a useful research tool is their open-ended nature. The definition of happiness is left up to the respondent—we do not impose an American concept of happiness on Chinese respondents or a Chinese definition on Chilean respondents. The open-ended nature of the definition results in consistent patterns in the basic explanatory variables across respondents worldwide, allowing us to control for those variables and explore variance in the effects of all sorts of other factors on happiness, ranging from crime rates to commuting time to the nature of governing regimes.

At the same time, if we think about happiness as a measure of welfare with relevance to policy (a topic that is increasingly in the public debate), the definition does matter. Are we thinking of happiness as contentment in the Benthamite sense or as a fulfilling life in the Aristotelian sense? There is much room for debate. My studies suggest that respondents' conceptions of happiness vary according to their norms, expectations, and ability to adapt, among other things. Our priors as economists and policy makers likely suggest that some conceptions of happiness (such as the opportunity to lead a fulfilling life) are worth pursuing as policy objectives, while others (such as contentment alone) are not. That choice entails normative judgments and a debate we have not yet had, and the answer is likely to vary across societies. Some societies (such as the United States) seem to place more value on the ability of individuals to pursue opportunities, while others place more value on guaranteeing at least some level of collective welfare. Those normative differences could influence varying conceptualizations of happiness across societies.

A related question is how to measure intertemporal trade-offs in happiness. Do we care more about happiness today or happiness tomorrow? Surely some objectives are worth pursuing (such as reducing fiscal deficits, reforming malfunctioning public sectors, and overthrowing despots) that are likely to increase unhappiness today but increase it in the future. Perhaps the answer is as simple as the income accounting framework suggests: People vary in their ability to trade off income today for income tomorrow, and they have different discount rates. The same might apply to happiness: Some people value contentment today more than fulfillment tomorrow, while others are more vested in the future. And, as in the case of discount rates, people's capacity to make these trade-offs depends to some extent on their prospects of upward mobility or their vision of the future.

On the other hand, there are complexities in trading off happiness today for happiness tomorrow. Trading off a dollar today for two tomorrow, for example, is different than making a sacrifice today (such as working very hard in graduate school) for an outcome you expect will make you happier in the future (such as higher status and more freedom in your future career), because the prospect of the future may make you less unhappy about your current sacrifice or state.[7] This question is not unresolvable, but it needs to be addressed.

Finally, there is the question of cardinality versus ordinality. Responses to happiness surveys are categorical and ordinal in nature; respondents place themselves in categories that range from very unhappy to very happy, but these categories do not have cardinal weights. Yet a policy framework would require choices, not least because resources are limited. Do we care more about reducing the unhappiness of the miserable or increasing the happiness of the already happy? From a development perspective, do we care as much about the misery of a millionaire who lives in a country with very high average levels of income and widely accessible public goods as we do about that of a person who lives in a very poor context and is unhappy? Again, it is possible to imagine both a theoretical framework and an empirical base upon which to test these questions, but we have not yet done so.

We cannot resolve all these questions at this juncture, but the discussion raises important issues for development policy. These conundrums will give economists fodder for debate—about happiness and income, and beyond—for years to come. Despite the difficulty that happiness as a concept poses for both method and economic philosophy, it forces us to think deeply about what measures of human well-being are the most accurate benchmarks of economic progress and human development. We may reach a point in the future where we are comparing happiness across and within countries in the same way we now compare income. For now, however, many unanswered questions remain that both researchers and broader publics must address.

Notes

1. The correlation coefficient between the two (based on research on British data for 1975–92, which includes both questions, and Latin American data for 2000–01, in which different phrasing was used in different years) ranges between 0.56 and 0.50.

2. Microeconometric happiness equations have the standard form: $W_{it} = \alpha + fIx_{it} + \varepsilon_{it}$, where W is the reported well-being of individual i at time t, and X is a vector of known variables, including sociodemographic and socioeconomic characteristics. Unobserved characteristics and measurement errors are captured in the error term.

3. The coefficients produced from ordered probit or logistic regressions are remarkably similar to those from ordinary least squares (OLS) regressions based on the same equations, allowing us to substitute OLS equations for ordered logit or probit and then attach relative weights to them. For an extensive and excellent discussion of the methodology underpinning happiness studies, and how it is evolving, see Van Praag and Ferrer-i-Carbonell 2004.

4. It is also possible that initially happier countries grew faster than initially unhappy countries with the same income (because they had happier, more productive workers?), and thus the coefficient on growth in a regression that compares the two with final income and final happiness is negative. I thank Charles Kenny for raising this point.

5. I thank both Justin Wolfers and Charles Kenny for thoughtful conversations on this point.

6. A related body of research examines the effects of inequality and relative income differences on well-being and studies how inequality mediates the happiness-income relationship. At some level, people probably adapt to inequality as they do to other things—and they are less skilled at adapting to changes in inequality. I do not cover this topic here; it merits an entire paper of its own (Graham and Felton 2006; Luttmer 2005).

7. I thank an anonymous reviewer for raising this excellent point.

References

Blanchflower, D., and A. Oswald. 2004. "Well-Being over Time in Britain and the USA." *Journal of Public Economics* 88: 1359–87.

Clark, Andrew, and Orsolya Lelkes. 2009. "Let Us Pray: Religious Interactions in Life Satisfaction." Mimeo, Paris School of Economics, January.

Clark, Andrew, and Andrew Oswald. 1994. "Unhappiness and Unemployment." *Economic Journal* 104: 648–59.

Daly, Mary C., Andrew Oswald, Daniel Wilson, and Stephen Wu. 2010. *The Happiness-Suicide Paradox*. Working paper, Department of Economics. Warwick, England: University of Warwick.

Davey, Gareth, Zhenghui Chen, and Anna Lau. 2009. "Peace in a Thatched Hut—That Is Happiness: Subjective Well-Being among Peasants in Rural China." *Journal of Happiness Studies* 10: 239–52.

Deaton, Angus. 2008. "Income, Health, and Well-Being around the World: Evidence from the Gallup World Poll." *Journal of Economic Perspectives* 22 (2, Spring): 53–72.

Diener, Edward. 2010. "Money Can Buy At Least One Kind of Happiness." *Journal of Personality and Social Psychology* 99 (July): 1–52.

Diener, Edward, and Martin Seligman. 2004. "Beyond Money: Toward an Economy of Well-Being." *Psychological Science in the Public Interest* 5 (1): 1–31.

DiTella, Rafael, and Robert MacCulloch. 2006. "Happiness and Adaptation to Income and Status: Evidence from an Individual Panel." Mimeo, Harvard University.

Easterlin, Richard. 1974. "Does Economic Growth Improve the Human Lot? Some Empirical Evidence." In *Nations and Households in Economic Growth*, ed. P. David and M. Reder. New York: Academic Press.

Eggers, Andrew, Clifford Gaddy, and Carol Graham. 2006. "Well-Being and Unemployment in Russia in the 1990's: Can Society's Suffering Be Individuals' Solace?" *Journal of Socio-economics* 35 (January): 209–42.

Frey, Bruno, and Alois Stutzer. 2002. *Happiness and Economics*. Princeton, NJ: Princeton University Press.

———. 2008. "Happiness and Health: Lessons—and Questions—for Policy." *Health Affairs* 27 (1, January–February): 72–87.

———. 2010. *Happiness around the World: The Paradox of Happy Peasants and Miserable Millionaires*. Oxford, England: Oxford University Press.

Graham, Carol. Forthcoming. "Adaptation to Prosperity and Adversity: Insights from Happiness Studies from around the World." *World Bank Research Observer*.

Graham, Carol, and Soumya Chattopadhyay. 2008a. "Gross National Happiness and the Economy." *The Globalist*. October 24. www.theglobalist.com/printStoryId.aspx?StoryId=7312.

———. 2008b. "Public Opinion Trends in Latin America (and the U.S.): How Strong Is Support for Markets, Democracy, and Regional Integration?" Paper prepared for the Brookings Partnership for the Americas Commission, Washington, DC, June.

Graham, Carol, and Andrew Felton. 2006. "Does Inequality Matter to Individual Welfare: An Exploration Based on Happiness Surveys in Latin America." *Journal of Economic Inequality* 4: 107–22.

Graham, Carol, and Eduardo Lora, eds. 2009. *Paradox and Perception: Measuring Quality of Life in Latin America*. Washington, DC: The Brookings Institution Press.

Graham, Carol, and Stefano Pettinato. 2002. *Happiness and Hardship: Opportunity and Insecurity in New Market Economies*. Washington, DC: The Brookings Institution Press.

Graham, Carol, and Sandip Sukhtankar. 2004. "Does Economic Crisis Reduce Support for Markets and Democracy in Latin America? Some Evidence from Surveys of Public Opinion and Well-Being." *Journal of Latin American Studies* 36: 349–77.

Graham, Carol, Soumya Chattopadhyay, and Mario Picon. 2010a. "Adapting to Adversity: Happiness and the 2009 Economic Crisis in the United States." *Social Research: An International Quarterly* 77 (2): 715–48.

———. 2010b. "The Easterlin Paradox Revisited: Why Both Sides of the Debate May Be Correct." In *International Differences in Well-Being*, ed. Ed Diener, John Helliwell, and Daniel Kahneman. Oxford, England: Oxford University Press.

Graham, Carol, Lucas Higuera, and Eduardo Lora. 2009. *Valuing Health Conditions: Insights from Happiness Surveys across Countries and Cultures*. Inter-American Development Bank (IDB) Research Working Paper Series, No. 100. Washington, DC: IDB.

Helliwell, John, A. Harris, and Haifang Huang. 2008. "International Differences in the Determinants of Life Satisfaction." Mimeo, University of British Columbia.

Kahneman, Daniel, and Angus Deaton. 2010. "Does Money Buy Happiness....Or Just a Better Life?" Mimeo, Princeton University, June.

Knight, J., and R. Gunatilaka. 2007. *Great Expectations? The Subjective Well-Being of Rural-Urban Migrants in China*. Discussion Paper Series No. 322, Department of Economics. Oxford, England: University of Oxford, April.

Lora, Eduardo. 2008. *Beyond Facts: Understanding Quality of Life in Latin America.* Washington, DC: Inter-American Development Bank.

Luttmer, Erzo. 2005. "Neighbors As Negatives: Relative Earnings and Well-Being." *Quarterly Journal of Economics* 120 (3, August): 963–1002.

Sacks, D., B. Stevenson, and J. Wolfers. 2010. "Subjective Well-Being, Income, Economic Development, and Growth." Presented at the Annual Bank Conference on Development Economics, Stockholm, Sweden, May 31–June 2.

Stevenson, Betsey, and Justin Wolfers. 2008. "Economic Growth and Subjective Well-Being: Reassessing the Easterlin Paradox." *Brookings Panel on Economic Activity,* April.

Stutzer, Alois, and Rafael Lalive. 2004. "The Role of Social Work Norms in Job Searching and Subjective Well-Being." *Journal of the European Economic Association* 2: 696–719.

Van Praag, Bernard, and Ada Ferrer-i-Carbonell. 2004. *Happiness Quantified: A Satisfaction Calculus Approach.* Oxford, England: Oxford University Press.

Whyte, M., and C. Hun. 2006. "Subjective Well-Being and Mobility Attitudes in China." Mimeo, Harvard University.

Individual Welfare and Subjective Well-Being: Comments on "Subjective Well-Being, Income, Economic Development, and Growth," by Daniel W. Sacks, Betsey Stevenson, and Justin Wolfers

PETER J. HAMMOND, FEDERICA LIBERINI, AND EUGENIO PROTO

Introduction

The Easterlin Paradox

Plenty of empirical work supports the proposition that, within any given country, a person with a higher income is more likely to report a higher level of happiness or other measure of life satisfaction. Easterlin's (1974) "paradox" arose because average reported happiness seemed to increase little, if at all, with growth in national income per head, at least for developed countries, in which most of the population has sufficient income to meet basic needs. In particular, although U.S. income per head rose steadily between 1946 and 1970, it seemed that average reported happiness showed no long-term trend and actually declined between 1960 and 1970. This suggests that, after basic needs have been met, further economic growth may fail to enhance the average of people's reports of their own happiness or life satisfaction. Easterlin's original paper appeared in a *Festschrift* for Moses Abramovitz, who devoted his career to understanding the process of economic growth in a historical context. At about the same time, the benefits of economic growth were also being questioned by scholars such as Hirsch (1977) and Scitovsky (1976).

The Easterlin paradox is the subject of the 2010 paper by Sacks, Stevenson, and Wolfers (henceforth SS&W), as well as a previous extensive article by Stevenson and Wolfers (2008). Under a wide variety of circumstances, they find that an increase in personal income does increase the average level of reported well-being. Indeed, if one were to give a specific numerical estimate of the ratio between the increase of the

Department of Economics, University of Warwick, Coventry CV4 7AL, UK

This commentary is loosely based on Peter Hammond's presentation to the 2010 ABCDE Conference in Stockholm during the fourth plenary session devoted to "New Ways of Measuring Welfare." Hammond received generous support for his research from a Marie Curie chair funded by the European Commission under contract number MEXC-CT-2006-041121. The helpful comments of Andrew Oswald and Justin Wolfers are gratefully acknowledged.

Annual World Bank Conference on Development Economics 2011, Global

average level of reported well-being (measured using their particular cardinal scale) and the increase in the logarithm of personal income, that number would probably be 0.35. This directly contradicts the Easterlin paradox, if it could be applied in unmodified form to the SS&W data sets.

Debates have been ongoing for several decades over the precise circumstances under which growth leads to increased subjective well-being when both are suitably measured. The recent survey by Clark, Frijters, and Shields (2008), along with Easterlin's prize-winning 2010 volume, suggests that the debates can be expected to continue. SS&W have done us all a great service by examining the data so carefully and in such detail.

An orthodox discussion might quibble with some of those details. For example, it might be important that SS&W follow Deaton (2008) and others in using proprietary data from the Gallup World Poll. Or, as Easterlin and colleagues (2010) suggest, to consider data over a long enough period to exclude any possibility of business cycle effects. We might have been expected to discuss such details, perhaps by taking up Justin Wolfers' very kind offer to use some of this proprietary data to run alternative regressions on our behalf. We did not do so because we see no particular reason to doubt the validity and robustness of SS&W's results, at least for the kind of data set they have chosen to analyze. Nor will we attempt to settle the differences between Easterlin and SS&W.

Instead, we raise the broader question of whether the debate matters. That is, we consider what significance, if any, this kind of empirical work could have for economic policy analysis. This, we believe, accords with the general theme of this plenary session, "New Ways of Measuring Welfare." Moreover, suppose we were to accept Easterlin's strongest empirical claims, along with the concomitant value judgment that development does nothing to enhance individual well-being. Then we would have to wonder what is left of the original raison d'être of the International Bank for Reconstruction and Development (IBRD) and the International Development Association (IDA), two of the oldest and most prominent agencies of what has become the World Bank Group. Clearly, much is at stake.

Separating Facts from Values

Hume (1739, book III, part I, section I, paragraph 27) remarks that "in every system of morality, which I have hitherto met with" there is an "imperceptible" change so that, "instead of the usual copulations of propositions, *is*, and *is not*, I meet with no proposition that is not connected with an *ought*, or an *ought not*." Thus, philosophers speak of Hume's Law as the claim that one cannot derive an "ought" from an "is." More precisely, the law refers to an "is–ought" or "fact–value" distinction between, on the one hand, descriptive or positive statements of fact and, on the other hand, prescriptive or normative judgments of ethical value.

Despite philosophers' criticisms of Hume's Law, one could argue that economists should be especially alert whenever the propositions put before us slip over the often unnoticed barrier between purely factual descriptions and the values that purport to describe our aspirations. A good example of how often the barrier goes unobserved comes in the familiar phrase "measuring welfare" in the title of this session. After all, measurement by itself can only answer descriptive or positive questions and so is definitely on the fact side of the fact–value distinction. Whereas we take the view that the whole purpose of any attempt to measure individual economic welfare should be to provide an indicator of how effectively an economic system provides the goods, services, and public environment that benefit its various individual participants in their attempts to pursue a good life. This obviously makes welfare an inherently normative concept, on the value side of the fact-value distinction.[1]

Well-Being As Evidence for Welfare?

Easterlin's (1974) title—"Does Economic Growth Improve the Human Lot?" is considerably more subtle than "Measuring Welfare." Slightly rephrased and expanded, his title could be "Is There Any Evidence That Economic Growth Causes Its Presumed Beneficiaries to Express More Satisfaction with Their Lives?" The rephrased question is obviously purely descriptive or positive. It acquires much more interest, however, if the objective evidence is thought to inform the answer to the prescriptive or normative question "Should economic policy be less or more oriented toward growth and development?"

These thoughts lead rather naturally to others more profound:

1. With Hume's Law in mind, can any kind of factual evidence ever be relevant for economic policy?
2. If some kind of evidence can be relevant, what kind would it be?
3. In particular, is there anything at all relevant in individuals' responses to questions about their own life satisfaction?

A negative answer to the first question would deprive economic science of most of its interest for those of us who were drawn to study it in the hope of learning how the world can be made better. And the second question can be answered in part by a positive response to the third, toward which we now turn. The rest of this commentary will consider attempts to measure subjective well-being (SWB) in ways that can provide evidence related to the normative concept of individual welfare.

In the next section, we briefly recapitulate the traditional welfare measures. Some of these purport to be objective, while others depend on preferences. Then we address the question of what, if anything, the new subjective measures might add to the old measures, considering their relevance to the normative concepts of individual and social welfare. We describe an empirical test that shows a strong positive association between income and subjective well-being. In the final section, we suggest how further work could help us understand the usefulness of measures of subjective well-being for providing factual evidence on which to base normative judgments of economic welfare.

Traditional Measures of Welfare

Real Income

A traditional and objective measure of welfare is annual income per head. In any given year, we can compare and even add the incomes of various individuals who face identical prices for all commodities. When prices vary over time or people face different prices, incomes need correcting for these variations. This is often done simply by dividing income by a consumer price index or deflator to produce a measure of real income. Provided this index is the value of an observable fixed commodity bundle or market basket—or even a more sophisticated price index based on observable aggregates such as mean expenditure shares for different kinds of goods—the result is an objective measure, as in Oulton (2008). In principle, one could even divide personal income by a different price index for each consumer. See, for example, the discussions in Boskin and colleagues (1996, 1998) and associated articles in the *Journal of Economic Perspectives* devoted to the Boskin commission.

However, only in a special case do such objective measures correspond to an exact price index based on the individual consumer's preferences. As discussed by Hulten (1973) and by Samuelson and Swamy (1974), following the pioneering work of Ville (1946, 1951), the consumer's preferences must be homothetic, which is equivalent to the very special case in which the demand for every commodity has an income elasticity of exactly 1. In that case, a Divisia or chain price index with continuously revised quantity weights will be exact.

Even when preferences may not be homothetic, real income can still be measured by what Samuelson (1974) calls a "money metric" utility function based on Hicks's (1956) measure equivalent variation—see, for example, Chipman and Moore (1980), Hammond (1994), and Weymark (1985). This money metric, however, is generally subjective to the extent that it depends on detailed estimates of parameters that determine the consumer's demand functions. It also depends on a reference price vector and, when extended to consider aspects of the public environment, a reference level for each aspect.

Human Development and Other Objective Measures

A self-sufficient farmer with no officially recorded income is obviously better off than somebody with no resources at all beyond a pittance in the form of an inadequate but officially recorded income. This neglect of what Sen (1977, 1981) calls "entitlements" is just one way in which a measure of real income overlooks important dimensions of human well-being. Other dimensions—including nutrition, health, functioning, capabilities, and dignity—feature prominently in writings such as Dasgupta (1993) and Sen (1980, 1981, 1987). All these additional dimensions can, in principle, be objectively measured on the basis of a person's observed circumstances. For example, the UN's Human Development Index includes life expectancy, adult literacy, and education, along with gross domestic product (GDP) per capita.

Especially in health economics and medical decisions, well-being is often measured using quality-adjusted life years (QALYs), which are also based on medical practitioners' observations and assessments of individual health states. A sampling of the relevant literature can be found in Bleichrodt and Quiggin (1997); Bleichrodt, Wakker, and Johannesson (1997); Broome (1993); Pliskin, Shepard, and Weinstein (1980); and Wakker (1996, 2008). Canning (2007) has proposed an interesting way of integrating QALYs into a real income measure of well-being.

New Measures of Well-Being

Subjective Well-Being

Psychologists' use of individuals' reports of their happiness or life satisfaction goes back at least to Watson (1930), who asked subjects to provide answers on a graphical scale. For an extensive review, see Wilson (1967), who emphasizes the reliability or intrapersonal consistency of "avowed" happiness. Later surveys by Diener (1984) and Diener and colleagues (1999) encourage us to use the term "subjective well-being" (SWB). Easterlin's (1974) results relied on measuring a similar concept. So does the richer interpersonal concept introduced by van Praag (1968) and explained more thoroughly in van Praag and Ferrer-i-Carbonell (2008).

One question raised by the work of Easterlin (1974), Simon (1974), van Praag (1971), and many successors is whether new ways of measuring welfare would make any difference. That is, if we measure SWB along with real income and other, older objective economic indicators of welfare, do we derive any information we can use to guide policy?

An Ordinal Objective Measure of SWB

For some specific value of n, such as 10, consider the question: "On a scale of 1 to n, how satisfied are you with your life in general?" We readily admit that we lack confidence in how to give this question any concrete interpretation and wonder what the "right" answer could possibly be even in our own case. About all one can say is that this is a relatively clear case in which more should always be better. This reflects how hard it is to give the concept of life satisfaction any objective meaning. Anyway, this leads us not to attach too much significance to our own putative responses or, by extension, to those of other individuals.

Nevertheless, suppose we were to consider the results of a large survey whose respondents report not only a degree of life satisfaction or happiness h in the set H: = \{1, 2, ..., n\}, but also what they believe to be their current annual income $y \geq 0$. For each $x \geq 0$ and for each $h \in \{1, 2, ..., n\}$, let $F_h(x)$ denote the proportion of individuals in the sample who combine reports of an annual income $y \leq x$ with a satisfaction level of h. Also, for each $h \in \{1, 2, ..., n\}$, let P_h denote the proportion of the overall sample who report SWB level h. By definition, note that the sum $F(x) := \sum_{h=1}^{n} F_h(x)$ is the overall cumulative distribution function for income. Of course, $F_h(0) \geq 0$, while $F(x)$ is nondecreasing in x. Furthermore, the definition of P_h implies that

$$F_h(x) \rightarrow P_h \quad \text{as} \quad x \rightarrow \infty \qquad (1)$$

Now, for each $x \geq 0$ with $F(x) > 0$ and for each $h \in \{1, 2, ..., n\}$, let

$$P_h(x): = F_h(x)/F(x) \tag{2}$$

denote the relative proportion, among all individuals with incomes $y \leq x$, who report life satisfaction levels h. We note that, because $F(x) \to 1$ as $x \to \infty$, equations (1) and (2) imply that

$$P_h(x) \to P_h \quad \text{as} \quad x \to \infty \tag{3}$$

With these definitions, an objective measure of SWB among all persons reporting incomes of $y \leq x$ is given by the n-dimensional vector[2]

$$P(x) = (P_1(x), P_2(x), P_3(x), ..., P_n(x)) \tag{4}$$

Next, consider the n-vector of cumulative measures

$$Q(x) = (Q_1(x), Q_2(x), Q_3(x), ..., Q_n(x)) \tag{5}$$

where, for each $h \in H$, we define

$$Q_k(x): = \sum_{h=1}^{k} P_h(x) \tag{6}$$

This is the proportion of individuals with incomes $y \leq x$ who report satisfaction levels $h \leq k$. Obviously, $Q_n(x) = 1$ for all income levels x. These cumulative measures are important because an obvious necessary and sufficient condition for SWB to rise with income is that $Q_k(x)$ falls as x increases for each $k = 1, 2, ..., n - 1$. That is, the proportion of individuals whose reported satisfaction level is low must fall as one moves up the income distribution.

Note that, like an ordinal equivalence class of utility functions that represent the same preference ordering because all are strictly increasing transformations of each other, the n-dimensional vector $P(x)$ is ordinal because its definition depends only on which happiness levels are ranked higher.

A Cardinal Objective Measure of SWB

A lot of empirical work, including most linear regression studies, ignores much of the richness in the data by simply replacing the different components of each vector $P(x)$ with the one-dimensional mean statistic

$$\bar{P}(x) = \sum_{h=1}^{n} P_h(x) \, h \tag{7}$$

This not only discards a lot of information, but constructing $\bar{P}(x)$ requires that happiness be measured on a cardinal scale. Specifically, for every possible comparison such as $\bar{P}(x) > \bar{P}(x')$ to be preserved whenever the happiness scale $H: = \{1, 2, ..., n\}$ is replaced by the new n-point happiness scale $H': = \{\eta_1, \eta_2, ..., \eta_n\}$ with $\eta_1 < \eta_2 < ... \eta_n$, it is necessary and sufficient that there be an additive constant α and a multiplicative constant $\rho > 0$ such that

$$\eta_h = \alpha + \rho h \quad \text{for all} \quad h \in H. \tag{8}$$

Finally, we note that virtually all existing work concerning the Easterlin paradox relies on cardinal measures of mean happiness such as $\bar{P}(x)$ defined by equation (7).

We do not know if, along with different data sets, this is really significant in helping to explain apparently inconsistent empirical results. For the following discussion, we make a point of keeping track of all n components in the vector $P(x)$ defined by equation (4) for all relevant different income levels x.

Could SWB Be Relevant? An Empirical Test

A Null Hypothesis

Consider the following rather extreme null hypothesis: for each $x \geq 0$, the relative proportions $P_h(x)$ of individuals with incomes $y \leq x$ who report different satisfaction levels $h \in H$ are all independent of x. Equation (3) implies in this case that $P_h(x) = P_h$, independent of x.

Suppose that for all $h \in H$ and $x \geq 0$, we define

$$G_h(x) := F_h(x)/P_h \tag{9}$$

as the proportion of all interviewees reporting satisfaction level h whose income is $y \leq x$. Then each $G_h(x)$ is a cumulative income distribution function for those interviewees, which satisfies $G_h(x) \to 1$ as $x \to \infty$. Using equation (2) to substitute for $F_h(x)$ in (9) gives

$$G_h(x) = P_h(x)F(x)/P_h \tag{10}$$

The null hypothesis that $P_h(x) = P_h$ independent of $x \geq 0$ is therefore equivalent to having $G_h(x) = F(x)$, independent of h. Under this null hypothesis, any reports of SWB would tell us nothing at all relevant to any statements regarding the relative subjective values of different income levels $y \geq 0$.

An Alternative Hypothesis

A natural alternative to the null hypothesis that $G_h(x) = F(x)$, independent of h, is that $G_h(x)$ decreases as h increases for each fixed $x \geq 0$. This corresponds to the hypothesis that, among people reporting happiness level h, the proportion of poorer persons with incomes $y \leq x$ decreases as h increases.

Data Sources

Two different versions of both the null and alternative hypotheses can be tested using data from the World Values Survey (WVS), a particularly accessible source. The data were collected from interviews conducted in five waves between 1981 and 2008, for a total of 117,876 observations. In an attempt to ensure representativeness, the data we used were restricted to wave–country combinations with at least 30 observations.

In addition to happiness measured on a 4-point scale, the interviewers collected income data measured on an interval scale. To arrive at corresponding distributions of annual individual income measured consistently in year 2000 US dollars, the raw WVS data were transformed as follows:

- Extract the lower and upper bounds of whatever income range was reported by the interviewee, then transform both bounds to measures of annual income.
- Use an interval regression to estimate a probability distribution of possible incomes for each interviewee.

Adjust for both exchange rates and price changes using data taken from World Development Indicators (WDI) 2010.

The first version of the null hypothesis uses the income data directly. However, at least one version of Easterlin's paradox considers whether people become happier as the country they live in experiences growth in GDP per capita. It would be interesting to see how our null hypothesis fares with the kind of long-run growth data whose use Easterlin advocates. For the time being, however, we have limited ourselves to a second static version of the null hypothesis, in which individual income is replaced by contemporaneous GDP per capita for the country in which the interviewee lives.

Results for the First Version of the Null Hypothesis

Figure 1 represents the transformed data graphically, with income x measured along the horizontal axis using a logarithmic scale. It displays the graphs of the four conditional cumulative income distribution functions, $G_h(x)$, corresponding to each of the four possible happiness levels, $h \in \{1, 2, 3, 4\}$.

The four graphs show a very clear positive association between happiness and income, at least for the 98 percent of interviewees whose income levels, measured in year 2000 US dollars, lie between about 50 cents and $300 a day. Indeed, the association is so strong that no two curves cross. Specifically, for every threshold income level x, among all the individuals who report the same happiness level h, the proportion $F_h(x)$ whose income is $y \leq x$ always decreases as h increases. In other words, those who report a higher h on the WVS 4-point happiness scale are less likely to have low incomes, regardless of what threshold we choose to distinguish between high and low incomes.

We applied a formal, two-sample, one-sided version of the Kolmogorov-Smirnov test three times to the different adjacent pairs of conditional income distributions to see whether each graph lies significantly above its successor, in accordance with the alternative hypothesis laid out earlier. The test was passed in every case with a p-value of 0.000.

Results for the Second Version of the Null Hypothesis

To consider the second version of the null hypothesis, figure 2 replaces the absolute income levels in figure 1 with national GDP per capita. The cumulative income distribution reports the proportion of interviewees living in countries whose contemporaneous GDP per capita, again measured in year 2000 US dollars, was no greater

FIGURE 1.
Four Income Distribution Functions

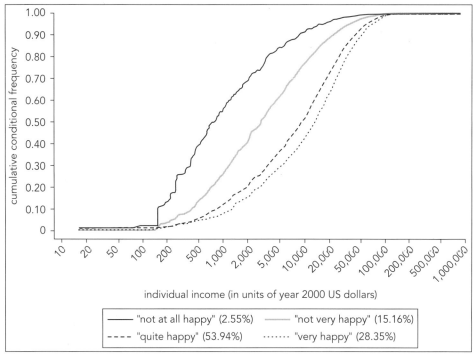

Source: WVS 1981–2008, official aggregate, 2009.

than the income level marked on the horizontal axis. Not surprisingly, there are some significant jumps in the constructed distribution, reflecting how every interviewee in some quite large countries shares the same national GDP per capita.

Once again, the four curves are not only distinct but clearly ordered in the same way they were in figure 1. The same three Kolmogorov-Smirnov tests were passed with a *p*-value of 0.000. Thus, reported life satisfaction is definitely positively associated with both personal income and with GDP per head. Of course, this does not contradict the version of Easterlin's negative findings that focuses on long-run growth trends, particularly in countries that were either already developed or have recently become much more developed.

Should SWB Be Relevant? Ethical Values

Two Extreme Views

Establishing a positive association between happiness and income is one thing. Its relevance for policy is quite another. We have not even distinguished the hypothesis that income causes happiness from the alternative possibility that happiness raises income, perhaps even at the national as well as the individual level. Nevertheless, let

FIGURE 2.
Four Distribution Functions Based on GDP per Capita

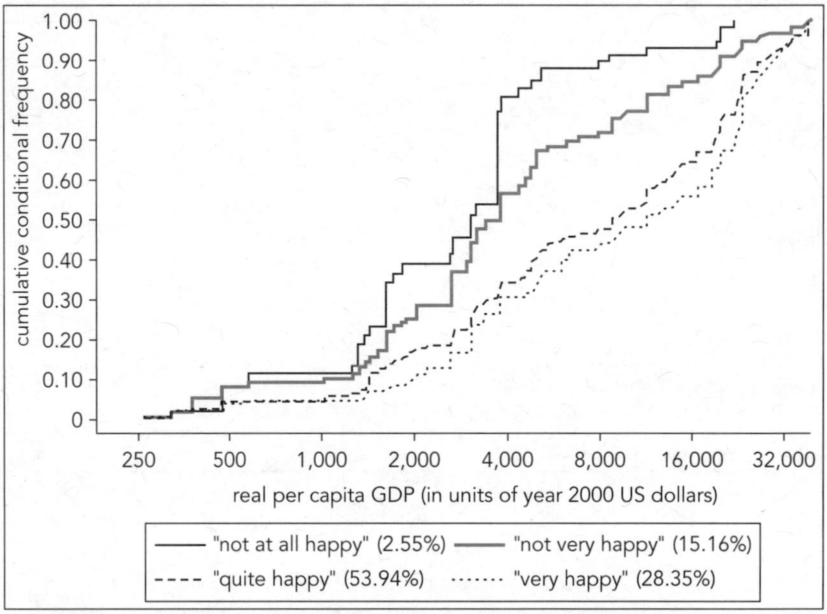

Source: WDI 2010, World Bank.

us provisionally accept the hypothesis that policies that increase economic opportunities will add to measured SWB. Does that make a case for basing policy recommendations on SWB measures? On this question there is room for two extreme opposing views, as well as, no doubt, many positions in between.

The first extreme is the skeptic's claim that any empirical SWB analysis is bound to lack normative significance. This is the implicit position of traditional welfare economics, based as it is on concepts such as revealed preference, willingness to pay, and money metric utility. It may be reinforced by the view that people's expressions of their own subjective well-being constitute no more than how Shakespeare chose to describe life itself: " ... a tale/Told by an idiot, full of sound and fury,/Signifying nothing" (*Macbeth*, act 5, scene 5).

The second extreme is the "hedonometric" claim that not only is SWB relevant; in fact, only the mean of all individuals' SWB reports matters, and any other measure can be disregarded. This appears to be the position advocated by Layard, among others—see, for example, Dolan, Layard, and Metcalfe (2011) and Layard (2005, 2010). As discussed earlier, this extreme attaches cardinal significance to the different happiness levels.

SWB and Pareto Dominance

Between these two extremes is the view that SWB measures are relevant to the comparisons one needs as a basis for policy recommendations.

For example, rather than base social welfare judgments on individuals' reported preferences, could we not use SWB measures instead? Then one might say that policy A has better effects than policy B for individual i, and so increases i's welfare if—and only if—the change from B to A would increase the estimated SWB, not necessarily of i personally in a world of unreliable reports, but of most people sufficiently like i for the comparison of SWB measures to be deemed relevant. Such personal comparisons of different policies are already enough to determine a modified Pareto criterion, according to which policy A Pareto dominates policy B if—and only if—the estimated SWB for every person under policy A is higher than it would be under B. Used in this limited way, estimated SWB might be a more reliable guide than the usual welfare measures based on concepts such as revealed preference, willingness to pay, and money metric utility.

Comparing Welfare Levels

For policy changes that are not Pareto improvements, however, some way of trading off different people's gains and losses is required. To see whether this is possible, we might first ask when one can say that person i has a higher welfare level than person j. Traditionally, the answer has been if—and only if—i's real income is higher than j's, but a fundamental difficulty is the lack of any objective measure of real income.

A new answer can use objective measures of SWB. Then we can say that person i has a higher welfare level than person j if—and only if—people whose objective circumstances are like those of i generally report higher SWB levels than do those whose objective circumstances are like those of j.

SWB and Suppes-Sen Dominance

Once we introduce comparisons between different people's estimated SWB levels, there may be an appealing way to express a preference between policies A and B, even though neither Pareto dominates the other. A first idea is to use Suppes' (1966) grading principle as discussed in Sen (1970). Specifically, policy A will dominate policy B if—and only if—A would Pareto dominate a (possibly infeasible) policy alternative B in which different people's SWB measures are derived by permuting those achieved under policy B. In particular, the distribution of SWB measures under policy A should dominate that of those under policy B.

A different way of expressing the same dominance condition involves multidimensional cumulative distributions such as the $Q_k(x)$ considered earlier. The idea is to reduce the proportion of individuals whose happiness levels falls below each possible different h. For similar ideas see Dasgupta, Sen, and Starrett (1973) and Saposnik (1983).

Progressive Transfers

Dalton (1920, p. 251), following an idea he ascribes to Pigou (1912), enunciated what has since become known as the Pigou-Dalton principle of progressive transfers.

This is the claim that transferring income costlessly from a richer to a poorer person will reduce inequality so long as the transfer is not large enough to reverse the ranking of the two persons' incomes. A similar idea can be applied with measured SWB replacing income. That is, one can regard favorably a different kind of progressive income transfer from individuals with higher SWB levels to those with lower levels, as long as the transfer is not large enough to reverse the ranking of their SWB levels. In this way, some pairs of policies can be ranked even though neither dominates the other according to the Suppes-Sen criterion.

An extension of the same idea would be to apply the equity axiom suggested by Sen (1973) but often ascribed to Hammond (1976). This would regard any policy change as beneficial provided it affects only two people's estimated SWB level and increases the minimum of the two SWB levels. Pushed all the way, this would take us to a modified "Rawlsian" policy that maximizes the lowest estimated SWB level in the whole population. This will usually differ from the usual maximun policy, because estimated SWB differs from individual utility, as usually measured, and also because the measure applies not just to each person separately but equally to a group of people who share similar objective circumstances.

Welfare Weights

We conclude with a final warning. The kind of ordinal estimated SWB measure we have been discussing cannot provide sufficient information, in general, to derive the welfare weights that are generally needed whenever policy choices force us to trade off some individuals' welfare gains against others' losses. Those trade-offs require some form of cardinal information or at least social marginal rates of substitution between estimated SWB measures for different groups of people whose objective circumstances are similar.

Notes

1. Some authors, citing the tradition of Robbins (1932), claim that one should instead give the word "welfare" purely descriptive content. But then, at the risk of oversimplifying Little's (1965) cogent critique in a mere metaphor, we are in danger of pursuing mirages in the arid desert of Archibald's (1959) "essentialism."
2. We ignore the loss of one dimension that arises because the n proportions must add up to 1.

References

Archibald, G. Christopher. 1959. "Welfare Economics, Ethics, and Essentialism." *Economica* 26: 316–27.

Bleichrodt, Han, and John Quiggin. 1997 "Characterizing QALYs under a General Rank Dependent Utility Model." *Journal of Risk and Uncertainty* 15: 151–65.

Bleichrodt, Han, Peter Wakker, and Magnus Johannesson. 1997. "Characterizing QALYs by Risk Neutrality." *Journal of Risk and Uncertainty* 15: 107–14.

Boskin, Michael J., Ellen R. Dulberger, Robert J. Gordon, Zvi Griliches, and Dale W. Jorgensen. 1996. *Toward a More Accurate Measure of the Cost of Living*. Final report to the Senate Finance Committee from the Advisory Commission to Study the Consumer Price Index. Retrieved from http://www.ssa.gov/history/reports/boskinrpt.html.

———. 1998. "Consumer Prices, the Consumer Price Index, and the Cost of Living." *Journal of Economic Perspectives* 12 (Winter): 3–26.

Broome, John. 1993. "QALYs." *Journal of Public Economics* 50: 149–67.

Canning, David. 2007. "Valuing Lives Equally and Welfare Economics." Harvard School of Public Health. http://www.hsph.harvard.edu/pgda/WorkingPapers/2007/PGDA_WP_27_2007.pdf.

Chipman, John S., and James C. Moore. 1980. "Compensating Variation, Consumer's Surplus, and Welfare." *American Economic Review* 70: 933–49.

Clark, Andrew E., Paul Frijters, and Michael A. Shields. 2008. "Relative Income, Happiness, and Utility: An Explanation for the Easterlin Paradox and Other Puzzles." *Journal of Economic Literature* 46: 95–144.

Dalton, Hugh. 1920. "The Measurement of the Inequality of Incomes." *Economic Journal* 30: 348–61.

Dasgupta, Partha. 1993. *An Inquiry into Well-Being and Destitution*. Oxford: Oxford University Press.

Dasgupta, Partha, Amartya K. Sen, and David Starrett. 1973. "Notes on the Measurement of Inequality." *Journal of Economic Theory* 6: 180–87.

Deaton, Angus. 2008. "Income, Aging, Health and Wellbeing Around the World: Evidence from the Gallup World Poll." *Journal of Economic Perspectives* 22(2): 53–72.

Diener, Ed. 1984. "Subjective Well-Being." *Psychological Bulletin* 95: 542–75.

Diener, Ed, Eunkook M. Suh, Richard Lucas, and Heidi Smith. 1999. "Subjective Well-Being: Three Decades of Progress." *Psychological Bulletin* 125: 276–302.

Dolan, Paul, Richard Layard, and Paul Metcalfe. 2011. "Measuring Subjective Well-Being for Public Policy." UK Office for National Statistics. Available at http://www.statistics.gov.uk/articles/social_trends/ measuring-subjective-wellbeing-for-public-policy.pdf.

Easterlin, Richard A. 1974. "Does Economic Growth Improve the Human Lot? Some Empirical Evidence" In *Nations and Households in Economic Growth: Essays in Honor of Moses Abramovitz*, ed. Paul A. David and Melvin W. Reder. New York: Academic Press.

———. 2010 *Happiness, Growth, and the Life Cycle*. New York: Oxford University Press.

Easterlin, Richard A., Laura Angelescu McVey, Malgorzata Switek, Onnicha Sawangfa, and Jacqueline Smith Zweig. 2010. "The Happiness-Income Paradox Revisited." *Proceedings of the National Academy of Sciences of the USA* 107: 22463–8.

Hammond, Peter J. 1976. "Equity, Arrow's Conditions, and Rawls' Difference Principle." *Econometrica* 44: 793–804.

———. 1994. "Money Metric Measures of Individual and Social Welfare Allowing for Environmental Externalities." In *Models and Measurement of Welfare and Inequality*, ed. W. Eichhorn, 694–724. Berlin: Springer-Verlag.

Hicks, John R. 1956. *A Revision of Demand Theory*. Oxford: Clarendon Press.

Hirsch, Fred. 1977. *Social Limits to Growth*. London: Routledge & Kegan Paul.

Hulten, Charles R. 1973. "Divisia Index Numbers." *Econometrica* 41: 1017–25.

Hume, David. 1739. *A Treatise of Human Nature*. London: John Noon.

Layard, Richard. 2005. *Happiness: Lessons from a New Science*. New York: Penguin.

Layard, Richard. 2010. "Measuring Subjective Well-Being." *Science* 327: 534–5.

Little, Ian M. D. 1965. "Welfare Economics, Ethics, and Essentialism: A Comment." *Economica* 32: 223–5.

Oulton, Nicholas. 2008. "Chain Indices of the Cost-of-Living and the Path-Dependence Problem: An Empirical Solution." *Journal of Econometrics* 144: 306–24.

Pigou, A. C. 1912. *Wealth and Welfare*. London: Macmillan.

Pliskin, Joseph S., Donald S. Shepard, and Milton C. Weinstein. 1980. "Utility Functions for Life Years and Health Status." *Operations Research* 28: 206–24.

Robbins, Lionel. 1932 (2nd ed. 1935). *An Essay on the Nature and Significance of Economic Science*. London: Macmillan.

Sacks, Daniel W., Betsey Stevenson, and Justin Wolfers. 2010. "Subjective Well-Being, Income, Economic Development, and Growth." CESifo Working Paper No. 3206. Available at http://www.ifo.de/portal/pls/portal/docs/1/1185210.PDF.

Samuelson, Paul A. 1974. "Complementarity: An Essay on the 40th Anniversary of the Hicks-Allen Revolution in Demand Theory." *Journal of Economic Literature* 12: 1255–289.

Samuelson, Paul A., and Subramanian Swamy. 1974. "Invariant Economic Index Numbers and Canonical Duality: Survey and Synthesis." *American Economic Review* 64: 566–93.

Saposnik, Rubin. 1983. "On Evaluating Income Distributions: Rank Dominance, the Suppes-Sen Grading Principle of Justice, and Pareto Optimality." *Public Choice* 40: 329–36.

Scitovsky, Tibor. 1976 (rev. 1992). *The Joyless Economy: The Psychology of Human Satisfaction*. Oxford: Oxford University Press.

Sen, Amartya K. 1970. *Collective Choice and Social Welfare*. San Francisco: Holden Day. (Republished in 1984, Amsterdam: North-Holland.)

Sen, Amartya K. 1973 (expanded ed. 1997). *On Economic Inequality*. Oxford: Oxford University Press.

Sen, Amartya K. 1977. "Starvation and Exchange Entitlements: A General Approach and Its Application to the Great Bengal Famine." *Cambridge Journal of Economics* 1: 33–59.

Sen, Amartya K. 1980. "Equality of What?" In *Tanner Lectures on Human Values*, ed. S. McMurrin. Cambridge: Cambridge University Press. pp. 187–220.

Sen, Amartya K. 1981. *Poverty and Famines: An Essay on Entitlement and Deprivation*. Oxford, Clarendon Press.

Sen, Amartya K. 1987. *Commodities and Capabilities*. Oxford: Oxford University Press.

Simon, Julian L. 1974. "Interpersonal Welfare Comparisons Can Be Made—and Used for Redistribution Decisions." *Kyklos* 27: 63–98.

Stevenson, Betsey, and Justin Wolfers. 2008. "Economic Growth and Subjective Well-Being: Reassessing the Easterlin Paradox." *Brookings Papers on Economic Activity* Spring: 1–87.

Suppes, Patrick. 1966. "Some Formal Models of Grading Principles." *Synthese* 16: 284–306.

Van Praag, Bernard, 1971. "The welfare function of income in Belgium: An empirical investigation,"European Economic Review, Elsevier, vol. 11(3), 337–69.

Van Praag, Bernard M. S. 1968. *Individual Welfare Functions and Consumer Behavior*. Amsterdam: North-Holland.

Van Praag, Bernard M. S., and Ada Ferrer-i-Carbonell. 2008. *Happiness Quantified: A Satisfaction Calculus Approach* (revised edition). Oxford: Oxford University Press.

Ville, Jean. 1946, 1951. "Sur les conditions d'existence d'une ophélimité totale et d'un indice de prix." *Les annales de l'Université de Lyon* 9: 32–39. Translated by Peter K. Newman as "The Existence-Conditions of a Total Utility Function." *Review of Economic Studies* 19: 123–8.

Wakker, Peter P. 1996. "A Criticism of Healthy-Years Equivalents." *Medical Decision Making* 16: 207–14.

———. 2008. "Lessons Learned by an Economist Working in Medical Decision Making." *Medical Decision Making* 28: 690–8.

Watson, Goodwin. 1930. "Happiness Among Adult Students of Education." *Journal of Educational Psychology* 21: 79–109.

Weymark, John A. 1985. "Money-Metric Utility Functions." *International Economic Review* 26: 219–32.

Wilson, Warner R. 1967. "Correlates of Avowed Happiness." *Psychological Bulletin* 67: 294–306.

World Bank. 2010. *World Development Indicators 2010*. Washington DC: World Bank.

Comment on "Happiness Measures as a Guide to Development Policy" by Carol Graham

LEONARDO GASPARINI

If we all seek happiness, and living a happy life is our ultimate goal, shouldn't happiness be at the center of development studies and be the guide for development policy? In a deep, comprehensive, and insightful essay, Carol Graham tackles these issues with the balance of someone who has extensively studied the topic and knows its promises as well as its limitations and pitfalls. Graham surveys the happiness literature, highlights its challenges, illustrates the main points with results from her own research, and provides an assessment of the current state of the debate. In this comment, I share some thoughts motivated by Graham's arguments and evidence, and illustrate some points with results from my own research.

Happiness As an Objective for Development Policy

A debate exists on the relevance of happiness measures as benchmarks for development. At one extreme, some people say that aggregate measures of happiness should be the only indicators to evaluate progress and policy (Layard 2005). If people behave so as to maximize utility, some aggregate indicator of happiness seems to be a reasonable measure for aggregate welfare. Others emphasize the several pitfalls of this position, ranging from serious measurement issues to the more conceptual problems of adaptation and awareness (Sen 1999). In fact, according to many analysts, happiness measures should not be of any concern for development policy. This was the overwhelming position in economics until recently, and it is probably still the most widespread view. In what follows, I address some of the "antihappiness" arguments.

As Graham notes, the "adaptation conundrum" is one of the main challenges for people advocating happiness as a benchmark for development. This phenomenon has

Leonardo Gasparini is director of the Center for Distributional, Labor and Social Studies (CEDLAS), Facultad de Ciencias Económicas, Universidad Nacional de La Plata (UNLP), La Plata, Argentina.

Annual World Bank Conference on Development Economics 2011, Global

been documented in recent papers. For instance, Di Tella, Haisken-De New, and MacCulloch (2007), using data from the German Socioeconomic Panel, find that life satisfaction adapts completely to income within four years: growth implies only a temporary boost to happiness. This phenomenon of "hedonistic habituation" is well-known in psychology (Myers 2000). Humans derive a great deal of enjoyment from any new form of positive experience. However, people quickly become familiar with the new source of joy, and the initial happiness fades away.

The conundrum triggered by adaptation is illustrated in figure 1. Suppose development policy boosts productivity and a person gets a permanent wage increase at time t_1. Then the credit market improves at time t_2 and the same person gets a loan to buy a house. Under full habituation, happiness jumps at both t_1 and t_2, but it always returns to the long-run level h_0.

Thus, if happiness is our social goal, what is the use of development policy? This conundrum has led many people to discard happiness as a sensible benchmark for development. In my view, and according to evidence provided by Graham and other researchers in this field, there are at least two reasons why discarding happiness indicators may be an overreaction. The first is that recent studies conclude that although there might be an overshooting after a positive change, long-run happiness *is* affected by economic changes. With new and better data, Deaton (2008), Stevenson and Wolfers (2008), and others challenge the Easterlin paradox, according to which happiness does not increase with development. These studies find that development is good for happiness. Figure 2—showing happiness under partial habituation—seems to be a better representation of the real world than figure 1. In this context, development policy can play a role if maximizing happiness is the social target. Policy makers might be frustrated by the fact that the initial boost in happiness does not last, but that is not a valid argument against policies that are successful in increasing long-run happiness.

The second argument against discarding happiness indicators has to do with the nature of happiness, a topic that Graham also discusses. In the world of figure 1, notice that even when happiness returns to its long-run value after a policy shock, lifetime average happiness is greater with policy than without it. If policy can provide a person with many happiness episodes, his or her life will be substantially happier

FIGURE 1.
Happiness under Full Habituation

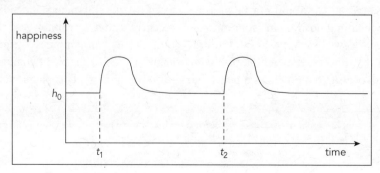

FIGURE 2.
Happiness under Partial Habituation

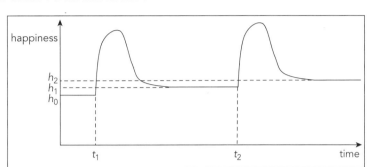

on average. In fact, some say that happiness is no more than brief moments of ful-fillment (see Morris 2004). We can hope to have more of these moments but not aspire to a permanent higher level of happiness.[1] In this framework, development policy has a role even when its impact on happiness is only temporary.

Other arguments against the use of happiness indicators are related to measure-ment issues. However, as Graham noted, many of the same concerns apply to other common measures of welfare, such as income or consumption. Measurement issues might be more serious in happiness than in income, but that will not necessarily be the case if we can improve surveys and apply new techniques and technology from psychology and neurosciences. In the future it might be easier to measure some dimensions of happiness than to estimate all sources of income.

If happiness is our welfare measure, should we give resources to rich people who feel sad? This question, although valid, also applies to income and consumption: if these welfare variables are used to guide policy, resources should be transferred to lazy or dishonest people whose incomes are low despite the fact that they have opportunities to work. There are several conceptual problems in having outcome variables such as happiness, income, or consumption as guides for policy. The devel-opment literature is increasingly dealing with opportunities rather than outcomes, and this will affect the happiness literature.

The previous paragraphs argue that some of the concerns about the use of happi-ness measures as a guide for development policy may not be too serious. In fact, some people disregard these concerns and support happiness measures as the *only* devel-opment goal. This extreme view also has problems. Suppose that some policy does not have any positive effect on happiness. For instance, sometimes it is even argued that certain areas of education make people less happy by making them more aware of the injustices in the world, the fragility of life, or their position in society. Even if these arguments were true, it is likely that most people will not support a reduction in education, because happiness is not the only thing that drives our lives. Other values are more or equally important. People are ready to compromise happiness for these other values, both in their lives and in the policies they support.

Research in psychology shows that about 50 percent of one's overall sense of happiness is genetically determined and cannot be changed; 10 percent is due to circumstances (e.g., income, education); and 40 percent comes from day-to-day experiences and behavior (Lyubomirsky, Sheldon, and Schkade 2005). This is bad news for development policy, because it implies that policy is not very important for people's happiness. However, we should not abandon policy but rather be aware of the size of the policy effects we can expect on happiness indicators. And policy should pay more attention to factors that significantly increase people's sense of happiness: mating, employment, friends, holidays. Of course, there are limits to public interventions, but policy can do many things in these areas. To start with, it can support evidence-based studies in psychology, neurosciences, economics, and other areas to learn more about what can be done to help people feel happier. This kind of research is almost nonexistent in most developing countries.

Dimensions of Welfare and Trade-Offs

Suppose we agree that self-reported happiness is one of the many dimensions of welfare. Is it possible to ignore it in the analysis, given that it is correlated with other objective measures of well-being? In a recent study for Latin America using data from the Gallup Poll and a simple factor analytic model, we concluded that welfare can be appropriately summarized by three dimensions: income, variables associated with basic needs, and subjective welfare measures (Gasparini and et al. 2010). This result acknowledges the importance of happiness measures but also suggests that welfare is a multidimensional phenomenon that cannot be fully captured by one dimension. Any policy aimed at one dimension would likely be suboptimal in the others.

In some cases, the inclusion of the happiness dimension may not affect the policy debate. For instance, investment in water and sanitation increases measures of objective welfare as well as subjective satisfaction, at least for awhile. In other cases, however, there might be a trade-off, and this is when the question of happiness as a benchmark for development policy becomes more interesting.

Graham mentions some of these trade-offs. For instance, development policy that promotes competition and productivity may reduce happiness, at least temporarily. A wide net of social protection and labor regulations may hinder economic growth but may reduce uncertainty and hence increase happiness.

Gasparini and others (2010) found several areas with potential conflict for policy recommendations when looking alternatively at income and happiness. In several Latin American countries, older people are among the most disadvantaged in terms of subjective welfare but not in terms of income or consumption. This reversion has implications for targeting social policies. The gap between rural and urban areas is enormous in terms of income, smaller but still large in terms of consumption, and substantially narrower in terms of happiness. For instance, while 66 percent of the income poor in Ecuador live in rural areas, just 42 percent of the "happiness poor" live in those areas. Large family size is associated with low welfare measured by income or consumption (adjusted for demographics), but the association with happiness is weaker. For instance, in Latin America, the difference in the average number of children between households in the bottom 30 percent of the income distribution and the rest of society is more than 1, but the happiness difference is just 0.2. Targeting social programs on the basis of family size may imply significant biases when other dimensions of deprivation beyond income and consumption are considered.

In many countries poor people (when we define poverty by income or access to goods and services) are, on average, more satisfied than the nonpoor with social policy. In Latin America the difference is not negligible: 7 to 9 points (Gasparini et al. 2010). When we consider the subjective definition, the results change: the happiness poor are less satisfied with efforts to deal with poverty and lack of employment. This result could be driven in part by unobservable personality traits; for example, those who are more likely to rank themselves as poor (even if they are not poor according to objective measures) are also more likely to be less satisfied with a range of other things, including efforts to deal with poverty. The result is challenging: Should we partially disregard the low levels of approval of the subjective poor because they are in part driven by unobservable individual factors, such as pessimism, that lead some of these people to incorrectly consider themselves poor? Or Should we give special attention to this negative view of the social policy because the happiness poor are the real poor, whom our weak scheme to measure poverty with incomes and consumption cannot properly identify?

New evidence seems to support the view that development is generally good for happiness.[2] However, as Graham stresses in her paper, the process by which an economy develops matters a lot. Giving happiness a greater weight as a social goal compared with, for instance, GDP will not affect the need for development policies but may affect decisions about the type of policies and the speed of growth. Large changes seem to be very traumatic. The paradox of unhappy growth documented by Graham and Lora (2009) and others should be taken seriously. Graham says that insecurity regarding a rapidly changing reward structure, volatility, and inequality are happiness-reducing factors during high-growth episodes. A factor she does not mention but one that is probably relevant is the reduction in leisure during growth episodes. People may feel that they have to take advantage of the boom and may overreact—working too many hours, feeling stressed and frustrated. As Graham acknowledges, people seem to be happier in low-growth equilibrium. Development policy should not ignore this fact, although we should not try to avoid any change because it might be traumatic: long-term gains in happiness may outweigh short-term losses.

In conclusion, including happiness in the benchmarks for development will not affect the need for development policy but may affect the speed, type, and nature of interventions.

Notes

1. This argument is related to the philosophical discussion on happiness as contentment or happiness as a fulfilling life.

2. The study of the causal effects of policy on happiness is plagued by empirical problems. One of the more serious is that of bicausality, noted in Graham's paper. A large body of evidence exists in psychology on the effect of happiness on income and other indicators of successful performance in the labor market. In a well-known survey of that literature, Lyubomirsky, King, and Diener (2005) conclude that if you make people feel happy, they perform better in many dimensions. Happiness not only is caused by success but actually causes it.

References

Deaton, A. 2008. "Income, Health, and Well-Being around the World: Evidence from the Gallup World Poll." *Journal of Economic Perspectives* 22 (2, Spring): 53–72.

Di Tella, R., J. Haisken-De New, and R. MacCulloch. 2007. "Happiness Adaptation to Income and to Status in an Individual Panel." NBER Working Paper 13159, National Bureau for Economic Research, Washington, DC.

Gasparini, L., M. Marchionni, W. Sosa Escudero, and S. Olivieri. 2010. "Objective and Subjective Deprivation." In *Paradox and Perception. Measuring Quality of Life in Latin America*, ed. C. Graham and E. Lora. Washington, DC: The Brookings Institution Press.

Graham, C., and E. Lora, eds. 2009. *Paradox and Perception: Measuring Quality of Life in Latin America*. Washington, DC: The Brookings Institution Press.

Layard, R. 2005. *Happiness: Lessons from a New Science*. New York: Penguin Press.

Lyubomirsky, L., A. King, and E. Diener. 2005. "The Benefits of Frequent Positive Affect: Does Happiness Lead to Success?" *Psychological Bulletin* 131: 803–55.

Lyubomirsky, L., K. Sheldon, and D. Schkade. 2005. "Pursuing Happiness: The Architecture of Sustainable Change." *Review of General Psychology* 9: 111–31.

Morris, D. 2004. *The Nature of Happiness*. London: Little Books.

Myers, D. 2000. "The Funds, Friends and Faith of Happy People." *American Psychologist* 55: 56–7.

Sen, A. 1999. *Development As Freedom*. New York: Knopf.

Stevenson, B., and J. Wolfers. 2008. "Economic Growth and Subjective Well-Being: Re-assessing the Easterlin Paradox." *Brookings Papers on Economic Activity*, April.

Social Programs and Transfers:
Are We Learning?

The Evolution and Impact of Unconditional Cash Transfers in South Africa

INGRID WOOLARD AND MURRAY LEIBBRANDT

At the time of the transition to democracy in 1994, the South African social security system was already notably well developed for a middle-income country (Case and Deaton 1998, Lund 1993; van der Berg 1997). It was originally developed under apartheid as a welfare state for whites, then incrementally expanded under social and political pressure to incorporate other groups. Thus, at the advent of the new postapartheid society, some important planks for a social assistance system were in place. Since then, policies have been implemented that have expanded this system substantially. Direct spending on cash transfers currently stands at 3.5 percent of gross domestic product (GDP). This is more than twice the median spending of 1.4 percent of GDP across developing and transition economies (World Bank 2009).

Most of these policies are implemented through unconditional cash transfers. The size, shape, and design aspects of the social assistance system make South Africa an interesting case study. Are cash transfers well targeted and redistributive? Do we know if they enhance human capital accumulation? Are they fiscally sustainable? Have changes in social policy been evidence-based or rights-based?

We begin by documenting the historical context for the current cash transfer programs. Then we look at evidence concerning the aggregate impact of these cash transfers on poverty levels. We review the literature on the impact of the cash transfers on specific socioeconomic outcomes and behaviors. We conclude by looking at the feasibility and appropriateness of introducing conditions into what is currently an unconditional cash transfer program.

Social Security, Social Assistance, and Social Insurance

There are two separate aspects of social security: the insurance concept (social insurance) and the redistribution concept (social assistance). The social insurance prong of

Ingrid Woolard is Associate Professor at the University of Cape Town and Murray Leibbrandt is Professor at the University of Cape Town.

Annual World Bank Conference on Development Economics 2011, Global

South Africa's social security system is far smaller than the social assistance prong. However, we provide a brief review of the social insurance programs to ensure that our discussion is located within a complete picture of the social security system. Figure 1 shows the basic architecture of this system.

The insurance concept focuses on insuring workers against the risk of income loss and hence increases lifetime income smoothing. Most programs based on this concept are financed from premiums and contributions, and benefits depend on contributions. In South Africa, the government is responsible for three primary social insurance mechanisms: the Unemployment Insurance Fund, the Compensation Funds, and the Road Accident Fund.

The Compensation Funds provide medical care and income benefits to workers who are injured at work or develop occupational diseases. These funds also pay survivor benefits to the families of workers who are fatally injured while on the job. The Road Accident Fund provides compensation for the loss of earnings and general damages to victims of road accidents caused by the negligent or wrongful driving of another person. We do not consider these funds further, because they provide very specific risk benefits that are not directly related to poverty alleviation.

For the purposes of this paper, the Unemployment Insurance Fund (UIF) is of much greater significance. All private-sector/formal-sector workers and their employers must contribute 1 percent of salary to the UIF. The UIF pays benefits to contributors in cases of unemployment, illness, maternity, or adoption of a child, and pays benefits to the worker's dependents if the worker dies in service. It is estimated that in 2009 approximately 8 million workers (and their employers) contributed to the fund, but only 10 percent of the 4.1 million unemployed received any unemployment benefits (Leibbrandt et al. 2010).[1] Part of the explanation for this large gap between

FIGURE 1.
Social Security in South Africa

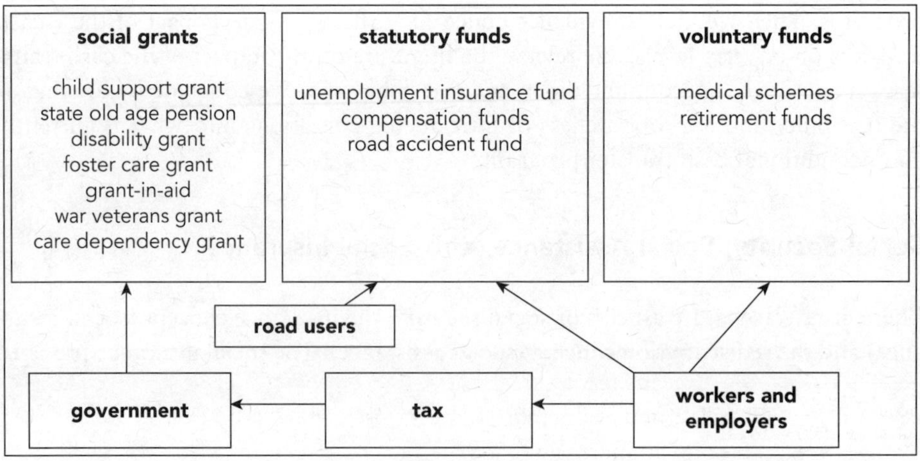

Source: Government of South Africa, 2010.

the number of unemployed and the number of people with claims on the fund lies in the fact that more than half of the unemployed report that they have never worked (Statistics SA 2008) and thus have not contributed to the UIF. Of those who have worked, almost half have been unemployed for more than a year and would have exhausted their benefits if they were ever eligible for them. Thus, while the UIF clearly plays an important role in providing replacement income to the short-term unemployed with work experience, the vast majority of the unemployed fall outside this system.

Redistribution programs, on the other hand, do not focus on workers alone, and the key element is poverty relief. In South Africa, the term "social assistance grants" refers to noncontributory and income-tested benefits provided by the state to vulnerable groups such as the disabled, the elderly, and children in poor households. Benefits are financed out of general tax revenues.

The major grant types in South Africa are the state old age pension (for income-eligible persons over age 60), the disability grant (for income-eligible working-age adults who are temporarily or permanently unable to work because of poor health or disability), the child support grant (currently for children under 16 but being phased in up to age 18) who are living with low-income caregivers, and the foster care grant (for children who have been placed with a foster parent by court order). By April 2010, 14 million people (out of a population of 49 million) were benefiting from social assistance grants. Of these, 2.5 million were receiving old age pensions, 1.3 million were receiving disability grants, 9.4 million children were benefiting from child support grants, and 570,000 children were benefiting from foster care grants.

The rest of the paper focuses on these social grants rather than the UIF or other aspects of South Africa's social insurance system. Fiscally, these grants are completely dominant. In the 2009/10 fiscal year, the UIF paid out benefits amounting to R8.2 billion (purchasing power parity [PPP] $1.7 billion), which is less than one-tenth of the amount spent on cash transfers in the same year. As UIF is the major prong of the social security system directed at vulnerable sections of the working-age population, the system as a whole is heavily skewed toward income support for the young, the elderly, and the disabled, with little direct support to the unemployed. We return to this point in our conclusion. The next section provides the historical context that gave rise to this broad coverage of the young and the elderly while providing little direct support to working-age adults.

How the System Developed

Noncontributory social pensions were instituted in 1928 for whites and coloreds who were not covered by occupational retirement insurance.[2] Pensions were subject to age criteria and a means test to ensure that only the poor were targeted. The proportion of the white population that was dependent on social pensions remained relatively small despite an increasingly liberal means test, as occupational retirement insurance covered the majority of the white population. In 1943, take-up rates among the elderly were 40 percent for whites and 56 percent for coloreds (van der Berg 1997). By that year, only 4 percent of all social assistance spending was on Africans, and this consisted of targeted relief and pensions for the blind (van der Berg 1997).

In 1944 the Smuts government extended social old age pensions to Africans, though benefit levels were less than one-tenth those for whites. By 1958 (a decade into the apartheid era), Africans made up 60 percent of the 347,000 social old age pensioners, although they received only 19 percent of all old age pension spending (van der Berg 1997).

In the 1970s and 1980s the apartheid government worked hard to give the "independent homelands" political legitimacy. Ironically, a major impetus for what Kruger (1992) describes as the "deracialization" of social assistance came from attempts to bolster the homeland system of racial separation. This led to a rapid increase in the funds flowing to the homelands for old age pensions. The coverage of the African elderly population increased steadily, and by 1993 there were almost twice as many African pensioners inside the homelands as outside (van der Berg 1997).

In the late 1970s the principle of moving to parity in social spending levels was reluctantly accepted (van der Berg 1997). From that time on, fiscal expenditures on social assistance rose rapidly in an attempt to incorporate all race groups into the system and to provide similar levels of benefits. Spending on social old age pensions rose from 0.6 percent of GDP in 1970 to 1.8 percent by 1993 (van der Berg 1997). Fiscal constraints precluded increasing the benefits for all race groups to the level of those previously enjoyed by white pensioners, and white benefits were eroded while African benefits were rapidly increased. As shown in figure 2, African pension benefits rose fivefold in real terms between 1970 and 1993, while white pension benefits fell by a third.

The 1992 Social Assistance Act finally did away with all discriminatory provisions. Thus, the social pensions and grants that were set up to protect the white population gradually expanded their eligibility rules to include all South Africans. "This [made] it . . . an unusually comprehensive system compared with that found in other developing countries" (Lund 1993, 22).

Figure 2 shows that the real value of the pension declined somewhat through the late 1990s but recovered from 2004 onward to retain the same real levels offered at the start of the postapartheid period. This grant, inherited from the apartheid era, was the core component around which the other components of the postapartheid social grant system were added or expanded.

One of the components that has expanded dramatically is the disability grant. This is the only grant intended for working-age adults. It goes to disabled and chronically ill persons over the age of 18 but below the age at which they would be eligible for the old age pension. The means test is the same as for the old age pension. The main criterion is that recipients must be disabled to the extent that they are unable to support themselves. Permanent grants are awarded to those who are permanently disabled. Temporary grants are awarded for a shorter period—for example, six months—to those who are expected to regain the ability to support themselves. Numbers for the disability grant increased significantly in the late 1990s but have

FIGURE 2.
Monthly Value of Pension Benefits by Race, 1960–2010 (constant 2010 PPP$ prices)

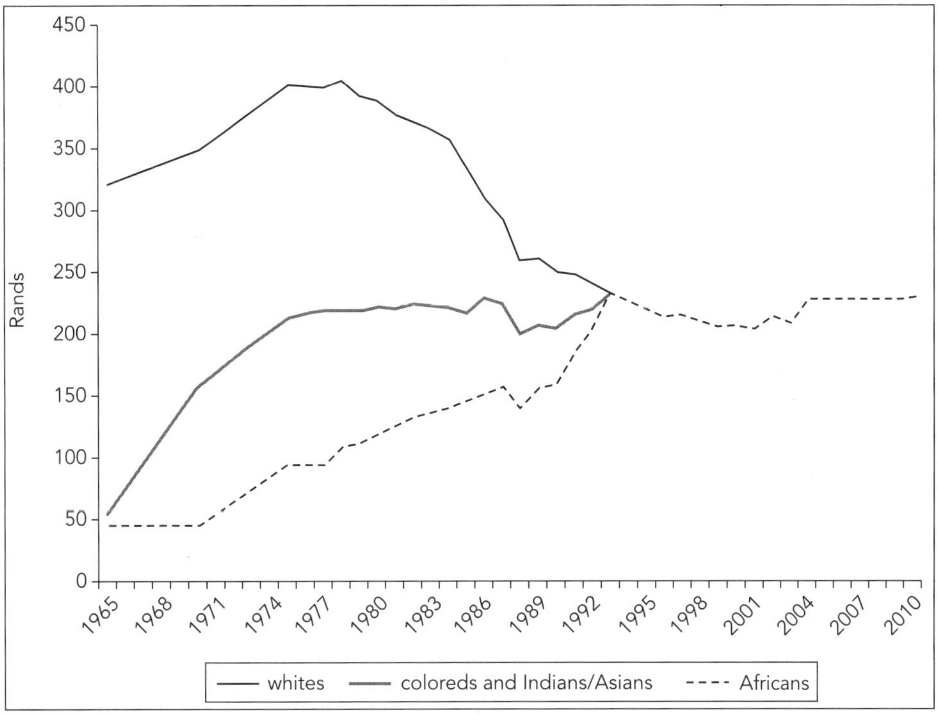

Sources: Nominal data from 1960 to 1994 kindly provided by Servaas van der Berg (personal communication); data from 1995 onward, Government of South Africa, various years.

Note: Data deflated to 2010 prices using headline consumer price index and a PPP$ exchange rate of 4.67 in 2010.

leveled off in the past decade. Today, about 6 percent of working-age adults receive a disability grant each month.

Thus, improved coverage and parity in benefits occurred in the case of the old age pension and the disability grant. However, in the case of child grants, the incoming postapartheid government confronted a highly inequitable inheritance. At the time of the political transition in 1994, little was being spent on children, and expenditure was highly unequal by race. At that time, three grants were directed at children. A foster care grant was available to children who had been placed with foster parents through a court order. A care dependency grant (CDG) was given to caregivers of children who were disabled enough to need full-time care. Finally, there was a state maintenance grant. We deal with this grant first as, fiscally, it is by far the most important of the three and its postapartheid evolution holds important lessons.

The state maintenance grant was intended for a parent or guardian living with a child under 18 years of age if the applicant was unmarried, widowed, or separated; had been deserted by a spouse for more than six months; had a spouse who received a social grant; or had a spouse who had been in prison, a drug treatment center, or similar institution for more than six months. Applicants had to prove that they had made efforts to apply for private maintenance from the other parent but had been unsuccessful. There were limitations not only on nonparents' receipt of the grant but also on eligibility with respect to children born outside marriage. As a result of significant differences in both the rules and how they were applied, very few African children and their caregivers received the grant. In 1993, the last year for which racially disaggregated welfare spending data are available, only 0.2 percent of African children were receiving maintenance grants, while 1.4 percent of white children, 4.0 percent of Indian children, and 5.0 percent of colored children received grants (Lund 2008).

The new African National Congress (ANC) government quickly recognized that providing equal access to the state maintenance grant would have large fiscal implications. Simulations based on household survey data suggested that there would be more than a 20-fold increase in expenditures if all caregivers became aware of their rights (Haarman and Haarman 1996). To be fair to the government, the fiscal implications were not their only consideration. The grant was also deemed inappropriate for the South African context, with its underlying basis that the only children in need were those living with single mothers. Many children in need lived with both or neither of their parents. As Simkins and Dlamini put it at the time, "[T]ransfer payments in support of children have traditionally assumed a nuclear family context, whereas this is by no means the only basis of social organization" (1992, 65).

The government moved swiftly to institute reform. In December 1995 the Lund Committee was established to evaluate the existing system of state support and explore alternative policy options targeting children and families. The committee recommended a new strategy that included a child-linked grant that had a lower monetary value than the state maintenance grant but targeted a much wider group of beneficiaries.

The child support grant (CSG) was introduced in April 1998 at a level of R100 (PPP$37) per month for each eligible child younger than seven years of age. The money was to be paid to the child's primary caregiver. Applicants for the grant were required to pass a means test (based on household income), produce certain documents, and demonstrate efforts to secure funds from other sources. The strict requirements prevented many genuine caregivers of poor children from applying for the grant. By 1999 only 21,997 children had been signed up. In response to the low take-up rate, the government altered the means test from a household measure to one that considered only the income of the primary caregiver and his or her spouse, net of other social assistance grants.

When the CSG was introduced, it included several conditions. Applicants were initially expected to participate in "development programs" and to have proof that the children for whom they were applying were immunized. The requirement regarding development programs was dropped after it became obvious that such programs simply did not exist in many areas. The immunization requirement was dropped because it often discriminated against children who were already disadvantaged in terms of access to services.

The CSG is a good example of how a program can be improved if it is found to be ineffective. Take-up of the CSG was very low in the first three years. Surveys of provincial social development offices showed that take-up was being severely undermined by contradictory interpretations of the means test and the conditions. Despite the changes to the law, some welfare offices still required single mothers to provide proof that they had tried to obtain private maintenance from the father of the child or were actively seeking work (Samson, van Niekerk, and McQuene 2006). As shown in figure 3, by 2000 (two years into the program) only 150,000 children were receiving their entitlement.

In 2000 the South African cabinet appointed a Committee of Inquiry into Comprehensive Social Security (the Taylor Committee), which examined the shortcomings of the system. Under the leadership of Viviene Taylor, the committee recommended the introduction of a universal grant to all South Africans (a basic income grant), beginning with the extension of the child support grant to all children. Following the submission of the report, the Department of Social Development extended the grant from age 7 to age 14, doubling its scope. In his January 2002 state-of-the-nation address, President Thabo Mbeki announced a government-led campaign to "register all who are eligible for the child grant" (Samson, van Niekerk, and McQuene 2006). The president's strong commitment sent a clear message to the bureaucracy that social grants were

FIGURE 3.
Number of Children Receiving the Child Support Grant, by Year and Age Group

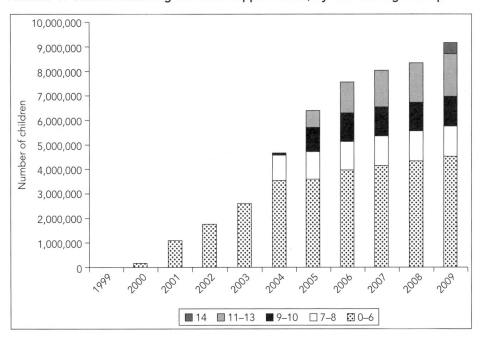

Source: South African Social Security Agency, special request.

the central pillar of the poverty eradication strategy. By April 2003, 2.6 million children had been signed up for the grant, and take-up continued to escalate.

Since then this grant has been further expanded and older age groups have been gradually included. Beginning in 2010, all income-eligible children born after 1996 will receive the CSG until they turn 18. The means test has also been relaxed. In October 2008 the test was increased to 10 times the value of the grant for single caregivers and double that for married caregivers. Until that time the means test had been fixed at R800 in urban areas and R1100 in rural areas for 10 years. In the most extreme situation, this meant that the means test for a married caregiver in an urban area changed from an income ceiling of R800 (PPP$183) per month to R4600 (PPP$1,053). Estimates based on survey data suggest that this change in the means test should have brought an additional 1.5 million children into the net (Leibbrandt et al. 2010).

Let us return briefly to the two other child grants that have been in existence since before the CSG was established. Both have seen marked increases in take-up over recent years. This can be partly attributed to an increase in general awareness of the grants, but it is also related to the HIV/AIDS pandemic, as both grants are used in some cases to provide for children affected or infected by AIDS.

The foster child grant (FCG) is paid to those who have gone through a court process to become registered as foster parents of a child. The grant is intended for children up to the age of 18 years who are "in need of care" and are not receiving such care from their biological parents. This includes children who are abused as well as children in trouble with the law. The grant is not primarily intended to deal with poverty and thus has no means test unless the child has independent income. Because the grant value is almost three times larger than the CSG, there is a clear incentive to caregivers to choose the FCG over the CSG if they can. The significant difference between the two amounts is a legacy of the haphazard way the grant system came into being. The Lund Committee was aware of this problem when it deliberated, but it could not propose a higher amount for the CSG and still stay within the budget limit in its terms of reference and did not want to recommend lowering the value of the FCG.

The care dependency grant is given to caregivers of children who are severely disabled to the extent that they need full-time care. If such care were not available in the home, they would have to be institutionalized. The grant is available for children from 1 to 18 years of age.

All in all then, over the postapartheid period social grant policy evolved in a way that continued and modified some inherited grants (the old age pension, the disability grant, and the foster care grant), removed the state maintenance grant, and replaced it with the child support grant. Table 1 provides a contemporary snapshot, showing the current value of the various cash transfer payments. The old age pension and the disability grant are regarded as quite generous, equating to 1.75 times the average per capita household income. Another way to benchmark the amount is to compare it with the minimum wage. In South Africa minimum wages differ according to sector. In 2010 one of the lowest wage determinations was for domestic workers in nonmetropolitan areas: at R1192 per month, which was only about 10 percent

TABLE 1. Value of the Grants in 2010

Grant type	2010 value in Rands (and PPP$) per month	Grant value as percentage of median monthly per capita income
Old age pension	R1080 (PPP$230)	1.75
Disability grant	R1080 (PPP$230)	1.75
Child support grant	R250 (PPP$53)	0.40
Foster care grant	R710 (PPP$150)	1.15

Source: Author calculations.

Note: Per capita income is from the 2008 National Income Dynamics Study, inflated to 2010 prices using headline Consumer Price Index.

more than the pension or disability benefit. The CSG is much smaller than the adult grants or the FCG.

Putting this system of grants in place over the postapartheid era meant a rapid increase in spending on social assistance (see figure 4). While spending on education and health has remained fairly constant in real terms, social assistance (excluding administration) now consumes 3.2 percent of GDP, up from 1.9 percent in fiscal year 2000/01.

Coverage

The grants have an extensive reach. Simulations based on survey data suggest that about three-quarters of the elderly are income-eligible for the old age pension, and almost all of them report receiving the grant. As noted earlier, about 6 percent of the working-age population receives disability grants. While 60 percent of age-eligible children receive a grant of some form, our survey estimates suggest that 70 percent are income-eligible for the child support grant. There are a number of reasons for this. First, take-up among infants is very low, partly because caregivers procrastinate or there is a delay in obtaining a birth certificate for the child. Second, our simulations use the new means test, which may not have been widely communicated. Third, and of greater concern, some groups seem to be outside the reach of the grant. One of the most at-risk segments of the child population is orphans. Figure 5 shows how many orphans under the age of 15 years are currently receiving social assistance, according to 2008 data from the National Income Dynamics Study (NIDS).[3] What is most striking is the high number of paternal orphans receiving grants, particularly the CSG, and the low number of maternal orphans receiving grants. This finding matches evidence in Case, Hosegood, and Lund (2005) that the probability of a child receiving a grant decreases when the mother is absent. Woolard, Carter, and Agüero (2005) draw the same conclusion using the KwaZulu-Natal Income Dynamic Study (KIDS) data. Children living with their widowed fathers are the least likely to be receiving grants. Unsurprisingly, orphans who have lost both parents are the most likely to be receiving the foster care grant. Surprisingly, though, orphans (outside of

FIGURE 4.
Social Expenditures As a Percentage of GDP

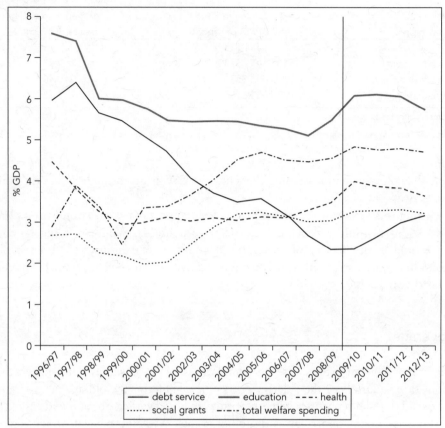

Source: Government of South Africa, 1999–2010.

paternal orphans) are less likely than children with both parents to be receiving the CSG. This may be a result of the more complex documentation required without the child's mother as caregiver.

Impact of Cash Transfers on Household Poverty

The immediate objective of cash transfer programs is to alleviate hardship among vulnerable groups. In this part of the paper, we take an aggregate look at the extent to which cash transfers in South Africa achieve this aim. Precise measurement of the impact of specific programs on poverty is a largely intractable problem because of the difficulties involved in establishing a legitimate counterfactual as a benchmark. As a result, studies tend to focus on determining whether cash transfer programs target the poor and on comparing the adequacy of household income with and without the pension income component (Barrientos and Lloyd-Sherlock 2002). We follow this approach here.

FIGURE 5.
Percentage of Children Receiving Social Assistance, by Vital Status of Parents

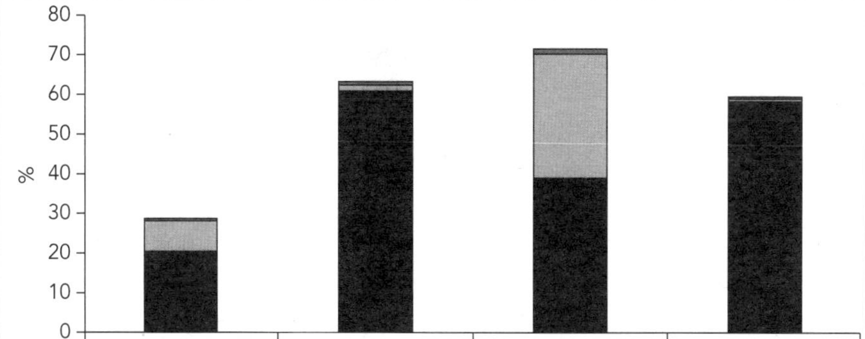

	maternal orphan	paternal orphan	dual orphan	not an orphan
CDG	0.3	0.7	1.4	0.4
FCG	7.6	1 7	30.9	0.5
CSG	20.7	60.7	39.1	58.2

Source: Author calculations using SALDRU 2008.

Note: CDG = care dependency grant, FCG = foster child grant, CSG = child support grant.

In figure 6 we disaggregate household income sources by income quintile to highlight the role of social assistance grants in providing income support to the poorest households. It is striking that fully two-thirds of income to the bottom quintile comes from social assistance grants, with most of this income coming from child grants (the CSG, FCG, and CDG combined). As households move up the income distribution, labor market income becomes increasingly important and reliance on social assistance is commensurately reduced.

Table 2 shows the proportion of households reporting access to cash transfers. Note that in 1997 households in quintile 2 were much more likely to be getting a grant than households in quintile 1. The reason is straightforward: The magnitude of the old age pension and the disability grant were enough to lift all but the biggest households out of the first quintile (Leibbrandt et al. 2010). The rapid roll-out of the much smaller child support grant from 2000 onward is clear in table 2; whereas in 1997 just under a third of households were receiving a grant, by 2006 this proportion had risen to about half. Significantly, the percentage of households in the bottom quintile with access to social assistance rose from 16 percent to 64 percent between 1997 and 2008.

Table 3 shows the percentage of households in each income quintile that received income from specific social assistance grants in 2008. More than half of the households in the bottom quintile received some income from the child support grant, in comparison with only 9 percent of households in the top quintile. Owing to the effect of the old age pension in lifting many households out of the poorest quintile,

FIGURE 6.
Sources of Household Income, by Quintile

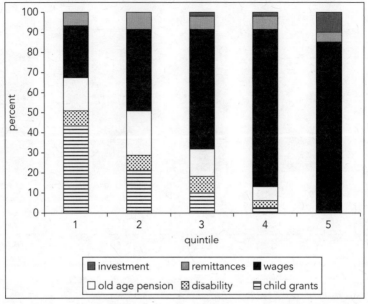

Source: Author calculations using SALDRU 2008.

TABLE 2. Percentage of Households Reporting Any Income from Grants

Quintile	1997	2002	2003	2004	2005	2006	2008
1	15.9	32.0	31.7	40.2	47.7	69.4	63.7
2	54.0	55.8	50.9	71.2	73.3	69.9	73.7
3	46.7	51.6	53.2	67.1	69.1	69.4	66.8
4	33.8	33.2	34.8	35.8	40.1	45.4	47.6
5	14.0	11.3	7.9	8.8	10.0	12.0	12.4
Total	32.9	36.8	32.0	38.6	45.5	55.2	52.2

Sources: Author calculations using Statistics SA 1997, 2002, 2003, 2004, 2005, and 2006, and SALDRU 2008.

TABLE 3. Percentage of Households Reporting Any Income from Social Grants, by Quintile

Quintile	% reporting any income from child grants	% reporting any income from disability grant	% reporting any income from old age pension
1	55.8	5.7	9.8
2	57.9	10.9	27.1
3	45.4	14.7	23.5
4	26.5	9.9	17.7
5	9.0	2.8	5.0
All	33.6	8.2	15.3

Source: Author calculations using SALDRU 2008.

households that received the old age pension were more likely to be in the second or third quintile than in the very poorest quintile.

In table 4 we present a "morning after" simulation of the increase in poverty if the grants were abruptly discontinued and households did not have the opportunity to dissolve and reconstitute. This is obviously a highly unrealistic counterfactual, since many households would not be sustainable economic units in the absence of grants. Nevertheless, such simulations give some sense of the significance of grants in poverty alleviation. The table shows that government grant income does not change the headcount measure (P_0) substantially. However, when the depth (P_1) and severity (P_2) of poverty measures are used, poverty is seen to diminish markedly as a result of government grants. This effect became stronger between 1993 and 2008, especially between 2000 and 2008, when the CSG was rolled out.

Table 4 suggests that without government grants, poverty would have worsened over time. primarily because the postapartheid labor market has operated in such a way as to leave an increasing number of South African households outside its ambit. Households can be linked directly to the labor market through employment and earnings or indirectly through remittance income from migrant workers and other remitters. Table 5 shows that the share of households with no direct or indirect link

TABLE 4. Poverty With and Without Government Grants

Poverty when income includes government grants

Year	Poverty line = PPP$223 per capita per month			Poverty line = PPP$121 per capita per month		
	P_0	P_1	P_2	P_0	P_1	P_2
1993	0.72	0.47	0.36	0.56	0.32	0.22
2000	0.71	0.45	0.33	0.54	0.29	0.19
2008	0.70	0.44	0.32	0.54	0.28	0.18

Poverty when income excludes government grants

	P_0	P_1	P_2	P_0	P_1	P_2
1993	0.73	0.53	0.43	0.60	0.4	0.32
2000	0.72	0.5	0.4	0.57	0.37	0.29
2008	0.71	0.54	0.46	0.60	0.44	0.37

Sources: Author calculations using SALDRU 1993 and 2008, and Statistics SA 2000.

TABLE 5. Household Labor Market Attachment and Access to Grants of the Unemployed (%)

	1997	2006	2008
No one employed, no remittances, no social grants	11.8	13.2	16.9
No one employed, no remittances, social grants	17.5	24.7	24.9
No one employed, remittances	21.3	11.2	12.9
One employed	35.8	39.4	36.6
Two or more employed	13.5	11.5	9.4
Total	100.0	100.0	100.0

Sources: Author calculations using Statistics SA 1997 and 2006, and SALDRU 2008.

Note: This table covers only selected years owing to lack of data in other surveys on either remittances or labor market status.

to the labor market has risen sharply, from 30 percent in 1997 to 42 percent in 2008. The rapid expansion of the grants has coincided with these substantial changes in the number of households with no link to the labor market. There is little doubt that the postapartheid record on poverty alleviation would have been much more dismal without the expansion of the social security system.

Impact of the Grants in the Long Run

The inability of poor households to invest in the productive capacity of their members, especially the education and health of children, has implications for the persistence of poverty. Cash transfer programs provide a predictable and reliable source of income that can significantly affect the capacity of households to invest in human and physical capital, and thus break the intergenerational cycle of poverty. In this section, we review the evidence on the effect of cash transfers on education and health. We also review the substantial literature on the effect of the grants on labor supply. Most of the literature has focused on the old age pension, which has been in place much longer than the child support grant. We focus on papers that take an econometric approach. For a broader review of both quantitative and qualitative studies, see Budlender and Woolard (2006).

Case and Deaton (1998), using data from the 1993 Project for the Study of Living Standards and Development (PSLSD), found that pension income is spent like other income—that is, "a Rand is a Rand." They also found that because of the very high prevalence of three-generation and skip-generation households among South Africa's African population, young children were found disproportionately in households receiving pensions, and pension money received by women was more likely to be spent in ways that enhance child outcomes (e.g., on food and school fees).

Also using the 1993 PSLSD data, and focusing on children under five, Duflo (2000) examines the extent to which allocating resources to women rather than to men affects the distributional outcome and, in particular, investments in children. More than a quarter of African children of this age group live in the same household as an old age pension recipient. The effect on children is measured through weight-for-height and height-for-age. The presence in the household of a woman who is eligible for the old age pension results in an increase in girls' (but not boys') weight-for-height and height-for-age z-scores. Duflo finds no effect on either boys' or girls' nutritional outcomes when men receive pensions. This paper is important for two reasons. First, Duflo presents robust evidence that children are benefiting from a cash transfer program intended for a completely different target group. Second, because these effects differ according to the gender of the person who receives the transfer, the paper rejects the unitary model of the household in which all household income is pooled and then allocated according to a joint household utility function.

Edmonds, Mammen, and Miller (2005) use a nonparametric regression discontinuity design to examine changes in household composition associated with the old age pension. They find that households in which a person reaches pension age experience a decrease in women aged 30 to 39 and an increase in children under 5 and women aged 18 to 23. Using data from a 1999 child labor survey, Edmonds (2006) identifies changes in schooling and child labor when a household member becomes eligible for the pension. School attendance and completed schooling rise, and market work declines. The effects are limited to pension-eligible men, a result that Edmonds attributes to greater liquidity constraints for men. Because Edmonds examines children over age five, his results are not necessarily inconsistent with Duflo's results for younger children.

Case and Ardington (2008) investigated whether having a pensioner in the household reduces the negative effect of maternal orphanhood on schooling. They find that having a female pensioner mitigates the impact of orphanhood with respect to school enrollment and progress but not with respect to school-related expenses. Having a male pensioner in the household has a negative effect on progress in school and an insignificant effect on enrollment and school-related expenditures.

Hamoudi and Thomas (2005) examined the effect of the pension on educational attainment of children using the 1998 National Demographic and Health Survey. They looked at children aged 6 to 19, and estimated total years of schooling on the basis of current or last grade. Overall, the authors find that pension income has a greater beneficial effect on girls' education than on boys' education. This accords with results of earlier analyses (such as Duflo 2000) but adds the nuance that for older children (aged 13 to 19), a male pension tends to increase education among boys and decrease education among girls, whereas a female pension has little effect on either. Among younger children (aged 6 to 12), a female pension has a positive effect on girls and no effect on boys. Further analysis shows that, overall, boys aged 6 to 15 who live with their mothers are further ahead in school than those who do not. Boys who live in pensioner households, however, are likely to have gone less far in education if they live with their mothers. The same pattern is found among girls, although it is not as marked.

Case (2001) investigated the effect of old age pensions on health status. Her analysis was based on a small sample of households in the Langeberg health district of the Western Cape. The study found that old age pension income was pooled in 84 percent of households. Where income was not pooled, beneficial health effects were experienced only by the pensioner; where income was pooled, children were taller, suggesting a beneficial effect on them. The study suggested that this effect works partly through improved sanitation, partly through improved nutritional status, and partly through reduction in psychosocial stress.

All in all, clear evidence exists of the positive effect of the old age pension on human capital outcomes. The evidence on the labor market effects of grant receipt is mixed. Early research on the old age pension suggested that it had substantial negative effects on adult labor supply. Bertrand, Mullainathan, and Miller (2003) found a reduction in working hours of members of working age when another member of the household reached pension age, suggesting that pension receipt represents an income shock on the household level. However, the reduction in hours is highest when the pensioner is a woman, evidence that is complementary to Duflo's in terms of a rejection of perfect household income pooling. Posel, Fairburn, and Lund (2006) followed the same methodology but expanded the definition of the household to include nonresident members. They found that African women were significantly more likely to be migrant workers when they were members of a household that received a pension, especially when the pension recipient was female. The authors hypothesized that the pension provided the means to migrate and freed the older person to care for the children of the migrant, freeing the migrant to seek work.

The work of Ardington, Case, and Hosegood (2009) also disputed the earlier findings of Bertrand and colleagues (2003). This study used data on nonresident (migrant) household members and panel data that allowed the authors to control for time-invariant differences between pension recipients and nonrecipients. Their results suggested that the old age pension had a positive effect on adult labor supply—the probability that working-age adults are employed is approximately 3 percentage points higher in households with at least one pension recipient. Like Posel, Fairburn, and Lund (2006), Ardington and colleagues argued that the old age pension relieved financial and child care constraints, which were short-run impediments to migrating.

Recently Ranchhod (2010) has used panel data from the national Labour Force Survey to look at the effect of the cessation of the pension (owing to the pensioner's death or outmigration) on household formation and labor supply. For people who maintained their residency status across waves, Ranchhod found large and statistically significant increases in employment rates for middle-aged women and men (9.3 and 8.1 percentage points, respectively), as well as for older adult women and men (10.3 percentage points for both). These findings are consistent with those of Bertrand and colleagues (2003) and not necessarily inconsistent with the findings of Posel and colleagues (2006) and Ardington and colleagues (2009), who broadened their definition of household membership to include migrants.

In one of the few analyses of the child support grant, Agüero, Carter, and Woolard (2007) used KIDS data to test whether receipt of the grant during the first 36 months of a child's life had an effect on child nutrition as measured by height-for-age. The paper conditioned on a measure for eagerness of the mother in an attempt to capture the true causal effect of the grant. The authors found that children who received the CSG during the first three years of their life (the so-called "nutritional window" during which adult height is largely determined) had significantly higher height-for-age than children who did not.

In summary, we do not know a great deal with a high degree of certainty. It seems clear that access to either a pension or a child support grant can improve the health status of beneficiaries and other household members by improving their nutrition and access to health care. And some evidence exists that older people, particularly women, are inclined to allocate this income in ways that directly benefit more vulnerable household members, such as young children. Evidence about the effect of cash transfers on the labor supply of beneficiaries and their household members is mixed. Basic economic theory suggests that cash transfers are an injection of nonlabor income into the households and should have an income effect on direct and indirect beneficiaries in the household. Thus, these transfers may have the effect of reducing incentives for work. The empirical analysis in two of the papers we reviewed supported this theory. On the other hand, a cash transfer might help overcome a liquidity constraint if migrant laborers initially need to draw resources from the original sending household. There seems to be some empirical support for this theory.

To Condition or Not to Condition?

The South African behavioral evidence is particularly interesting because it shows behavioral responses from cash transfers that are means-tested but unconditional. Behavioral responses are therefore seen to be outcomes of a pure income effect. This is unusual in the contemporary international policy milieu and has stimulated a discussion of whether behavioral responses to grants could have been more effectively shaped by imposing conditions on recipients. In this section we draw out some of the implications of the implementation of the CSG for this issue.

As discussed earlier, when the CSG was introduced, it was intended to be a conditional cash transfer. Applicants had to provide proof that the child had been immunized, that they were participating in development programs, that they had not refused employment without good reason, and that they had attempted to secure private maintenance for the child from the other parent if they were separated or divorced. The development program requirement was dropped after it became obvious that such programs simply did not exist in many areas. The immunization requirement was dropped because it often discriminated against children who were already disadvantaged in terms of access to health services. As noted earlier, initial take-up of the grant was slow, in part because of these conditions. Once the regulations were changed and increased effort was put into rolling out the grant, take-up increased rapidly.

Grants are an important element of the post-1994 South African government's rights-based approach, in line with the right to social security granted in the constitution. This rights-based approach does not square easily with the imposition of conditions. Despite this (and despite the early problems associated with implementing behavioral conditions), the issue of conditions has resurfaced regularly over the past decade. The recent extension of the CSG to children until they turn 18 coincided with renewed efforts by the government to impose behavioral conditions.

Having decided that it would be good to impose conditions, the government considered what conditions might be appropriate. In Budlender's (2008) interviews with high-ranking government officials, several said that reproductive health issues and knowledge are especially important for young adults, but none had workable suggestions for conditions that might be imposed. Eventually it became clear that any conditions attached to a CSG for children aged 15–17 years should focus on education.

The question then arose as to whether an education condition should relate to enrollment, attendance, or performance. One argument against enrollment as a condition is that this is a once-off measure at the beginning of the year, and that enrollment without regular attendance brings little benefit. The argument for enrollment is that it is easy to measure. Almost all schools are now covered by a centralized information system that can provide individual enrollment information, including school and grade. Similar comprehensive information systems with respect to attendance and performance will not be in place in the foreseeable future.

Beginning in January 2010, caregivers of CSG beneficiaries "need to ensure that children for whom they are in receipt of a grant are enrolled and attending school. Regular proof of school enrollment needs to be submitted to the Department of Social Development, along with reports from the school. Upon receipt of any information regarding a child not attending school, the Department of Social Development will send a social worker to investigate and put in place steps to ensure that the child attends school. While punitive measures such as stopping the grant are not envisaged, these provisions will allow government to improve school attendance and provide the necessary support to households where needed" (Republic of South Africa 2010, 104).

This is a very soft condition, since the grant will not be stopped if a child does not attend school. In addition, it seems that "regular proof of enrollment" will be annual submission of a school report card, meaning that the intervention of a social worker may come too late to be effective. Also, given the shortage of social workers and the demands on them, it seems unlikely that monitoring and intervention will be a priority area for the Department of Social Development.

Nevertheless, even a soft condition may have some effect if caregivers believe they are required to send their children to school to get the grant. However, it is unclear that there is a demand-side problem with school enrollment. As shown in figure 7, it is already very high.

FIGURE 7.
School Enrollment, Ages 0–17

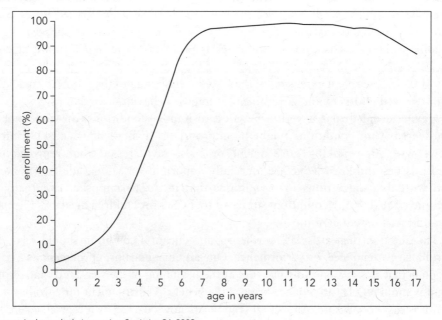

Source: Author calculations using Statistics SA 2009.

School attendance is a much bigger problem than school enrollment (Budlender 2008); however, conditioning on school attendance would entail a significant administrative burden on the Department of Education and would require intersectoral coordination between the Department of Social Development and the Department of Education. It is unclear that the administrative capacity exists to implement a proper monitoring and reporting system. It would also be much more costly to implement than a condition related to enrollment.

Conclusion

In some respects, South Africa is an exceptional case for a developing country. The first exceptional factor for this paper is the extent of its social assistance provision, with cash transfers going to more than a quarter of the population. The second factor is that it is a middle-income country with almost no public debt, so the cash transfer programs are financed from tax revenue rather than donor funding or borrowing. The third factor is the extreme inequality in the country. The South African government is committed to reducing inequality and poverty, and redistribution through progressive taxes and pro-poor cash transfers is seen to be an efficient way to accomplish this.

We have shown that the reduction in poverty over the postapartheid period has been strongly associated with the expansion of social grants. Also, drawing on the benefit-incidence literature (van der Berg 2001, 2009), it seems clear that the disbursement of these grants has been strongly redistributionist. Thus, at the aggregate level, there is no doubt that they have had a positive effect on poverty and inequality. However, these outcomes are the result of very large increases in social spending, so it would have been surprising to see no aggregate effect. In addition, providing evidence of these effects is not the same as making a case that these social grants are the best policy instruments for alleviating poverty. This case would require an assessment of the grants against a set of alternative policies. We have not done this in the paper.

Rather, we have discussed the body of work that has assessed the effects of the grants on key micro-outcomes such as health, education, and labor supply. Evidence exists that the money flowing into households through grants is used in part to improve health and education outcomes for household members other than the direct beneficiary. These effects are crucial for longer-run poverty alleviation. The evidence on the labor supply effects of grants is mixed: Grants seem to promote migration in search of employment but also seem to provide some disincentive for working-age household members to look for work.

Thus, at the end of the day we face a dilemma. There is no doubt that the social assistance system in South Africa is channeling grant income into needy households and that this income changes the behavior of some members of such households. Nonetheless, the current system, which focuses on children and the elderly, is an artifact of history rather than a coherently designed system. In the absence of comprehensive social insurance, working-age adults can benefit from social assistance grants only if they are disabled or live with a child or an elderly person. Many people believe that the social grant system should be extended to focus directly on the unemployed who are not covered by other grants. Such arguments are strengthened by the limitations of the unemployment insurance fund discussed earlier.

However, we should remember that the contemporary context is one of a massive post-2000 expansion of the cash transfer system. Further expansion in the future will face the issue of fiscal sustainability. So far, economic growth has supported the increase in the grant system, and the high returns in social well-being have justified this expenditure. But the country will face a tougher growth environment over the medium term, and it is unlikely that the fiscal space exists for expanding cash transfers. The overriding goal of economic and social policy must be the assimilation of many more of the unemployed into the labor market. It seems that a positive employment environment is the key parameter for sustainable social transformation. We would therefore argue for a stronger focus on active labor market policies to complement the extensive system of cash transfers.

In sum, we are cautious about further expansion of social grants. However, we are also cautious about internal reforms to current systems. We looked briefly at the possibility of imposing behavioral conditions. There are costs associated with the imposition of these conditions, and they are likely to be high in the South African context. The desire to introduce conditions seems to be driven by political economy considerations; that is, the belief that taxpayers may be more likely to support transfers to the poor if they are linked to efforts to overcome poverty in the long term, particularly if those efforts involve actions to improve the welfare of children. This approach is not helpful to the poor, and, in the absence of sensible conditions that are easy and inexpensive to monitor and enforce, there seems little reason to tamper with the current system of unconditional cash transfers.

Notes

1. Since the maximum benefit period is 238 days, this implies that fewer than 10 percent of the unemployed are receiving unemployment benefits at any given time.

2. South Africa under apartheid used race as a primary classification of the population into African, colored, Indian, and white groups. Statistics continue to be collected using these classifications. The term "black" is used to signify African, colored, and Indian people in the context of signifying previously disenfranchised groups.

3. Unfortunately, there is no information on grant receipt by children over the age of 15.

References

Agüero, Jorge, Michael Carter, and Ingrid Woolard. 2007. *The Impact of Unconditional Cash Transfers on Nutrition: The South African Child Support Grant.* Working Paper 39. Brasilia, Brazil: International Policy Centre for Inclusive Growth.

Ardington, Cally, Anne Case, and Victoria Hosegood. 2009. "Labor Supply Responses to Large Social Transfers: Longitudinal Evidence from South Africa." *American Economic Journal: Applied Economics* 1 (1): 22–48.

Barrientos, Armando, and Peter Lloyd-Sherlock. 2002. *Noncontributory Pensions and Social Protection*. Paper in the Issues in Social Protection series, Social Protection Sector. Geneva: International Labour Organization.

Bertrand, Marianne, Sendhil Mullainathan, and Douglas Miller. 2003. "Public Policy and Extended Families: Evidence from Pensions in South Africa." *World Bank Economic Review* 17 (1): 27–50.

Budlender, Debbie. 2008. "Feasibility and Appropriateness of Attaching Behavioural Conditions to a Social Support Grant for Children Aged 15–17 Years." Unpublished report commissioned by the Department of Social Development, Community Agency for Social Enquiry, Johannesburg.

Budlender, Debbie, and Ingrid Woolard. 2006. *The Impact of the South African Child Support and Old Age Grants on Children's Schooling and Work*. Paper prepared for International Program on the Elimination of Child Labour. Geneva: International Labour Organization.

Case, Anne. 2001. *Does Money Protect Health Status? Evidence from South African Pensions*. National Bureau for Economic Research (NBER) Working Paper 8495. Washington, DC: NBER.

Case, Anne, and Cally Ardington. 2008. "The Impact of Parental Death on School Enrolment and Achievement: Longitudinal Evidence from South Africa." *Demography* 43 (3): 401–20.

Case, Anne, and Angus Deaton. 1998. "Large Cash Transfers to the Elderly in South Africa." *Economic Journal* 108 (450): 1330–61.

Case, Anne, Victoria Hosegood, and Frances Lund. 2005. "The Reach and Impact of Child Support Grants: Evidence from KwaZulu-Natal." *Development Southern Africa* 22 (4): 467–82.

Duflo, Esther. 2000. "Child Health and Household Resources in South Africa: Evidence from the Old Age Pension Program." *American Economic Review* 90 (2): 393–98.

Edmonds, Eric. 2006. "Child Labor and Schooling Responses to Anticipated Income in South Africa." *Journal of Development Economics* 81 (2): 386–414.

Edmonds Eric, Kristen Mammen, and Douglas Miller. 2005. "Rearranging the Family? Income Support and Elderly Living Arrangements in a Low-Income Country." *Journal of Human Resources* 40 (1): 186–207.

Haarman, Claudia, and Dirk Haarman. 1996. *A Contribution Towards a New Family Support System in South Africa*. Report for the Lund Committee on Child and Family Support.

Hamoudi, Amar, and Duncan Thomas. 2005. *Pension Income and the Well-Being of Children and Grandchildren: New Evidence from South Africa*. Online working paper series 043-05, California Center for Population Research. Los Angeles: University of California.

Kruger, John. 1992. "State Provision of Social Security: Some Theoretical, Comparative and Historical Perspectives with Reference to South Africa." Master's thesis, University of Stellenbosch, Stellenbosch, South Africa.

Leibbrandt, Murray, Ingrid Woolard, Arden Finn, and Jonathan Argent. 2010. *Trends in South African Income Distribution and Poverty Since the Fall of Apartheid*. Working Paper 101. Paris: Organisation for Economic Co-operation and Development, Social, Employment and Migration.

Lund, Frances. 1993. "State Social Benefits in South Africa." *International Social Security Review* 46 (1): 5–25.

———. 2008. *Changing Social Policy: The Child Support Grant in South Africa*. Pretoria, South Africa: Human Sciences Research Council Press.

Posel, Dori, James Fairburn, and Frances Lund. 2006. "Labour Migration and Households: A Reconsideration of the Effects of the Social Pension on Labour Supply in South Africa." *Economic Modelling* 23 (5): 836–53.

Ranchhod, Vimal. 2010. "Household Responses to Adverse Income Shocks: Pensioner Out-migration and Mortality in South Africa." Unpublished mimeograph, University of Cape Town, Cape Town.

Republic of South Africa. 1999–2010. *Budget Review.* Pretoria: Government Printer.

SALDRU (Southern Africa Labour and Development Research Unit). 1993. *Project for Statistics on Living Standards and Development.* Cape Town: University of Cape Town.

———. 2008. *National Income Dynamics Study.* Cape Town: University of Cape Town.

Samson, Michael, Ingrid van Niekerk, and Kenneth McQuene. 2006. *Designing and Implementing Social Transfer Programs: A Guide to Management Arrangements for Social Transfers in the Form of Cash.* Cape Town: Economic Policy Research Institute.

Simkins, Charles, and Themba Dlamini. 1992. "The Problem of Supporting Poor Children in South Africa. In *Questionable Issue: Illegitimacy in South Africa*, ed. Sandra Burman and Eleanor Preston-Whyte, 16–42. Cape Town: Oxford University Press.

———. 1997. *October Household Survey.* Pretoria: Statistics SA.

Statistics SA (South Africa). 2000. *Income and Expenditure Survey.* Pretoria: Statistics SA.

———. 2002. *General Household Survey.* Pretoria: Statistics SA.

———. 2003. *General Household Survey.* Pretoria: Statistics SA.

———. 2004. *General Household Survey.* Pretoria: Statistics SA.

———. 2005. *General Household Survey.* Pretoria: Statistics SA.

———. 2006. *General Household Survey.* Pretoria: Statistics SA.

———. 2007. *General Household Survey.* Pretoria: Statistics SA.

———. 2008. *General Household Survey.* Pretoria: Statistics SA.

van der Berg, Servaas. 1997. "South African Social Security under Apartheid and Beyond." *Development South Africa* 14 (4): 481–503.

———. 2001. "Redistribution through the Budget: Public Expenditure Incidence in South Africa, 1993–1997." *Social Dynamics* 27 (1): 140–164.

———. 2009. *Fiscal Incidence of Social Spending in South Africa, 2006.* Stellenbosch Economic Working Paper 10/09. Stellenbosch, South Africa: University of Stellenbosch.

Woolard, Ingrid, Michael Carter, and Jorge Agüero. 2005. *Analysis of the Child Support Grant: Evidence from the KwaZulu-Natal Income Dynamics Study, 1993–2004.* Report to the Department of Social Development, Pretoria.

World Bank. 2009. "Levels and Patterns of Safety Net Spending in Developing and Transition Countries." In *Safety Net Primer.* Washington, DC: World Bank.

Comment on "The Evolution and Impact of Unconditional Cash Transfers in South Africa" by Ingrid Woolard and Murray Leibbrandt

JANE FORTSON

In their paper, "The Evolution and Impact of Unconditional Cash Transfers in South Africa," Ingrid Woolard and Murray Leibbrandt describe the origins and recent history of the South African social security system. They draw a distinction between social insurance (which is intended to protect against risk of income loss and is often a contributory system) and social assistance (which is intended to combat poverty through redistribution and is usually noncontributory and means-tested). In South Africa, the social security system includes both social insurance and social assistance funds, though social assistance accounts for the bulk of social security spending. The South African social insurance system includes three main funds: the Unemployment Insurance Fund, the Compensation Funds, and the Road Accident Fund. The social assistance system includes numerous types of grants, the most prominent of which are the child support grant, the state old age pension, the disability grant, and the foster care grant.

After describing the evolution of the current social security system, Woolard and Leibbrandt provide a rich picture of social assistance programs in South Africa, highlighting spending levels and program details. They present descriptive statistics for several of the key social assistance programs, including take-up rates and characteristics of beneficiaries. Finally, they present evidence on the effect of these grants on poverty and other outcomes, including health, education, and labor supply. In addition to reducing poverty and inequality, evidence suggests that social assistance grants have improved some educational and health outcomes, at least for certain subgroups (see, e.g., Agüero, Carter, and Woolard 2009; Case 2001; Duflo 2000; Edmonds 2006). Evidence on the effect of social assistance grants on labor supply is mixed and is complicated by the presence (or absence) of migrant workers in the household (see, e.g., Ardington, Case, and Hosegood 2009; Ranchhod 2010).

Though South Africa—with high rates of income inequality and extensive social assistance financed by tax revenue—may be a special case, the origins and effects of

Jane Fortson is an economist at Mathematica Policy Research, Oakland, CA.

Annual World Bank Conference on Development Economics 2011, Global
© 2013 The International Bank for Reconstruction and Development/The World Bank

the South African social assistance system can nevertheless provide lessons for other countries. South Africa shares some of the same challenges faced by other countries in Sub-Saharan Africa, including HIV/AIDS and unemployment (Tortora 2009). Understanding the effect of grants in South Africa may provide an indication of what the effect might be elsewhere in Sub-Saharan Africa, particularly in southern Africa.

As we think about how these lessons might be generalized in designing social assistance systems elsewhere, the authors' work generates two key questions: (1) Should transfers be conditional or unconditional? (2) Are transfers the best way to achieve improvements in the outcomes we care about?

Should Transfers Be Conditional or Unconditional?

Conditional cash transfers have been shown to be an effective policy tool in other settings, particularly in Latin America (e.g., Schultz 2004). Making payments to households conditional on certain behaviors—such as school attendance or immunizations—can incentivize behavior and may be an effective way to encourage behavior when there are social benefits not internalized by the household. The South African child support grant (CSG) was originally introduced as a conditional cash transfer program. However, the conditions (including proof of immunization and proof of efforts to secure employment) hindered take-up, and there were concerns that some of the neediest children would not be able to access grants because of their inability to access services. Since 2000, all age- and income-eligible children have been able to receive the grant unconditionally. Imposing conditions could enhance the behavioral benefits of the CSG and could generate additional support for the program among taxpayers. However, as Woolard and Leibbrandt explain, imposing conditions has numerous drawbacks. First, the South African Constitution grants a right to social security, and conditioning grants on behavior is not in line with a rights-based approach. Second, if access to services is limited, imposing conditions may effectively exclude households without access to services, which may be among the neediest. Third, imposing conditions would introduce administrative costs to assess compliance. Finally, conditions are effective in improving outcomes only if they are closely related to outcomes and if we can monitor compliance. The outcomes we might be most interested in improving, such as school attendance and sexual behavior, may be the most difficult to monitor. Outcomes that are easier to monitor, such as school enrollment, may not be the ones we are most interested in improving. For example, in South Africa, a cash transfer conditional on school enrollment would not likely result in increased enrollment, since enrollment is already nearly universal among children aged 7–14.

The solution recently adopted in South Africa is "soft" conditionality, which in this case means that school enrollment and attendance are said to be required, but the CSG will not be stopped if the child does not attend school. Though this conditionality will not affect grant receipt, it might affect outcomes if caregivers believe that their children are required to attend school to receive the CSG.

Several studies in South Africa have shown that unconditional cash transfers can lead to improved health and education outcomes for children (e.g., Agüero, Carter, and Woolard 2009; Case, Hosegood, and Lund 2005); in other settings, conditional cash transfers have also been shown to lead to improvements in outcomes (e.g., Schultz 2004). Given the nonnegligible costs associated with imposing conditions (including the costs of compliance as well as the potential exclusion of the neediest households), we may want to measure the marginal benefit of conditionality.

A recent paper by Baird, McIntosh, and Özler (2010) provides the first experimental evidence on the marginal effect of conditionality. Enumeration areas (EAs) in a region of Malawi were randomly assigned to three study arms: a group eligible for conditional cash transfers; a group eligible for unconditional cash transfers; and a control group. Adolescent girls enrolled in school at baseline in treatment EAs were eligible to receive grants ($5–$15 monthly); in the conditional cash transfer EAs, grants were conditional on school attendance. (In both treatment arms, the size of the transfer was also randomized at the individual level.) The authors found that both unconditional and conditional cash transfers led to increases in enrollment and attendance, but the marginal effect of the conditionality was not significant. Their results suggest that, in some settings, unconditional cash transfers may generate some of the same improvements as conditional cash transfers.

Previous nonexperimental evidence from Latin America has suggested that conditionality has positive marginal effects. Baird and colleagues (2010) is the first experimental study of the effects of conditionality; differences between their study and earlier work could reflect differences in methods. However, the effect of conditionality might also vary depending on the context. In Latin America, where much of the previous work was conducted, enrollment rates and income levels may be higher and teen marriage rates may be lower than rates in Malawi, where Baird and colleagues conducted their study. These and other factors could affect the marginal impact of conditionality. Nevertheless, the study suggests that, at least in some contexts, unconditional cash transfers and conditional cash transfers may generate similar impacts. Because the administrative and political costs of imposing conditions can be substantial, unconditional cash transfers might be preferable to conditional cash transfers when their effects are likely to be similar.

Are Transfers the Best Way to Achieve Improvements in the Outcomes We Care About?

While transfers (unconditional or conditional) may generate positive effects on education and health among children, they are among many policy instruments that can generate improvements in child outcomes. The design of the optimal social assistance system depends on our objectives. For example, redistribution might be a very effective way to reduce poverty in the short term. However, if the goal of social assistance is to increase intergenerational mobility by influencing children's outcomes, cash transfers are just one of many possible strategies and might not be the most cost-effective strategy available.

For instance, a range of strategies could be used to generate increases in educational attainment for children in poverty. If demand-side impediments to schooling exist, possible strategies to increase educational attainment include cash transfers (conditional and unconditional), deworming, and informational interventions. Through their Deworm the World initiative, the Young Global Leaders have drawn attention to deworming as a potential strategy to improve health and increase schooling in developing countries in which intestinal worms are prevalent. Deworming can achieve educational gains similar to those from cash transfers at a fraction of the cost (Abdul Latif Jameel Poverty Action Lab 2005; Miguel and Kremer 2004). Providing information about the perceived returns to schooling may increase schooling at a low cost. For example, Jensen (2010) found that providing information to adolescent boys in the Dominican Republic about the returns to schooling led to large increases in educational attainment. In addition to these kinds of interventions, other strategies might stimulate demand for schooling, including interventions that improve health or improve labor market prospects.

However, in some settings, significant supply-side impediments to schooling exist. Cash transfers and other strategies to stimulate demand may not achieve much in places where good-quality schooling is not provided. In those places, improving the supply of schooling is likely to achieve greater benefits. School-building programs and programs that monitor and incentivize teacher attendance are two of many possible strategies to improve the supply of schooling (Duflo, Hanna, and Ryan 2010; Levy et al. 2009).

As these examples illustrate, the appropriate policy instrument depends on our objectives and on the context. If social assistance is aimed at increasing educational attainment for children in poverty, cash transfers may not be the cheapest or most effective way to generate improvements in many settings.

Concluding Remarks

Woolard and Leibbrandt describe the characteristics of the social assistance system in South Africa, documenting its reach and highlighting some of the key considerations in designing social assistance systems. Their discussion centers on the child support grant, a cash transfer program that recently introduced soft conditionality for benefit receipt. They discuss the challenges in imposing conditions for receipt of social assistance grants, raising important questions about the marginal benefits of conditions and whether these benefits offset their limitations.

Existing evidence suggests that conditional cash transfers might be a useful policy tool in settings in which demand-side impediments to schooling exist and the costs of compliance (logistical or political) are low. However, new evidence from Malawi suggests that unconditional cash transfers may achieve similar benefits with fewer costs, at least in some settings (Baird the McIntosh, and Özler 2010). Cash transfers—unconditional or conditional—redistribute income and can improve children's outcomes. However, they are among many possible strategies that can increase intergenerational mobility by improving children's outcomes. Therefore, policy makers should think broadly about the policy instruments they use to influence outcomes, paying careful attention to demand- and supply-side factors that may threaten child well-being.

References

Abdul Latif Jameel Poverty Action Lab. 2005. *Fighting Poverty: What Works? Issue 1.* http://www.povertyactionlab.org/sites/default/files/publications/Fighting%20Poverty%2C%20What%20works%20Issue%201.pdf.

Agüero, Jorge, Michael Carter, and Ingrid Woolard. 2009. *The Impact of Unconditional Cash Transfers on Nutrition: The South African Child Support Grant.* Working Paper 06/08. School of Development Studies, University of KwaZulu-Natal.

Ardington, Cally, Anne Case, and Victoria Hosegood. 2009. "Labor Supply Responses to Large Social Transfers: Longitudinal Evidence from South Africa." *American Economic Journal: Applied Economics* 1 (1): 22–48.

Baird, Sarah, Craig McIntosh, and Berk Özler. 2010. *Cash or Condition? Evidence from a Randomized Cash Transfer Program.* Policy Research Working Paper 5259. Washington, DC: World Bank.

Case, Anne. 2001. *Does Money Protect Health Status? Evidence from South African Pensions.* National Bureau for Economic Research (NBER) Working Paper 8495. Cambridge, MA: NBER.

Case, Anne, Victoria Hosegood, and Frances Lund. 2005. "The Reach and Impact of Child Support Grants: Evidence from KwaZulu-Natal." *Development Southern Africa* 22 (4): 467–82.

Duflo, Esther. 2000. "Child Health and Household Resources in South Africa: Evidence from the Old Age Pension Program." *American Economic Review* 90 (2): 393–98.

Duflo, Esther, Rema Hanna, and Stephen Ryan. 2010. "Incentives Work: Getting Teachers to Come to School." Unpublished mimeograph. Massachusetts Institute of Technology.

Edmonds, Eric. 2006. "Child Labor and Schooling Responses to Anticipated Income in South Africa." *Journal of Development Economics* 81 (2): 386–414.

Jensen, Robert. 2010. "The (Perceived) Returns to Education and the Demand for Schooling." *Quarterly Journal of Economics* 125 (2): 515–48.

Levy, Dan, Matt Sloan, Leigh Linden, and Harounan Kazianga. 2009. *Impact Evaluation of Burkina Faso's BRIGHT Program.* Mathematica Policy Research Document No. PR09-29. Princeton, NJ: Mathematica Policy Research.

Miguel, Edward, and Michael Kremer. 2004. "Worms: Identifying Impacts on Education and Health in the Presence of Treatment Externalities." *Econometrica* 72 (1): 159–217.

Ranchhod, Vimal. 2010. "Household Responses to Adverse Income Shocks: Pensioner Out-Migration and Mortality in South Africa." Unpublished mimeograph. University of Cape Town.

Schultz, T. Paul. 2004. "School Subsidies for the Poor: Evaluating the Mexican Progresa Poverty Program." *Journal of Development Economics* 74 (1): 199–250.

Tortora, Robert. 2009. *Sub-Saharan Africans Rank the Millennium Development Goals (MDGs).* Washington, DC: Gallup.

Closing Remarks

JOAKIM STYMNE

Ladies and gentlemen, dear friends, the 2010 ABCDE conference is coming to an end. Three very full days have passed. Five Nobel laureates have shared their findings. Some 20 parallel sessions have been held with almost 600 participants. Myriad ideas have been aired. I trust that you will leave Stockholm with new insights and inspiration, reassured that we will continue our joint drive toward global development. For those of us staying behind—representatives of the Swedish government, of institutions and agencies—your research and thinking will be important contributions to our policy formulation and our continued reform of development cooperation.

The ABCDE has been something of a checkpoint—an opportunity to pause and reflect. Are we on the right path toward a global society in which economic growth occurs together with poverty reduction and empowered individuals? I think we are, but there are twists and turns in the road ahead and choices to be made. We need to keep an eye on the map and perhaps redraw it once in a while. Difficult? Yes, but a little less so after these three days.

On one level it is easy to summarize this conference in a few words: It's been marvelous. But at the same time it's impossible to do justice to the totality of the discussions. How does one summarize three days of conversation in a brief closing statement? Given the sheer number of speeches and contributions, any selection of highlights will be subjective.

In an attempt to bring some scientific method to the process, Ann and I have compared notes. We have also had tremendous help from three Ph.D. students from the Institute of International Economic Studies here in Stockholm. Of course, a full written report on the conference will be forthcoming. I hope you will agree with me that the following issues deserve to be mentioned. I'll start with the first half of the conference, and Ann will continue.

At the time of the Conference, Joakim Stymne was State Secretary for International Development Cooperation at the Ministry for Foreign Affairs of Sweden.

Annual World Bank Conference on Development Economics 2011, Global
© 2013 The International Bank for Reconstruction and Development/The World Bank

After the welcome addresses from World Bank chief economist Justin Lin, Swedish minister for finance Anders Borg, and minister for international development cooperation Gunilla Carlsson, we turned our attention to Nobel laureate Elinor Ostrom. In her keynote address, "Overcoming the Samaritan's Dilemma in Development Aid," she reminded us of the necessity to continuously question our basic assumptions and terminology. We must look deeper into questions of ownership, sustainability, and evaluation, as well as the complex structure of incentives and motivations. She emphasized the need to make better use of our knowledge base and identified processes and methods for individual and organizational learning as critical components of more effective development cooperation.

In the plenary session on "Environmental Commons and the Green Economy," Thomas Sterner challenged our thinking on climate change and the options available to address it. He stressed the need for global coordination, binding agreements, voluntary pledges, and green growth, and called for strict measures. As one concrete example, he suggested substantial increases in fuel costs; we look forward to his upcoming book, in which he promises to explore the effects of such decisions on poverty. In the same plenary session, Ramón López discussed the complex relationship among consumption, production, and environmental impact. He argued that over the past few decades, production in advanced countries has become dematerialized while consumption has not, implying that rich countries have not become cleaner but rather better at dumping dirt elsewhere. In his comment, Simon Levin stressed the necessity to achieve cooperation at the global level, which in turn calls for adaptive, adequate institutions.

In "Postcrisis Debates on Development Strategy," Abhijit Banerjee summed up lessons learned in development policy over the past 20 years and described the gradual shift away from the Washington Consensus. We now have a more nuanced view of the role of private enterprise and export promotion, and more attention is being directed toward institutions and human resources.

Shang-Jin Wei enhanced our understanding of the concept of leapfrogging—the use of policy instruments to engineer a faster industrial transformation than what might emerge naturally. However, there does not seem to be strong, uncontestable evidence that a leapfrogging industrial policy results in faster economic growth. Discussants Geoffrey Heal and Franjo Štiblar highlighted the shift from macro to micro perspectives and noted issues of deregulation and outsourcing, challenges with growth models, and the need for a wider analytical framework.

In the second keynote address, Torsten Persson shared his theories about weak states, strong states, and development. He argued that state capacity—in the form of extractive capacity (or physical power) and productive capacity (or legal power)—has been overlooked in most mainstream economic models. A lack of state capacity is often accompanied by low gross domestic product and political violence.

It was a pleasure for me to chair the third plenary session yesterday morning on "The Political Economy of Fragile States." Stephen Ndegwa presented key findings from the forthcoming *World Development Report 2011*. He said expectations for progress will have to shift in terms of both time horizon and size of the effect.

James Fearon showed that a country's level of income has little or no relevance in trying to predict the outbreak of violent conflict. Poor countries are more often prone to conflict because of weak political institutions rather than poverty per se. Aid in conflict-affected countries, therefore, needs to do more than just raise income levels. Conditionality should be based on institution-building rather than policy. In their comments, Alan Gelb and Louise Anten added their perspectives on the need to address dilemmas and trade-offs, the complexity of emerging from fragility, and the relationship between governance and conflict.

As we near the end of this conference, I'd say that the strength and beauty and dynamism of a research conference like this one are the differences and disagreements, the courage to challenge conventional wisdom, the enthusiasm for new possibilities, the readiness to question and be questioned, the integrity to defend one's convictions, and the openness to change one's mind. But I think we do have consensus about one thing: the need for more meetings and platforms like this one.

In that context, I'd like to mention that while today is the last day of the ABCDE, it is the first day of YES, the global Youth Employment Summit, "Rework the World." The summit is organized by the Tällberg Foundation and YES, Inc., with support from the Swedish government. It will be an arena for discussing another burning global issue: youth employment. Some one hundred initiatives from around the world will be presented and examined—all with the objective of creating the jobs of tomorrow and building a more socially, financially, and ecologically sustainable society. I know that some of you will attend the summit, and I hope you will take some inspiration from ABCDE with you.

Before I officially close ABCDE 2010, one important task remains: thanking everyone who helped organize this event. It has been a pleasure to cohost this conference with the World Bank. With ABCDE 2010, we have added yet another layer to an excellent long-standing relationship. Ann, with you and your collaborators—including Leita Jones—by our side, we've had the greatest support and experience to lean on. Thank you very much. And to Mia: you, Julia, Kerstin, and the rest of your team already know how much we appreciate your efforts. You all have a close to magical ability to make things happen in the most effective, efficient way.

Our sincere thanks also to the entire steering committee. You've done a tremendous job securing the highest level of participants, putting together an impressive program, and foreseeing potential problems and preventing them from materializing. Also, of course, a big thank-you to Boris Pleskovic, who's been a driving force behind this conference for so many years and who is still around, despite having retired. And last but not least, a warm, sincere thanks to all of you distinguished Nobel laureates, renowned professors, researchers, students, colleagues from government offices and agencies, friends, and members of civil society. The past few days have reminded us again of the need for close relationships between policy makers and researchers. In this interaction, new ideas are born, conventional wisdom is challenged, and possibilities are created.

I hope we'll all meet again at ABCDE 2011. Thank you, and have a safe trip home.

Closing Remarks

ANN HARRISON

Joakim, thank you very much for your summary of the first half of the conference. I will continue with the second half. Following the session on fragile states, Joseph Stiglitz gave a keynote address in honor of Partha Dasgupta entitled "Learning, Growth, and Development." He asked questions that are important themes of this conference: How can developing countries catch up with developed countries? Does industrial policy work, and if so, which policies have proved to be most effective?

Stiglitz began by referring to the heady days in Cambridge, when he and his colleagues anticipated "putting a golden nail in the coffin of capitalism." He argued that markets by themselves do not yield efficient solutions for promoting innovation, in part because knowledge is a public good. There are large spillovers and externalities, as well as imperfections in the industrial structure. To overcome these imperfections, he proposed creating incentives to expand parts of the economy that generate spillovers. In particular, he proposed an industrial policy whose goal is not to pick winners but to identify these externalities and support them. One goal would be to use instruments that give broad-based support, such as the subsidies and other forms of support used in East Asia. Since the World Trade Organization has restricted the use of subsidies, he suggested using the exchange rate as a tool of industrial policy.

The fourth plenary was part of a larger movement that advocates going beyond the use of standard welfare measures, such as gross domestic product (GDP) or GDP growth. The session focused on subjective measures of well-being or happiness. Following the work of Richard Easterlin, social science research on happiness has taken off in the past 20 years. The impetus has been the development of surveys that ask people how happy or how good they feel.

At the time of the conference, Ann Harrison was Director of Development Policy, Development Economics, World Bank. I am grateful to Jean Jacques Dethier for helping in preparing these remarks.

Annual World Bank Conference on Development Economics 2011, Global
© 2013 The International Bank for Reconstruction and Development / The World Bank

Justin Wolfers explored the relationship between happiness and income—across individuals within a given country, between countries in the same year, and over time. He showed that richer people are more satisfied with their lives than poorer people in the same country. This relationship is similar in most countries around the world, except Belgium. His results suggest that material wealth and subjective well-being go hand in hand.

On the other side of the coin, Carol Graham presented an overview of her new book, *Happiness Around the World: The Paradox of Happy Peasants and Miserable Millionaires.* She also reported on what happened to happiness in the United States when the stock market fell at the onset of the global financial crisis in 2008 (people were less happy) and documented the interesting fact that uncertainty makes people very unhappy. The critical role of uncertainty in reducing happiness is important in an increasingly volatile and globally interconnected world. When developing countries grow, the process may lead to significant increases in living standards, but the process of growth is full of uncertainty and creates a lot of stress. The results presented by Carol Graham and Justin Wolfers can be reconciled if we take into account the fact that they use different measures of well-being and different specifications.

In his keynote address on poverty traps, Partha Dasgupta focused on a phenomenon that is all too prevalent in developing countries: child malnutrition. Irreversible malnutrition and infection at the earliest stages of life lead to many problems in early childhood, including an inability to acquire socio-emotional competencies, and have a stranglehold effect on a person's acquisition of human capital later in life. He showed that, in some contexts, preventing the collapse of local institutions should be the object of policy design; in others, the provision of meals to schoolchildren should be the immediate investment. (In his presentation, he relied on the world development indicators; those indicators are free and universally available on the World Bank's new open data website: http://data.worldbank.org/data-catalog/.)

The fifth plenary session was dedicated to issues of empowerment and social policy. It began with a presentation by Esther Duflo, who received the John Bates Clark medal this year for being the top economist under the age of 40; she is only the second woman to receive the medal. In her presentation, she looked at the links between women's empowerment and economic development. She asked whether development alone is enough to reduce inequality between men and women, and whether empowerment not only promotes equity but also accelerates development. She concluded by saying that neither economic development nor women's empowerment is the magic bullet. To bring about equity between men and women, it will be necessary to continue to take policy actions that favor women at the expense of men, possibly for a very long time. This may result in benefits that are not sufficient to compensate for the cost of distortions, but she said we should care about equity for its own sake, not simply because it is good for efficiency or for growth. This presentation will be a valuable input for the 2012 World Development Report on gender equality.

Ingrid Woolard and Murray Leibbrandt looked at the evolution and impact of unconditional cash transfers in South Africa, where more than a quarter of the population receives such social assistance. They are cautious about extending the system to focus directly on the unemployed or further expanding social grants, and argue against imposing behavioral conditions because the limited benefits may not be worth the cost. In her comments, Jane Fortson reinforced this view.

Finally, we launched the global development debates on development challenges in a post-crisis world, the theme of this year's conference. This was a joint effort with the World Bank Institute, with Stephanie Flanders from the BBC moderating, and five luminaries—Eric Maskin, James Mirrlees, Robert Solow, Partha Dasgupta, and Abhijit Banarjee—joining her on the stage. It was a very exciting debate.

ECO-AUDIT
Environmental Benefits Statement

The World Bank is committed to preserving endangered forests and natural resources. **Annual World Bank Conference on Development Economics 2011, Global: Development Challenges in a Postcrisis World** is printed on recycled paper made with 50-percent post-consumer waste. The Office of the Publisher follows the recommended standards for paper usage set by the Green Press Initiative, a nonprofit program supporting publishers in using fiber that is not sourced from endangered forests. For more information, visit www.greenpressinitiative.org.

Saved:
- **14** trees
- **6 million** BTUs of energy
- **1,189** pounds of greenhouse gases (CO_2 equivalent)
- **6,450** gallons of waste water
- **432** pounds of solid waste